EBD 10/18/89

INSTRUMENTAL
VIRTUOSI

Recent Titles in the Music Reference Collection

INSTRUMENTAL VIRTUOSI

A Bibliography of Biographical Materials

Compiled by Robert H. Cowden

Music Reference Collection, Number 18

Greenwood Press
New York • Westport, Connecticut • London

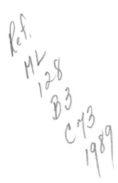

Library of Congress Cataloging-in-Publication Data

Cowden, Robert H.
  Instrumental virtuosi.

  (Music reference collection, ISSN 0736-7740 ; no. 18)
  Bibliography: p.
  Includes index.
  1. Musicians—Biography—Bibliography.   I. Title.
II. Series.
ML128.B3C73   1989   016.78 '092 '2   88-34816
ISBN 0-313-26075-3 (lib. bdg. : alk. paper)

British Library Cataloguing in Publication Data is available.

Library of Congress Catalog Card Number: 88-34816
ISBN: 0-313-26075-3
ISSN: 0736-7740

First published in 1989

Greenwood Press, Inc.
88 Post Road West, Westport, Connecticut 06881

Printed in the United States of America

The paper used in this book complies with the
Permanent Paper Standard issued by the National
Information Standards Organization (Z39.48-1984).

10 9 8 7 6 5 4 3 2 1

To my students in CSSSA and SJSU
for challenging my parameters,
for respecting my visions,
but most of all
for keeping all of us
involved and young

Contents

Preface

As with its two predecessors, this third volume of comprehensive bibliographies about performers is a compilation of sources from a variety
of dictionaries, encyclopedias, periodicals, and the published materials
by and about the individuals selected. Instrumental Virtuosi completes
my project, which began with Concert and Opera Singers (1985) and con-
tinued with Concert and Opera Conductors (1987), both also published by
Greenwood Press; however, revised and expanded editions are future pos-
sibilities. The realization of this vast undertaking is especially
gratifying as there exists nothing in the field of similar scope. For
those who are curious, I personally compiled and annotated all of the
entries because I felt that one had to interact with the materials.
Data banks are helpful, but entries can be misleading or incorrect as
anyone who has consulted shelf lists at major libraries can testify.
Catalogers -- if I may be permitted a slightly heretical observation --
have been moderately less consistent over the decades than even we
bibliographers! My latest compilation posed some problems of choice
that I had not previously encountered. Singers have, after all, been
around since before recorded history, and the experiments of the Italian
'Camerata' thrust them into prominence some four hundred years ago.
Conductors are a more recent phenomenon and evolved in direct relationship to the increasing sophistication of musical compositions during the
classical and early romantic periods. Instrumentalists, on the other
hand, pursue a variety of acoustical (and recently electronic) instruments, and quite different ones have dominated at different times. For
example, the seventeenth and eighteenth centuries were clearly the age
of the violinist and to a lesser extent the other strings; the nineteenth century brought pianists to the forefront; and our own century
has experienced, perhaps, the beginning of the end of the acoustical
instrument era, at least as traditionally practiced.

In contrast to the earlier volumes which excluded artists from the pop
and commercial fields (a revised and expanded edition of Concert and
Opera Singers which will include such performers is in preparation), the
Louis Armstrongs, the Duke Ellingtons, and the Stéphane Grappellis are
in this bibliography. Grove 6 correctly points out that "...the true
virtuoso has always been prized not only for his rarity but also for his
ability to widen the technical and expressive boundaries of his art."
Many of the innovations in instrumental performance have come from the
popular side of the street where real widening has taken place. Tarr/
Armstrong and Rubinstein/Ellington are interesting analogies indeed in
this regard. As in my previous efforts, I have tried to err on the side
of inclusion rather than exclusion, but it remains difficult to draw a
hard and fast line between performers who are and who are not virtuosi.

CHOICE OF VIRTUOSI

Artists included in "PART C: Individual Virtuosi, A-Z" had to be cited
in at least one of the standard music biographical dictionaries or encyclopedias, had to have written an autobiography or substantive contribution to the understanding of style or interpretation, and/or had to
have been the subject of a biographical study. Articles in major
musical periodicals and/or mention in some other publication, e.g., the
extensive material on Louis Armstrong in the published criticism of
Whitney Balliett (A0003-0007), were not considered adequate recognition
by themselves. Occasionally -- fortunately very seldom -- biographical
material about an intriguing figure whom one would wish to include does
exist (Ohm, J.H.M. Die 13 jaehrige Pianistin Alwine Ohm aus Hannover und
deren 4 jaerige Kunstreise durch Deutschland.... Hamburg: Carl Fischer's
Buch-druckerei, 1860. viii, 128 p., portrait), but no other sources were
discovered that fit my guidelines. On the other hand, many instrumentalists are included in two of the standard reference works who are not
mentioned in any other published materials, and such individuals are a
part of this compilation.

Several important restrictions have been adopted for this bibliography:
(1) virtuosi from the Renaissance, such as the lutenist John Dowland and
the organist Francisco Correa de Arauxo, are generally excluded; (2)
talented performers whose reputations rest on their involvement as
chamber music players -- Ignaz Schuppanzigh comes immediately to mind --
are not included; (3) composers who excelled on one or more instruments
are excluded. Brahms and Beethoven performed brilliantly at the keyboard as attested to by Konrad Huschke who authored Beethoven als
Pianist und Dirigent (Berlin: Schuster & Loeffler, 1919) as well as
Johannes Brahms als Pianist, Dirigent und Lehrer (Karlsruhe: F.G.
Verlag, 1935). As in the case of Mozart, however, each was primarily a
composer and will not be found here. Exceptions, however, must be
addressed in this special area as they must be and were with conductors.
Who being of right mind could not include Chopin, Rachmaninoff, and
Liszt, not to mention von Buelow, Barenboim, Clementi, and Rostropovich.
All of these gentlemen were and are known as virtuosi; (4) and finally,
I did not list band leaders who also performed, such as Glenn Miller.
Unquestionably, there will be some honest disagreement, not so much with
inclusions as with exclusions, but the guidelines are, overall, quite
broad and fair: a minimum of two entries from the first four categories
of information which will be explained later in this preface, or a
single entry plus an autobiography or biographical study of the artist.

I learned early on in this series that compilations that were literally
crammed with a myriad of fussy details implied, indeed required, hard
choices which might result in some degree of human error. I therefore
encourage each reader to check back, consider the alternatives, and
understand that reasoned selections are an inevitable part of the
process of generating a major bibliography of this type.

There is one final point that should be addressed with regard to the
inclusion of book titles. Again over ninety-eight percent of the books
listed have been personally inspected. A lack of specifics or a comment
on the unavailability of the titles make the unseen items obvious. In
the case of major instrumentalist/conductors or instrumentalist/com-

posers, such as von Buelow, Chopin, Clementi, and Liszt, however, the
sheer number of books made any attempt at comprehensiveness both
impractical and inappropriate. Most studies deal almost exclusively
with each individual as a composer or conductor rather than as a
performer. Therefore, a concentrated attempt was made to select only
those titles that dealt specifically with performance involvement and/or
shed light on personal life and artistic orientation. I am well aware
of a number of titles that would have been included had I been able to
secure a copy; and the numerous references to a bibliography after the
dictionary and encyclopedia entries suggest further avenues for the
serious researcher. The cross that any bibliographer must bear is
engraved with the countless titles that have not or cannot be located.
They are probably somewhere, but where? This bibliography includes most
of what has been published in this area, and omissions certainly suggest
where additional work must be done.

REFERENCE WORKS AND PERIODICALS

Initially, twenty reference works in seven languages and eighteen
periodicals in six languages were reviewed for inclusion; the final list
includes fifteen and twelve respectively. Please note that in the area
of jazz, three of the works themselves (the compilations by Bernhard
Hefele and Eddie S. Meadows as well as the publication of Donald
Kennington and Danny L. Read) are bibliographies, and it seemed dupli-
cative to list all their citations again. Each of the twenty-six titles
has been assigned a bibliographical abbreviation, and a coded list of
the reference works with their abbreviations immediately follows this
preface.

FACTUAL DATA AND LANGUAGES

Baker 7, which was edited by the justly renowned lexicographer Nicolas
Slonimsky, has been the primary, although not exclusive, source for the
spelling of names, as well as date and place of birth and death. I
should mention that the indication of nationality reflects the last
known citizenship, e.g., Egon Petri was born in Germany of Dutch descent
but became a naturalized American citizen. Very few of the twelve
hundred fifteen virtuosi listed here are not found in Baker 7 in which
case the source of data is indicated specifically: e.g., Harry Adaskin
(C0001) is found in the Encyclopedia of Music in Canada. Perhaps because the talented performer has gained the spotlight in every generation almost all of the instrumentalists listed in this bibliography are
to be found in at least two basic encyclopedias or biographical dictionaries.

A conscious effort was made to include all known biographical material
in the Germanic and Italic branches of the Indo-European language
family. Those that I have seen personally are here; most of the others
are mentioned in the detailed annotations and cross-references.

ORDER OF MATERIALS

This work is divided into three major sections. The first, "COLLECTIVE
WORKS: Books on Virtuosi," includes thirty-seven titles devoted to all
performers regardless of their instrument; four titles devoted to brass

players; fifty titles which deal exclusively with the keyboard artists; a single title for percussionists; sixty-five titles encompassing string players; and eight books for woodwind players, a total of 165 titles. The entries are code numbered A0001 through A0165 (please refer to the brief headnote which introduces this section); authors, co-authors, and editors in this section also appear in the Index. Some of the titles include the name of each artist in the annotation, and these names are cross-indexed under the entries for individual virtuosi. Annotations are specifically designed to be informational. The second section, "COLLECTIVE WORKS: Related Books," contains one hundred thirty-five titles, with additional material on many of the instrumentalists mentioned in section one. As in the previous section, the entries are code numbered (B0001 through B0134; a late addition is numbered B0003A) and authors, co-authors, and editors are listed in the Index. Any artists mentioned in the annotations are cross-referenced in section three.

The final section, "Individual Virtuosi: A-Z," contains twelve hundred fifteen artists from Harry Adaskin to Otto Zykan listed alphabetically and numbered from C0001 through C1215. Along with essential birth and death information, each entry may include information from five different types of sources: (1) entries in any of the fifteen reference works listed in the bibliographical abbreviations section, with the edition and volume number if appropriate. Bibliographic references not duplicated in this compilation are indicated, e.g., Baker 7 (Bibliography); (2) articles of a biographical or autobiographical nature from any of the eleven periodicals listed in the abbreviations section; (3) autobiographies or books by the performer related directly to pedagogy or interpretation; (4) biographies about the performer and compilations of memorabilia, scores, reviews, etc.; (5) other books containing important material; for example, because Pablo Casals is mentioned prominently in Gerald Moore's autobiography, this reference appears under the code number C0227.5. This section can act as its own index and, used in conjunction with the collective works, should provide an abundance of sources to pursue for information. Appendix I suggests a few additional reference sources which may be unknown to even the serious amateur, items D0001 to D0022. Appendix II provides a comprehensive index to the sixteen hundred seven instrumentalists included in Nicolas Slonimsky's seventh edition of Baker's Biographical Dictionary of Musicians. Any commonality with the twelve hundred fifteen artists listed in this bibliography is indicated by the appropriate code number which precedes the name. The fact that fewer than five percent of the artists are not to be found in Baker 7 attests to Slonimsky's comprehensive work. Appendix III is an index to the New Grove Dictionary of American Music with any commonality of artists again indicated by the appropriate code number. Appendix IV classifies the 1,215 individual virtuosi by instrument so that all the specialists are listed in one place. An index to authors, co-authors, editors, and compilers in all sections of the bibliography completes the work.

I will continue to add artists and expand the number of encyclopedias, dictionaries, and periodicals that are cross-referenced; therefore, readers are encouraged to inform me, through the publisher, of any additions, deletions, or corrections. The number of titles that have come to light during my research has been a constant source of pleasure.

Bibliographies are by definition process rather than product, and I trust that this particular project will continue ad infinitum. A final thought relates to ideas that have surfaced as a result of my long love affair with this peculiar area of research, namely valuable additional projects that can and should be explored: (1) an indexing of biographical materials which accompany recordings and which are often the only authoritative information available; (2) an annotated listing of the thousands of artists' brochures generated by booking agencies. This would be a challenging task indeed as the only major holdings of such materials that I have encountered are in private hands; (3) definitive compilations of instrumental pedagogical materials such as Thomas E. Warner's <u>Bibliography of Woodwind Instruction Books</u> (Detroit, 1967). Regarding pedagogical materials, many of these are mentioned in the encyclopedia articles that I have cross-referenced in this book, but even the massive collection at the Library of Congress has serious gaps and omissions suggesting that this will be a long-term research project of formidable scope.

ACKNOWLEDGMENTS

Expressions of gratitude tend to assume the character of "reruns" when one works on a series. Compiling a comprehensive bibliography, one which sailed in uncharted waters as this one did, entails the input and cooperation of a number of libraries, funding sources, and individuals. I should first of all like to thank Lim M. Lai for his fine support and expertise; he is a true friend and valued colleague indeed. Marilyn Brownstein, humanities editor at Greenwood Press, had the faith to publish my initial volume as well as the vision to continue the series, and I am deeply grateful. And I must express special gratitude to the following: the Library of Congress in Washington and the Music Library at the University of California/ Berkeley; Barry Kernfeld, editor of <u>The New Grove Dictionary of Jazz</u>, who was kind enough to confirm entries in that work prior to publication so that references could be made in this compilation; the San Jose State University Foundation; and Professor Gus C. Lease, Music Department Chairman at San Jose State University.

I had intended to dedicate this last volume to my wife, but she demurred in her accustomed way for whatever reason(s) I do not fully understand – perhaps because she likes my poetry better as I write it exclusively for her. Be that as it may, much of my work as a performer, a director, a producer, an administrator, a teacher, and a writer resulted from her encouragement, her tenacity, her faith in my abilities, and her willingness to put up with my.... Anyway –– "Dein Bildnis wunderseelig, Hab' ich im Herzensgrund."

Robert H. Cowden
Monte Sereno, California
October, 1988

Bibliographical Abbreviations

The abbreviations listed below are used in the text of this bibliography, especially in the third section on individual conductors. The abbreviations chosen are widely used, and readers should find them easy to remember and use.

Encyclopedias and Dictionaries

Baker 7
Baker's Biographical Dictionary of Musicians. 7th edition. Revised by Nicolas Slonimsky. New York: Schirmer Books, 1984.

DEU
Basso, Alberto, ed. Dizionario enciclopedico universale della musica e dei musicisti. Le biografie. 4 vols. (A-Bur/Je-Ma). Torino: Unione Tipografico, 1985- .

EdS
Enciclopedia dello spettacolo. 9 vols. Roma: Casa Editrice le Maschere, 1954-62. Aggiornamento 1955-1965. Roma: Unione Editoriale, 1966.

Fetis 2
Fétis, Francois-J. Biographie universelle des musiciens et bibliographie général de la musique. 8 vols. deuxieme edition. Paris: Librairie De Firmin Didot Fréres, Fils Et Cie, 1873. Supplément et Complément. Publies sous la direction de M. Arthur Pougin. 2 vols. Paris, 1881.

Grove 6
Sadie, Stanley, ed., The New Grove Dictionary of Music and Musicians. 20 vols. London: Macmillan Publishers Limited, 1980.

Grove-AM
Hitchcock, H. Wiley and Stanley Sadie, eds. The New Grove Dictionary of American Music. 4 vols. London: Macmillan Publishers Limited, 1986.

Grove-Jazz
Kernfeld, Barry, ed. The New Grove Dictionary of Jazz. 2 vols. London: Macmillan Publishers Limited, 1988.

JB
   Hefele, Bernhard, comp. Jazz-Bibliographie. Munich: K.G. Saur Verlag
   KG, 1981.

   An outstanding compilation which forms the basis for ongoing
   research. 6,600 individual entries including (a) 133 bibliographies;
   (b) ninety-nine dictionaries/encyclopedias; (c) ninety-eight collective works; (d) 157 discographies; (e) 552 general titles on jazz;
   (f) 540 titles on cultural background; (g) 700+ individual artists.

JRRM
   Meadows, Eddie S., comp. Jazz Reference and Research Materials: a
   Bibliography. New York: Garland Publishing, Inc., 1980.

   2,563 entries focus primarily on American publications from the turn
   of the century through 1978.

LJ2
   Kennington, Donald and Danny L. Read. The Literature of Jazz: a
   Critical Guide. 2nd rev. ed. Chicago: American Library Association,
   1980.

MGG
   Blume, Friedrich, ed. Die Musik in Geschichte und Gegenwart:
   allgemeine Enzyklopaedie der Musik.... 14 vols. Kassel: Baeren-
   reiter Verlag, 1949-67. Supplement. Kassel, 1973/1979. Register.
   Kassel, 1986.

PAB-MI/2
   McNeil, Barbara and Miranda C. Herbert, eds. Performing Arts
   Bibliography Master Index: a Consolidated Guide to over 270,000
   Bibliographical Sketches of Persons Living and Dead, as They
   Appear in over 100 of the Principal Biographical Dictionaries
   Devoted to the Performing Arts. 2nd edition. Detroit: Gale Research
   Company, 1982.

Riemann 12
   Gurlitt, Wilibald, ed. Riemann Musik-Lexikon: Personenteil. 2 Vols.
   12. voellig neubearbeitete Auflage. Mainz: B. Schott's Soehne, 1959-
   1967. Ergaenzungsband. Mainz, 1972/1975.

Schmidl
   Schmidl, Carol. Dizionario universale dei musicisti. 2 vols. Milano:
   Sonzono, 1928/1929. Supplemento. Milano, 1938.

Periodicals

CL
       Clavier. Vol. 1 (1962) to Vol. 26 (1987).

DB
       Downbeat. Vol. 22 (1955) to Vol. 54 (1987).
       Note: This began as an informational trade magazine; with 22/8
             the new format included biographical articles/interviews.

GR

    The Gramophone. Vol. 44 (1966–67) to Vol. 64 (1986–87).
    Note: Prior to volume 45 there was no table of contents.

HiFi

    High Fidelity. Vol. 1 (1951) to Vol. 36 (1986).

HiFi/MusAm

    High Fidelity and Musical America.
    Note: Musical America was merged into High Fidelity with Vol.
        15/2 (February 1965).

HiFi/MusRev;
HiFi/Rev;
HiFi/SR

    HiFi/Stereo Review. Vol. 1 (1958) to Vol. 52 (1987).
    Note: Magazine began as HiFi and Music Review; with 1/11 became
        HiFi Review; HiFi/Stereo Review from February 1960.

CK(KB);
KB

    Keyboard. Vol. 1 (1920) to Vol. 68 (1987).
    Note: Magazine began as Contemporary Keyboard; with Vol. 10
        (1984) became Keyboard.

JJS

    Journal of Jazz Studies. Vol. 1 (1973) to Vol. 6, #1.

ML

    Music and Letters. Vol. 1 (1920) to Vol. 28 (1979–80).

MM

    Music and Musicians. Vol. 13 (1964–65) to Vol. 28 (1979–80).

PQ

    Piano Quarterly. #43 (Spring 1963) to #139 (1986–87).

RS

    British Institute of Recorded Sound. As of 1961 the
    publication was called Recorded Sound. No. 1 (Summer
    1956) to No. 86 (1984).

Strad

    Vol. 76 (1965) to Vol. 98 (1984).

INSTRUMENTAL
VIRTUOSI

PART A.

COLLECTIVE WORKS:
Books on Virtuosi

This brief headnote is intended to clarify the number code sequence thus enabling the reader to go immediately to those collective works which might contain information on artists specializing in a particular class of instrument. Titles which include all performers regardless of their instrument are numbered A0001-A0037; those including brass players are numbered A0038-A0041; keyboard artists are numbered A0042-A0091; percussionists are numbered A0092; string virtuosi are numbered A0093-A0157; and woodwinds are numbered A0158-0165. Every reasonable effort was made to list the individual artists in the annotations, but often the sheer number made this impractical. Each reader is therefore urged to consult any titles which offer the promise of additional information of a biographical or bibliographical nature.

ALL PERFORMERS

A0001. Améry, Jean. Im Banne des Jazz: Bildnisse grosser Jazz-Musiker. Rueschikon-Zuerich: Albert Mueller Verlag. 128 p., 20 illus.

Armstrong, Ella Fitzgerald, Parker, Billy Holiday, Ellington, Bessie Smith, Young, Tristano, Hampton, Sarah Vaughan, Reinhardt, Ory, Krupa, Beiderbecke, Miles Davis, Bechet, Mahalia Jackson, Gillespie, Mezzrow, and John Lewis.

A0002. Avgerinos, Gerassimos. Kuenstler-Biographien: die Mitglieder im Berliner Philharmonischen Orchester von 1882-1972. Berlin: Gerassimos Avgerinos, 1972. 188 p., bibliography.

A0003. Balliett, Whitney. American Musicians: Fifty-six Portraits in Jazz. New York: Oxford University Press, 1986. 415 p.

Important artists from the birth of jazz to Cecil Taylor. Author of nine books, Balliett has been one of the most stylish and perceptive critics of jazz since his work for the Saturday Review (1953-57).

A0004. Balliett, Whitney. Improvising: Sixteen Jazz Musicians and Their Art. New York: Oxford University Press, 1977. vi, [i], 263 p., index.

Allen, Oliver, Hines, Mary Lou Williams, Russell, Jess Stacy, Norvo, Catlett, Rich, Grapelli, Jim Hall, and Bob Wilber.

A0005. Balliett, Whitney. New York Notes: a Journal of Jazz, 1972-1975. Boston: Houghton Mifflin Company, 1976. [ii], 250 p.

Based on articles originally written for the New Yorker.

A0006. Balliett, Whitney. Night Creature: a Journal of Jazz, 1975-1980. New York: Oxford University Press, 1981. 285 p., index.

Mentions almost everyone but especially Armstrong, Basie, Ellington, Gillespie, Goodman, Hampton, Hines, Parker, Tatum, and Wilson.

A0007. Balliett, Whitney. Such Sweet Thunder: Forty-nine Pieces on Jazz. New York: The Bobbs-Merrill Company, Inc., 1966. 366 p., index.

Articles from the New Yorker 1962-66.

A0008. Blaukopf, Kurt. Grosse Virtuosen. Teufen: A. Niggli und W. Verkauf, 1954. 195 p., 16 illus., discography, 56-item bibliography.

Backhaus, Besrodny, Campoli, Casals, Cortot, Demus, Edwin Fischer, Gieseking, Grumiaux, Gulda, Heifetz, Horowitz, Kempff, Kreisler, Mainardi, Menuhin, Neveu, David Oistrakh, Helmut Roloff, Szigeti, Schneiderhahn, and Thibaud.

A0009. Brashovanova, Lada. Bulgarische Instrumentalisten. Translated by Erika Moskova. Sofia: Komitee fuer Freundschaft und Kulturelle Ver-bindungen mit dem Ausland, 1969. 46 p., portraits.

Forty-three artists are included with a short biography, repertoire, and portrait for each. Good reference for regional artists.

A0010. Brush, Gerome. Boston Symphony Orchestra: Charcoal Drawings of Its Members with Biographical Sketches. Boston: Privately Printed for the Orchestra, 1936. vii, 218, [i] p., portraits.

A0011. Chilton, John. Who's Who of Jazz: Storyville to Swing Street. New York: Da Capo Press, Inc., 1985 [original London, 1972]. [v], 375 p. + [16] plates, 98 illus., 68-item bibliography of periodicals and newspapers.

Over one thousand jazz musicians in America prior to 1920.

A0012. Čižik, Vladimír. Slovenski koncertni umelci. 2 vols. Bratislava: Slovensky Hudobny Fond, 1974/76. 145, [3] p., illus.; 300 p., illus.

Volume one includes forty-four artists many with a short bibliography and discography; volume two covers forty-five instrumentalists and chamber groups.

A0013. Claghorn, Charles Eugene. Biographical Dictionary of Jazz. Englewood Cliffs (NJ): Prentice-Hall, Inc., 1982. 377 p., index of jazz and combo groups.

Short profiles "of more than 3,400 jazz musicians, composers, vocalists, and bands."

A0014. de Bremont, Anna. The World of Music: the Great Virtuosi. New York: Brentanos [London: W.W. Gibbings], 1892. 257 p.

Ascher, Charles-August de Bériot, Ole Bull, Buxtehude, Clementi, Chopin, Ernst, Gottschalk, Gung'l, Herz, Hummel, Kalkbrenner, Liszt, Moscheles, Paganini, Spohr, Tausig, Thalberg, and Vieuxtemps.

A0015. Doružka, Lubomír. Panoráma populární hudby 1918/1978 aneb nevšední písničkáři všedních dní. Praha: Mladá Fronta, 1981. 284 p., 72 illus., index.

Major artists with a variety of instruments and styles.

A0016. Escudier, Léon. Mes souvenirs: les virtuoses. Paris: E. Dentu, Libraire-Editeur, 1868. 358 p.

Important period material on Bottesini, Chopin, Godefroid, Herz, Gottschalk, Paganini, Vieuxtemps, and Vivier.

A0017. Ewen, David. Famous Instrumentalists. New York: Dodd, Mead & Company, 1965. 159 p., 21 illus., index.

Twenty-three artists' "biographies for young people."

A0018. Ewen, David, ed. Living Musicians. New York: The H.W. Wilson Company, 1940. 390 p., photo of each musician, classified list by type of musician.

Ninety-two pianists, fifty violinists, fourteen cellists, nine organists, six violinists, six flutists, six harpsichordists, three harpists, two guitarists, one lutenist, one clarinetist, one oboist, one saxophonist, and one xylophonist. Artists from Clarence Adler to Efrem Zimbalist.

A0019. Ewen, David, ed. Living Musicians. First Supplement. New York: The H.W. Wilson Company, 1957. 178 p., necrology [2nd printing 1964], list of new biographies, classified list of new biographies.

Approximately 150 new additions from Geza Anda to Tossy Spivakovsky.

A0020. Feather, Leonard. The Encyclopedia of Jazz in the Sixties. New York: Bonanza Books, 1966. 312 p., 257 illus., poll winners, jazz record companies, [major] recordings of the sixties, 57-item bibliography.

A0021. Feather, Leonard and Ira Gitler. The Encyclopedia of Jazz in the Seventies. New York: Horizon Press, 1976. 393 p., 245 illus., jazz education, jazz films, recommended recordings 1966-1975, 102-item bibliography 1966-1975.

A0022. Feather, Leonard. The New Encyclopedia of Jazz. New York: Bonanza Books, 1960. 527 p., 500 illus., recommended jazz recordings, jazz organizations, jazz record companies, 113-item bibliography.

The 1955 edition [New York: Horizon Press] revised and enlarged.

A0023. Ferris, George T. The Great Violinists and Pianists. New York: D. Appleton and Company, 1881. Reprint 1972. iv, 326 p.

Ole Bull, Chopin, Clementi, de Bériot, Gottschalk, Liszt, Moscheles, Paganini, Clara Schumann, Spohr, Thalberg, and Viotti.

A0024. Handy, D. Antoinette. Black Women in American Bands & Orchestras. Metuchen (NJ): The Scarecrow Press, 1981. xii, 319 p., illus., appendices, 433-item bibliography, index to profiles, general index.

A0025. Knauss, Zane, comp. Conversations with Jazz Musicians. Detroit: Gale Research Company, 1977. 281 p.

Interviews with Louis Belson, Leon Breeden, Gillespie, Eric Kloss, Jimmy McPartland, Barry Miles, Sy Oliver, Charlie Spivak, Billy Taylor, Phil Woods, and Sol Yaged.

A0026. Larsson, Lars Erik. Upplaendske spelmaen under 4 arhundraden. Uppsala: Upplands Grafiska AB, 1980. 336 p., illus., indices.

An important biographical dictionary for Scandanavian artists.

A0027. Mannucci, Michele and Furio Fossati. I grandi della musica jazz da Scott Joplin a Gil Evans. Vol. 2: I grandi della musica jazz da Miles Davis a Douglas Ewart. Milano: Longanesi & C., 1979. 134, [2] p., 28 illus., discographies; 135-317 p., bibliography, index of names, index of terms, general index for volumes one and two.

Volume one includes fifty artists; volume two adds fifty more.

A0028. Marmontel, A. Virtuoses contemporains. Paris: Heugel et Fils, 1882. 301, [2] p.

Twenty-six artists are mentioned but especially Diemer, Duvernoy, Jaell, Planté, Anton Rubinstein, and Wieniawski.

A0029. McCarthy, Albert J. Kings of Jazz. Revised and edited by Stanley Green. South Brunswick (NJ): A.S. Barnes and Co., Inc., 1978. 367 p., illus., selected discographies, bibliography.

Beiderbecke, Miles Davis, Johnny Dodds, Ellington, Gillespie, Jelly Roll Morton, Oliver, Parker, and Waller.

A0030. Miller, Mark. Jazz in Canada: Fourteen Lives. Toronto: University of Toronto Press, 1982. 245 p., discographies, index.

Trump and Teddy Davidson, Paul and P.J. Perry, Herbie Spanier, Wray Downes, Larry Dubin, Nelson Symonds, Gary Nadon, Claude Ranger, Sonny Greenwich, Brian Barley, and Ron Park. None of these artists is included in PART C, but information on most of them can be found in Encyclopedia of Music in Canada [Toronto: University of Toronto Press, 1981] edited by Helmut Kallmann, Gilles Potvin and Kenneth Winters. A worthy research project would be to compile a biographical dictionary of notable jazz artists in the world other than Americans.

A0031. Ortiz Oderigo, Nester R. <u>Profiles del jazz</u>. Buenos Aires:
Ricordi Americana, 1955. 189 p.

   Bunk Johnson, Keppard, Oliver, Armstrong, Tommy Ladnier, Ory, Bechet,
   Johnny Dodds, George Lewis, Omer Simeon, Jelly Roll Morton, James P.
   Johnson, Bud Scott, Lonnie Johnson, Pops Foster, and Baby Dodds.

A0032. Rusch, Robert D. <u>Jazztalk: the "Cadence" Interviews</u>. Secaucus
(NJ): Lyle Stuart Inc., 1983. 190 p., discography, index.

   Hubbard, Paul Quinichette, Jackson, Cecil Taylor, Sun Ra, Milt
   Hinton, Von Freeman, Billy Harper, Blakey, and Bill Dixon.

A0033. Sachs, Harvey. <u>Virtuoso: the Life and Art of Niccolo Paganini,
Franz Liszt, Anton Rubinstein, Ignace Jan Paderewski, Fritz Kreisler,
Pablo Casals, Wanda Landowska, Vladimir Horowitz, [and] Glenn Gould</u>.
London: Thames and Hudson, 1982. 208 p., 45 illus., notes, 77-item
bibliography, index.

A0034. Shapiro, Nat and Nat Hentoff, eds. <u>The Jazz Makers</u>. New York:
Rinehart & Company, Inc., 1957. Reprint 1975/1979. 368 p., 21 illus.

   Twenty-one major artists but most helpful for Jelly Roll Morton,
   Baby Dodds, Armstrong, Jack Teagarden, Beiderbecke, and Russell.

A0035. Viujsje, Bert, ed. <u>Jazzportretten</u>. Amsterdam: Van Gennep bv,
1983. 143 p.

   Ben Webster interviews Illinois Jacquet, Dexter Gordon, Getz, Gil
   Evans, Bill Evans, Abbey Lincoln, Piet Noordijk, Rein de Graaff,
   Maarten Altena, Phillip Wilson, George Lewis, and Wynton Marsalis.

A0036. Weissmann, Adolf. <u>Der Virtuose</u>. Berlin: Paul Cassirer, 1918.
174 p., 39 illus.

   Many famous artists, but really helpful for Paganini, Liszt, Anton
   Rubinstein, Busoni, Joachim, and von Buelow.

A0037. Zidek, Frantisek. <u>Cesti housliste tri stoleti</u>. Praha: Panton,
1979. 350 p., 33 illus., 42-item bibliography, index of names.

   A revised edition was published in 1982. Good source for obscure
   artists as well as many performers unknown in the West.

BRASS PLAYERS

A0038. Baker, David. <u>Jazz Styles and Analysis: Trombone, a History of
the Jazz Trombone via Recorded Solos</u>. Chicago: Maher Publications, 1973.
144 p., illus.

   This survey from Fernando Arbello to Trummy Young offers a valid and
   interesting way to approach the historical evolution of styles.

A0039. Bridges, Glenn D. Pioneers in Brass. Detroit: Sherwood Publications, 1965. v, 113 p., illus.

Fifty-nine outstanding players including women.

A0040. Coar, Birchard. A Critical Study of the Nineteenth Century Horn
Virtuosi in France. De Kalb (IL): Privately Printed for the Author,
1952. ix, 168 p., 29 illus., 3 appendices including twenty-six short
biographies, 67-item bibliography.

A0041. Fitzpatrick, Horace A. The Horn and Horn-Playing and the Austro-
Bohemian Tradition from 1680-1830. London: Oxford University Press,
1970. xiv, 256 p., 17 illus., bibliography, index.

KEYBOARD

A0042. Anon. Celebridades del piano: esbozos biográficos por un
dilettanti. Barcelona: Imprenta Elzeviriana de Borrás, Mestres y Ca.,
1914. 176 p., 32 portraits.

Thirty-two keyboard artists from Clementi to Paderewski each with
a portrait.

A0043. Anon. Sketches in Miniature of Present-Day Musicians. Boston:
Mason & Hamlin, n.d. [1926]. 23 p., 21 portraits.

Twenty-one performers are represented in this publicity release.

A0044. Benjamin, William Howard. Biographies of Celebrated Organists of
America. Albany (NY): The Benjamin Publishing Co., 1908. 155 p., illus.

Of great interest regarding the history of performance in America, a
topic which would benefit from a new comprehensive survey. '

A0045. Bie, Oscar. A History of the Pianoforte and Pianoforte Players.
Translated by E.E. Kellett and E.W. Naylor. London: J.M. Dent & Company,
1899 [original published in Munich: Verlagsanstalt F. Bruckmann A.-G.].
Reprint 1966. xi, 336 p., 133 illus., index.

A0046. Bouvet, Charles. Une dynastie de musiciens français: les
Couperin organistes de l'église Saint-Gervais. Paris: Librairie
Delagfave, 1919. Reprint 1977. 304 p., 16 illus., bibliography, notes,
index.

A0047. Brook, Donald. Masters of the Keyboard. London: Rockliff, 1946.
Reprint 1971 with bibliography. 183 p., illus.

John Bull, J.S. Bach, Domenico Scarlatti, Mozart, Moscheles, Chopin,
Liszt, Clara Schumann, Anton Rubinstein, Leschetizky, Busoni, Hess,
Paderewski, Rachmaninoff, Harriet Cohen, Curzon, Hambourg, Eileen
Joyce, Louis Kentner, Moiseiwitsch, Leff Pouishnoff, and Solomon.

A0048. Brower, Harriette Moore. Modern Masters of the Keyboard. New York: Frederick A. Stokes Company, 1926. Reprint 1969. viii, [i], 303 p., 16 illus.

Rachmaninoff, Rosenthal, Cortot, de Pachmann, Ignaz Friedman, Brailowsky, Gieseking, Josef Lhevinne, Landowska, Lamond, von Dohnanyi, Siloti, Schmitz, Medtner, Samaroff, Schnabel, Mitja Nikisch, and Moiseiwitsch.

A0049. Brower, Harriette Moore. Piano Mastery: Talks with Master Pianists and Teachers. New York: Frederick A. Stokes Company Publishers, 1915. x, 299 p., 16 illus.

Thirty-one artists are interviewed.

A0050. Burch, Gladys. Famous Pianists: for Boys and Girls. New York: A.S. Barnes & Company, 1943. Reprint 1956 as Famous Pianists for Young People. vii, 156p., illus.

A0051. Chapin, Victor. Giants of the Keyboard. Philadelphia: Lippincott, 1967. 189 p., illus., discography, index.

Clementi, Dussek, Johann Cramer, Hummel, Field, Czerny, Moscheles, Liszt, Clara Schumann, Gottschalk, Anton Rubinstein, Carreño, Busoni, Paderewski, J.C. Bach, and Schnabel.

A0052. Chasins, Abram. Speaking of Pianists. New York: Alfred A. Knopf, 1957. 291, xiv p., index.

The second edition [1961] includes a supplementary chapter to update materials with its own index. Also see the third edition [1981].

A0053. Cooke, James Francis. Great Pianists on Piano Playing: Study Talks with Foremost Virtuosos. Philadelphia: Theodore Presser Co., 1917. 418 p., illus.

Twenty-eight artists including Backhaus, Busoni, Hofmann, and Rachmaninoff. Cooke edited the Etude (1908-49) which was a landmark publication bridging the amateur and professional musical worlds.

A0054. Doerschuk, Bob, ed. Rock Keyboard. New York: Quill/William Morrow and Company, Inc., 1984. 187 p., illus., index.

Twenty-four performers are highlighted among a host of lesser talent.

A0055. Dubal, David. Reflections from the Keyboard: the World of the Concert Pianist. New York: Summit Books, 1984. 399 p., portraits, biographical notes, selected discography, index.

Interviews with thirty-five pianists from Claudio Arrau to Earl Wild.

A0056. Ehrlich, A. [pseud. for Albert Payne]. Beruehmte Klavierspieler der Vergangenheit und Gegenwart: eine Sammlung von 116 Biographien und 114 Portraets. Leipzig: A.H. Payne, 1893. viii, 367 p., illus.

An enlarged American edition, Celebrated Pianists of the Past and Present: a Collection of One Hundred and Thirty-nine Biographies with Portraits [Philadelphia: Theodore Presser, 1894. viii, 423 p., illus.], presented "...to its readers those pianists, resident in America, who are not included in the original edition." Both editions are very important period sources.

A0057. Elder, Dean. Pianists at Play: Interviews, Master Lessons, and Technical Regimes. Evanston (IL): The Instrumentalist Company, 1982. 324 p., illus., index.

Materials originally published in Clavier. Elder has attempted "... first and foremost a reference work on piano playing. It includes some of the best master class lessons...and technical regimes." Twenty-seven interviews with twenty-five artists; thirteen master lessons with twelve artists; and five technical regimes.

A0058. Gerig, Reginald. Famous Pianists and Their Technique. Washington: Robert B. Luce, Inc., 1974. xvi, 560 p., illus., 342-item bibliography, index.

A0059. Grigorev, Lev Grigorevich. Sovremennye pianisty. Moskva: Gos. muzykal'noe izd-vo, 1977. 286 p., 52 illus.

A0060. Kaiser, Joachim. Grosse Pianisten in unserer Zeit. Muenchen: Ruetten und Loening Verlag, 1965. Reprint 1967 in a limited edition. 230, [1] p., 28 illus., discography, index.

This edition was translated by David Wooldridge and George Unwin [London: George Allen & Unwin Ltd, 1971] as Great Pianists of Our Time with an expanded discography by Francis F. Clough.

A revised and expanded German edition [Muenchen: R. Piper & Co., Verlag, 1972] includes an index. Artur Rubinstein, Backhaus, Arrau, Horowitz, Kempff, Rudolf Serkin, Curzon, Richter, Gilels, Casadesus, Michelangeli, Gould, Barenboim, Stephen Bishop, Brendel, Argerich, Gelber, Watts, Ashkenazy, Pollini, Pommier, and Anda.

A0061. Kehler, George, comp. The Piano in Concert. 2 vols. Metuchen (NJ): The Scarecrow Press, Inc., 1982. xxxiv, 786 p.,; 787-1,143 p.

This monumental and invaluable reference work lists over two thousand pianists. Each artist is annotated with a short biography and a list of representative repertoire. "This work is meant for pianists, musicologists, researchers, and others interested in those who have played the piano publicly and the programs they have played. It has four major purposes. They are (1) to identify and include those pianists who have made outstanding contributions by their performances; (2) to provide a brief biographical sketch of each pianist; (3) to determine and list the programs played by these performers; and (4) to give as completely as possible bibliographical citations from published reviews of the programs here included. It embraces primarily nineteenth and twentieth-century pianists, with a limited number of eighteenth-century performers."

A0062. Lahee, Henry Charles. Famous Pianists of Today and Yesterday. Boston: The Page Company Publishers, 1900. vi, [iv], 11-345 p., 9 illus., chronological table of famous pianists, index.

A0063. von Lenz, Wilhelm. Die grossen Piano-virtuosen unserer Zeit aus persoenlicher Bekanntschaft. Berlin: B. Behr's Buchhandlung, 1872. 111 p.

Liszt, Chopin, Tausig, and von Henselt. The first English translation was published by G. Schirmer in New York in 1899. A revised translation edited by Philip Reder as The Great Piano Virtuosos of Our Time [New York: Regency Press, 1971] was reprinted in 1973.

A0064. Locard, Paul. Les maîtres contemporains de l'orgue. Paris: Editions du Corrier musical, 1901. 48 p., 3 portraits.

A0065. Loesser, Arthur. Men, Women and Pianos: a Social History. New York: Simon and Schuster, 1954. xvi, 654 p., 352-item bibliography, index.

Loesser's professional entry is C0745. His talented brother wrote the music for "Guys and Dolls" and "The Most Happy Fella"!

A0066. Lorenz, Paul. Grosse Pianisten dreier Jahrunderte. Wien: Bergland Verlag, 1979. 143 p., illus., 20-item bibliography, index of names.

A0067. Lyle, Wilson. A Dictionary of Pianists. New York: Schirmer Books, 1984. 343, [32] p., 50 illus., winners of international piano competitions and medalists of conservatories and schools.

Over twenty-five hundred performers are included.

A0068. Lyons, Len. The Great Jazz Pianists Speaking of Their Lives and Music. New York: William Morrow and Company, Inc., 1983. 321 p., illus., individual discographies, appendix, index.

Twenty-seven artists from Ran Blake to Josef "Joe" Zawinul.

A0069. Mach, Elyse. Great Pianists Speak for Themselves. 2 vols. New York: Dodd, Mead & Company, 1980/1988. xvi, 204 p., 26 illus., index; 258 p., 25 illus., index.

Arrau, Ashkenazy, Brendel, Browning, de Larrocha, Dichter, Firkusny, Gould, Horowitz, Janis, Lili Kraus, Tureck, and Watts.

The second volume adds Badura-Skoda, Bolet, Egorov, Fialkowska, Fleisher, Gilels, Hough, Kocsis, Ohlsson, Ousset, Perahia, and Pogorelich.

A0070. Marcus, Adele. Great Pianists Speak with Adele Marcus. Neptune (NJ): Paganiniana Publications, 1979. 160 p., 58 illus.

Bachauer, Karl Ulrich Schnabel, Frank, Bolet, Firkusny, de Larrocha, Ohlsson, Browning, and Adele Marcus.

A0071. **Marmontel, Antoine François.** Les pianistes célèbres: silhouettes et médaillons. Paris: Heugel et fils, 1878. vii, 310, [2] p.

Thirty artists from Field to Liszt. 2nd enlarged edition 1887.

A0072. **Méreaux, Amédée.** Les clavecinistes de 1637 à 1790: histoire du clavecin, portraits et biographies des célèbres clavecinistes. Paris: Heugel et Cie Editeurs, 1867. 87 p.

Folio edition with biographies of twenty-five major figures.

A0073. **Methuen-Campbell, James.** Chopin Playing from the Composer to the Present Day. New York: Taplinger Publishing Company, 1981. [2], 13, 289 p., pupils of Chopin, Prizewinners of the Frederic Chopin International Piano Competition, notes, discography, 153-item bibliography, index.

This is essential reading for those wishing to trace the various national schools which have trained artists in this literature. Note titles under C0236.

A0074. **Niemann, Walter.** Meister des Klaviers: die Pianisten der Gegenwart und der letzten Vergangenheit. Berlin: Verlegt bei Schuster & Loeffler, 1919. 245 p., index.

A0075. **Noyle, Linda J.** Pianists on Playing: Interviews with Twelve Concert Artists. Metuchen (NJ): The Scarecrow Press, Inc., 1987. xii, 175 p., discography, index.

Ashkenazy, Bolet, Browning, Davidovich, Dichter, Janina Fialkowska, Firkusny, Fleisher, André-Michel Schub, Abbey Simon, Votapek, and Watts.

A0076. **Papp, Viktor.** Liszt Ferenc élo magyar tanitványai. Budapest: Dante Kiad, 1938. 191 p., illus.

Fourteen important Hungarian pianists.

A0077. **Pauer, Ernst.** A Dictionary of Pianists and Composers for the Pianoforte, with an Appendix of Manufacturers of the Instrument. London: Novello, Ewer and Co., 1895. v, 159 p.

This is a marvelous resource for obscure performers.

A0078. **Rabinovich, David Abramovich.** Portrety pianistov. Moskva: Gos. muzykal'noe izd-vo, 1970. 266 p., illus.

Trained originally as a concert pianist with Anna Essipova, the author turned to writing about composers and performers.

A0079. **Range, Hans Peter.** Die Konzertpianisten der Gegenwart: ein Musikliebhaber berichtet ueber Konzertmilieu und 150 Klavier-Virtuosen. Lahr/Schwarzwald: Moritz Schauenburg, 1964. 218, [1] p. 40 portraits.

The second edition [1966] includes 173 pianists and 54 portraits.

A0080. Range, Hans Peter. Pianisten im Wandel der Zeit. Lahr/Schwarz-
wald: Moritz Schauenburg Verlag, 1982. 102 p., 8 illus., index of names.

A0081. Rattalino, Piero. Da Clementi a Pollini: duecento anni con i
grandi pianisti. Milano: G. Ricordi & C., 1983. 479, [16] p., 25 illus.,
88-item bibliography, index of names

A0082. Raugel, Félix. Les organistes. Paris: Librairie Renouard, 1923.
Reprint 1962. 126, [2] p., 17 illus., 66-item bibliography.

A0083. Ritter, August Gottfried. Zur Geschichte des Orgelspiels, vor-
nehmlich des deutschen, im 14. bis zum Anfange des 18. Jahrhunderts. 2
vols. Leipzig: Max Hesse's Verlag, 1884. Reprint 1969. 225 p., index;
230 p. (musical examples).

A0084. Schang, F.C. Visiting Cards of Pianists from the Collection of
F.C. Schang with Comment by Him. New York: Joseph Patelson Music House,
1979. 112 p., illus., 23-item bibliography.

   Thirty-five artists were selected.

A0085. Schonberg, Harold C. The Great Pianists. New York: Simon and
Schuster, 1963. 448 p., 62 illus., index.

   A bibliography would have enhanced this otherwise fine effort.

A0086. Unterbrink, Mary. Jazz Women at the Keyboard. Privately Printed
for the Author, n.d. viii, 184 p., 29 illus., 42-item bibliography,
index of names.

A0087. Villanis, Luigi Alberto. L'Arte del pianoforte in Italia (da
Clementi a Sgambati). Bologna: Libreria Forni Editrice, 1969 [original
Torino, 1907]. [ii], 253, [4] p.

A0088. West, John Ebenezer. Cathedral Organists Past and Present: a
Record of the Succession of Organists of the Cathedrals, Chapels Royal,
and Principal Collegiate Churches of the United Kingdom. London: Novello
and Company, Limited, 1899. xi, [1], 141, [1] p., bibliography, index.

A0089. Wier, Albert E. The Piano: Its History, Makers, Players and
Music. New York: Longmans, Green and Co., 1940.

   See pp. 375-417 for a biographical dictionary of pianists.

A0090. Young, Percy M. Keyboard Musicians of the World. London:
Abelard-Schuman, 1967. 184 p., 28 illus., discography, index.

   This falls into the category of a music appreciation guide.

A0091. Zilberquit, Mark. Russia's Great Modern Pianists. Neptune (NJ):
Paganiniana Publications, 1983. 511 p., illus., index of names.

   Berman, Bashkirov, Gilels, Andrei Gavrilov, Tikhon Khrennikov,
   Vladimir Krainev, Nikolai Petrov, Mikhail Pletnyov, Richter, Gregory
   Sokolov, Rodion Shchedrin, and Eliso Virsaladze.

PERCUSSION

A0092. Brown, Theodore Dennis. A History and Analysis of Jazz Drumming to 1942. Ph.D. diss., University of Michigan, 1976. x, 605 p.

STRINGS

A0093. Allen, Julia C. Famous Violinists: Short Sketches of Some of the Most Celebrated Violin Virtuosi. New York: The John Church Company, 1893. [1], 31 p.

Corelli, Tartini, Viotti, Spohr, Paganini, de Bériot, Bull, Leonard, Vieuxtemps, Wieniawski, Joachim, Sarasate, Musin, and Urso.

A0094. Anon. Blues Guitarists: Collected Interviews from the Pages of Guitar Player Magazine. Saratoga (CA): Guitar Player Productions, n.d. [1975]. 72 p., illus., index.

Nineteen guitarists from Elvin Bishop to Johnny Winter are included.

A0095. Anon. Guitar Notables: Brief Interviews from Guitar Player Magazine's "Pro's Reply" Column. Saratoga (CA): Guitar Player Productions, n.d. [1975]. 63 p., illus.

Forty-eight "notables" from Chet Atkins to Johnny Winter.

A0096. Anon. Jazz Guitarists: Collected Interviews from Guitar Player Magazine. Introduction by Leonard Feather. Saratoga (CA): Guitar Player Productions, n.d. [1975]. 119 p., illus., index.

Forty-one artists are included some in multiple interviews.

A0097. Anon. Rock Guitarists: Revised from the Pages of Guitar Player Magazine. 2 vols. Saratoga (CA): Guitar Player Magazine, n.d. [1978]. 171 p., illus., index of 70 guitarists; 214 p., illus., index of 66 guitarists.

A0098. Anon. The International Library of Music: Music Literature, Volume III -- the Violinists Guide. New York: The University Society, 1925. viii, 311 p., illus.

A0099. Applebaum, Samuel and Sada. The Way They Play. 12 vols. Neptune City (NJ): Paganiniana Publications, Inc., 1972-83. 380 p., illus.; 384 p., illus.; 320 p., illus., discography; 320 p., illus.; 299, [21] p., illus.; 352 p., illus.; 283, [2] p., illus., index; 285 p., illus., index; 285 p., illus., index; 253 p., illus., index; 253 p., illus., index; 253 p., illus., index.

"The purpose of this series of books is quite diverse -- to show how many of the world's great string players achieve their interpre-tations...to reveal personality glimpses of the artists...that will provide a deeper understanding of their activities."

Volume one includes sixteen violinists, four violists, and five
cellists; volume two includes eleven violinists, two violists, four
cellists, and three bassists; volume three includes twelve artists;
volumes four, five, and six each have nine artists; volumes seven,
nine, and ten include six artists each AND have a cumulative index
(as do all volumes beginning with #7); volume eight has seven
artists; volume eleven, five, and volume twelve, four. This fan-
tastic undertaking is a "must" for all serious string buffs!

A0100. Applebaum, Samuel and Ida. "With the Artists": World Famed
String Players Discuss Their Art. New York: John Market & Co., 1955.
vii, 318 p., illus., index.

Corigliano, Eisenberg, Elman, Francescatti, Joseph Fuchs, Galamian,
Carroll Glenn, Heifetz, Hilsberg, Katims, Kaufman, Kreisler, Kurtz,
Menuhin, Milstein, Mischakoff, Morini, Persinger, Piatigorsky,
Primrose, Ricci, Leonard Rose, Schuster, Spalding, Spivakowsky,
Stern, Szigeti, Patricia Travers, and Zimbalist.

A0101. Bachmann, Alberto. An Encyclopedia of the Violin. Introduction
by Eugéne Ysaÿe. Translated by Frederick H. Martens. New York: D.
Appleton and Company, 1925. Reprint 1966 with preface by Stuart Canin.
xiv, 470 p., 78 plates, biographical dictionary of violinists, bibliography, index.

Bachmann, a student of Ysaye, Hubay, and Adolf Brodsky, also composed
three violin concertos. His professional entry is C0054.

A0102. Bachmann, Alberto. Les grands violinistes du passé. Paris:
Librarie Fischbacher, 1913. 468, [1] p., illus.

A basic source which includes forty-three of the finest artists.
He also published Le secret de la virtuosité: le violon, ses
maîtres et ses ancêtres a copy of which I have not located.

A0103. Bachmann, Alberto. Le violin (lutherie-oeuvres-biographies):
guide a l'usage des artistes & des amateurs. Paris: Librairie Fischbacher, 1906. xi, 198 p., index of names.

Short biographies of 188 important performers.

A0104. Baechi, Julius. Von Boccherini bis Casals: Essais ueber 17
Meistercellisten und die Entwicklung des Cellospiels mit einem Anhang
zur Geschichte des Violoncellos. Zuerich: Panton-Verlag, 1961. 91 p.,
illus., bibliography, discography.

Boccherini, Jean-Pierre Duport, Jean-Louis Duport, Romberg, Lee,
Dotzauer, Joseph Merk, Friedrich Kummer, Servais, Franchomme, Piatti,
Gruetzmacher, Davidov, David Popper, Klengel, and Hugo Becker.

The second edition, Behruemte Cellisten: Portraets der Meistercellisten von Boccherini bis Casals und Paul Gruemmer bis Rostro-
povitch [Zuerich: Atlantis Musikbuch-Verlag AG, 1973], adds fifteen
cellists. The third edition [1981] adds two more and an index.

A0105. Bonaventura, Arnoldo. Storia del violino dei violinisti e della musica per violino. Milano: Ulrico Hoepli Editore-Libraio, 1925 [2nd edition 1953]. 282 p., 262-item bibliography, fold-out plate of violin schools.

The bibliography is very important especially for early biographies!

A0106. Bone, Philip J. The Guitar and Mandolin: Biographies of Celebrated Players and Composers. London: Schott & Co., Ltd., 1972 [original 1914; enlarged 1954]. [vi], 388 p., 132 illus., index.

A0107. Boyden, David Dodge. The History of Violin Playing from Its Origins to 1761 and Its Relationship to the Violin and Violin Music. London: Oxford University Press, 1965. xxiii, 569 p., 50 illus., phono-disk, appendix, 264-item bibliography, glossary, index.

An absolutely basic history through the end of the Baroque era.

A0108. Britt, Stan. The Jazz Guitarists. Poole (Dorset): Blandford Press, 1984. 128 p., illus., partial discographies.

Important material on George Benson, Teddy Bunn, Kenny Burrell, Charlie Christian, Tal Farlow, Freddy Green, Jim Hall, Lonnie Johnson, Eddie Lang, John McLaughlin, Wes Montgomery, and Django Reinhardt.

A0109. Brook, Donald. Violinists of Today. London: Rockliff, 1948. Reprint 1972. xiii, 192 p., 28 portraits of 28 artists.

A0110. Budis, Ratibor. Housle v promenách staletí. Praha: Supraphon, 1975. 153, [24] p., illus., phonodisk, bibliography, index.

Includes a variety of string players.

A0111. Budis, Ratibor. Slavní cesti houslisté. Praha: Státní Hudebni vydavatelství, 1966. 194, [1] p., 12 illus., 27-item bibliography.

Famous as well as little-known Czech string players.

A0112. Campbell, Margaret. The Great Violinists. Foreword by Ruggiero Ricci. Garden City: Doubleday & Company, Inc., 1981. xxix, 366 p., 70 illus., notes, 68-item bibliography, discography, index.

A0113. Clarke, A. Mason. A Biographical Dictionary of Fiddlers Including Performers on the Violoncello and Double Bass, Past and Present. London: Wm. Reeves, n.d. [1895]. vii, [i], 360 p., 9 illus.

A0114. Cosma, Viorel. Figuri de lautari. Bucuresti: Editura Muzicala a Uniunii Compozitorilor din R.P.R., 1960. 228, [4] p., illus., 47-item bibliography, discography.

A0115. Creighton, James Lesley. Discopaedia of the Violin 1889-1971. Foreword by Yehudi Menuhin. Toronto: University of Toronto Press, 1974. xvi, 987 p., index of composers, index of popular titles, index of manufacturers, index of artists.

"The recorded works of almost seventeen hundred violinists are listed in this discopaedia, from cylinders of 1889 to the quadrasonic disks of our own time." Encompassing artists from Vasco Abadiev to Paul Zukofsky, this is an absolutely monumental work! One of the few such compilations consistently cross-indexed in the major dictionaries and encyclopedias.

A0116. Ehrlich, A. [pseud. for Albert Payne]. Beruehmte Geiger der Vergangenheit und Gegenwart: eine Sammlung von 88 Biographien und Portraits. Leipzig: Verlag von A.H. Payne, 1893. xi, 316 p., illus.

The second edition [1902] was expanded to 104 artists from De Ahna to Florian Zajic. Robin H. Legge translated the original edition with notes and additions [London: The Strad, 1897].

A0117. Farga, Franz. Violins and Violinists. Translated by Egon Larsen. New York: The Macmillan Company, 1950. xvi, 223 p., 140 illus., index.

A0118. Flood, W.H. Grattan. The Story of the Harp. Boston: Longwood Press, 1905. Reprint 1977. xx, 207 p., 32 illus., 71-item bibliography, index.

A0119. Gelrud, Paul Geoffrey. A Critical Study of the French Violin School (1782-1882). Ph.D. diss. Cornell University, 1941. 651 p., illus., bibliography.

A0120. Ginsburg, Lev. History of the Violoncello. Translated by Tanya Tchistyakova. Neptune (NJ): Paganiniana Publications, Inc., 1983. 384 p., illus., footnotes, index.

Details regarding many individual artists not found elsewhere.

A0121. Gruenberg, Max. Meister der Violine. Stuttgart: Deutsche Verlags-Anstalt, 1925. 257 p., index of names.

A0122. Grunfeld, Frederic V. The Art and Times of the Guitar: an Illustrated History of Guitars and Guitarists. New York: The Macmillan Company, 1969. [iv], 340 p., illus., notes, 310-item bibliography, index.

A0123. Hartnack, Joachim W. Grosse Geiger unserer Zeit. Muenchen: Ruetten & Loening Verlag, 1967 [rev. ed. Zuerich, 1977]. 335, [1] p., 33 illus., discography, 44-item bibliography, index.

A number of artists, but thirty-six are given special treatment.

A0124. Kienzel, Rich. Great Guitarists. New York: Facts on File, 1985. 246 p., illus., index.

Fifteen performers from blues, seventeen from country, fifteen from jazz, and sixteen from rock are included.

A0125. Lahee, Henry C. Famous Violinists of Today and Yesterday. Boston: L.C. Page and Company, 1899. Revised/expanded ed. 1925. Reprint 1977. x, [iv], 11-384 p., 10 illus., index.

AO126. Liégeois, C. & E. Nogué. Le violoncelle: son histoire, ses virtuoses. Paris: Costallat & Cie, 1913. xiv, 315 p., table of names.

Approximately 500 performers are included.

AO127. Martens, Frederick H. String Mastery: Talks with Master Violinists, Viola Players and Violoncellists. New York: Frederick A. Stokes Company, 1923. ix, [ii], 360 p., 16 illus.

One of the better American writers on music of his generation.

AO128. Marx, Karl. Die Entwicklung des Violoncell und seiner Spiel-technik bis Jean-Louis Duport. Ph.D. diss. University of Saarbruecken, 1963.

AO129. McCutcheon, Meredith Alice. Guitar and Vihuela: an Annotated Bibliography. New York: Pendragon Press, 1985. xlv, 353 p., 13 illus., appendix of periodicals, appendix of music, index.

An excellent work, but artists such as Siegfried Behrend, Ernesto Bitetti, John McLaughlin, and Carlos Montoya are not included.

AO130. Mongan, Norman. The History of the Guitar in Jazz. New York: Oak Publications, 1983. ix, 274 p., 237 illus., sources, discography, index.

AO131. Moser, Andreas. Geschichte des Violinspiels. 2 vols. Tutzing: Hans Schneider, 1966/67 [original Berlin, 1923].

The second volume is particularly helpful: Das Violinspiel von 1800 (Deutschland) bis in die erste Helfte des 20. Jahrhunderts. 371 p., 11 fold-out plates of violin schools, footnotes, index of names.

AO132. Østvedt, Arne. Fiolinens trollmenn i var tid: elleve portretter. Oslo: Gyldendal, 1959. 170, [1] p., illus.

Kreisler, Elman, Szigeti, Heifetz, Milstein, Francescatti, Oistrakh, Szymon Goldberg, Schneiderhan, Menuhin, and Stern.

AO133. Phipson, Thomas Lamb. Biographical Sketches and Anecdotes of Celebrated Violinists. London: Richard Bentley and Son, 1877. xii, 254 p.

Covers sixty famous violinists from Lulli to Joachim and Wieniawski.

AO134. Phipson, Thomas Lamb. Famous Violinists and Fine Violins: Historical Notes, Anecdotes, and Reminiscences. London: Chatto & Windus, 1896. xvi, 254 p., index.

AO135. Pincherle, Marc. Les violonistes: compositeurs et virtuoses. Paris: Henri Laurens, Editeur, 1922. 126, [2] p., 12 illus., 23-item bibliography, index.

AO136. Pougin, Arthur. Le violon: les violonistes et la musique de violon du XVIe au XVIIIe siècle. Paris: Librairie Fischbacher, 1924. 358, [1] p., illus., 211-item bibliography, index of names.

A0137. Prat, Domingo. Diccionario Biografico-Bibliografico-Historico-Critico de Guitarristas. Buenos Aires: Casa Romero y Fernandez, 1934. 468, [3] p., portrait, appendix.

This rarity was published in a numbered and signed edition of 1,605 copies. Literally hundreds of guitarists are listed [pp. 11-345], and there is an appendix of additional entries [pp. 349-396].

A0138. Raaben, Lev Nikolaevich. Zhizn' zamechatel'nykh skripache. Leningrad: Muzyka, 1969. 310, [2] p., 18 illus., bibliographical references.

Good source for minor cellists and violinists.

A0139. Regli, Francesco. Storia del violino in Piemonte. Torino: Tipografia di Enrico Dalmazzo, 1863. 204 p., portrait.

A0140. Reuchsel, Maurice. L'Ecole classique du violon. 2nd ed. Paris: Librairie Fischbacher, 1906 [original 1905]. 100, [1] p., illus.

Reuchsel (b. November 22, 1880, Lyons; d. July 12, 1968, Lyons) published what appears to be an autobiography, Un violoniste en voyage, which I have been unable to locate. His brother Amédée was a fine organist.

A0141. Roth, Henry. Great Violinists in Performance: Critical Evaluations of over 100 Twentieth-Century Virtuosi. Los Angeles: Panjandrum Books, 1987. xii, 266 p., illus., 24-item bibliography, index.

A major contribution to the literature.

A0142. Roth, Henry. Master Violinists in Performance. Foreword by Josef Gingold. Neptune City (NJ): Paganiniana Publications, 1982. 320 p., illus., 25-item bibliography, index.

Especially valuable for Ysaÿe, Kubelik, Thibaud, Huberman, Elman, Heifetz, Szigeti, and Menuhin.

A0143. Sallis, James. The Guitar Players: One Instrument and Its Masters in American Music. New York: William Morrow and Company, Inc., 1982. 288 p., 14 illus., index.

Among the highlighted artists are Lonnie Johnson, Eddie Lang, Roy Smeck, Charlie Christian, Riley Puckett, T-Bone Walker, George Barnes, Hank Garland, Wes Montgomery, Michael Bloomfield, Ry Cooper, Ralph Towner, and Lenny Breau.

A0144. Schang, F.C. Visiting Cards of Violinists from the Collection of F.C. Schang. Privately Published for the Author, 1975. 80 p., illus.

Twenty-eight artists are represented with comments by the author.

A0145. Schwarz, Boris. Great Masters of the Violin from Corelli and Vivaldi to Stern, Zukerman and Perlman. Foreword by Yehudi Menuhin. New York: Simon and Schuster, 1983. 671 p., illus., notes, bibliog., index.

One of the most readable and authoritative general surveys by a scholar who was also a fine violinist. The ten page bibliography should be consulted by anyone interested in the field. Schwarz (b. March 26, 1906, St. Petersburg, Russia; d. December 31, 1983, New York City) was a student of Carl Flesch, Jacques Thibaud, and Lucien Capet and was a member of the first violin section of the NBC Symphony under Toscanini.

A0146. Stoeving, Paul. The Story of the Violin. London: The Walter Scott Publishing Co., Ltd., 1904. xix, 323, [1] p., portrait, chronological table of masters and pupils, index.

A0147. Stoeving, Paul. The Violin: Its Famous Makers and Players. Westport (CT): Greenwood Press, 1970 [original Boston, 1928]. 100 p.

A0148. Stowell, Robin. The Development of Violin Technique from L'Abbé le fils (Joseph Barnabe Saint-Sévin) to Paganini. Ph.D. diss. Cambridge University, 1979.

A0149. Summerfield, Maurice J. The Jazz Guitar: Its Evolution and Its Players. Newcastle upon Tyne: Campbell Graphics, Ltd., 1978. 238 p., illus., selected discographies and readings, index of [116] players.

A0150. Tobler, John. Guitar Heroes. New York: St. Martin's Press, Inc., 1978. 88 p., illus., representative albums.

This initial version contains thirty-two biographies.

A0151. Tobler, John and Stuart Grundy. The Guitar Greats. London: British Broadcasting Corporation, 1983. 191 p., illus., discographies, index.

Comprehensive chapters on B.B. King, Scotty Moore, James Burton, Hank B. Marvin, Eric Clapton, Jeff Beck, Pete Townshend, Jimmy Page, Ry Cooper, Ritchie Blackmore, Steve Miller, Carlos Santana, Joe Walsh, and Brian May. Clapton is the only one who made my list.

A0152. Van der Straeten, Edmund Joseph. The History of the Violin: Its Ancestors and Collateral Instruments from Earliest Times to the Present Day. 2 vols. London: Cassell and Company, Ltd., 1933. xvii, 416 p., 48 plates, 33 illus.; ix, 473 p., 73 illus., biographical index.

Volume one covers famous performers from c.1550 to 1700; volume two continues from 1700 to the 1930s.

A0153. Van der Straeten, Edmund Joseph. The History of the Violoncello, the Viol da Gamba, Their Precursors and Collateral Instruments, with Biographies of All the Most Eminent Players of Every Country. London: William Reeves Bookseller Ltd., 1914. Reprint 1971. xvii, 700 p., 59 plates, 65 illus., index.

There was also a special two volume edition [1914] with extra plates. A cellist and gambist himself, Van der Straeten frequently performed early music with his own trio.

A0154. Van der Straeten, Edmund Joseph. The Romance of the Fiddle: the
Origin of the Modern Virtuoso and the Adventures of His Ancestors. New
York: Benjamin Bloom, Inc., 1971 [original London, 1911]. xvi, 315, [34]
p., illus., index.

A0155. von Wasielewski, Waldemar. Die Violine und ihre Meister. 8th
enlarged edition. Leipzig: Druck und Verlag von Breitkopf & Haertel,
1927 [original 1868]. xvi, 745 p., 162-item bibliography, index.

   The bibliography of violin methods is especially valuable! An
   earlier edition [1920?] was translated by Isobella S.E. Stigand
   as The Violincello and Its History. Reprint New York, 1968. A
   student of David, he was concertmaster in Duesseldorf. His memoirs,
   Aus 70 Jahren, were published in Stuttgart in 1897.

A0156. von Wasielewski, Waldemar. Das Violoncell und seine Geschichte.
Leipzig: Druck und Verlag von Breitkopf & Haertel, 1889. 245 p., 47-item
bibliography, index.

   The bibliography of cello methods is quite valuable.

A0157. Zingel, Hans Joachim. Harfe und Harfenspiel vom Beginn des 16.
bis ins zweite Drittel des 18. Jahrhunderts. Halle: Laaber-Verlag, 1932.
Reprint 1979. 269, 36, vii p., illus., bibliography, index of names.

WOODWINDS

A0158. Estock, Joseph James. A Biographical Dictionary of Clarinetists
Born before 1800. Ph.D. diss. University of Iowa, 1972. xi, 392 p.,
tables, list of works, bibliography.

A0159. Giddins, Gary, Peter Keepnews and Dan Morgenstern. The Sax
Section: Biographical Sketches. New York: New York Jazz Museum, 1974.
37 p., discographies, bibliographies.

   Johnny Hodges, Carter, Charlie Parker, Dolphy, Coleman, Hawkins,
   Freeman, Ben Webster, Young, Dexter Gordon, Getz, Sonny Rollins,
   Coltrane, Carney, Mulligan, Chaloff, Adrian Rollins, and Bechet.

A0160. Langwill, Lyndesay Graham. The Bassoon and the Contrabassoon.
London: Ernest Benn Limited, 1965. xiv, 23, 269 p., illus., discography,
5 appendices including an index.

   Chapter twelve: "Some Noted Players Past and Present."

A0161. de Lorenzo, Leonard. My Complete Story of the Flute: the Instrument, the Performer, the Music. New York: The Citadel Press, 1951. xvi,
493, [32] p., 35 illus.

   There is an extensive section on performers [pp.63-346]. de Lorenzo
   was first flutist of the New York Philharmonic as well as a respected
   teacher at the Eastman School. His professional entry is C0750.

A0162. Mueller, Regula, ed. Gespraeche mit Floetisten. Bern-
Ostermundigen: Salm Verlag, 1983. 114 p., 6 portraits, discographies.

   Peter-Lukas Graf, Irena Grafenauer, Andre Jaunet, Paul Meisen,
   Aurèle Nicolet, and Gustav Scheck.

A0163. Rockstro, Richard Shepherd and Georgina M. A Treatis on the
Construction of the Flute Including...Critical Notices of Sixty Celebrated Flute-Players. London: Rudall, Carte and Co., Ltd., 1928
[original 1889]. xli, 664 p., 67 illus., chronological bibliography,
index.

A0164. Weston, Pamela. Clarinet Virtuosi of the Past. London: Robert
Hale, 1971. 291, [1], [64] p., illus., index, chapter bibliography, 29-
item general bibliography.

   Concentrates on the unquestioned greats.

A0165. Weston, Pamela. More Clarinet Virtuosi of the Past. London:
Printed for the author by Halstan & Co., Ltd., 1977. 392, [64] p.,
illus., 54-item bibliography, index.

   Coverage of numerous minor figures. Supplement to A0906.

PART B.
COLLECTIVE WORKS:
Related Books

B0001. Aldrich, Richard. Concert Life in New York 1902-1923. New York:
G.P. Putnam's Sons, 1941. Reprint 1971. 795 p., index, list of Sunday
New York Times articles.

Reviews by one of the outstanding American critics. Especially
important for Hofmann, Kreisler, Ysaÿe, and Zimbalist.

B0002. Anon. The NBC Symphony Orchestra. New York: National Broadcasting Company, 1938. 120 p., portraits.

Includes "Biographies of Personnel" by Philip Kerby.

B0003. Aronson, Rudolph. Theatrical and Musical Memoirs. New York:
McBride, Nast and Company, 1913. [vi], 283 p., 72 illus., index.

An interesting period source.

B0003A. Bachmann, Robert C. Grosse Interpreten im Gespraech. Bern:
Hallwag Verlag, 1977 [original 1976]. 224 p., 52 illus., index.

Seven instrumentalists are included: Anda, Arrau, Menuhin, Milstein,
Szeryng, Weissenberg, and Zuckerman.

B0004. Bagdanskis, Jonas. The Lithuanian Musical Scene. Translated by
Olimpija Armalyté. Vilnius: Mintis Publishers, 1974. 120 p., illus.

Five pianists: Juozapénaité, Aldona & Halina Radvilaité, Vainiunaité,
and Bialobzeskis. Three organists: Vasiliauskas, Luksaité, and
Digrys.

B0005. Bennwitz, Hanspeter. Interpretenlexikon der Instrumentalmusik.
Bern: Francke Verlag, 1964. 326 p.

This rare volume includes regional performers.

B0006. Berutto, Guglielmo. Il Piemonte e la musica, 1800-1984. Torino:
privately printed for the author, 1984. 419, [2] p., illus.

Numerous major and minor instrumentalists.

B0007. Bescoby-Chambers, John. The Archives of Sound Including a
Selective Catalogue of Historical Violin, Piano, Spoken, Documentary,

Orchestral, and Composer's Own Recordings. Bolton (Lancashire): The Oakwood Press, n.d. [1964]. 153 p., 7 illus., 28-item bibliography.

An unusual compilation which is full of factual information and short biographical sketches. Suggests a needed research project to document this critical aspect of each artist's career.

B0008. Buffen, Frederick F. Musical Celebrities. London: Chapman & Hall, Limited, 1889. 116 p., 18 illus.

Joachim, Bottesini, Anton Rubinstein, Hofmann, and Sarasate. The "second series" [1893] includes Paderewski and de Pachmann.

B0009. Bumpus, John Skelton. The Organists & Composers of St. Paul's Cathedral. London: Printed for the author by Bowden, Hudson & Co., 1891. 272 p. + 5 plates, illus.

B0010. Canas, Luis Arrieta. Criticas y crónicas musicales. Santiago De Chile: Imp. "Cisneros", 1927. 214, [1] p.

Paderewski, Thibaud, Kubelik, and Elman.

B0011. Chorley, Henry F. Thirty Years' Musical Recollections. 2 vols. London: Hurst and Blackett, Publishers, 1862. xv, [ii], 312 p., portrait; vi, [ii], 323 p., portrait.

Important for mid-19th century performers. Ernest Newman edited a version of this work [New York, 1926. Reprint 1983]. As the outspoken conservative critic of the Athenaeum (1831-68), Chorley evaluated the finest artists of his day. Readers might also consult Music and Manners.... [London, 1844] and his Autobiography.... [London, 1873].

B0012. Chotzinoff, Samuel. A Little Night Music. New York: Harper & Row, Publishers, 1964. 151 p., illus.

Heifetz, Horowitz, Artur Rubinstein, and Segovia.

B0013. Clews, Frank. The Golden Disk. London: Brown, Watson. 155 p., 32 illus.

Artists and groups who have sold one million or more copies of a song.

B0014. Cohen, Joel and Herb Snitzer. Reprise: the Extraordinary Revival of Early Music. Boston: Little, Brown & Company, 1985. xvi, 227 p., illus., glossary, index.

Numerous contributors to the revival, but especially Arnold Dolmetsch, Noah Greenberg, Thomas Binkley, the Harnoncourts, the Kuijkens, Frans Brueggen, and Gustav Leonhardt.

B0015. Cross, Colin, with Paul Kendall & Mick Farren. Encyclopedia of British Beat Groups and Solo Artists of the Sixties. London: Omnibus Press, 1980. 95, [1] p., illus., index of names.

B0016. Dance, Stanley. The World of Swing. New York: Charles Scribner's Sons, 1974. xii, 436 p., 88 illus., relevant records, index.

This was the first of a projected series of volumes.

B0017. Danzi, Michael. American Musician in Germany 1924-1939: Memoirs of the Jazz, Entertainment, and Movie World of Berlin during the Weimar Republic and the Nazi Era -- and in the United States as Told to Rainer E. Lotz. Schnitten: Norbert Ruecker, 1986. ix, 292 p. + 8 plates, 32 illus., index.

A little known but fascinating memoir.

B0018. Davison, Henry, comp. From Mendelssohn to Wagner Being the Memoirs of J.W. Davison Forty Years Music Critic of "The Times". London: Wm. Reeves, 1912. xviii, 539 p., 61 illus., [incomplete] list of articles, index.

A general source for the period 1835-1885 in England. Davison was one of the most influential music critics of his generation.

B0019. de Gral, Hugo. Musicos Mexicanos. Mexico, D.F.: Editorial Diana, S.A., 1965. 275, [8] p.

Many instrumentalists are included among the 129 artists mentioned.

B0020. della Corte, Andrea. L'Interpretazione musicale e gli interpreti. Torino: Unione Tipografico-Editrice Torinese, 1951. xvi, 574 p., 12 portraits, 263 illus.

Keyboard: Mozart, Clementi, Beethoven, Chopin, Field, Moscheles, Liszt, Thalberg, Tausig, von Buelow, Anton Rubinstein, Brahms, Paderewski, and Busoni.

Violin: Corelli, Vivaldi, Geminiani, Veracini, Somis, Tartini, Nardini, Pugnani, Viotti, Paganini, Jaochim, Huberman, Ysaÿe, and Sarasate. As the influential critic of La Stampa (1919-67)in Turin, della Corte tended toward intellectual evaluations.

B0021. Diehl, Alice Mangold. Musical Memories. London: Richard Bentley and Son, 1897. xii, 319 p., index.

Period source for Anton Rubinstein, von Henselt, and Thalberg.

B0022. Diosy, Bella, ed. Ungarischer Kuenstler Almanach: das Kuenstler Ungarns in Wort und Bild. Budapest: Koeniglich Ungarische Universitaets-druckerei, 1929. 283 p., illus., index of names.

Sixty-one instrumentalists are included.

B0023. Downes, Irene, ed. Olin Downes on Music: a Selection of His Writings during the Half-Century 1906-1955. New York: Simon and Schuster, 1957. xxxi, 473 p., index.

Numerous instrumentalists are evaluated by the "Dean" of critics.

B0024. Eberhardt, Goby. Erinnerungen an bedeutende Maenner unserer Epoche. Luebeck: Otto Quissow-Verlag, Kom.-Ges., 1926. 309, [7] p., illus.

Ysaÿe, Wieniawski, Paganini, von Vecsey, Jan Kubelik, Vasa Prihoda, Karl Unthan, Heinrich Bandler, and Felix Berber.

B0025. Elder, Arnfried. Der nordelbische Organist: Studien zu Sozialstatus, Funktion und kompositorischer Produktion eines Musikerberufes von der Reformation bis zum 20. Jahrhundert. Kassel: Baerenreiter-Verlag, 1982. xi, 447 p., bibliography, music, index of names.

B0026. Elson, Howard and John Brunton. Whatever Happened to ... ? The Great Rock and Pop Nostalgia Book. New York: Proteus Publishing Co., Inc., 1981. 159 p., illus.

197 individual artists and groups.

B0027. Epstein, Helen. Music Talks: Conversations with Musicians. New York: McGraw-Hill Book Company, 1987. xiii, 241 p., illus., index.

Cecylia Arzewski, Ivan Galamian, James Galway, Vladimir Horowitz, Yo-Yo Ma, and Itzhak Perlman.

B0028. Ertel, Paul. Kuenstler-Biographien. 10 vols. Berlin: Concert-Direction Hermann Wolff, 1898-1907.

Vol. 1: Gabrilowitsch.
Vol. 3: Busoni and Kreisler.
Vol. 4: Cortot, Godowsky, Lamond, Pugno, and Thibaud.
Vol. 5: Josef Lhevinne, de Greef, and Capet.
Vol. 6: Vianna da Motta.
Vol. 8: Backhaus and Hambourg.
Vol. 9: Flesch.

B0029. Espinosa, Adolfo Parra. Antologia de artistas, compositores y profesionales Ecuatorianos. Cuenca: Publicaciones y Papeles, 1983. 296 p., illus.

B0030. Ewen, David. Men and Women Who Make Music. New York: Thomas Y. Crowell Company, 1939. Reprint 1945. xiv, 274 p., 16 illus., index.

Kreisler, Heifetz, Menuhin, Szigeti, Milstein, Hofmann, Horowitz, Artur Rubinstein, Schnabel, Rudolf Serkin, Casals, and Piatigorsky. "In all probability, Ewen has publ. more books on music and edited more reference publications than anyone else in the 20th century..." BAKER 7.

B0031. Ewen, David. Encyclopedia of Concert Music. New York: Hill and Wang, 1959. ix, 566 p., selected readings on music and musicians.

Over 250 instrumentalists included, each with a short biography.

B0032. Ewen, David. Musicians since 1900: Performers in Concert and Opera. New York: The H.W. Wilson Company, 1978. ix, 974 p., portraits.

Among the 432 performers are ten cellists, two flutists, three guitarists, two harpists, four harpsichordists, sixty-seven pianists, four violists, and twenty-six violinists.

B0033. **Fenner, Theodore.** Leigh Hunt and Opera Criticism: the "Examiner" Years, 1808-1821. Lawrence: The University Press of Kansas, 1972. xiv, 253 p., 20 illus., notes, 163-item select bibliography, general index, index of performers, index of operas.

Another valuable period source.

B0034. **Fernett, Gene.** Thousand Golden Horns: the Exciting Age of America's Greatest Dance Bands. Midland (MI): The Pendell Company, 1966. 171, [4] p., illus.

B0035. **Finck, Henry T.** Success in Music and How It is Won. New York: Charles Scribner's Sons, 1909. xiv, 471 p., index.

Chopin, Liszt, von Buelow, Anton Rubinstein, Paderewski, Paganini, Jan Kubelik, Remenyi, Ole Bull, Spohr, Joachim, August Wilhelmj, Kreisler, and Leschetizky. Music editor of the New York Evening Post (1881-1924), Finck was especially comfortable with vocal rather than instrumental music, and he wrote extremely well about composers and performers who were up front and emotional.

B0036. **Fisher, Renee B.** Musical Prodigies: Masters at an Early Age. Foreword by Yehudi Menuhin. New York: Association Press, 1973. 240 p., 19 illus., 81-item bibliography, index of names.

B0037. **Flesch, Carl.** The Memoirs of Carl Flesch. Translated by Hans Keller. New York: The Macmillan Company, 1958 [original London, 1957]. Reprint 1973. xiii, 393 p., 21 illus., 3 appendices, index.

Mentions literally everyone, but especially Auer, Hugo Becker, Busoni, Richard Burmeister, Capet, Casals, Elman, Enesco, Heifetz, Hofmann, Joseph Hellmesberger, Joachim, Huberman, Kreisler, Leschetizky, Rosé, Paganini, Sarasate, Schnabel, Szigeti, Thibaud, and Ysaÿe.

B0038. **Gaisberg, F.W.** Music on Record. London: Robert Hale Limited, 1946. Reprint 1977. 269 p., 33 illus., index.

Chapter eleven: "Masters of the Keyboard." Chapter twelve: "Kreisler and Others."

B0039. **Gaisberg, F.W.** The Music Goes Round. New York: The Macmillan Company, 1942. 273 p., 16 illus., index.

This is the source for B0038. Numerous artists, but especially Casals, Heifetz, Kreisler, Menuhin, Artur Rubenstein, Schnabel, and Paderewski.

B0040. **Garcia, Francisco Moncada.** Pequeñas biografias de grandes musicos Mexicanos. Primera Serie. México, D.F.: Ediciones Framong, 1966. 291 p., 62 illus., 21-item bibliography.

Excellent for obscure Mexican instrumentalists.

B0041. Gavoty, Bernard. L'arme à gauche. Paris: Beauchesne, 1971.
143 p.

Cortot, Segovia, Artur Rubinstein, Argenta, Chopin, Marcel Dupré,
Casals, Fournier, François, Gieseking, Landowska, Kempff,
Malcuzynski, and Menuhin. As music critic for Le Figaro in Paris
(1945-1981), Gavoty knew all of the prominent artists of his time.
He was responsible for a series of excellent monographs about
performers (Les Grandes Interpretes) as well as documentary films.

B0042. Gavoty, Bernard. Vingt grands interprètes. Lausanne: Les
Editions Rencontre, 1966. 127 p., illus.

Cortot, Kempff, Gieseking, Artur Rubinstein, Richter, Michelangeli,
Cziffra, Casals, David Oistrakh, Segovia, Landowska, and Dupré.

B0043. Geitvik, Sivert Hansson. Spelemenn pa Søre Sunnmøre i Honndalen
og i Sunnylven. Volda: S.H. Geitvik, 1952. 119, [1] p.

Norwegian string players.

B0044. Gelatt, Roland. Music Makers: Some Outstanding Musical
Performers of Our Day. New York: Alfred A. Knopf, 1953. Reprint 1972.
xvi, 286, xiv p., 21 illus., index.

"Each chapter attempts to anlayze its subject's special gifts, the
reasons why he performs as he does, and his influence on other
musicians." Szigeti, Casals, Kell, Segovia, Robert Casadesus,
Gieseking, Hess, Horowitz, Artur Rubinstein, and Landowska.

B0045. Giesen, Hubert. Am Flugel, Hubert Giesen: meine Lebenserinn-
erung. Frankfurt/M., S. Fischer Verlag, 1972. 300, [2] p., 28 illus.,
discography by Ute Mayer, index.

Adolf Busch, Heifetz, Kreisler, and the Menuhin family.

B0046. Gitler, Ira. Jazz Masters of the Forties. New York: The
Macmillan Company, 1966. Reprint 1983. 290 p., illus., 87-item
bibliography, index.

B0047. Given, Dave. The Dave Given Rock 'n' Roll Stars Handbook: Rhythm
and Blues Artists and Groups. Smithtown (NY): Exposition Press, 1980. v,
328 p., discographies.

B0048. Goldberg, Joe. Jazz Masters of the Fifties. New York: The
Macmillan Company, 1965. 246 p., discographies.

Mulligan, Monk, Blakey, Davis, Rollins, Modern Jazz 4tet, Mingus,
Desmond, Ray Charles, Coltrane, Cecil Taylor, and Coleman.

B0049. Graham, Alberta Powell. Strike up the Band! Bandleaders of
Today. New York: Thomas Nelson & Sons, 1949. 160 p., 81-item
bibliography.

Thirty-five of the most prominent leaders from Armstrong and Ellington to Hampton and Woody Herman.

B0050. Grew, Sydney. Favorite Musical Performers. London: T.N. Foulis, Limited, 1923. 266 p., 10 illus.

Violinists: Corelli, Vivaldi, Veracini, Tartini, Viotti, Paganini, and Ole Bull.
Keyboard: Froberger, Marchand, Scarlatti, P.E. Bach, Mozart, Clementi, Dussek, Steibelt, Czerny, and Moscheles.

B0051. Grew, Sydney. Makers of Music: the Story of Singers and Instrumentalists. London: G.T. Foulis & Co., Ltd., 1924. 365 p., illus., index.

Numerous pianists and violinists but especially Ferrari, Pugnani, Leclaire, and Viotti.

B0052. Grubb, Suvi Raj. Music Makers on Record. London: Hamish Hamilton Ltd., 1986. Introduction by Daniel Barenboim. [vii], 244 p. + 8 plates, 32 illus., discography, index.

Moore, Perlman, Barenboim, Jacqueline DuPré, and Zukerman.

B0053. Hadden, J. Cuthbert. Modern Musicians. Edinburgh: T.N. Foulis, 1918 [original 1913]. 267 p., 21 illus.

Paderewski, de Pachmann, Sauer, Rosenthal, Hambourg, Siloti, D'Albert, Carreño, Busoni, Backhaus, Ysaÿe, Kubelik, von Vecsey, Marie Hall, Elman, Thibaud, Kreisler, Burmeister, Cesar Thomson, Jean Gerardy, Casals, and Hugo Becker.

B0054. Hadlock, Richard. Jazz Masters of the Twenties. New York: The Macmillan Company, 1965. 255 p., 14 illus.

Armstrong (1924-31), Hines, Beiderbecke, Waller, James P. Johnson, Teagarden, Fletcher Henderson, Don Redman, Eddie Lang.

B0055. Haggin, B.H. 35 Years of Music. New York: Horizon Press, 1974 [first published as Music Observed, 1964]. 297, [4] p., index.

Backhaus, Ellington, Gould, Heifetz, Horowitz, Richter, Schnabel, and Szigeti.

B0056. Henderson, Archibald Martin. Musical Memories. London: The Grant Educational Co., Ltd., 1938. xii, 143 p., 12 illus.

Pugno, Busoni, Paderewski, D'Albert, Lamond, and Fanny Davies.
Full of comments on organists and pianists.

B0057. Hughes, Langston. Famous Negro Music Makers. New York: Dodd, Mead & Company, 1955. 179 p., 23 illus., index.

Jelly Roll Morton, Ellington, and Armstrong.

B0058. Jacobson, Robert. Reverberations: Interviews with the World's Leading Musicians. New York: William Morrow & Company, Inc., 1974. 308 p.,

An index would have been most helpful in using this otherwise valuable compilation. Graffman, de Larrocha, Istomin, Rosina Lhevinne, Janos Starker, Menuhin, Artur Rubinstein, Segovia, and Rudolf Serkin.

B0059. Jakob, Friedrich. Die Orgel und der Blinde. Maennedorf: Th. Kuhn AG, 1973. 39 p., illus., bibliography.

B0060. Kaufmann, Helen. Artists in Music of Today. New York: Grosset & Dunlop Publishers, 1933. 111 p., 50 illus.

"The choice has been limited to pianists, violinists, singers, and conductors." Fifty instrumentalists are included.

B0061. Key, Pierre. Pierre Key's Music Year Book 1925-26: the Standard Music Annual. New York: Pierre Key, Inc., 1925. 379 p., illus.

Key was a music critic in Chicago and New York (New York World 1907-1919). His music annuals provide valuable source materials on performers active between the two world wars. The initial volume includes Cortot, Dushkin, Gabrilowitsch, Rudolf Ganz, Gieseking, Heifetz, Hutcheson, Kochanski, Levitzki, Josef Lhevinne, Ney, Novaes, Max Rosen, Salmond, Samaroff, and Zimbalist. The title of the third edition was changed to Pierre Key's International Music Year Book 1928: the Standard Music Annual. Anyone doing research on this period should consult each volume in the series.

B0062. Key, Pierre. Pierre Key's Musical Who's Who: a Biographical Survey of Contemporary Musicians. New York: Pierre Key, Inc., 1931. 498 p., illus.

"Material compiled and arranged by Irene E. Haynes."

B0063. Klein, Herman. Thirty Years of Musical Life in London 1870-1900. New York: The Century Company, 1903. Reprint 1978. xvii, 483 p., 106 illus., index.

A respected critic recalls many of the foremost virtuosi who appeared in London. The index is a veritable Who's Who of that era.

B0064. Kohut, Adolph. Beruehmte israelitsche Maenner und Frauen in der Kulturgeschichte der Menschheit: Lebens- und Charakterbilder aus Vergangenheit und Gegenwart. 2 vols. Leipzig-Reudnitz: Druck und Verlag von A.H. Payne, n.d. 433 p., illus.; 432 p., illus.

Seventeen violinists, five cellists, seventeen pianists, and four other instrumentalists. A very rare and important compilation.

B0065. Kornfeld, James. Erinnerungen und Begegnungen mit.... Swinemuende: Verlag J. Kornfeld, 1933. 18 p.

David, Moscheles, Joachim, Liszt, and Sarasate.

B0066. Krehbiel, Henry Edward. Review of the New York Musical Season 1885-1886 Containing Programmes of Noteworthy Occurrences, with Numerous Criticisms. New York: Novello, Ewer & Co., 1886. xxi, 233 p., index.

Essentially reprints of articles from the New York Tribune. The five volumes, 1885-86 through 1889-90, record the instrumentalists who triumphed or failed in New York City. A marvelous writer, Krehbiel completed and published Thayer's original English MS on Beethoven (1921) which remains a standard biography, and he served as the American editor of the second edition of Grove's Dictionary of Music and Musicians (1904-10).

B0067. Lahee, Henry C. The Organ and Its Masters. Boston: L.C. Page & Company, 1902. 345 p., 14 illus., chronological table, index.

Note his books on pianists (A0320) and violinists (A0732).

B0068. Leigh, Spencer. Stars in My Eyes: Personal Interviews with Top Music Stars. Liverpool: Raven Books, 1980. 160 p., illus., glossary.

Twenty-three interviews from Charles Aznavour to Don Williams.

B0069. Leisner, Otto. 50 Grammofon Stgener. København: Samlereus Vorlag, 1959. 54, [1] p., illus.

B0070. Lengyel, Cornel, ed. W.P.A. Project 10377: the History of Music in San Francisco.

Vol. 1. Music of the Gold Rush Era. San Francisco: W.P.A., 1939. [vi], 212 p., illus., bibliography. Chapter 11 "Visiting Virtuosi" mentions a number of artists but especially Hauser, Herz, and Ole Bull. The W.P.A. provided employment for over eight million Americans including actors, artists, musicians, and writers. This is a landmark series, and original copies are very rare!

Vol. 4. Celebrities in El Dorado 1850-1906. New York: AMS Press, 1972 [original 1938 with illus.]. 270 p., selected bibliography, index. Many instrumentalists from Harold Bauer and Ole Bull to Ysaÿe.

Vol. 5. Fifty Local Prodigies 1906-1940. San Francisco: W.P.A., 1940. [viii], xii, [i], 203 p., illus., bibliography. Material on Ricci, Menuhin, and Slenczynski.

B0071. Lipovsky, Alexander, comp. Lenin Prize Winners: Soviet Stars in the World of Music. Translated by Olga Shartse. Moscow: Progress Publishers, n.d. [c.1966]. 286, [1] p., 12 illus.

David Oistrakh, Kogan, Richter, and Rostropovich.

B0072. Mann, Ernst and Bruno Vogler, Heinz Voss, Hans Gerloff. Deutschlands Oesterreich-Ungarns und der Schweiz: Musiker in Wort und Bild. Eine illustrierte Biographie der gesamten alldeutschen Musikwelt.

1. Ausgabe 1909/10. Leipzig–Gohlis: Bruno Vogler Verlagsbuchhandlung, 1909. vi, 525 p., illus.

Numerous instrumentalists each with a portrait. This is another of those reference titles which should be reprinted.

B0073. **Martin, Jules.** Nos artistes: annuaire des théâtres et concerts 1901–1902. Paris: Société d'Editions Litteraires et Artistiques. Librairie Paul Ollendorf, 1901. 410 p., 375 portraits.

A rare period source which includes instrumentalists.

B0074. **Martin, Jules.** Nos artistes: portraits et biographies suivis d'une notice sur les droits d'auteurs, l'Opéra, la Comédie-Française, les associations artistiques, etc.... Paris: Librairie de l'Annuaire Universel, 1895. 448 p., 369 portraits.

Filled with obscure nineteenth-century performers. Martin's work provides significant information unavailable elsewhere.

B0075. **McGrath, Noel.** Australian Encyclopedia of Rock: the Complete Biographies and Discographies of Every Popular Australian Recording Artist and Group Since 1958. Victoria: Outback Press Pty Ltd, 1978. 376 p., illus.

B0076. **Meyer, Torben** and Josef Mueller-Marein, Hannes Reinhardt. Musikalske selvportraetter. København: Jul. Gjellerups Forlag, 1966. 325 p., 40 illus.

Curzon, Stern, and Helmut Walcha.

B0077. **Mildberg, Bod.** Das Dresdner Hoftheater in der Gegenwart: Biographien und Charakteristiken. Dresden: F. Piersons Verlag, 1902. 270 p., 112 portraits.

B0078. **Moogk, Edward B.** Roll Back the Years: History of Canadian Recorded Sound and Its Legacy (Genesis to 1930). Ottawa: National Library of Canada, 1975. xii, 443 p., illus., phonodisk.

A pioneer work in its field by the discographer who was chiefly responsible for the National Library of Canada's extensive and valuable collection of recordings. He was an expert on Canadian recordings, and his vast personal collection formed the basis for his work at the NLC. Biographical notes are in chapter five, and performer's discographies are in chapter six.

B0079. **Morley, Paul.** Ask: the Chatter of Pop. London: Faber and Faber Limited, 1986. 127 p., illus.

Thirty-three individual artists and groups.

B0080. **Mueller, Martin** and Wolfgang Mertz, eds. Diener der Musik: unvergessene Soloisten und Dirigenten unserer Zeit im Spiegel der Freunde. Tuebingen: Rainer Wunderlich Verlag Hermann Leins, 1965. 275 p., 20 illus., 13-item bibliography, discography.

A delightful collection of essays each written by a personal friend of the artist: Guenther Ramin, Gieseking by Demus, Cortot, Steuermann, Edwin Fischer by Kempff, Kulenkampff by Fischer, Lipatti, Haskil by Igor Markevitch, and Schnabel.

B0081. Mueller-Marein, Josef and Hannes Reinhardt. Das Musikalische Selbstportrait von Komponisten, Dirigenten, Instrumentalisten, Saenger-innen und Saengern unserer Zeit. Hamburg: Nannen-Verlag GmbH, 1963. 508 p., 55 illus., select bibliography, index of names.

Fifty distinguished artists including Schneiderhan, Rosbaud, Menuhin, and Helmut Walcha.

B0082. Nanquette, Claude. Anthologie des interprètes. Paris: Editions Stock, 1979. 745, [4] p., index.

A comprehensive work which includes sixty-nine instrumentalists.

B0083. Nanquette, Claude. Les grands interprètes romantiques. Paris: Librairie Arthème Fayard, 1982. 367 p., 60 illus., 406-item bibliography.

Principal conductors, singers, and instrumentalists from the early nineteenth century to the present. Paganini, Vieuxtemps, Joachim, Sarasate, Ysaÿe, Kreisler, Liszt, Thalberg, Clara Schumann, Anton Rubinstein, Planté, Pugno, Paderewski, D'Albert, and Busoni.

B0084. Noglik, Bert and Heinz-Juergen Lindner. Jazz im Gespraech. Berlin: Verlag Neue Musik, 1978. 184, [15] p., 12 illus.

Twelve largely unknown German jazz musicians: Conrad Bauer, Guenther Fischer, H.-J. Graswurm, Ulrich Gumpert, Manfred Hering, Hubert Katzenbeier, Hermann Keller, Klaus Koch, E.-L. Petrowsky, Friedhelm Schoenfeld, Manfred Schulze, and Guenter Sommer.

B0085. Noglik, Bert. Jazzwerkstatt International. Berlin: Verlag Neue Musik, 1981. 490 p., 26 illus., discography.

A series of interviews with journeymen as well as the famous.

B0086. O'Connell, Charles. The Other Side of the Record. New York: Alfred A. Knopf, 1947. Reprint 1970. xi, 332, xi p., index.

A former music director at RCA Victor recalls fifteen outstanding artists: Rachmaninoff, Heifetz, Iturbi, and Artur Rubinstein.

B0087. Page, Drew. Drew's Blues: a Sideman's Life with the Big Bands. Baton Rouge: Louisiana State University Press, 1980. 226 p. + 8 plates, 35 illus., index.

Numerous artists but good material on Benny Goodman and Harry James.

B0088. Pape, Werner. Die Entwicklung Violoncellspiels im 19. Jahrhundert. Ph.D. diss. University of Saarbruecken, 1962.

B0089. Parker, **H.T.** Eighth Notes: Voices and Figures of Music and the Dance. New York: Dodd, Mead and Company, 1922. 238 p.

Reprinted from the Boston Evening Transcript, our critic shares "...the impressions received and recorded by a reviewer..." Paderewski, Gabrilowitsch, Bauer, Rachmaninoff, Hofmann, Busoni, Moiseiwitsch, Novães, Auer, Kreisler, Heifetz, Zimbalist, Spalding, Thibaud, Elman, Ysaÿe, and Casals.

Para Espinosa, Adolfo. SEE: Espinosa, Adolfo Para (B0029).

B0090. Pascall, Jeremy. The Stars & Superstars of Black Music. London: Phoebus Publishing Limited, 1979. 113 p., illus.

B0091. Picart, **Hervé** and Bertrand Alary, Jean-Yves Legras. Hard & Heavy: les dieux de rock lourd. Paris: Jacques Grancher, Editeur, 1985. 127 p., illus.

B0092. Pincherle, Marc. The World of the Virtuoso. Translated by Lucile H. Brockway. New York: W.W. Norton & Company, Inc., 1963 [original Paris, 1961]. 192 p. + 4 plates, 9 illus.

Menuhin, Kreisler, Landowska, Georges Enesco, Giovanni Giornovichi, Boucher, and Paganini. As a musicologist, Pincherle has written extensively on the history of violin music. Unfortunately, neither Les violonistes compositeurs et virtuoses (Paris, 1922) nor Jean-Marie Leclair l'aine (Paris, 1952) were located.

B0093. Porter, Andrew. Music of Three Seasons: 1974-1977. New York: Farrar Strauss Giroux, 1978. xix, 667, [1] p., index.

As music critic for the New Yorker since 1972, Porter has earned a high reputation as one of the finest contemporary writers in his field. Vignettes on a host of performers!

B0094. Porter, Andrew. Music of Three More Seasons. New York: Alfred A. Knopf, 1981. 613 p., index.

B0095. Ranta, Sulho. Saevelten taitureita: esittaeviae taiteilijoita kahden ja puolen vuosisadan ajalta. 2. lisaetty ja uudistettu painos. Porvoo: Werner Soederstroem, 1960. 684 p., 738 illus., 173-item bibliography.

113 conductors, instrumentalists, and singers.

B0096. von Reuter, Florizel. Great People I Have Known. Waukesha: Freeman Printing Co., 1961. 231 p., 69 illus.

B0097. Riccio, Giancarlo. Percorsi del rock italiano. Milano: Edizioni il Formichiere, 1980. 158 p., illus.

B0098. Riess, Curt. Knauers Weltgeschichte der Schallplatte. Zuerich: Droemersche Verlagsanstalt AG, 1966. 447 p., 150 illus., 52-item bibliography, index of names.

The generation of Kubelik, Paderewski, Kreisler, and Artur Rubinstein.

B0099. Rohozinski, L., ed. Cinquante ans de musique française de 1874 à 1925. 2 vols. Paris: Les Editions Musicales de la Librairie de France, 1925. 394 p., illus.; 424 p., illus.

Chapter eleven: "Grands virtuoses."

B0100. Rosenberg, Deena and Bernard. The Music Makers. New York: Columbia University Press, 1979. xiii, 466 p., 32 illus., index.

Piatigorsky, Arrau, Lydia Artymiw, Doriot Anthony Dwyer, Kurt Loebel, Julius Levine, Kermit Moore, and Larry Adler. "This book was created by a sociologist and his musicologist daughter who have sought to document the patterns and panorama of contemporary musical life exclusively through the techniques of oral history." They set out "deliberately to create a body of significant evidence", evidence which will provide an added dimension for future historians.

B0101. de Ruyter, Michiel. Een leven med jazz. Amsterdam: Uitgeverij en Boekhandel Van Gennep bv, 1984. 86, [1] p. + 12 plates, 30 illus., index.

B0102. Ryan, Thomas. Recollections of an Old Musician. New York: E.P. Dutton & Company, 1899. Reprint 1979. xvi, 274 p. + 45 plates, 46 illus.

Ole Bull, Wieniawski, Anton Rubinstein, Joachim, Herz, and Paganini.

B0103. Saleski, Gdal. Famous Musicians of a Wandering Race: Biographical Sketches of Outstanding Figures of Jewish Origin in the Musical World. New York: Block Publishing Company, 1927. xiv, 463 p., portraits.

Seventy-three violinists from Leopold Auer to Oscar Zuccarini; nineteen cellists from Evsei Beloussoff to Mila Wellerson; sixty-five pianists from Isidor Achron to Joseph Wieniawski.

2nd edition: Famous Musicians of Jewish Origin. New York, 1949. Sixty-eight violinists; fourteen cellists; eighty-six pianists. Both editions must be consulted!

B0104. Salter, Norbert, ed. The World Musical and Theatrical Guide. 2 vols. New York: p.p., 1929. 327 p.; 332 p., illus., index to both vols.

Volume two includes forty-three instrumentalists.

B0105. Samazeuilh, Gustave, ed. Les écrits de Paul Dukas sur la musique. Paris: Société d'Editions Françaises et Internationales, 1948. 691, [10] p., portrait, index.

Interesting material on Pugno, Paderewski, Ysaÿe, and Edouard Risler.

B0106. Sandu, Augustin. Arpegii pentru patru anotimpuri. 2 vols. Iasi (Romania): Editura Junimea, 1976. 253 p., illus.; Arpegii II .... 1981. 335, [1] p., illus.

Interviews with twenty-six composers, conductors, and instrumentalists. Twenty-nine additional artists are in volume two.

B0107. Schickel, Richard. The World of Carnegie Hall. New York: Julian
Messner, Inc., 1960. [iii], 438 p., illus., index.

B0108. Schonberg, Harold C. Facing the Music. New York: Summit Books,
1981. 464 p., index.

The first music critic awarded a Pulitzer Prize (1971), he exercised
enormous influence as critic for the New York Times (1950-1980).
Fine insights on Hofmann, Horowitz, Josef Lhevinne, and Artur
Rubinstein. His work "...reveals a profound knowledge of music...
[and] his intellectual horizon is exceptionally wide." BAKER 7.

B0109. Schonberg, Harold C. The Glorious Ones: Classical Music's
Legendary Performers. New York: Times Books, 1985. xviii, 509, [1] p.,
illus., 194-item bibliography, index.

Thirty-nine artists are covered in some depth including Paganini,
Liszt, Joachim, Anton Rubinstein, Paderewski, Sarasate, Kubelik,
Ysaÿe, Kreisler, Hofmann, Rachmaninoff, Heifetz, Artur Rubinstein,
and Horowitz.

B0110. Schwaiger, Egloff. Warum der Applaus: beruehmte Interpreten
ueber ihre Musik. Muenchen: Ehrenwirth Verlag, 1968. 349 p., 48 illus.,
section of short biographies.

Anda, Arrau, Fournier, Holliger, Kempff, Kirkpatrick, Magaloff,
Menuhin, Anton Nowakowski, Edith Peinemann, Rudolf Serkin, Szeryng,
Schneiderhan, and Helmut Walcha.

B0111. Schwarz, Boris. Music and Musical Life in Soviet Russia 1917-
1970. New York: W.W. Norton & Company, Inc., 1973 [original London,
1972]. [v], 550 p., notes on sources, selected bibliography, index.

Valuable for Soviet instrumentalists since the 1917 Revolution.
Although primarily a musicologist, Schwarz (b. March 26, 1926,
St. Petersburg, Russia; d. December 31, 1983, New York City) was
a fine violinist. A student of Flesch, Thibaud, and Capet, he
was a member of the NBC Symphony under Toscanini.

B0112. Scudo, P. L'Année musicale. 3 vols. Paris: Librairie de L.
Hachette et cie, 1860/1861/1862. iii, 340. p.; 405 p.; 361 p.

A rare and excellent period source for artists such as Vieuxtemps,
Alfred Jaëll, and Planté.

B0113. Seidl, Anton. The Music of the Modern World Illustrated in the
Lives and Works of the Greatest Modern Musicians and in Reproductions of
Famous Paintings, etc.. vol. 1 Text; vol. 2 Music. New York: D. Appleton
and Company, 1895. xi, 236 p., 52 illus.; vii, 348 p., 27 illus.

Originally issued in twenty-five fasciles in 1895, this folio work
is important for pianists and violinists.

B0114. Servières, Georges. Documents inédits sur les organistes français des XVII et XVIII siècles. Paris: Au Bureau d'édition de la "Schola cantorum", n.d. [c.1922]. 44 p. + 2 plates.

B0115. Shaw, George Bernard. London Music in 1888-89 as Heard by Corno di Bassetto (Later Known as Bernard Shaw) with Some Further Autobiographical Particulars. London: Constable and Company Limited, 1950 [original 1937]. 420 p., index.

Written before Shaw became famous as a playwright, these reprints from the Star are amusing and insightful period sources.

B0116. Shaw, George Bernard. Music in London 1890-94. 3 vols. London: Constable and Company Limited, 1956 [original 1932]. 302; 325; 320 p., index to the complete work is in vol. 3.

Reprints from The World full of witty and abusive comments.

B0117. Silver, Caroline. The Pop Makers. New York: Scholastic Book Services, 1967. 127 p., illus.

B0118. Slonimsky, Nicolas. A Thing or Two About Music. Westport (CT): Greenwood Press, Publishers, 1972 [original 1948]. iv, 304, [i] p.

Slonimsky, one of the greatest music lexicographers, has touched elbows with every significant musician available. His latest autobiography, Perfect Pitch: A life Story, just appeared. His own biographical entry in BAKER 7 as well as his delightful prefaces to both BAKER 6 and BAKER 7 should be required reading!

B0119. Stallings, Penny. Rock 'n' Roll Confidential. Boston: Little, Brown and Company, 1984. 256 p., illus., index.

B0120. Stargardt-Wolff, Edith. Wegbereiter grosser Musiker: unter Verwendung von Tagebuchblaettern, Briefen und vielen persoenlichen Erinnerungen von Hermann und Louise Wolff, den Gruendern der ersten Konzertdirektion 1880-1935. Berlin: Ed. Bote & G. Bock, 1954. 312 p., 26 illus., index of names.

The daughter of the first great German agent shares some insights into a "Who's Who" of the period. SEE: B0028. The Hermann Wolff Concert Management (later known as H. Wolf & J. Sachs) was founded in 1881 and represented many of the finest artists of the period.

B0121. Stewart, Charles and Paul Carter Harrison. Chuck Stewart's Jazz Files. Foreword by Billy Taylor. Boston: Little Brown and Company, 1985. 144 p., index of photographs, notes.

B0122. Taylor, Arthur R. Notes and Tones: Musician to Musician Interviews. New York: Coward, McCann & Geoghegan, 1982 [originally privately printed for the author, 1977]. 296 p., 9 illus., index.

B0123. Tosches, Nick. Unsung Heroes of Rock 'n' Roll. New York: Charles Scribner's Sons, 1984. 245 p., chronology, discorgraphies, index.

Twenty-six musicians who were part of the evolution of the form.

B0124. Upton, George P. Musical Memories: My Recollections of
Celebrities of the Half Century 1850-1900. Chicago: A.C. McClurg
& Co., 1908. xiv, 345 p., 47 illus., index.

Music critic for the Chicago Tribune, Upton authored several
interesting reference works including Women in Music.

B0125. Van Doorn, Boud. Le Tien Bekende Nederlanders in gesprek met ...
10 bekende landgenoten. Den Haag: Omniboek, 1977. 134 p., illus.

B0126. Vásárhelyi, Julius. Ungarn ein Land der Musik: Ungarischer
Kuenstleralmanach. Budapest: Koeniglich Ungarische Universitaets-
druckerei, 1930. 340 p., illus., alphabetical list of artists.

Among the many artists are fifty-four instrumentalists each with a
portrait and a short biographical sketch.

B0127. Wagner, Charles L. Seeing Stars. New York: G.P. Putnam's Sons,
1940. Reprint 1977. ix, 403 p., 11 illus., index.

Insights from the talented manager of numerous "stars". Although
normally considered a singer's manager, he handled a number of
famous pianists and violinists.

B0128. Walker, Bettina. My Musical Experiences. London: Richard Bentley
and Son, 1892. x, 324 p.

Tausig, Sgambati, Liszt, Henselt, and Xavier Scharwenka.

B0129. Weinschenk, Harry Erwin, ed. Kuenstler Plaudern. Berlin: Wilhelm
Limpert Verlag, 1938. 338 p., 177 illus.

Fifty artists were asked to discuss their lives and careers: Lamond,
Ney, Backhaus, Edwin Fischer, Gieseking, and Georg Kulenkampff.

B0130. van Westering, Paul Christian. De mens schter de musicus:
gesprekken met.... Haarlem: De Toorts, 1964. 309 p., illus.

Starker, Menuhin, Casadesus, Shura Cherkassky, and Van Cliburn.

B0131. Whelbourn, Hubert. Standard Book of Celebrated Musicians Past
and Present. Revised and enlarged edition. New York: Garden City
Publishing Co., Inc., 1937. xiii, 305 p., 7 illus.

This was originally published in London as Celebrated Musicians, Past
and Present in 1930. There are over 100 instrumentalists included in
the 340 chosen. Coverage is minimal.

B0132. Wiener, Hilda and D. Miller Craig. Pencil Portraits of Concert
Celebrities. London: Sir Isaac Pitman & Sons, Ltd., 1937. xii, 198, [1]
p., 100 portraits by Wiener.

Numerous instrumentalists from Ysaye to Jelly d'Aranyi.

B0133. Zemzare, Ingrida and Guntars Pupp. <u>Jauno Muzika</u>. Riga: "Liesma", 1979. 269 [2] p., illus.

   Twenty-seven major artists plus numerous others are included in this valuable resource which is particularly helpful for researchers who are knowledgeable only about the "West."

B0134. Zwerin, Mike. <u>Close Enough for Jazz</u>. London: Quartet Books Limited, 1983. vii, [i], 246 p., illus., index.

PART C.
Individual Virtuosi, A-Z

This brief headnote is intended for those readers who bypassed the Preface which contains a detailed explanation of the type of information one will encounter in PART C: INDIVIDUAL VIRTUOSI, A-Z. The entries are alphabetical, are code numbered C0001 through C1215, and include at least two entries from the five sources of material which relate to that individual. These distinct categories will always be listed in the following order: (1) A coded entry which indicates one of fifteen major performing arts' reference works. Titles and codes are in the Bibliographical Abbreviations section which follows the Preface. Titles were selected for their reliability and availability, and each entry will give the edition and volume number where appropriate. To alert the reader to additional bibliographic references NOT DUPLICATED in this work, the entry ("Bibliography") will appear after the code, e.g. Baker 7 (Bibliography); (2) A coded entry which refers to one of eleven periodicals which have been checked for articles of a biographical or autobiographical nature. There are a few occasional references, e.g. Time or Newsweek where a special issue is concerned; (3) Autobiographies and some titles written by the performer which relate directly to interpretation. As mentioned in the Preface, a bibliography of books about instrumental pedagogy is a massive research project in its own right; (4) Biographies about instrumentalists including historical novels if there was good reason to believe that the content was based upon or influenced by actual events; (5) Additional sources as well as cross-references from Parts A, B, and C. Please note that any cross-references particularly with regard to Parts A and B are not complete and mention only those artists itemized in the individual annotations.

C0001.
Adaskin, Harry. Canadian Violinist; b. October 6, 1901, Riga, Latvia.

1. Encyclopedia of Music in Canada (Bibliography); PAB-MI/2 (Bibliography).

3. Adaskin, Harry. A Fiddler's World. 2 vols. Vancouver (BC): November House, 1977/1980. 293 p. + 8 plates, 35 illus.; 187 p. + 15 plates, 44 illus.

   Memoirs to 1938 are in volume one; 1938 to 1980 are in volume two. He attended master classes under Thibaud and Georges Enesco. Among his better known pupils is Maurice Solway.

C0002.
Adderley, Cannonball [Julian Edwin]. American Jazz Alto Saxophonist;
b. September 15, 1928, Tampa, Florida; d. August 8, 1975, Gary, Indiana.

1. Baker 7; DEU (Bibliography); Grove 6/1 (Bibliography); Grove-AM
   (Bibliography, 15 entries); Grove-Jazz (Bibliography); JB (Bibliog-
   raphy); JRRM; LJ/2; PAB-MI/2 (Bibliography); Riemann 12/Supp.
   (Bibliography).

2. DB 24/18, 26/21, 27/11, 28/12, 13, 29/13, 34/23, 37/1, 39/12, 40/12.

4. Kernfeld, Barry. Adderley, Coltrane, and Davis at the Twilight of
   Bebop: the Search for Melodic Coherence (1958-59). Ph.D. diss.
   Cornell University, 1981.

C0003.
Adler, Larry. American Harmonica Player; b. February 10, 1914,
Baltimore, Maryland.

1. Baker 7; Grove 6/1; Grove-AM (Bibliography); Grove-Jazz; PAB-MI/2.

3. Adler, Larry. It Ain't Necessarily So: an Autobiography. New York:
   Grove Press, Inc., [c.1984, published 1987]. xi, 222 p. + 16 plates,
   26 illus., index.

C0004.
Aeschbacher, Adrian. Swiss Pianist; b. May 10, 1912, Langenthal.

1. Baker 7; DEU; Grove 6/1 (Bibliography); MGG/Supp.; Riemann 12 +
   Supp.

C0005.
Agosti, Guido. Italian Pianist; b. August 11, 1901, Forli.

1. Baker 7; DEU; Grove 6/1; MGG/Supp.; PAB-MI/2 (Bibliography); Riemann
   12 + Supp.; Schmidl/Supp.

C0006.
Aguado y Garcia, Dionisio. Spanish Guitarist; b. April 8, 1784, Madrid;
d. December 29, 1849, Madrid.

1. Baker 7; DEU (Bibliography); Fetis 2/1; Grove 6/1 (Bibliography);
   Mendel; MGG (Bibliography); Riemann 12; Schmidl.

5. A0129, A0137.

C0007.
Ahlgrimm, Isolde. Austrian Harpsichordist; b. July 31, 1914, Vienna.

1. Baker 7; Grove 6/1 (Bibliography); PAB-MI/2 (Bibliography); Riemann
   12 + Supp. (Bibliography).

C0008.
Ahrens, Joseph Johannes Clemens. German Organist; b. April 17, 1904,
Sommersell, Westphalia.

1. Baker 7; DEU; Grove 6/1 (Bibliography); MGG/Supp. (Bibliography);
   PAB-MI/2 (Bibliography); Riemann 12 + Supp. (Bibliography).

C0009.
Alain, Marie-Claire. French Organist; b. August 10, 1926, St. Germain-
en-Laye.

1. Baker 7; DEU (Bibliography); Grove 6/1 (Bibliography); PAB-MI/2
   (Bibliography); Riemann 12 + Supp. (Bibliography).

C0010.
Alard, Jean-Delphin. French Violinist; b. March 8, 1815, Bayonne;
d. February 22, 1888, Paris.

1. Baker 7; DEU; Fetis 2/1 + Supp.; Grove 6/1 (Bibliography); Mendel;
   MGG/Supp. (Bibliography); PAB-MI/2 (Bibliography); Riemann 12;
   Schmidl.

5. A0102, A0131.

C0011.
Alberghi, Paolo Tommaso. Italian Violinist; b. December, 1716, Faenza;
d. October 11, 1785, Faenza.

1. Baker 7; Grove 6/1.

C0012.
Alborea, Francesco. Italian Cellist; b. March 7, 1691, Naples; d. July
20, 1739, Vienna, Austria.

1. Baker 7; Grove 6/1; Schmidl/Supp.

C0013.
Albu, Sandu. Romanian Violinist; b. August 22, 1897, Sinaia.

1. DEU.

3. Albu, Sandu. Cu vioara prin lume.... Edited by Alexandru Bilciurescu.
   Bucuresti: Muzicala a uniuni compozitorilor, 1972. 289 p. + 4 plates,
   32 illus.

C0014.
Alcock, Walter Galpin. English Organist; b. December 29, 1861, Eden-
bridge; d. September 11, 1947, Salisbury.

1. Baker 7; Grove 6/1; Schmidl.

C0015.
Alkan, Charles Henri Valentin. French Pianist; b. November 30, 1813,
Paris; d. March 29, 1888, Paris.

1. Fetis 2/1; Mendel; PAB-MI/2 (Bibliography); Riemann 12 + Supp.
   (Bibliography).

2. HiFi/SR 15/2.

4. Schilling, Britta. Das Konzertprinzip der Brillanz der Pianist
   Charles H.V. Alkan 1813-1888. Ph.D. diss. University of Cologne.

C0016.
Allen, Red [Henry James]. American Jazz Trumpeter; b. January 7, 1908,
New Orleans, Louisiana; d. April 17, 1967, New York City.

1. Baker 7; DEU (Bibliography); EdS (Bibliography); Grove 6/1 (Bibliography); Grove-AM (Bibliography); Grove-Jazz; JB; LJ; PAB-MI/2
   (Bibliography); Riemann 12 + Supp.

2. DB 26/1, 32/2.

4. Evensmo, Jan and Per Borthen. The Trumpet and Vocal Art of Henry Red
   Allen 1927-1942. Holse (Norway): Jazz Solography Series, 1977. 52,
   [2] p., discography.

5. A0004.

   SEE: Williams, Martin T. Jazz Masters of New Orleans. New York:
        Collier-Macmillan, 1967. 287 p.

C0017.
Almenraeder, Karl. German Bassoonist; b. October 3, 1786, Ronsdorf, near
Dusseldorf; d. September 14, 1843, Biebrich.

1. Baker 7; DEU (Bibliography); Grove 6/1 (Bibliography); Fetis 2/1 +
   Supp.; Mendel; MGG/Supp. (Bibliography); PAB-MI/2 (Bibliography);
   Riemann 12; Schmidl.

5. A0160.

C0018.
Amfiteatrov, Massimo. Italian Cellist; b. February 27, 1907, Paris,
France.

1. Baker 7; DEU; Grove 6/1; MGG/Supp.; Riemann 12/Supp.

C0019.
Ammons, Albert. American Jazz Pianist; b. 1907, Chicago, Illinois;
d. December 2, 1949, Chicago.

1. Baker 7; DEU; EdS (Bibliography); Grove 6/1 (Bibliography);
   Grove-AM (Bibliography); Grove-Jazz; JB; PAB-MI/2 (Bibliography).

C0020.
Anda, Geza. Hungarian Pianist; b. November 19, 1921, Budapest; d. June
13, 1976, Zurich, Switzerland.

1. Baker 7; DEU; Grove 6/1 (Bibliography); MGG/Supp.; PAB-MI/2 (Bibliography); Riemann 12 + Supp.

2. HiFi/SR 23/3; MM 23/10.

3. He published cadenzas to Mozart's piano concertos [Berlin, 1973].

4. Ruefenacht, Peter, ed. Geza Anda: ein Erinnerungsbild. Zuerich:
   Artemis Verlag, 1977. 118, [1] p., illus., repertoire, discography.

5. A0060, B0110.

C0021.
Andersen, Carl Joachim. Danish Flutist; b. April 29, 1847, Copenhagen;
d. May 9, 1909, Copenhagen.

1. Baker 7; DEU; Grove 6/1; MGG/Supp. (Bibliography); Riemann 12;
   Schmidl.

C0022.
Andersen, Vigo. Danish Flutist, brother of Carl; b. April 21, 1852,
Copenhagen; d. January 28, 1895, Chicago, Illinois.

1. Baker 7; DEU; Grove 6/1.

C0023.
Anderson, Lucy. English Pianist; b. December 12, 1797, Bath; d. December
24, 1878, London.

1. Baker 7; Grove 6/1 (Bibliography); Schmidl.

C0024.
André, Maurice. French Trumpeter; b. May 24, 1933, Alès, near Nîmes.

1. Baker 7; DEU (Bibliography); Grove 6/1; PAB-MI/2 (Bibliography);
   Riemann 12/Supp.

C0025.
Andrée, Elfrida. Swedish Organist; b. February 19, 1841, Visby;
d. January 11, 1929, Goeteborg.

1. Baker 7; DEU (Bibliography); Grove 6/1 (Bibliography); MGG/Supp.
   (Bibliography); Riemann 12 + Supp.; Schmidl.

C0026.
Andreoli, Carlo. Italian Pianist; b. January 8, 1840, Mirandola;
d. January 22, 1908, Reggio Emilia.

1. Baker 7; DEU; Grove 6/1 (Bibliography); Schmidl.

   His brother, Guglielmo (1835-1860), was also a virtuoso pianist.

C0027.
Anet, Jean-Baptiste [known as Baptiste Anet]. French Violinist;
baptized January 2, 1676, Paris; d. August 14, 1755, Lunéville.

1. Baker 7; DEU (Bibliography); Fetis 2/Supp.; Grove 6/1 (Bibliography);
   MGG/Supp. (Bibliography); Riemann 12 + Supp. (Bibliography); Schmidl
   + Supp. (under Baptiste).

5. SEE: de la Laurencie, L. L'Ecole française de violon de Lully à
   Viotti. Paris, 1922. pp. 350-65.

C0028.
d'Anglebert, Jean-Henri. French Clavecinist; b. 1628, Paris; d. April 23, 1691, Paris.

1. Baker 7 (Bibliography); DEU (Bibliography); Fetis 2/1; Grove 6/5 (under D'Anglebert - Bibliography); Mendel; MGG + Supp; PAB-MI/2 (Bibliography); Riemann 12 (Bibliography) + Supp.; Schmidl (under D'Anglebert) + Supp.

C0029.
Anievas, Augustin. American Pianist; b. June 11, 1934, New York City.

1. Baker 7 (out-of-order between Amfiteatrov and Amiot); Grove 6/1; Grove-AM.

C0030.
Ansorge, Conrad Eduard Reinhold. German Pianist; b. October 15, 1862, Buchwald, near Loebau, Silesia; d. February 13, 1930, Berlin.

1. Baker 7; DEU (Bibliography); Grove 6/1 (Bibliography); MGG (Bibliography); Riemann 12 (Bibliography); Schmidl.

2. Die Musik 20/7 (1930).

C0031.
Aranyi, Francis. Hungarian Violinist; b. March 21, 1893, Budapest; d. May 5, 1966, Seattle, Washington.

1. Baker 7; Riemann 12 + Supp.; Schmidl/Supp.

C0032.
d'Aranyi, Jelly. Hungarian Violinist; b. May 30, 1893, Budapest; d. March 30, 1966, Florence, Italy.

1. Baker 7; DEU; Grove 6/1 (Bibliography); Riemann 12 + Supp.

4. Macleod, Joseph Todd Gordon. The Sisters d'Aranyi. London: Allen & Unwin, 1969. 320 p. + 4 plates, 11 illus., music index, notes, general index.

The third sister is listed under **Adila Fachiri** (C0372).

5. A0115.

C0033.
Arban, Joseph Jean-Baptiste. French Cornetist; b. February 28, 1825, Lyons; d. April 9, 1889, Paris.

1. Baker 7; DEU (Bibliography); Fetis 2/Supp. Grove 6/1; Schmidl.

C0034.
Arbós, Enrique Fernández. Spanish Violinist; b. December 24, 1863, Madrid; d. June 2, 1939, San Sebastian.

1. Baker 7; DEU (Bibliography); EdS; Grove 6/1; Riemann 12.

4. Espinós Moltó, V. El meastro Arbós: memorias (1863-1939). Madrid:
   Ediciones Cid, 1963. xxiii, 538 p., 62 illus., list of premiere
   performances, index of names.

C0035.
Arbuckle, Matthew. American Cornetist; b. 1828; d. May 23, 1883, New
York City.

1. Baker 7; Grove-AM (Bibliography); PAB-MI/2 (Bibliography).

C0036.
Argerich, Martha. Argentinian Pianist; b. June 5, 1941, Buenos Aires.

1. Baker 7; DEU; Grove 6/1; PAB-MI/2 (Bibliography); Riemann 12/Supp.

2. CL 18/6; CK(KB) 7/7.

5. A0060.

C0037.
Armingaud, Jules. French Violinist; b. May 3, 1820, Bayonne; d. February
27, 1900, Paris.

1. Baker 7; DEU; Fetis 2/1 + Supp.; Grove 6/1 (Bibliography); Mendel.

C0038.
Armstrong, Louis "Satchmo". American Jazz Trumpeter; b. July 4, 1900,
New Orleans, Louisiana; d. July 6, 1971, New York City.

1. Baker 7 (Bibliography); DEU (Bibliography); EdS; Grove 6/1 (Bibliography); Grove-AM (Bibliography - 26 entries); Grove-Jazz; JB (Bibliography - 96 entries); JRRM (Bibliography - 131 entries); LJ
   (Bibliography - 25 entries); MGG/Supp. (Bibliography); PAB-MI/2
   (Bibliography); Riemann 12 + Supp. (Bibliography).

2. DB 26/1, 29/5, 32/15; HiFi/SR 5/4, 25/2; JJS 3/1; MM 18/12.

3. Armstrong, Louis. Satchmo: My Life in New Orleans. New York:
   Prentice-Hall, Inc., 1954. 240 p. + 16 plates., illus.

   Copyrighted in 1951, this leaves out much of his magical career.

   Armstrong, Louis. Swing That Music. New York: Longmans, Green, 1936.
   136 p.

4. Biamonte, Salvatore G. Louis Armstrong, l'ambasciatore del jazz.
   Milano: U. Mursia & C., 1973. 165, [1] p., illus.

   Boujut, Michel. Pour Armstrong. Paris: Filipacchi, 1976. 128 p.,
   illus., discography 1923-1971 by Daniel Nevers, index of cited
   authors, 37-item bibliography, filmography.

   Collier, James Lincoln. Louis Armstrong: an American Genius. New
   York: Oxford University Press, 1983. ix, 383 p. + 8 plates, 24
   illus., notes, discography, index.

Eaton, Jeanette. Trumpeter's Tale: the Story of Young Louis Armstrong. New York: William Morrow & Company, 1955. 191 p., illus.

Faber, Anne. Louis Armstrong. Hamburg: Cecilie Dressler Verlag, 1977. 173 p., illus., discography.

Goffin, Robert. Horn of Plenty: the Story of Louis Armstrong. Translated by James F. Bezou. New York: Allen, Towne & Heath, Inc., 1947. Reprint 1977/1978. 304 p., portrait.

Hoskins, Robert. Louis Armstrong: Biography of a Musician. Los Angeles: Holloway House Publishing Co., 1979. 222 p., filmography, select discography.

Joensen, Bendt. Louis Armstrong. København: Gyldendal, 1958. 32, [1] p., 8 illus.

Jones, Max and John Chilton. Louis: the Louis Armstrong Story, 1900–1971. Boston: Little, Brown and Company, 1971. 256 p., illus., chronology, film list, index.

The English edition [St. Albans: Mayflower, 1975] was expanded to 302 p. + 16 plates.

Jones, Max, John Chilton and Leonard Feather. Salute to Satchmo. London: I.P.C. Specialist & Professional Press Ltd., 1970. 155 p., 24 illus., index of names.

Mauro, Walter. Louis Armstrong: el rey del jazz. Milano: Rusconi Libri S.p.A., 1979. 216, [1] p. + 6 plates, 13 illus., discography, filmography, 35-item bibliography.

McCarthy, Albert J. Louis Armstrong. New York: A.S. Barnes and Company, Inc., 1960. 85, [1] p. + 2 plates, 4 illus., selected discography.

Meryman, Richard. Louis Armstrong: a Self Portrait [interview by Richard Meryman]. New York: The Ekins Press, 1971. 59 p. + 8 plates, 16 illus.

Expanded and edited from Life (April 15, 1966).

Panassié, Hugues. Louis Armstrong. Paris: Editions du Belvédère, 1947. 107 p., 9 illus., discography by Charles Delaunay.

Panassié, Hugues. Louis Armstrong. Paris: Nouvelles éditions latines, 1969. 220, [1] p. + 4 plates, 15 illus., discography.

There is an English translation [New York: Charles Scribner's Sons, 1971] which is abridged.

Richards, Kenneth G. Louis Armstrong. Chicago: Children's Press, 1967. 95 p., illus., 49-item bibliography, index.

Slawe, Jan [pseud. for Jan Sypniewski]. Louis Armstrong: Zehn mono-
graphische Studien. Basel: Papillons-Verlag, 1953. 127 p., portrait,
genealogy, chronology, filmography, discography, 18-item bibliography, index.

Winkler, Hans Juergen. Louis Armstrong: ein Portraet. Wetzler:
Pegasus Verlag, 1962. 47 p. + 8 plates, 16 illus., discography.

C0039.
Arrau, Claudio. Chilean Pianist; b. February 6, 1903, Chillan.

1. Baker 7; DEU (Bibliography); Grove 6/1 (Bibliography); Grove-AM
   (Bibliography); MGG (Bibliography); PAB-MI/2 (Bibliography);
   Riemann 12 + Supp.

2. CL 7/2, 9/1, 11/8, 22/3; GR 49/February, 55/February, 60/February;
   HiFi/MusAm 17/2; CK(KB) 4/7, 9/7, MM 26/8; PQ 83, 88, 106, 120.

4. Cardone, Inés María. Claudio Arrau: lo que nunca se dijo de su viaje
   a Chile. Santiago: Fondo Cultural Diario la Tercera/Editorial Andrés
   Bello, 1985. 157 p., illus.

   Gavoty, Bernard. Claudio Arrau. Geneva: Verlag René Kister, 1962.
   34 p., 24 illus., discography.

   Horowitz, Joseph. Conversations with Arrau. New York: Alfred A.
   Knopf, 1982. xv, 317 p., discography by T.W. Scragg, index.

5. A0055, A0060, A0069, B0100, B0110.

   SEE: 50 entrevistas con gente importante del mundo de la musica.
   Barcelona: Edita Ediciones de Nuevo Arte Thor, 1980. 236, [1]
   p., illus.

   Reprints from the periodical Monsalvat.

C0040.
Artôt, Alexandre-Joseph Montagney. Belgian Violinist; b. January 25,
1815, Brussels; d. July 20, 1845, Ville-d'Avray.

1. Baker 7; DEU; Fetis 2/1 + Supp.; Grove 6/1; Mendel; MGG/Supp.;
   Riemann 12.

C0041.
Asciolla, Dino. Italian Violinist; b. June 9, 1920, Rome.

1. Baker 7; DEU; Grove 6/1.

C0042.
Ashkenazy, Vladimir. Soviet Pianist (currently holding Icelandic
citizenship); b. July 6, 1937, Gorky, USSR.

1. Baker 7; DEU (under Askenazij); Grove 6/1; PAB-MI/2 (Bibliography);
   Riemann 12/Supp.

2. CL 8/7, 15/1, 18/8, 19/9; GR 45/August, 55/October, 63/September;
   HiFi/MusAm 28/5; CK(KB) 3/6; KB 13/3; MM 18/9; PQ 103.

4. Parrott, Jasper and Vladimir Ashkenazy. Beyond Frontiers. London:
   William Collins Sons & Co. Ltd., 1984. 239 p., 17 illus., discography by John Kehoe, recordings in progress, index.

5. A0060, A0069, A0075.

   SEE: Matheopoulos, Helena. Meastro: incontri con i grandi direttori
        d'orchestra. Milano: Garzanti Editore s.p.a., 1983.

C0043.
Askenase, Stefan. Belgian Pianist; b. July 10, 1896, Lwow, Poland;
d. November 18, 1985, Cologne, Germany.

1. Baker 7; DEU; Grove 6/1; PAB-MI/2 (Bibliography); Riemann 12 + Supp.

C0044.
Atkins, Chet [Chester Burton]. American Country-Western/Popular Music
Guitarist; b. June 20, 1924, Luttrell, Tennessee.

1. Baker 7; Grove-AM (Bibliography); PAB-MI/2 (Bibliography).

3. Atkins, Chet with Bill Neely. Country Gentleman. Chicago: H. Regnery,
   1974. xiii, 226 p., illus.

   O'Donnell, Red. Chet Atkins. Nashville: Athens Music Company, 1967.
   46 p., illus.

C0045.
Auberlen, Samuel Gottlob. German Violinist/Organist; b. November 23,
1758, Fellbach, near Stuttgart; d. August 23, 1829, Ulm.

1. Fetis 2/1; Mendel; MGG/Supp. (Bibliography); Riemann 12 (Bibliog.)

3. Auberlen, Samuel G. Samuel Gottlob Auberlen: Musikdirektors und
   Organisten am Muenster in Ulm. Leben, Meinungen und Schicksale.
   Ulm: In Commission der Stettinischen Buchhandlung, 1824. viii, 248 p.

C0046.
Aubert, Jacques. French Violinist; b. September 30, 1689, Paris;
d. (buried May 19, 1756), Belleville, near Paris.

1. Baker 7; DEU; Fetis 2/1 (Bibliography); Grove 6/1; MGG; PAB-MI/2
   (Bibliography); Riemann 12 (Bibliography) + Supp. (Bibliography);
   Schmidl.

C0047.
Auer, Leopold. Hungarian Violinist; b. June 7, 1845, Veszprem; d. July
15, 1930, Loschwitz, near Dresden, Germany.

1. Baker 7; DEU (Bibliography); Fetis 2/Supp.; Grove 6/1; Grove-AM
   (Bibliography); Mendel; MGG/Supp.; PAB-MI/2 (Bibliography); Riemann
   12 (Bibliography) + Supp. (Bibliography); Schmidl + Supp.

3. Auer, Leopold. My Long Life in Music. New York: Frederick A. Stokes Company, 1923. xii, 377 p., 47 illus., index.

Auer, Leopold. Violin Playing as I Teach It. New York: Frederick A. Stokes Company Publishers, 1921. vi, [iii], 225 p., 10 illus.

4. Raaben, Lev Nikolaevich. Leopol'd Semenovich Auer. Leningrad: Muzyka, 1962. 176 p., illus.

Rakos, Miklós. Veszprémtoel szentpétervarig (Auer lipót élete és muevészete). Kiadja: Veszprém megyei tanács V.B., 1981. 194 p., 49 illus.

5. A0115, A0145, B0037, B0089.

C0048.
Aulin, Tor Bernhard. Swedish Violinist; b. September 10, 1866, Stockholm; d. March 1, 1914, Saltsjobaden.

1. Baker 7; DEU (Bibliography); Grove 6/1 (Bibliography); MGG/Supp. (Bibliography); PAB-MI/2 (Bibliography); Riemann 12 + Supp. (Bibliography); Schmidl + Supp.

His sister Laura Valborg (b. January 9, 1860, Gaevle; d. January 11, 1928, Oerebro) was a well-known pianist. SEE: Grove 6/1.

C0049.
Ax, Emanuel. American Pianist; b. June 8, 1949, Lwow, Poland.

1. Baker 7; Grove-AM (Bibliography).

2. CL 19/1, 26/5; HiFi/MusAm 27/10; CK(KB) 6/2; KB 10/9.

C0050.
Ayler, Albert. American Jazz Saxophonist; b. July 13, 1936, Cleveland, Ohio; d. November 25, 1970, New York City.

1. Baker 7; DEU (Bibliography); Grove 6/1 (Bibliography); Grove-AM (Bibliography, 10 entries); JB (11 entries); JRRM; LJ; PAB-MI/2 (Bibliography).

2. DB 33/23, 38/7.

C0051.
Babbi, Pietro Giovanni. Italian Violinist; b. May 6, 1745, Cesena; d. November 19, 1814, Dresden, Germany.

1. Baker 7; DEU; Fetis 2/1; Grove 6/1 (Bibliography); Mendel; MGG (Bibliography); Riemann 12 (Bibliography); Schmidl + Supp.

C0052.
Bachauer, Gina. Greek Pianist; b. May 21, 1913, Athens; d. August 22, 1976, Athens.

1. Baker 7; DEU; PAB-MI/2 (Bibliography); Riemann 12 + Supp.

2. CL 9/3; HiFi 13/11.

5. A0070.

C0053.
Bache, Constance. English Pianist; b. March 11, 1846, Birmingham;
d. June 28, 1903, Montreux, France.

1. DEU; Schmidl.

3. Bache, Constance. Brother Musicians: Reminiscences of Edward and
Walter Bache. London: Methuen & Co., 1901. x, [i], 330 p., 16
illus., index.

Her brother, Walter (b. June 19, 1842, Birmingham; d. March 26,
1888, London), was a pianist. SEE: Riemann 12.

C0054.
Bachmann, Alberto Abraham. Swiss Violinist; b. March 20, 1875, Geneva;
d. November 24, 1963, Neuilly-sur-Seine.

1. Baker 7; DEU; Schmidl/Supp.

3. Bachmann published several pedagogical books: An Encyclopedia of the
Violin (A0708), Les grands violinistes du passe (A0709), and Le
violin (lutherie-oeuvres-biographies) (A0710).

C0055.
Bachrich, Sigismund. Hungarian Violinist; b. January 23, 1841,
Zsambokreth; d. July 16, 1913, Vienna.

1. Baker 7; MGG/Supp.; Riemann 12; Schmidl.

3. Bachrich, Sigismund. Aus verklungenen Zeiten: Erinnerungen eines
alten Musikers. Wien: Paul Knepler Verlag, 1914.

No copy of these posthumous memoirs cited in MGG was located.

C0056.
Backhaus, Wilhelm. German-born Swiss Pianist; b. March 26, 1884,
Leipzig; d. July 5, 1969, Villach, Austria.

1. Baker 7; DEU (Bibliography); Grove 6/2 (Bibliography); MGG; PAB-MI/2
(Bibliography); Riemann 12 + Supp.; Schmidl.

2. MM 18/3.

4. Eichmann, Arnold Heinz. Wilhelm Backhaus. Geneva: René Kister, 1958.
31 p., 23 illus., recordings.

Ricolo, Gennaro. Wilhelm Backhaus: una vita per Beethoven. Benevento:
Stabilimento lito-tipografico editoriale De Martini, 1969. 31 p.

5. A0008, A0053, A0060, B0028, B0053, B0055, B0129.

C0057.
Badura—Skoda, Paul. Austrian Pianist; b. October 6, 1927, Vienna.

1. Baker 7; DEU (Bibliography); Grove 6/2 (Bibliography); MGG/Supp.
(Bibliography); PAB—MI/2 (Bibliography); Riemann 12 + Supp.
(Bibliography).

2. CL 12/3, 25/9; CK(KB) 6/1.

3. Badura—Skoda, Paul. Interpreting Mozart on the Keyboard. Translated
by Leo Black. London: Barrie and Rockliff, 1962 [original Vienna,
1957]. ix, 319 p. + 24 plates, references, bibliography, index of
works.

C0058.
Baehr, Franz Josef. Austrian Clarinetist; b. February 19, 1770, Vienna;
d. August 7, 1819, Vienna.

1. Baker 7; Grove 6/2 (Bibliography); Mendel.

C0059.
Baermann, Heinrich Joseph. German Clarinetist; b. February 14, 1784,
Potsdam; d. June 11, 1847, Munich.

1. Baker 7 (Bibliography); DEU; Fetis 2/1; Mendel; MGG/Supp. (Bibliography); Riemann 12 (Bibliography) + Supp. (Bibliography).

His son, **Karl** (b. October 24, 1811, Munich; d. May 23, 1855, Munich),
was also a clarinetist. He published Vollstaendige Clarinettschule.
5 vols. Offenbach/M., 1864-75.

C0060.
Bailey, Buster [William C.]. American Jazz Clarinetist; b. July 19,
1902, Memphis, Tennessee; d. April 12, 1967, New York City.

1. Grove—AM (Bibliography); Grove—Jazz; Riemann 12.

C0061.
Baillot, Pierre—Marie—François de Sales. French Violinist; b. October 1,
1771, Passy, near Paris; d. September 15, 1842, Paris.

1. Baker 7 (Bibliography); DEU (Bibliography); Fetis 2/1 (Bibliography)
+ Supp. (Bibliography); Grove 6/2 (Bibliography); Mendel; MGG
(Bibliography); Riemann 12 (Bibliography) + Supp. (Bibliography);
Schmidl.

4. Tajan—Rogé, D. Hommage à la mémoire de Baillot; discours prononcé par
M.D. Tajan—Rogé à la soirée musicale qui a eu lieu dans la petite
salle du Conservatoire nationale de musique.... Paris: Armand Le
Chevalier, Editeur, 1872. 24 p.

C0062.
Baker, Chet [Chesney H.]. American Jazz Trumpeter; b. December 23, 1929,
Yale, Oklahoma.

1. Grove-AM; Grove-Jazz; JB; PAB-MI/2 (Bibliography); Riemann/Supp.

2. DB 31/20, 31/22, 48/10.

C0063.
Baker, Israel. American Violinist; b. February 11, 1921, Chicago, IL.

1. Baker 7; Grove 6/2; Grove-AM.

C0064.
Baker, Julius. American Flutist; b. September 23, 1915, Cleveland, OH.

1. Baker 7; Grove-AM (Bibliography); PAB-MI/2 (Bibliography).

C0065.
Baker, Robert Stevens. American Organist; b. July 7, 1916, Pontiac, IL.

1. Baker 7; Grove 6/2; Grove-AM; PAB-MI/2 (Bibliography).

C0066.
Ballista, Antonio. Italian Pianist; b. March 30, 1936, Milan.

1. Baker 7; DEU; Grove 6/2.

C0067.
Balokovič, Zlatko. Yugoslavian Violinist; b. March 21, 1895, Zagreb;
d. March 29, 1965, Venice, Italy.

1. Baker 7; Riemann 12 + Supp.

C0068.
Balsam, Artur. American Pianist; b. February 8, 1906, Warsaw, Poland.

1. Baker 7; DEU; Grove 6/2; Grove-AM; PAB-MI/2 (Bibliography); Riemann
   12 + Supp.

C0069.
Banister, Henry Joshua. English Cellist; b. 1803, London; d. 1847,
London.

1. Baker 7; DEU.

C0070.
Barcewicz, Stanislaw. Polish Violinist; b. April 16, 1858, Warsaw;
d. September 1, 1929, Warsaw.

1. Baker 7; DEU (Bibliography); Grove 6/2 (Bibliography); MGG/Supp.
   (Bibliography); Riemann 12/Supp.; Schmidl (under Barcevicz).

C0071.
Barenboim, Daniel. Israeli Pianist; b. November 15, 1942, Buenos Aires,
Argentina.

1. Baker 7; DEU; Grove 6/2; PAB-MI/2 (Bibliography); Riemann 12/Supp.

2. GR 50/September; HiFi/MusAm 22/1; MM 16/12.

5. A0060, B0052.

   SEE: Meyer-Josten, Juergen. Musiker im Gespraech: Daniel Barenboim; Maurizio Pollini. Foreword by Claudio Arrau. Frankfurt: Henry Litolff's Verlag, 1980. 20 p., 4 illus.

   SEE: William Wordsworth under Jacqueline DuPré (C0343.4).

C0072.
Bar-Illan, David. Israeli Pianist; b. February 7, 1930, Haifa.

1. Baker 7; Grove 6/2; Grove-AM (Bibliography).

2. HiFi/MusAm 17/7, 18/4.

C0073.
Barkel, Charles. Swedish Violinist; b. February 6, 1898, Stugun; d. March 7, 1973, Stockholm.

1. Baker 7; Grove 6/2 (Bibliography); Riemann 12 + Supp.

C0074.
Barker, Danny [Daniel]. American Jazz Guitarist; b. January 13, 1909, New Orleans, Louisiana.

1. JB; JRRM; LJ; PAB-MI/2 (Bibliography).

3. Barker, Danny. A Life in Jazz. Edited by Alyn Shipton. New York: Oxford University Press, 1986. viii, 223 p. + 8 plates, 20 illus., chronological discography, index.

C0075.
Barmas, Issaye. Russian Violinist; b. May 1, 1872, Odessa; d. July 3, 1946, London, England.

1. Baker 7; Riemann 12; Schmidl/Supp.

3. Barmas, Issaye. Die Loesung des Geigentechnischen Problems. Berlin: F.H. Schneider, 1913.

C0076.
Baron, Samuel. American Flutist; b. April 27, 1925, New York City.

1. Baker 7; Grove 6/2; Grove-AM (Bibliography); PAB-MI/2 (Bibliography); Riemann 12/Supp.

C0077.
Barrère, Georges. French Flutist; b. October 31, 1876, Bordeaux; d. June 14, 1944, Kingston, New York.

1. Baker 7; Grove 6/2; Grove-AM (Bibliography); Riemann 12; Schmidl/Supp.

C0078.
Barret, Apollon Marie-Rose. French Oboist; b. c.1803, Paris; d. March 8, 1879, London, England.

1. Baker 7; Fetis 2/1; Mendel; Riemann 12; Schmidl.

3. Barret, Apollon. A Complete New Method for the Oboe Comprising All the New Fingerings, New Tables of Shakes, Scales, Exercises. London: Jullien and Company, n.d.

C0079.
Barrière, Jean. French Cellist; b. c.1705; d. June 6, 1747, Paris.

1. Baker 7; DEU; Fetis 2/1; Grove 6/2 (Bibliography); Mendel; MGG/Supp. (Bibliography); Riemann 12 + Supp.; Schmidl.

C0080.
Barrows, John. American French-horn Player; b. February 12, 1913, Glendale, California; d. January 11, 1974, Madison, Wisconsin.

1. Baker 7; Grove-AM; PAB-MI/2 (Bibliography).

C0081.
Barth, Christian Samuel. German Oboist; b. January 11, 1735, Glauchau; d. July 8, 1809, Copenhagen, Denmark.

1. Baker 7; DEU; Fetis 2/1; Grove 6/2; Mendel; MGG/Supp. (Bibliography); Riemann 12 + Supp.

C0082.
Barth, Karl Heinrich. German Pianist; b. July 12, 1847, Pillau, near Koenigsberg; d. December 23, 1922, Berlin.

1. Baker 7; DEU; Riemann 12; Schmidl.

C0083.
Barth, Richard. German Violinist; b. June 5, 1850, Grosswanzleben; d. December 25, 1923, Marburg.

1. Baker 7; DEU; Grove 6/2 (Bibliography); Riemann 12; Schmidl.

4. Deggeller-Engelke, Eleonora. Zur Brahmsfolge: Richard C. Barth (1850-1923), Leben, Wirken und Werk. Ph.D. diss. University of Marburg, 1942 [published 1949 by Elwert, Graefe und Unzer]. 94 p.

C0084.
Barthélémon, François-Hippolyte. French Violinist; b. July 27, 1741, Bordeaux; d. July 20, 1808, London, England.

1. Baker 7; DEU (Bibliography); EdS (Bibliography); Fetis 2/1; Grove 6/2 (Bibliography); Mendel; MGG/Supp. (Bibliography); PAB-MI/2 (Bibliography); Riemann 12 (Bibliography); Schmidl + Supp.

5. D0003.

C0085.
Barwahser, Hubert. Dutch Flutist; b. September 28, 1906, Herzogenrath, Germany.

1. Baker 7; Grove 6/2; Riemann 12/Supp.

C0086.
Bashkirov, Dmitri. Soviet Pianist; b. November 1, 1931, Tiflis.

1. Baker 7; Grove 6/2 (Bibliography); Riemann 12/Supp.

5. A0091.

C0087.
Basie, Count [William]. American Jazz Pianist; b. August 21, 1904, Red Bank, New Jersey; d. April 26, 1984, Hollywood, California.

1. Baker 7 (Bibliography); DEU (Bibliography); Grove 6/2 (Bibliography mentions a discography in preparation by B. Scherman); Grove-AM (Bibliography - 21 entries); Grove-Jazz; JB (17 entries); JRRM (26 entries); LJ; MGG/Supp. (Bibliography); PAB-MI/2 (Bibliography); Riemann 12 + Supp. (Bibliography).

2. DB 22/22, 25/19, 30/15, 32/9, 35/8, 37/7, 37/8, 42/15, 46/15; CK(KB) 3/7, 4/3.

4. Dance, Stanley. The World of Count Basie. New York: Charles Scribner's Sons, 1980. xxi, 399 p., 48 illus., selected discography, 72-item bibliography, index.

   Grunnet, Jorgen and J.G. Jepsen. Discography of Count Basie. Brande: Debut Records, 1959. 32 p.

   Horricks, Raymond. Count Basie and His Orchestra: Its Music and Its Musicians. New York: The Citadel Press, 1957. 320 p. + 8 plates, 13 illus., discography.

   Morgan, Alun. Count Basie. Tunbridge Wells, Kent: Spellmount Ltd, 1984. 94 p., 11 illus., discography, 14-item bibliography.

   Morgenstern, Dan and Jack Bradley, eds. Count Basie and His Bands. New York: New York Jazz Museum [exhibition catalogue], 1974. 20 p., chronology, selected compositions, selected 25-item bibliography.

   Sheridan, Chris, comp. Count Basie: a Bio-Discography. Westport (CT): Greenwood Press, 1986. xxvi, 1350 p. + 10 plates.

5. A0006.

C0088.
Batta, Alexandre. Dutch Cellist; b. July 9, 1816, Maastricht; d. October 8, 1902, Versailles, France.

1. Baker 7; Fetis 2/1 + Supp.; Mendel; Schmidl.

4. Eyma, Xavier and Arthur de Lucy. Alexandre Batta. Paris: Librairie Universelle, 1840. 16 p., portrait.

C0089.
Baudiot, Charles-Nicolas. French Cellist; b. March 29, 1773, Nancy; d. September 26, 1849, Paris.

1. Baker 7; DEU (Bibliography); Fetis 2/1; Grove 6/2 (Bibliography); Mendel; MGG/Supp. (Bibliography); Riemann 12 (Bibliography) + Supp.; Schmidl.

5. A0153.

C0090.
Bauer, Harold. American Pianist; b. April 28, 1873, Kingston on Thames, near London; d. March 12, 1951, Miami, Florida.

1. Baker 7; DEU; Grove 6/2 (Bibliography); Grove-AM (Bibliography); PAB-MI/2 (Bibliography); Riemann 12.

2. MQ (April 1943).

3. Bauer, Harold. Harold Bauer, His Book. New York: W.W. Norton & Company, Inc., 1948. Reprint 1969. 306 p., 11 illus., index.

5. A0058, B0089.

C0091.
Baumann, Hermann. German French-horn Player; b. August 1, 1934, Hamburg.

1. Baker 7; DEU; Grove 6/2 (Bibliography); Riemann 12/Supp.

C0092.
Baumgartner, Paul. Swiss Pianist; b. July 21, 1903, Altstaetten; d. October 19, 1976, Locarno, Italy.

1. Baker 7; DEU; Grove 6/2; MGG/Supp. (Bibliography); PAB-MI/2 (Bibliography); Riemann 12 + Supp.

C0093.
Bazzini, Antonio. Italian Violinist; b. March 11, 1818, Brescia; d. February 10, 1897, Milan.

1. Baker 7; DEU (Bibliography); EdS (Bibliography); Fetis 2/1 + Supp.; Grove 6/2 (Bibliography); Mendel; MGG/Supp. (Bibliography); PAB-MI/2 (Bibliography); Riemann 12 + Supp. (Bibliography); Schmidl + Supp.

4. Toni, Alceo. Antonio Bazzini: la vita - il violinista - il didatta - il compositore. Milano: Editrice Athena, 1946. 74, [5] p., 14 illus., compositions.

C0094.
Bean, Hugh. English Violinist; b. September 22, 1929, Beckenham.

1. Baker 7; Grove 6/2; PAB-MI/2 (Bibliography).

2. Strad Oct/1979.

C0095.
Beauvarlet-Charpentier, Jean-Jacques. French Organist; b. June 28, 1734, Abbeville; d. May 6, 1794, Paris.

1. Baker 7; DEU (Bibliography); Fetis 2/1; Grove 6/2 (Bibliography); Mendel (under Charpentier); MGG (Bibliography); Riemann 12 (Bibliography); Schmidl.

C0096.
Bechet, Sidney Joseph. American Jazz Clarinet/Soprano Saxophonist; b. May 14, 1897, New Orleans, Louisiana; d. May 14, 1959, Paris, France.

1. Baker 7; DEU (Bibliography); EdS (Bibliography); Grove 6/2 (Bibliography); Grove-AM (Bibliography - 13 entries); Grove-Jazz; JB (19 entries); JRRM (17 entries); LJ; MGG/Supp. (Bibliography); Riemann 12 + Supp. (Bibliography).

3. Bechet, Sidney. Treat It Gentle. Edited by Joan Reid, Desmond Flower and John Ciardi. London: Cassell & Company Ltd, 1960. Reprint 1975. vi, [iii], 245 p., 15 illus., discography by David Mylne, index.

4. Delaunay, Charles. Histoire de Sidney Bechet. Paris: Vogue, 1959. 12 p.

   Grunnet, Jorgen and J.G. Jepsen. Sidney Bechet: eine Diskographie. Luebeck: Uhle & Kleinmann, 1960. 38 p.

   Kunst, Peter. Sidney Bechet, ein Portraet. Wetzlar: Pegasus Verlag, 1959. 47 p. + 8 plates, 15 illus., discography.

   Mouly, Raymond. Sidney Bechet, notre ami. Paris: La Table Ronde, 1959. 124, [49] p., chronology, discography.

5. A0001, A0031, A0159.

C0097.
Becker, Hugo. German Cellist; b. February 13, 1863, Strasbourg; d. July 30, 1941, Geiselgasteig, near Munich.

1. Baker 7; DEU (Bibliography); Grove 6/2 (Bibliography); MGG (Bibliography); Riemann 12; Schmidl + Supp.

5. A0104, B0037, B0053.

C0098.
Becker, Jean. German Violinist, father of Hugo; b. May 11, 1833, Mannheim; d. October 10, 1884, Mannheim.

1. Baker 7; DEU; Grove 6/2 (Bibliography); Mendel; MGG (Bibliography); Riemann 12; Schmidl.

C0099.
Beckmann, Johann Friedrich Gottlieb. German Organist; b. September 6, 1737, Celle; d. April 25, 1792, Celle.

1. Baker 7; DEU (Bibliography); Fetis 2/1; Mendel; MGG/Supp. (Bibliography); Schmidl.

4. Mueller, Harald, ed. Das Testament des Celler Stadtorganisten Johann Friedrich Gottlieb Beckmann.... Celle: Selbstverlag, 1972. 20 p., illus., 10-item bibliography.

C0100.
Beer, Johann Joseph. German Clarinetist; b. May 18, 1744, Gruenwald; d. October 28, 1812, Berlin.

1. Baker 7; DEU (Bibliography); Fetis 2/1; Grove 6/2 (Bibliography); Mendel; MGG/Supp. (Bibliography); Riemann 12 (Bibliography) + Supp.; Schmidl.

C0101.
Behrend, Siegfried. German Guitarist; b. November 19, 1933, Berlin.

1. Baker 7; DEU (Bibliography); Grove 6/2; PAB-MI/2 (Bibliography); Riemann 12 + Supp. (Bibliography).

4. Eggers, Heino. Belinda, Siegfried Behrend: mit der Gitarre um die Welt. Berlin: Arani-Verlags GmbH, 1965. 40 p., illus.

C0102.
Beiderbecke, Bix [Leon Bismark]. American Jazz Cornetist; b. March 10, 1903, Davenport, Iowa; d. August 6, 1931, New York City.

1. Baker 7 (Bibliography); DEU (Bibliography); Grove 6/2 (Bibliography); Grove-AM (Bibliography - 15 entries); Grove-Jazz; JB (16 entries); JRRM (16 entries); LJ (16 entries); PAB-MI/2 (Bibliography); Riemann 12 + Supp. (Bibliography).

2. DB 28/17.

4. Berton, Ralph. Remembering Bix: a Memoir of the Jazz Age. New York: Harper & Row, Publishers, 1974. xiii, 428 p. + 8 plates, 27 illus., source notes, annotated bibliography and discography, index.

Burnett, James. Bix Beiderbecke. London: Cassell & Company Limited, 1959. 90 p. + 2 plates, 4 illus., discography.

Perhonis, J.P. The Bix Beiderbecke Story: the Jazz Musician in Legend, Fiction, and Fact. Ph.D. diss. University of Minnesota, 1978.

Sudhalter, Richard M. and Philip R. Evans. Bix: Man & Legend. New Rochelle (NY): Arlington House, 1974. 512 p., illus., daily diary, comprehensive discography, index of people, index of places.

Wareing, Charles H. and George Garlick. Bugles for Beiderbecke.

5. A0001, A0029, A0034, B0054.

C0103.
Belcke, Friedrich August. German Trombonist; b. May 27, 1795, Lucka,
Altenburg; d. December 10, 1874, Lucka.

1. Baker 7; Fetis 2/1 + Supp.; Grove 6/2; Schmidl.

C0104.
Bellison, Simeon. American Clarinetist; b. December 4, 1883, Moscow,
Russia; d. May 4, 1953, New York City.

1. Baker 7; Grove 6/2; Grove-AM (Bibliography).

C0105.
Benda, Franz. Bohemian Violinist; baptized November 22, 1709, Alt-
Benatek, Bohemia; d. March 7, 1786, Neuendorf, near Potsdam, Germany.

1. Baker 7 (Bibliography); DEU (Bibliography); Fetis 2/1; Grove 6/2
   (Bibliography); Mendel; MGG (Bibliography); PAB-MI/2 (Bibliography);
   Riemann 12 + Supp. (Bibliography); Schmidl.

3. His autobiography, written in 1763, was published in Neue Berliner
   Muzikzeitung, X (1856); English translation by Paul Nettl: Forgotten
   Musicians. New York: Philosophical Library, 1951.

4. Berten, Franzi. Franz Benda: sein Leben und seine Kompositionen.
   Ph.D. diss. University of Cologne, 1928. 65 p.

   Laserstein, Alfred. Franz Benda: sein Leben und seine Werk mit
   thematischen Verzeichnis seiner Kompositionen. Ein Beitrag zur
   Geschichte der Instrumentalmusik im 18. Jahrhundert. Ph.D. diss.
   University of Breslau, 1924. v, 200 p.

   Murphy, T.C. The Violin Concertos of Franz Benda and Their Use in
   Violin Pedagogy. Ph.D. diss. University of Southern California, 1968.

   Nissel-Nemenoff, Elfriede. Die Violintecknik Franz Benda's und seiner
   Schule. Ph.D. diss. University of Koenigsberg, 1930. 103 p.

C0106.
Bendel, Franz. German Pianist; b. March 23, 1833, Schoenlinde, Bohemia;
d. July 3, 1874, Berlin.

1. Baker 7; Fetis 2/1; Mendel; PAB-MI/2 (Bibliography); Schmidl.

C0107.
Bendinelli, Cesare. Italian Trumpeter; b. c.1550, Verona; d. 1617,
Monaco.

1. Baker 7 (Bibliography); DEU; Grove 6/2 (Bibliography).

3. Bendinelli wrote the first known trumpet method, Tutta l'arte della
   Trombetta, published in Documenta Musicologica, 2nd series, v,
   1975; English translation 1976.

C0108.
Bendix, Otto. Danish Pianist; b. July 26, 1845, Copenhagen; d. March 1, 1904, San Francisco, California.

1. Baker 7; DEU.

C0109.
Bennewitz [Benevic], Antonín. Czechoslovakian Violinist; b. March 26?, 1833, Přívaty, near Litomyše; d. May 29, 1926, Dosky, near Litoměřice.

1. Baker 7; Grove 6/2 (Bibliography); Mendel; Schmidl.

C0110.
Benoist, André. French Pianist; b. April 4, 1879, Paris; d. June 19, 1953, Monmouth Beach, New Jersey.

1. Baker 7.

3. Benoist, André. The Accompanist: an Autobiography of André Benoist. Edited by John Anthony Maltese. Neptune (NJ): Paganiniana Publications, Inc. 1978. 383 p., 200+ illus., discography, index.

4. Additional materials are in the Library of Congress.

C0111.
Berber, Felix. German Violinist; b. March 11, 1871, Jena; d. November 2, 1930, Munich.

1. Baker 7; MGG (Bibliography); Riemann 12 (Bibliography); Schmidl.

5. B0024.

C0112.
Berbiguier, Benoit-Tranquille. French Flutist; b. December 21, 1782, Caderousse, Vaucluse; d. January 28, 1838, Point-Levoy, near Blois.

1. Baker 7; DEU (Bibliography); Fetis 2/1; Grove 6/2 (Bibliography); Mendel; Riemann 12 (Bibliography); Schmidl (Bibliography).

C0113.
Berghout, Phia [Sophia] Rosa. Dutch Harpist; b. December 14, 1909, Amsterdam.

1. Grove 6/2.

4. Rijpstra-Verbeek, Mimi. Harpe diem, Phia Berghout's arpeggio. 's-Gravenhage: Nijgh & Van Ditmar, 1974. 139, [1] p. + 4 plates, 18 illus.

C0114.
Berigan, Bunny [Rowland Bernart]. American Jazz Trumpeter; b. November 2, 1908, Hilbert, Wisconsin; d. June 2, 1942, New York City.

1. Baker 7; Grove 6/2 (Bibliography); Grove-AM (Bibliography); Grove-Jazz; JB; JRRM; LJ; PAB-MI/2 (Bibliography).

4. Danca, Vince. Bunny: a Bio-Discography of Jazz Trumpeter Bunny
   Berigan. Rockford (IL): p.p., 1978. 64 p., 6 illus., discography.

CO115.
Beringer, Oscar. English Pianist; b. July 14, 1844, Furtwangen, Baden,
Germany; d. February 21, 1922, London.

1. Baker 7; DEU; Grove 6/2 (Bibliography); MGG/Supp. (Bibliography);
   PAB-MI/2 (Bibliography); Riemann 12; Schmidl.

3. Beringer, Oscar. Fifty Years' Experience of Pianoforte Teaching and
   Playing. London: Bosworth & Co., 1907. 72 p., 14 illus.

CO116.
de Bériot, Charles-Auguste. Belgian Violinist; b. February 20, 1802,
Louvain; d. April 8, 1870, Brussels.

1. Baker 7 (Bibliography); DEU (Bibliography); Fetis 2/1 + Supp.; Grove
   6/2 (Bibliography); Mendel; MGG (Bibliography); PAB-MI/2 (Bibliography); Riemann 12 (Bibliography); Schmidl + Supp.

4. Cowden, Robert H. Concert and Opera Singers: a Bibliography of Biographical Materials. Westport (CT): Greenwood Press, 1985.

   Note the entries under Maria Felicita Malibran (CO378).

   Heron-Allen, Edward. A Contribution towards an Accurate Biography of
   Charles Auguste de Bériot and Maris Felecita Malibran-Garcia:
   Extracted from the Correspondence of the Former. London: 125 copies
   reprinted from The Violin Times for the author by F.W. Wakeham,
   1894. 24 p. + facsimile of a letter [unbound].

   Méreaux, Amédée. Biographies musicales: Labarre, De Bériot,
   Moscheles, Stamaty. Rouen: Imp. de D. Briere et Fils, n.d. 28 p.

5. A0014, A0023, A0093.

CO117.
de Bériot, Charles-Wilfride. French Pianist; b. February 21, 1833,
Paris; d. October 22, 1914, Sceaux de Gatinais.

1. Baker 7; DEU; Fetis 2/Supp.; Grove 6/2; MGG; PAB-MI/2 (Bibliography); Riemann 12.

   He was the son of Charles-Auguste and Maria Malibran who became
   involved in 1830 but did not marry until 1836.

CO118.
Berman, Lazar. Soviet Pianist; b. February 26, 1930, Leningrad.

1. Baker 7; DEU; Grove 6/2 (Bibliography); PAB-MI/2 (Bibliography).

2. CL 15/4; GR 54/February; HiFi/MusAm 36/1; CK(KB) 3/10; MM 25/5.

5. A0091.

C0119.
Béroff, Michel. French Pianist; b. May 9, 1950, Epinal, Vosges.

1. Baker 7; Grove 6/2; PAB-MI/2 (Bibliography).

C0120.
Berr, Friedrich. German Clarinetist/Bassoonist; b. April 17, 1794,
Mannheim; d. September 24, 1838, Paris, France.

1. Baker 7; DEU (Bibliography); Fetis 2/1 + Supp.; Grove 6/2 (Bibliography); Mendel; Riemann 12; Schmidl.

3. Berr, Friedrich. Traité complet de la clarinette à 14 clefs: manuel
   indispensable aux personnes qui professent cet instrument et à celles
   qui l'étudient. Paris: Duverger, 1836. 104 p.

C0121.
Berry, Chuck [Charles Edward Anderson]. American Rock-and-Roll Guitarist
and Singer; b. January 15, 1926, San Jose, California.

1. Baker 7 (Bibliography); DEU (Bibliography); Grove 6/2 (Bibliography);
   Grove-AM (Bibliography); PAB-MI/2 (Bibliography).

5. SEE: Lydon, Michael. Boogie Lightning. New York: The Dial Press,
        1974. 229 p., illus.

   SEE: Lydon, Michael. Rock Folk: Portraits from the Rock 'n' Roll
        Pantheon. New York: The Dial Press, 1971. 200 p., illus.

C0122.
Berteau, Martin. French Cellist; b. c.1700; d. January 23, 1771, Angers.

1. Baker 7; DEU; Fetis 2/1; Grove 6/2 (Bibliography); Mendel; MGG/Supp.
   (Bibliography); Riemann 12 + Supp.; Schmidl.

C0123.
Bertheaume, Isidore. French Violinist; b. 1752, Paris; d. March 20,
1802, St. Petersburg, Russia.

1. Baker 7; DEU; Fetis 2/1 (under Berthaume); Grove 6/2 (Bibliography);
   Mendel (under Berthaume); Riemann 12 (under Berthaume - Bibliography); Schmidl (under Berthaume).

C0124.
Bertini, Henri-Jérôme. French Pianist; b. October 28, 1798, London;
d. October 1, 1876, Meylau, near Grenoble.

1. Baker 7; DEU (Bibliography); Fetis 2/1; Grove 6/2 (Bibliography);
   MGG; PAB-MI/2 (Bibliography); Riemann 12 (Bibliography); Schmidl.

C0125.
Bertrand, Aline. French Harpist; b. 1798, Paris; d. March 13, 1835,
Paris.

1. Baker 7; Fetis 2/1; Mendel; Schmidl/Supp.

C0126.
Besozzi, Alessandro. Italian Oboist; b. July 22, 1702, Parma; d. July 26, 1793, Turin.

1. Baker 7; DEU (Bibliography); Fetis 2/1; Grove 6/2 (Bibliography); Mendel; MGG/Supp. (Bibliography); Riemann 12 + Supp. (Bibliography); Schmidl + Supp.

C0127.
Bessems, Antoine. Belgian Violinist; b. April 6, 1809, Antwerp; d. October 19, 1868, Antwerp.

1. Baker 7; Fetis 2/1 + Supp.; Mendel; Schmidl.

C0128.
Best, William Thomas. English Organist; b. August 13, 1826, Carlisle; d. May 10, 1897, Liverpool.

1. Baker 7; DEU (Bibliography); Fetis 2/Supp.; Grove 6/2 (Bibliography); Mendel; MGG/Supp. (Bibliography); PAB-MI/2 (Bibliography); Riemann 12 (Bibliography) + Supp. (Bibliography); Schmidl.

2. MQ 4/April.

4. Levien, John Joseph Mewburn. Impressions of W.T. Best (1826-1897) Organist at St. George's Hall, Liverpool, the Handel Festival &c. London: Novello and Company, Limited, 1942. 59 p., portrait, index.

5. SEE: Knauff, Theodore. Three Great Organists [Alexandre Guilmant, William T. Best, Charles M. Widor]. n.p.: n.pub., 1892. 16 p.

C0129.
Bethune, Blind Tom [Thomas Greene]. American Pianist; b. May 25, 1849, Columbus, Georgia; d. June 13, 1908, Hoboken, New Jersey.

1. Baker 7 (Bibliography); Grove 6/2 (Bibliography); Grove-AM (Bibliography); PAB-MI/2 (Bibliography).

4. Fuell, Melissa. Blind Boone: His Early Life and His Achievements. Kansas City (MO): Burton Publishing Company, 1915. 12 p.

Southall, Geneva H. Blind Tom: the Post-Civil War Enslavement of a Black Musical Genius. Book 1. Minneapolis: Challenge Productions, Incorporated, 1979. xx, 108 p., 263 bibliographical notes, 3 appendices.

Southall also wrote The Continuing "Enslavement" of Blind Tom, 1865-1887 (Minneapolis: Challenge Productions, Inc., 1982). No copy located.

The Marvelous Musical Prodigy, Blind Tom, the Negro Boy Pianist, Whose Performances at the Great St. James and Egyptian Halls, London, and Salle Hertz, Paris, Have Created Such a Profound Sensation.... New York: French & Wheat, Printers, 1868. 80 p.

5. SEE: Trotter, James M. Music and Some Highly Musical People...
   [Including]...Sketches of the Lives of Remarkable Musicians
   of the Colored Race. Boston: Lee and Shepard, Publishers,
   1881. Reprint 1968. 352, 152 p., 12 illus., index of music.

C0130.
Betti, Adolfo. Italian Violinist; b. March 21, 1873, Lucca; d. December
2, 1950, Lucca.

1. Baker 7; DEU.

2. Strad Oct-Nov-Dec/1972, Jan-Feb-March-April-May/1973, June/1975.

3. He wrote a short biography of Francesco Geminiani (C0443.4).

C0131.
Bezekirsky, Vasili. Russian Violinist; b. January 26, 1835, Moscow;
d. November 8, 1919, Moscow.

1. Baker 7; Grove 6/2 (Bibliography).

   His son, Vasily (b. January 15, 1880, Moscow; d. November 8, 1960,
   East Windham, New York), was also a violinist.

3. Bezekirsky, V.V. From the Notebook of a Russian Violinist 1850-
   1910. Translated by Samuel Wolf. Linthicum Heights (MD): Swand
   Publications, 1984. 74 p., translator's comments.

   He also wrote a survey of the art of the violin from the 17th to the
   20th century published in Kiev in 1913.

C0132.
von Biber, Heinrich Ignaz Franz. Bohemian Violinist; b. August 12, 1644;
d. May 3, 1704, Salzburg, Austria.

1. Baker 7 (Bibliography); DEU (Bibliography); Fetis 2/1; Grove 6/2
   (Bibliography); Mendel; MGG (Bibliography); PAB-MI/2 (Bibliography); Riemann 12 (Bibliography) + Supp. (Bibliography); Schmidl.

2. MQ Jan/1938; Strad July/1977.

4. Dann, Elias. Heinrich Biber and the Seventeenth-Century Violin.
   Ph.D. diss. Columbia University, 1968. 406 p., bibliography.

5. SEE: Paul Nettl under Franz Benda (C0105.3).

C0133.
Biernacki, Nikodem. Polish Violinist; b. 1826, Tarnopol; d. May 6, 1892,
Sanok.

1. Baker 7; Grove 6/2.

C0134.
Bigard, Barney [Alban Leon]. American Jazz Clarinetist; b. March 3,
1906, New Orleans, Louisiana; d. June 27, 1980, Los Angeles, California.

1. Baker 7; DEU (Bibliography); Grove 6/2 (Bibliography); Grove-AM (Bibliography); Grove-Jazz; JRRM; PAB-MI/2 (Bibliography).

2. DB 33/18, 36/12.

3. Bigard, Barney. With Louis and the Duke: the Autobiography of a Jazz Clarinetist. Edited by Barry Martyn. Introduction by Earl Hines. New York: Oxford University Press, 1986. x, 152 p. + 8 plates, 20 illus., index.

C0135.
Biggs, E. Power [Edward George Power]. American Organist; b. March 29, 1906, Westcliff, England; d. March 10, 1977, Boston, Massachusetts.

1. Baker 7; DEU; Grove 6/2; Grove-AM (Bibliography); PAB-MI/2 (Bibliography); Riemann 12/Supp.

Widely known for his weekly organ recitals on CBS (1942-58).

2. HiFi 5/1; HiFi/MusAm 22/8.

C0136.
Bignami, Carlo. Italian Violinist; b. December 6, 1808, Cremona; d. October 2, 1848, Voghera.

1. Baker 7; DEU (Bibliography); Grove 6/2 (Bibliography); MGG/Supp. (Bibliography); Schmidl.

C0137.
Bigot de Morogues, Marie. Alsatian Pianist; b. March 3, 1786, Colmar, Alsace; d. September 16, 1820, Paris, France.

1. Baker 7; DEU (Bibliography); Fetis 2/1; Grove 6/2 (Bibliography); Mendel; MGG/Supp. (Bibliography); Riemann 12 (Bibliography) + Supp. (Bibliography); Schmidl.

C0138.
Bihari, Janos. Hungarian Violinist; baptized October 21, 1764, Nagyabony; d. April 26, 1827, Pest.

1. Baker 7; DEU (Bibliography); Fetis 2/Supp.; Grove 6/2 (Bibliography); Mendel; MGG/Supp. (Bibliography); PAB-MI/2 (Bibliography); Riemann 12 (Bibliography) + Supp. (Bibliography); Schmidl + Supp.

C0139.
Bilson, Malcolm. American Pianist; b. October 24, 1935, Los Angeles, CA.

1. Baker 7; Grove-AM.

C0140.
Bini, Pasquale. Italian Violinist; b. June 21, 1716, Pesaro; d. April 1770, Pesaro.

1. Baker 7; DEU (Bibliography); Fetis 2/1; Grove 6/2 (Bibliography); Mendel; MGG/Supp. (Bibliography); Schmidl + Supp.

C0141.
Binns, Malcolm. English Pianist; b. January 29, 1936, Gedling,
Nottingham.

1. Baker 7; Grove 6/2; PAB-MI/2 (Bibliography).

C0142.
Birkenstock, Johann Adam. German Violinist; b. February 19, 1687,
Alsfeld; d. February 26, 1733, Eisenach.

1. Baker 7; DEU (under Birckenstock - Bibliography); Fetis 2/1; Grove
   6/2 (Bibliography); Mendel (under Birckenstock); MGG (under
   Birckenstock - Bibliography); Riemann 12 (under Birckenstock);
   Schmidl (under Birckenstock).

C0143.
Bishop-Kovacevich, Stephen. American Pianist; b. October 17, 1940, Los
Angeles, California.

1. Baker 7; Grove 6/2; Grove-AM; PAB-MI/2 (Bibliography).

2. HiFi/SR 28/2.

5. A0060.

C0144.
Bitetti [Ravina], Ernesto. Argentine Guitarist; b. July 20, 1943,
Rosario.

1. Baker 7; Grove 6/2; PAB-MI/2 (Bibliography).

C0145.
Blades, James. English Timpanist/Percussionist; b. September 9, 1901,
Peterborough.

1. Grove 6/2 (Bibliography); PAB-MI/2 (Bibliography).

3. Blades, James. Drum Roll. London: Faber and Faber Limited, 1977. xvi,
   275 p. + 8 plates, 34 illus., index.

   He also authored a history of percussion instruments as well as a
   pedagogical book on percussion technique.

C0146.
Blaes, Arnold Joseph. Belgian Clarinetist; b. December 1, 1814,
Brussels; d. January 11, 1892, Brussels.

1. Baker 7; Fetis 2/1; Grove 6/2; Mendel; Schmidl.

3. Blaes, Arnold. Souvenirs de ma vie artistique. Brussels, 1888. No
   copy located.

C0147.
Blagrove, Henry Gamble. English Violinist; b. October 20, 1811,
Nottingham; d. December 15, 1872, London.

1. Baker 7; Grove 6/2 (Bibliography); Schmidl.

C0148.
Blake, Eubie [James Hubert]. American Ragtime Pianist; b. February 7,
1883, Baltimore, Maryland; d. February 12, 1983, Brooklyn, New York.

1. Baker 7; Grove 6/2 (Bibliography); Grove-AM (Bibliography - 15
   entries); Grove-Jazz; JB (10 entries); IJ; PAB-MI/2 (Bibliography).

2. CK(KB) 3/8, 8/12.

3. The Eighty-Six Years of Eubie Blake. Recording made in 1969. Blake
   made his last public appearance at Lincoln Center on June 19, 1982!

4. Carter, Lawrence T. Eubie Blake: Keys of Memory. Detroit: Belcamp
   Publishing, 1979. 116. p.

   Kimball, Robert and William Bolcom. Reminiscing with Sissle & Blake.
   New York: The Viking Press, 1973. 254, [2] p., illus.

   Rose, Al. Eubie Blake. Foreword by Eubie Blake. New York: Schirmer
   Books, 1981. xvi, 214 p. + 10 plates, 36 illus., compositions, discography, piano rollography, filmography, index.

5. SEE: Southern, Eileen. The Music of Black Americans: a History. New
   York, 1971.

C0149.
Blakey, Art [Abdullah Ibn Buhaina]. American Jazz Drummer; b. October
11, 1919, Pittsburgh, Pennsylvania.

1. Baker 7; DEU (Bibliography); Grove 6/2 (Bibliography); Grove-AM
   (Bibliography - 15 entries); Grove-Jazz; JB; JRRM; IJ; PAB-MI/2
   (Bibliography); Riemann 12/Supp. (Bibliography).

2. DB 24/21, 28/10, 29/13, 38/6, 43/6, 46/17, 52/7.

5. A0032, B0048.

C0150.
Blanton, Jimmy [James]. American Jazz Double Bassist; b. October 1918,
Chattanooga, Tennessee.

1. Baker 7; Grove 6/2 (Bibliography); Grove-AM (Bibliography); Grove-
   Jazz; PAB-MI/2 (Bibliography); Riemann 12/Supp. (Bibliography).

C0151.
Blatt, František Tadeáš. Bohemian Clarinetist; b. 1793, Prague; d. March
9, 1856, Prague.

1. Baker 7; DEU (Bibliography); Fetis 2/1; Grove 6/2 (Bibliography);
   Mendel; MGG/Supp. (Bibliography); Riemann 12; Schmidl.

3. Blatt, František. Neue vollstaendige Clarinettenschule. Mainz: B.
   Schotts Soehne, 1828.

C0152.
Blumental, Felicja. Brazilian Pianist; b. December 28, 1918, Warsaw,
Poland.

1. Baker 7; Grove 6/2.

C0153.
Blumenthal, Jacob. German Pianist; b. October 4, 1829, Hamburg; d. May
17, 1908, London, England.

1. Baker 7; Fetis 2/1; Mendel; PAB-MI/2 (Bibliography); Riemann 12;
   Schmidl.

C0154.
Bochsa, Robert-Nicolas-Charles. French Harpist; b. August 9, 1789,
Montmedy, Meuse; d. January 6, 1856, Sydney, Australia.

1. Baker 7 (Bibliography); DEU (Bibliography); Fetis 2/1 + Supp.; Grove
   6/2 (Bibliography); Mendel; MGG/Supp.; PAB-MI/2 (Bibliography);
   Riemann 12; Schmidl.

There is a description of his method for harp in the MGG/Supp.

C0155.
Bodky, Erwin. American Pianist/Scholar; b. March 7, 1896, Ragnit, East
Prussia; d. December 6, 1958, Lucerne, Switzerland.

1. Baker 7; DEU (Bibliography); Grove 6/2 (Bibliography); Grove-AM; MGG
   + Supp.; Riemann 12 + Supp.

3. Bodky, Erwin. The Interpretation of J.S. Bach's Keyboard Works.
   Cambridge (MA): Harvard University Press, 1960. ix, 421 p. + 7
   plates, 2 appendices, selective bibliography, index.

4. Slosberg, Helen S., Mary V. Ullman and Isabel K. Whiting, eds.
   Erwin Bodky: a Memorial Tribute. Waltham (MA): Brandeis University,
   1965. 167, [1] p., 1 illus., discography.

C0156.
Boehm, Joseph. Hungarian Violinist; b. March 4, 1795, Budapest; d. March
28, 1876, Vienna, Austria.

1. Baker 7; DEU (Bibliography); Fetis 2/1 + Supp.; Mendel; Riemann 12;
   Schmidl.

C0157.
Boehm, Theobald. German Flutist/Inventor; b. April 9, 1794, Munich;
d. November 25, 1881, Munich.

1. Baker 7 (Bibliography); DEU (Bibliography); Fetis 2/1; Grove 6/2
   (Bibliography); Mendel; MGG (Bibliography); PAB-MI/2 (Bibliography); Riemann 12 (Bibliography) + Supp. (Bibliography); Schmidl.

3. Boehm, Theobald. Ueber der Floetenbau und die neusten Verbesserungen
   derselben. Mainz: B. Schotts Soehne, 1847. 57 p.

C0158.
Bolden, Buddy [Charles]. American Jazz Cornetist; b. c.1868, New
Orleans, Louisiana; d. November 4, 1931, Jackson, Louisiana.

1. Baker 7; DEU; Grove 6/2 (Bibliography); Grove-AM (Bibliography);
   Grove-Jazz; JB; JRRM; LJ; PAB-MI/2 (Bibliography); Riemann 12 +
   Supp. (Bibliography).

2. JJS 2/1.

4. Marquis, Donald M. In Search of Buddy Bolden, First Man of Jazz.
   Baton Rouge: Louisiana State University Press, 1978. xix, 176 p.
   + 12 plates, illus.

C0159.
Bolet, Jorge. American Pianist; b. November 15, 1914, Havana, Cuba.

1. Baker 7; Grove-AM (Bibliography); PAB-MI/2 (Bibliography); Riemann
   12/Supp.

2. CL 14/1, 22/8; HiFi/SR 29/1; MM 25/5, 25/9; PQ 133.

5. A0069, A0070, A0075.

C0160.
Bomtempo, João Domingos. Portuguese Pianist; b. December 28, 1775,
Lisbon; d. August 18, 1842, Lisbon.

1. Baker 7; DEU (Bibliography); Fetis 2/2 (under Bontempo); Grove 6/3
   (Bibliography); Mendel (under Bontempo); MGG/Supp. (Bibliography);
   Riemann 12 + Supp.; Schmidl.

C0161.
di Bonaventura, Anthony. American Pianist; b. November 12, 1930,
Follansbee, West Virginia.

1. Baker 7; Riemann 12/Supp.

C0162.
Bonnet, Joseph Elie. French Organist; b. March 17, 1884, Bordeaux;
d. August 2, 1944, Ste. Luce-sur-Mer, Quebec, Canada.

1. Baker 7; DEU (Bibliography); MGG/Supp. (Bibliography); PAB-MI/2
   (Bibliography); Riemann 12.

2. MQ July/1918.

5. SEE: Autobiography of Louis Vierne (C1155.3).

C0163.
Bordes-Pène, Léontine Marie. French Pianist; b. November 25, 1858,
Lorient; d. January 24, 1924, Rouen.

1. Baker 7 (Bibliography); Grove 6/3 (Bibliography)

C0164.
Borgatti, Renata. Italian Pianist; b. March 2, 1894, Bologna.

1. Baker 7; DEU.

C0165.
Borovsky, Alexander. American Pianist; b. March 18, 1889, Mitau, Russia; d. April 27, 1968, Waban, Massachusetts.

1. Baker 7; DEU (Under Borovskij); Riemann 12 (under Borowskij) + Supp.; Schmidl (under Borowski) + Supp.

C0166.
Borwick, Leonard. English Pianist; b. February 26, 1868, Walthamstow; d. September 15, 1925, Le Mans, France.

1. Baker 7; DEU; Grove 6/3; Riemann 12; Schmidl.

C0167.
Bos, Coenraad Valentyn. Dutch Pianist/Accompanist; b. December 7, 1875, Leiden; d. August 5, 1955, Chappaqua, New York.

1. Baker 7; Riemann 12; Schmidl.

3. Bos, Coenraad V. with Ashley Pettis. The Well-Tempered Accompanist. Foreword by Helen Traubel. Bryn Mawr (PA): Theodore Presser Co., 1949. x, 11-162 p., 17 illus., discography.

C0168.
Boskoff, George. Romanian Pianist; b. September 2, 1882, Jassy; d. August 27, 1960, Paris, France.

1. Baker 7; Grove 6/3 (Bibliography); Schmidl/Supp.

C0169.
Bosquet, Emile. Belgian Pianist; b. December 8, 1878, Brussels; d. July 18, 1958, Uccle, near Brussels.

1. Baker 7; Riemann 12 + Supp.; Schmidl/Supp.

C0170.
Bottesini, Giovanni. Italian Double Bassist; b. December 22, 1821, Crema; d. July 7, 1889, Parma.

1. Baker 7 (Bibliography); DEU (Bibliography); EdS (Bibliography); Fetis 2/2 + Supp.; Grove 6/3 (Bibliography); Mendel; MGG/Supp. (Bibliography); PAB-MI/2 (Bibliography); Riemann 12 (Bibliography) + Supp. (Bibliography); Schmidl.

As the first great virtuoso on his instrument, Bottesini demonstrated the potentials of the double bass. His pedagogical manual (Metodo completo per contrabasso. Milano: G. Ricordi e Cie, c.1866?) remains a classic.

2. Strad June/1968.

5. A0016, B0008.

SEE: Phipson, T.L. Voice and Violin: Sketches, Anecdotes, and Reminiscences. London: Chatto & Windus, 1898.

C0171.
Boucher, Alexandre-Jean. French Violinist; b. April 11, 1778, Paris; d. December 29, 1861, Paris.

1. Baker 7 (Bibliography); DEU (Bibliography); Fetis 2/2; Grove 6/3 (Bibliography); Mendel; MGG/Supp. (Bibliography); Riemann 12 (Bibliography).

3. Vallat, Gustave, ed. Etudes d'histoire, de moeurs et d'art musical sur la fin du XVIIIe siècle et la première moitié du XIXe siècle d'après des documents inédits: Alexandre Boucher et son temps. Paris: Maison Quantin, 1890. 248 p. + 3 plates, illus.

5. B0092.

C0172.
Braga, Gaetano. Italian Cellist; b. June 9, 1829, Giulianova, Abruzzi; d. November 21, 1907, Milan.

1. Baker 7 (Bibliography); DEU (Bibliography); Fetis 2/Supp.; Grove 6/3 (Bibliography); MGG/Supp. (Bibliography); Riemann 12 (Bibliography); Schmidl.

C0173.
Brailowsky, Alexander. Russian Pianist; b. February 16, 1896, Kiev; d. April 25, 1976, New York City.

1. Baker 7; DEU; Grove 6/3 (Bibliography); Grove-AM (Bibliography); MGG/Supp. (Bibliography); PAB-MI/2 (Bibliography); Riemann 12 + Supp.; Schmidl/Supp.

5. A0048.

C0174.
Brain, Aubrey Harold. English French-horn Player; b. July 12, 1893, London; d. September 20, 1955, London.

1. Baker 7; DEU; Grove 6/3; Riemann 12.

C0175.
Brain, Dennis. English French-horn Player, son of Aubrey; b. May 17, 1921, London; d. September 1, 1957, Hatfield, Hertfordshire.

1. Baker 7; DEU (Bibliography); Grove 6/3 (Bibliography); MGG/Supp. (Bibliography); PAB-MI/2 (Bibliography); Riemann 12 + Supp. (Bibliography).

One of the foremost virtuosos, his early death was a tragedy.

2. GR 46/July, 59/April, 61/July; HiFi/SR 15/4.

4. Pettitt, Stephen. <u>Dennis Brain: a Biography</u>. London: Robert Hale
   Limited, 1976. 192 p. + 4 plates, 14 illus., discography, index.

C0176.
Brandukov, Anatol. Russian Cellist; b. December 22, 1856, Moscow;
d. February 16, 1930, Moscow.

1. Baker 7 (Bibliography); DEU (Bibliography); Grove 6/3 (Bibliography);
   MGG/Supp. (Bibliography); Riemann 12 + Supp.; Schmidl.

C0177.
Brassin, Louis. French Pianist; b. June 24, 1840, Aix-la-Chapelle;
d. May 17, 1884, St. Petersburg, Russia.

1. Baker 7; Fetis 2/Supp.; Grove 6/3; Mendel; Schmidl.

C0178.
Bream, Julian. English Guitarist/Lutenist; b. July 15, 1933, London.

1. Baker 7; Grove 6/3 (Bibliography); PAB-MI/2 (Bibliography); Riemann
   12/Supp.

Responsible for the revival of interest in Elizabethan lute music.

2. GR 46/July, 59/April, 61/July; HiFi/SR 15/4.

4. Palmer, Tony. <u>Julian Bream: a Life on the Road</u>. Photographs by
   Daniel Meadows. New York: Franklin Watts, Inc., 1982. 216 p., illus.,
   discography.

5. A0129.

C0179.
Brendel, Alfred. Austrian Pianist; b. January 5, 1931, Wiesenberg,
Moravia.

1. Baker 7; DEU (Bibliography); Grove 6/3 (Bibliography); PAB-MI/2
   (Bibliography).

2. CL 12/9, 18/2; GR 46/February, 60/September, 61/April, 63/March;
   HiFi/MusAm 34/5; CK(KB) 9/5; MM 21/4, 25/4; PQ 106.

3. Brendel, Alfred. <u>Musical Thoughts and Afterthoughts</u>. Princeton:
   Princeton University Press, 1976. 168 p., 56-item bibliography,
   index.

5. A0060, A0069.

C0180.
Breval, Jean-Baptiste Sébastien. French Cellist; b. November 6, 1753,
Paris; d. March 18, 1823, Colligis, Aisne.

1. Baker 7; DEU; Fetis 2/2; Grove 6/3 (Bibliography); Mendel; MGG/Supp.
   (Bibliography); Riemann 12 (Bibliography) + Supp.; Schmidl.

3. Breval, Jean-Baptiste. Traité du violoncelle. Paris, 1804 [translated as New Introduction for the Violoncello, Being a Complete Key of the Knowledge of That Instrument. London, 1810].

Breval claimed that this was the first cello manual designed to instruct the player from elementary to virtuoso status.

C0181.
Brevig, Per. Norwegian Trombonist; b. September 7, 1936. Berg, near Halden.

1. Baker 7.

Included due to his intense involvement in contemporary music in support of which he has published Avant-Garde Techniques in Solo Trombone Music and Problems of Notations and Executions.

C0182.
Briccialdi, Giulio. Italian Flutist; b. March 2, 1818, Terni, Papal States; d. December 17, 1881, Florence.

1. Baker 7; DEU (Bibliography); Fetis 2/2 + Supp.; Grove 6/3 (Bibliography); Mendel; MGG/Supp. (Bibliography); Riemann 12; Schmidl.

C0183.
Bridgetower, George Auguste Polgreen. English Violinist; b. October 11, 1778, Biala, Poland; d. February 28, 1860, Peckham, Surrey.

1. Baker 7 (Bibliography); DEU (Bibliography); Grove 6/3 (Bibliography); MGG/Supp. (Bibliography); Riemann 12 (Bibliography) + Supp. (Bibliography); Schmidl.

C0184.
Brodsky, Adolf. Russian Violinist; b. April 2, 1851, Taganrog; d. January 22, 1929, Manchester, England.

1. Baker 7; DEU (Bibliography); Grove 6/3; MGG/Supp. (Bibliography); Riemann 12 (Bibliography) + Supp. (Bibliography); Schmidl.

4. Brodsky [Skadovsky], Anna. Recollections of a Russian Home (a Musician's Experiences). Manchester: Sherratt & Hughes, 1904. [ii], 202 p. The 2nd edition (London, 1914) is expanded to 238 p. + 3 plates, illus.

C0185.
Brosa, Antonio. Spanish Violinist; b. June 27, 1894, Canonja, Tarragona; d. March 26, 1979, Barcelona.

1. Baker 7; Grove 6/3 (Bibliography); PAB-MI/2 (Bibliography).

2. Strad July/1979.

C0186.
Brown, Brownie [Clifford]. American Jazz Trumpeter; b. October 30, 1930, Wilmington, Delaware; d. June 26, 1956, Pennsylvania (car accident).

1. Baker 7; DEU; Grove 6/3 (Bibliography); Grove-AM (Bibliography - 10 entries); Grove-Jazz; JB; JRRM; LJ; PAB-MI/2 (Bibliography); Riemann 12/Supp. (Bibliography).

2. DB 23/17, 28/21, 47/7.

4. Montalbano, Pierre. Clifford Brown: Biography and Discography. Marseille: Jazz Club Aix-Marseille, 1969. 12 p.

   Stewart, Milton Lee. Structural Development in the Jazz Improvisational Technique of Clifford Brown. Ph.D. diss. University of Michigan, 1973. 225 p., bibliography.

CO187.
Brown, Eddy. American Violinist; b. July 15, 1895, Chicago, Illinois; d. June 14, 1974, Albano Terme, Italy.

1. Baker 7; PAB-MI/2 (Bibliography); Riemann 12.

CO188.
Browning, John. American Pianist; b. May 22, 1933, Denver, Colorado.

1. Baker 7; Grove 6/3; Grove-AM (Bibliography); PAB-MI/2 (Bibliography); Riemann 12/Supp.

2. CL 20/1, 26/7; MM 18/8; PQ 91.

5. AO069, AO070, AO075.

CO189.
Brubeck, Dave [David Warren]. American Jazz Pianist; b. December 6, 1920, Concord, California.

1. Baker 7; DEU (Bibliography); EdS/Supp. (Bibliography); Grove 6/3; Grove-AM (Bibliography); Grove-Jazz; JB (17 entries); JRRM; PAB-MI/2 (Bibliography); Riemann 12/Supp. (Bibliography).

2. CL 26/2; DB 17/1-2, 22/16, 24/13, 24/15, 24/16, 24/18, 28/13, 28/15, 39/10, 43/6; HiFi/MusAm 19/1; CK(KB) 3/12; Time November 10, 1952.

4. Anon. Dave Brubeck. New York: Broadcast Music, Inc., 1961. 20 p.

CO190.
de la Bruchollerie, Monique. French Pianist; b. April 20, 1915, Paris; d. December 15, 1972, Paris.

1. Baker 7; Riemann 12/Supp (under la Bruchollerie).

2. Time April 30, 1965.

CO191.
Brueggen, Frans. Dutch Recorder Player; b. October 30, 1934, Amsterdam.

1. Baker 7; DEU (Bibliography); Grove 6/3 (Bibliography); PAB-MI/2 (Bibliography); Riemann 12/Supp. (Bibliography).

2. HiFi/MusAm 34/11.

5. BO014.

C0192.
Brymer, Jack. English Clarinetist; b. January 27, 1915, South Shields.

1. Baker 7; Grove 6/3; PAB−MI/2 (Bibliography).

3. Brymer, Jack. From Where I Sit. London: Cassell & Company Limited, 1979. vii, 183 p. + 4 plates, illus.

C0193.
von Buelow, Hans [Guido]. German Pianist; b. January 8, 1830, Dresden; d. February 12, 1894, Cairo, Egypt.

1. Baker 7 (Bibliography); DEU (Bibliography); EdS (Bibliography); Fetis 2/2; Grove 6/3 (Bibliography); Mendel; MGG (Bibliography); PAB−MI/2 (under Bulow − Bibliography); Riemann 12 (Bibliography).

A rare exception to our list as von Buelow was primarily known as a fine conductor. Among other triumphs, however, he premiered Tchai-kovsky's first piano concerto on October 25, 1875.

2. PQ 125.

3. von Buelow, Marie, ed. Hans von Buelows Briefe und Schriften. 8 vols. Leipzig: Druck und Verlag Breitkopf und Haertel, 1895−1908.

4. von Buelow, Marie. Hans von Buelows Leben dargestellt aus seinen Briefen. Leipzig: Druck und Verlag von Breitkopf und Haertel, 1919. xxi, 600 p., index.

von Buelow, Marie. Hans von Buelow in Leben und Wort. Stuttgart: J. Engelhorns Nachf., 1925. 298 p., 8 illus., 11−item bibliography, index.

Da Motta, Vianna J. Nachtrag zu Studien bei Hans von Buelow von Theodor Pfeiffer. Berlin: Verlag von Friedrich Luckhardt, 1896. viii, 84 p., index of names.

Pfeiffer, Theodor. Studien bei Hans von Buelow. 2nd edition. Berlin: Verlag von Friedrich Luckhardt, 1894. vii, 123 p., portrait.

Pfeiffer (b. October 20, 1853, Heidelberg; d. November 9, 1929, Baden−Baden) penned his recollections as a piano student.

Vogel, Bernhard. Hans von Buelow: sein Leben und sein Entwicklungs-gang. Leipzig: Max Hesses Verlag, 1887. vi, 69 p., portrait, index.

5. A0035, B0020, B0035.

SEE: Cowden, Robert H. Concert and Opera Conductors: a Bibliography of Biographical Materials. Westport (CT): Greenwood Press, 1987. NOTE: Entries under Hans von Buelow (C0157).

C0194.
Buhlig, Richard. American Pianist; b. December 21, 1880, Chicago,
Illinois; d. January 30, 1952, Los Angeles, California.

1. Baker 7; Grove-AM; PAB-MI/2 (Bibliography).

C0195.
Bull, John. English Keyboard Virtuoso; b. c.1562, Old Radnor,
Radnorshire; d. March 12, 1628, Antwerp, Belgium.

1. Baker 7 (Bibliography); DEU (Bibliography); Fetis 2/2; Grove 6/3
   (Bibliography); Mendel; MGG (Bibliography); PAB-MI/2 (Bibliography);
   Riemann 12 (Bibliography) + Supp. (Bibliography); Schmidl.

One of the early geniuses of contrapuntal keyboard music.

C0196.
Bull, Ole [Bornemann]. Norwegian Violinist; b. February 5, 1810, Bergen;
d. August 17, 1880, Lyso, near Bergen.

1. Baker 7 (Bibliography); DEU (Bibliography); EdS (Bibliography); Fetis
   2/2; Grove 6/3 (Bibliography); Mendel; MGG; PAB-MI/2 (Bibliography);
   Riemann 12 (Bibliography) + Supp. (Bibliography); Schmidl.

4. Aarvig, Christian Andreas. Den unge Ole Bull: en violinspillers
   ungdomskampe. København: Wilhelm Hansen Musikforlag, 1934. 114,
   [5] p., portrait.

   Bjørndal, Arne. Ole Bull, og norsk folkemusikk. Bergen: A.S. Lunde
   & Co. Forlag, 1940. 94 p., illus.

   Bjørndal, Arne. Ole Bull og Valestrand. Stord: S. Botnens Bok-
   trykkeri, 1950. 46 p., 12 illus.

   Bull, Inez. Ole Bull Returns to Pennsylvania: the Biography of a
   Norwegian Violin Virtuoso and Pioneer in the Keystone State. New
   York: Exposition Press, 1961. 124, [1] p., 17 illus.

   Bull, Inez. Ole Bull's Activities in the United States between 1843
   and 1880: a Great Norwegian Violinist's Triumphs in America. Smithtown (NY): Exposition Press, n.d. xxv, 115 p., 12 illus., 149-item
   bibliography.

   Bull, Sara Chapman. Ole Bull, a Memoir: with Ole Bull's Violin Notes
   and A.B. Crosby's Anatomy of the Violinist. Boston: Houghton Mifflin
   and Company, 1883. Reprint 1978. v, 417 p., illus., appendix, index.

   Danell, Eric. Ole Bull och Pratté: nagra kritiska randanmaerkningar.
   Stockholm: Seelig & Co., 1954. 50 p., 4 illus.

   Headland, Helen. Ole Bull: Norwegian Minstrel. Rock Island: Augustana
   Book Concern, 1949. 142, [12] p., illus.

   Lange, Ola. Ole Bull: livshistoria, mannen, kunstnaren. Oslo: Eige
   Forlag - Edition "Gamma", 1953. 414, [1] p., illus.

Lie, Jonas. Ole Bulls breve i uddrag udgivne af hans søn Alexander Bull: med en karakteristik og biografisk skitse af Jonas Lie. Kjøbenhavn: Glydendalske Boghandels Forlag, 1881. 410 p.

Ottmann, L. Ole Bull, der Geigerkoenig: ein Kuenstlerleben. Stuttgart: Verlag von Robert Luss, 1886. 233, [1] p., portrait.

Based upon the book by Bull's second wife, Sarah Chapman Bull.

Smith, Mortimer Brewster. The Life of Ole Bull. Princeton: Princeton University Press [for the American-Scandinavian Foundation, New York] 1943. Reprint 1973. ix, [iv], 220 p., 11 illus., index.

5. A0014, A0023, A0093, B0035, B0050, B0070, B0102.

C0197.
Bunk, Gerard. German Pianist/Organist; b. March 4, 1888, Rotterdam, Holland; d. September 13, 1958, Kamen, near Dortmund.

1. Riemann 12 + Supp.; Schmidl/Supp.

3. Bunk, Gerard. Liebe zur Orgel: Erinnerungen aus einem Musikerleben. 2. Aufl. Dortmund: Ardey Verlag, 1958. 185, [1] p., 3 illus.

C0198.
Buonamici, Giuseppe. Italian Pianist; b. February 12, 1846, Florence; d. March 17, 1914, Florence.

1. Baker 7; DEU (Bibliography); Grove 6/3 (Bibliography); Riemann 12; Schmidl.

C0199.
Burge, David Russell. American Pianist; b. March 25, 1930, Evanston, Illinois.

1. Grove 6/3; Grove-AM; PAB-MI/2 (Bibliography).

2. CL 2/2, 26/2, 26/7.

C0200.
Burgin, Richard. American Violinist; b. October 11, 1892, Warsaw, Poland; d. April 29, 1981, Gulfport, Florida.

1. Baker 7; Grove-AM.

C0201.
Burmester, Willy. German Violinist; b. March 16, 1869, Hamburg; d. January 16, 1933, Hamburg.

1. Baker 7; MGG/Supp. (Bibliography); Riemann 12 (Bibliography); Schmidl.

3. Burmester, Willy. Fuenfzig Jahre Kuenstlerleben. Berlin: A. Scherl g.m.b.h., 1926. 213, [2] p. + 10 plates + 4 foldouts, 23 illus.

Translated by Roberta Franke and Samuel Wolf as Fifty Years as a Concert Violinist [Linthicum Heights (MD): Swand Publications, 1975].

5. BO053.

C0202.
Busch, Adolf. German Violinist; b. August 8, 1891, Siegen, Westphalia; d. June 9, 1952, Guilford, Vermont.

1. Baker 7; DEU (Bibliography); Grove 6/3 (Bibliography); Grove-AM (Bibliography); PAB-MI/2 (Bibliography); Riemann 12 + Supp. (Bibliography); Schmidl + Supp.

One of the distinguished musical families of the twentieth-century.

2. RS 86.

4. Im Memoriam Adolf Busch. Dahlbruch: Brueder-Busch-Gesellschaft e.V., 1969 [original 1966]. 64 p., illus., discography.

5. BO045, DO012.

C0203.
Busch, Hermann. German Cellist, brother of Adolf; b. June 24, 1897, Siegen, Westphalia; d. June 3, 1975, Bryn Mawr, Pennslyvania.

1. Baker 7; DEU; PAB-MI/2 (Bibliography); Riemann 12 + Supp.

2. RS 86.

C0204.
Busoni, Ferruccio [Dante Michelangelo Benvenuto]. Italian Pianist; b. April 1, 1866, Empoli, near Florence; d. July 27, 1924, Berlin, Germany.

1. Baker 7 (bibliography); DEU (Bibliography); EdS (Bibliography); Grove 6/3 (Bibliography); MGG (Bibliography); PAB-MI/2 (Bibliography); Riemann 12 (Bibliography) + Supp. (Bibliography); Schmidl + Supp. (Bibliography).

2. Musical Observer (June 1925), PQ 108; RS 58.

3. Busoni, Ferruccio. Letters to His Wife. Translated by Rosamond Ley. London: Edward Arnold & Co., 1938. 319 p., 8 illus., index.

Busoni, Ferruccio. The Essence of Music and Other Papers. Translated by Rosamond Ley. London: Rockliff Publishing Corporation, 1957 [original Munich, 1922]. vii, 204 p., index.

4. Bibliothek Ferruccio Busoni. Berlin: Max Perl Antiquariat Auktion 96 (30. und 31. Maerz 1925). 111 p. [1421 entries].

Dent, Edward J. Ferruccio Busoni: a Biography. London: Oxford University Press, 1933. xv, 367, [1] p. + 23 plates, 42 illus., 5 appendices including repertoire and list of compositions, index.

Stuckenschmidt, H.H. Ferruccio Busoni: Zeittafel eines Europäers. Zuerich: Atlantis Verlag AG, 1967. 179, [1] p., 10 illus., index.

5. A0035, A0047, A0051, A0053, B0020, B0028, B0037, B0053, B0056, B0083, B0089, C0433.4.

SEE: Autobiography of Alfred Brendel (C0179.3).

C0205.
Bustabo, Guila. American Violinist; b. February 25, 1919, Manitowee, WI.

1. Baker 7; Riemann + Supp.

C0206.
Buswell, James Oliver IV. American Violinist; b. December 4, 1946, Fort Wayne, Indiana.

1. Baker 7; Grove 6/3; Grove-AM; PAB-MI/2 (Bibliography).

C0207.
Callaway, Paul [Smith]. American Organist; b. August 16, 1909, Atlanta, Georgia.

1. Baker 7; Grove 6/3; Grove-AM; PAB-MI/2 (Bibliography).

C0208.
Callender, Red [George]. American Jazz Double Bassist; b. March 6, 1918, Richmond, Virginia.

1. Grove-Jazz; PAB-MI/2 (Bibliography).

3. Callender, Red and Elaine Cohen. Unfinished Dream: the Musical World of Red Callender. London: Quartet Books Limited, 1985. xv, 239 p. + 8 plates, illus., select discography, index.

C0209.
Camden, Archie. English Bassoonist; b. March 9, 1888, Newark-upon-Trent; d. February 16, 1979, Wheathampstead.

1. Baker 7; Grove 6/3.

3. Camden, Archie. Blow by Blow -- the Memories of a Musical Rogue and Vagabond. London: Foreword by Yehudi Menuhin. Thames Publishing. 208 p., 27 illus., discography.

C0210.
Camidge, Matthew. English Organist; b. May 25, 1764, York; d. October 23, 1844, York.

1. Baker 7; DEU; Fetis 2/2; Grove 6/3; Mendel; MGG/Supp. (Bibliography); PAB-MI/2 (Bibliography); Riemann 12; Schmidl.

C0211.
Campagnoli, Bartolommeo. Italian Violinist; b. September 10, 1751, Cento di Ferrara; d. November 6, 1827, Neustrelitz, Germany.

1. Baker 7; DEU (Bibliography); Fetis 2/2; Grove 6/3 (Bibliography); MGG (Bibliography); Riemann 12 + Supp. (Bibliography); Schmidl + Supp.

4. Atti, Gaetano. Biografia di Bartolommeo Campagnoli da Cento, celebre violinista. Bologna: Tipografia Antonio Chierici, 1852.

No copy located.

C0212.
Campanella, Michele. Italian Pianist; b. June 5, 1947, Naples.

1. Baker 7; DEU (Bibliography); Grove 6/3; PAB-MI/2 (Bibliography).

C0213.
Campoli, Alfredo. English Violinist; b. September 30, 1923, Tortona, Italy.

1. Baker 7; DEU; Grove 6/3; PAB-MI/2 (Bibliography); Riemann 12.

2. Strad Dec/1975, March/1979, Oct/1981.

5. A0008.

C0214.
Capet, Lucien. French Violinist; b. January 8, 1873, Paris; d. December 18, 1928, Paris.

1. Baker 7; DEU (Bibliography); Grove 6/3 (Bibliography); MGG/Supp. (Bibliography); Riemann 12; Schmidl + Supp.

4. Anon. Lucien Capet (Notice Biographique). Paris: A. Dandelot, 1903. 47, [1] p., portrait.

5. B0028, B0037.

   SEE: Anon. La technique supérieure de l'archet. Paris: Editions Maurice Senart, 1916.

   Includes a biography of Capet by H. Expert who edited a number of Senart's publications.

C0215.
Capocci, Filippo. Italian Organist; b. May 11, 1840, Rome; d. July 25, 1911, Rome.

1. DEU (Bibliography); Grove 6/3 (Bibliography); MGG/Supp. (Bibliography); Riemann 12 (Bibliography); Schmidl.

4. de Santi, P. Angelo. Il Mo. Filippo Capocci e le sue composizioni per organo. Roma: Tipografia A. Befani, 1888. 33 p.

C0216.
Carle, Frankie [Francis Nunzio Carlone]. American Jazz Pianist; b. March 25, 1903, Providence, Rhode Island.

1. Grove-AM; PAB-MI/2 (Bibliography).

4. Catrambone, Gene. The Golden Touch: Frankie Carle. Roslyn Heights (NY): Libra Publishers, Inc., 1981. xviii, 262 p., 50 illus., compositions, discography, index of names.

C0217.
Carmirelli, Pina. Italian Violinist; b. January 23, 1914, Varzi.

1. Baker 7; DEU; Grove 6/3; PAB-MI/2 (Bibliography); Riemann 12/Supp.

C0218.
Carney, Harry. American Jazz Baritone Saxophonist; b. April 1, 1910, Boston, Massachusetts; d. October 8, 1974, New York City.

1. Baker 7; DEU; Grove 6/3 (Bibliography); Grove-AM (Bibliography); Grove-Jazz; PAB-MI/2 (Bibliography).

2. DB 25/24, 34/22.

5. A0159.

C0219.
Carreño, (Maria) Teresa. Venezuelan Pianist; b. December 22, 1853, Caracas; d. June 12, 1917, New York City.

1. Baker 7 (Bibliography); DEU: Fetis 2/Supp.; Grove 6/3 (Bibliography); MGG; PAB-MI/2 (Bibliography); Riemann 12 + Supp. (Bibliography); Schmidl.

4. Calcaño, José Antonio. Palabras pronuncidas...en el cementerio general del sur al ser repatriadas las cenizas de Teresa Carreño, el 15 de febrero de 1938. MS, 1938. 7 p.

Marciano, Rosario. Teresa Carreño, o un ensayo sobre su personalidad a los 50 años de su muerte. Caracas: Instituto Nacional de Cultura y Bellas Artes, 1966. 28 p., illus.

Mathews, W.S.B. Teresa Carreño: Biographical and Critical. Chicago: Curtis & Mayer, c.1885. Library of Congress: ML 417; C4M4.

Milinowski, Marta. Teresa Carreño, "by the grace of God". New Haven: Yale University Press, 1940. Reprint 1977. xvii, 410 p., 29 illus., chronology, 98-item bibliography, index.

Peña, Israel. Teresa Carreño (1853-1917). Caracas: Ediciones de la "Fundación Eugenio Mendoza," 1953. 64 p., illus.

Plaza, Juan Bautista. Teresa Carreño. Caracas: Tipografia Americana, 1938. 33 p., portrait.

Travieso, Carmen Clemente. Teresa Carreño (1853-1917): ensayo biográfico. Caracas: Editorial "Ancora," 1953. 80 p., 4-item bibliography.

5. AO051, BO053.

C0220.
Carrodus [né Carruthers], John Tiplady. English Violinist; b. January
20, 1836, Keighley, Yorkshire; d. July 12, 1895, London.

1. Baker 7; Grove 6/3; Schmidl.

4. Carrodus, Ada. J.T. Carrodus, Violinist: a Life Story 1838-1895.
London: A.J. Bowden, 1897. [iii], 117, iii p., portrait, index.

C0221.
Carter, Benny [Bennett Lester]. American Jazz Alto Saxophonist;
b. August 8, 1907, New York City.

1. Baker 7; DEU (Bibliography); Grove 6/3 (Bibliography); Grove-AM (Bibliography - 10 entries); Grove-Jazz; JB; JRRM; LJ; MGG/Supp.;
PAB-MI/2 (Bibliography); Riemann 12 + Supp.

2. DB 18/10, 25/9, 28/11, 32/21, 44/4; JJS 4/1, 5/1.

4. Berger, Morroe, Edward Berger and James Patrick. Benny Carter: a Life
in American Music. 2 vols. Metuchen (NJ): The Scarecrow Press, 1982.
xiii, 422 p. + 8 plates. illus., chapter notes, index; 417 p.,
chronology, discography, filmography, 358-item bibliography, addenda.

5. AO159.

C0222.
Cartier, Jean-Baptiste. French Violinist; b. May 28, 1765, Avignon;
d. 1841, Paris.

1. Baker 7; DEU (Bibliography); Fetis 2/2; Grove 6/3 (Bibliography);
MGG/Supp. (Bibliography); Riemann 12; Schmidl.

Cartier compiled an early anthology of excerpts from well-known 17th
and 18th century violin literature (Paris: Decombe et Cie, 1798).
GROVE 6 also mentions that "Cartier was also the author of an Essai
historique on the violin which has remained unpublished..." The
actual title of the MS is Dissertation sur le violin, tirée de
l'Essai historique sur cet instrument.

C0223.
Carulli, Ferdinando. Italian Guitarist; b. February 20, 1770, Naples;
d. February 17, 1841, Paris, France.

1. Baker 7; DEU (Bibliography); Fetis 2/2; Grove 6/3 (Bibliography);
Mendel; MGG/Supp.; Riemann 12; Schmidl + Supp.

5. AO129.

C0224.
Casadesus, Jean. French Pianist, son of Robert; b. July 7, 1927, Paris;
d. January 20, 1972, near Renfrew, Ontario, Canada.

1. Baker 7; DEU; Grove 6/3; MGG; PAB-MI/2 (Bibliography); Riemann 12/ Supp.

C0225.
Casadesus, Marius. French Violinist, uncle of Robert; b. October 24, 1892, Paris; d. October 13, 1981, Suresnes (Paris).

1. Baker 7; DEU; Grove 6/3; MGG; PAB-MI/2 (Bibliography); Riemann 12 + Supp. (Bibliography).

C0226.
Casadesus, Robert. French Pianist, father of Jean; b. April 7, 1899, Paris; d. September 19, 1972, Paris.

1. Baker 7; DEU; Grove 6/3; MGG; PAB-MI/2 (Bibliography); Riemann 12 + Supp.; Schmidl/Supp.

His wife Gaby [née L'Hôté] (b. August 1901, Marseilles) was also a talented painist. SEE: Grove 6/3; CL 14/7, 23/9; PQ 80.

2. CL 10/3, 18/2; PQ 119 (Special Issue).

5. A0060, B0044, B0130.

C0227.
Casals, Pablo [Pau Carlos Salvador Defilló]. Spanish Cellist; b. December 29, 1876, Vendrell; d. October 22, 1973, San Juan, Puerto Rico.

1. Baker 7 (Bibliography); DEU (Bibliography); Grove 6/3 (Bibliography); Grove-AM (Bibliography); MGG (Bibliography); PAB-MI/2 (Bibliography); Riemann 12 (Bibliography) + Supp. (Bibliography); Schmidl.

A legend during his own lifetime, Casals fused an almost religious dedication to music with great humanitarian vision.

2. HiFi/MusAm 24/7; HiFiRev 2/5; HiFi/SR 18/4; ML 2/4; Strad Jan/1967, Nov/1975, April/1980; MQ 72, 73, 75.

3. Casals, Pablo. Joys and Sorrows: Reflections. As Told to Albert E. Kahn. New York: Simon and Schuster, 1970. 314 p., 32 illus., index.

4. Alavedra, Joan. L'extraordinaria vida de Pau Casals. Barcelona: Edicions Proa, 1969. 107 p., illus.

Alavedra, Joan. Pau Casals. Próleg de Pau Casals. Barcelona: Editorial Aedos, 1962. 416, [1] p., illus., index of names, chronology.

Alavedra, Joan. Qui era Pau Casals? Barcelona: Ajuntament de Barcelona, 1977. 55, [2] p., 16 illus.

Albet, Montserrat. Pau Casals, una vida musical. Barcelona: Fundació Pau Casals, n.d. 69, [2] p., 24 illus.

A descriptive catalogue of the museum dedicated to his career.

Blum, David. Casals and the Art of Interpretation. New York: Holmes & Meier Publishers, Inc., 1977. xvi, 223 p. + 2 plates, 5 illus., 50-item bibliography, index to musical works, general index.

Casals, Enric. Pau Casals: dades biogràfiques inèdites cartes íntimes i records viscuts. Barcelona: Editorial Pòrtic, 1979. 347 p., illus., list of 23 biographies, index.

Christen, Ernest. Pablo Casals: l'homme, l'artiste. Genève: Labor et Fides, 1956. 174, [3] p. + 2 plates, 2 illus., 6-item bibliography.

Conte, Arthur. La légende de Pablo Casals. Perpignan: Editions Proa, 1950. 139, [2] p. + 6 plates, 6 illus.

Corredor, José María. Casals: biografiá ilustrada. Barcelona: Ediciones Destino, 1967. 149 p., illus., chronology, index of names.

Corredor, José María. Conversations avec Pablo Casals: souvenirs et opinions d'un musicien. Paris: A. Michel, 1955 [English translation by André Mangeot as Conversations with Casals. New York: E.P. Dutton & Co., Inc., 1957]. 343 p., illus.

The English edition is shorter and includes an index.

Corredor, José María. Pablo Casals cuenta su vida: conversaciones con el maestro. Carta-prefacio de Pablo Casals. Barcelona: Editorial Juventud, 1975. 319 p. + 8 plates, illus., bibliography.

Dalmau, Josefina. Pau Casals, l'home del violoncel. Barcelona: Editorial Blume, 1981. 93 p., chronology, 9-item bibliography.

Forsee, Aylesa. Pablo Casals: Cellist for Freedom. New York: Thomas Y. Crowell Company, 1965. 229 p. + 4 plates, 11 illus., 9-item reading list, index.

Garcia Borrás, José. Pablo Casals: peregrino en América: tres semanas con el maestro. Mexico, D.F.: Talleres Gráficos Victoria, 1957. Reprint 1967. 349, [2] p., illus.

Gavoty, Bernard. Pablo Casals. Genève: René Kister, 1955. 30, [2] p., 38 illus., list of recordings.

Ginsburg, Lev Solomonovich. Pablo Kazal's. Moscow: Muzyka, 1966. 244 p., illus., discography, bibliographical footnotes.

Kirk, H.L. Pablo Casals: a Biography. New York: Holt, Rinehart and Winston, 1974. xi, 692 p., illus., compositions, discography, notes, 191-item bibliography, index.

Littlehales, Lillian. Pablo Casals. New York: W.W. Norton & Co., Inc., 1929. 2nd revised and enlarged edition, 1948. Reprint 1970. 216, [1] p., 8 illus.

Liongueras, Joan. Pau Casals: eis homes i les obres. Barcelona: Edicions de "La Nova revista," 1927. 63 p. + 4 plates, 10 illus.

Lloyd Webber, Julian, comp./ed. Song of the Birds: Sayings, Stories and Impressions of Pablo Casals. London: Robson Books Ltd, 1985. 120 p. + 3 plates, 7 illus.

Mauron, Marie. La cloche aux étoiles de Pablo Casals. Avignon: Palais du Roure, 1956. 19, [1] p., illus.

Mueller-Blattau, Joseph Maria. Casals. Berlin: Rembrandt Verlag, 1964. 64 p., 33 illus., discography, 7-item bibliography.

Seehaus, Lothar. Pablo Casals. Hamburg: Cecilie Dressler Verlag, 1980. 155, [2] p., 106 illus., selected discography.

Seiler, Alexander J. P. Casals. Olten: Walter Verlag, 1956. 113 p., illus., chronology, discography.

Sopeña Ibáñez, Federíco. Pablo Casals: homenaje en el centenario de su nacimiento. Madrid: Comision Nacional Española, 1977. 64 p., illus.

Strongin, Theodore. Casals. New York: Grossman Publishers, Inc., 1966. unpaginated [93 p.], illus.

Taper, Bernard. Cellist in Exile: a Portrait of Pablo Casals. New York: McGraw-Hill Book Company, Inc., 1962. 120, [1] p., 36 illus.

von Tobel, Rudolf. Pablo Casals. Erlenbach-Zuerich: Rotapfel-Verlag, A.G., 1941. 128 p. + 10 plates, 41 illus., 8-item bibliography.

Vives de Fabregas, Elisa. Pau Casals. Barcelona: Rafael Dalmau, Editor, 1966. 453, [15] p. + 58 plates, 97 illus., index of names.

5. A0008, A0033, B0030, B0037, B0039, B0041, B0042, B0044, B0053, B0089.

   SEE: Autobiography of Gerald Moore (C0822.3).

   SEE: Ribas, Antoni. Catalans Universals. Barcelona: Editorial HMB, S.A., 1980. 154 p., illus.

C0228.
Cassadó, Gaspar. Spanish Cellist; b. September 30, 1897, Barcelona; d. December 24, 1966, Madrid.

1. Baker 7; DEU (Bibliography); Grove 6/3; MGG/Supp. (Bibliography); Riemann 12 + Supp. (Bibliography); Schmidl/Supp.

4. Anon. Gaspar Cassadó 1897-1966: Homenaje de "Música En Compostela". Madrid: Artes Gráficas Arges, 1968. 34 p., publications.

C0229.
Castleman, Charles. American Violinist; b. May 22, 1941, Quincy, MA.

1. Baker 7; Grove 6/3; Grove-AM; PAB-MI/2 (Bibliography).

2. HiFi/MusAm 31/12.

CO230.
Catlett, Big Sid[ney]. American Jazz Drummer; b. January 17, 1910, Evansville, Indiana; d. March 25, 1951, Chicago, Illinois.

1. Baker 7; DEU; Grove 6/4; Grove-AM (Bibliography); Grove-Jazz; PAB-MI/2 (Bibliography).

2. DB 33/6, 33/23.

5. A0004.

CO231.
Cesi, Beniamino. Italian Pianist; b. November 6, 1845, Naples; d. January 19, 1907, Naples.

1. Baker 7 (Bibliography); DEU (Bibliography); Riemann 12 (Bibliography); Schmidl.

   DEU Mentions an unpublished MS, Storia ed origine del pianoforte.

CO232.
Chapuis, Michel. French Organist; b. January 15, 1930, Dole, Jura.

1. DEU, Grove 6/4; MGG/Supp.; PAB-MI/2 (Bibliography).

4. Duchesneau, Claude. Claude Duchesneau interroge Michel Chapuis. Vendome: Editions du Centurion, 1979. 220 [3] p., discography.

CO233.
Chasins, Abram. American Pianist; b. August 17, 1903, New York City; d. June 21, 1987, New York City.

1. Baker 7 (Bibliography); Grove 6/4; Grove-AM; PAB-MI/2 (Bibliography); Riemann 12.

2. PQ 85.

3. SEE: A0310 and his biography of Van Cliburn (CO250.4).

CO234.
Cherkassky, Shura. American Pianist; b. October 7, 1911, Odessa, Russia.

1. Baker 7; DEU; Grove 6/4; Grove-AM; MGG/Supp. (Bibliography); PAB-MI/2 (Bibliography); Riemann 12 + Supp.

2. MM 17/8; New York Times April 2, 1978.

5. B0130.

CO235.
Cherry, Don[ald Eugene]. American Jazz Trumpeter; b. November 18, 1936, Oklahoma City, Oklahoma.

1. Baker 7; DEU (Bibliography); Grove 6/4 (Bibliography); Grove-AM (Bibliography); Grove-Jazz; JB; LJ; PAB-MI/2 (Bibliog.); Riemann 12/Supp.

2. DB 33/15, 42/16, 42/21, 45/13, 50/6, 55/13.

C0236.
Chopin, [François] Frédéric. Polish Pianist; b. March 1?, 1810, Zelazowa Wola, near Warsaw; d. October 17, 1849, Paris, France.

1. Baker 7 (Bibliography); DEU (Bibliography); Grove 6/4 (Bibliography - 6 entries on Chopin as a pianist and teacher); Mendel;
MGG (Bibliography); PAB-MI/2 (Bibliography); Riemann 12 (Bibliography) + Supp. (Bibliography); Schmidl + Supp.

2. CL 18/8.

4. Eigeldinger, Jean-Jacques. Chopin: Pianist and Teacher. Translated
by Naomi Shohet. London: Cambridge University Press, 1986. xvi, 324
p., 18 illus., over 400-item bibliography; index of names.

Hipkins, Edith J. How Chopin Played, from Contemporary Impressions
Collected from the Diaries and Note-Books of the Late A.J. Hipkins.
London: J.M. Dent and Sons Ltd., 1937. viii, 39 p., 4 illus.

Holland, Jeanne. Chopin's Teaching and His Students. Ph.D. diss.
University of North Carolina, 1973. vi, 329 p., musical examples,
bibliography.

Niecks, Frederick. Frederick Chopin as a Man and Musician. 2 vols.
London: Novello and Company, Limited, 3rd edition, 1902 [original
1888]. xx, 340 p., portrait; viii, 380 p., appendices, published
works, index.

5. A0014, A0016, A0023, A0047, A0063, A0073, B0020, B0035, B0041.

SEE: Bone, Audrey Evelyn. Jane Wilhelmina Sterling 1804-1859. Chip-
stead, Surrey: p.p. for the author by Starrock Services, 1960.

C0237.
Christian, Charlie. American Jazz Guitarist; b. July 29, 1916, Bonham,
Texas; d. March 2, 1942, New York City.

1. Baker 7; DEU; Grove 6/4 (Bibliography); Grove-AM (Bibliography - 13
entries); Grove-Jazz; JB; JRRM; LJ; PAB-MI/2 (Bibliography).

2. DB 33/17; Saturday Review May 17, 1958.

4. Callis, John. Charlie Christian 1939-1941. London: Middleton, 1977.
51 p.

5. A0108, A0143

C0238.
Christiani, Lise. French Cellist; b. December 24, 1827, Paris; d. 1853,
Tobolsk, Siberia, Russia.

1. Mendel, Schmidl.

C0239.
Chung, **Kyung-Wha**. Korean Violinist, sister of **Myung-Wah** and **Myung-Whun**; b. March 26, 1948, Seoul.

1. Baker 7; Grove 6/4 (Bibliography); Grove-AM; PAB-MI/2 (Bibliography).

2. HiFi/MusAm 24/2; HiFi/SR 31/4; Strad Sept/1977.

C0240.
Chung, **Myung-Wha**. American Cellist; b. March 19, 1944, Seoul, Korea

1. Baker 7; Grove-AM; PAB-MI/2 (Bibliography).

C0241.
Chung, **Myung-Whun**. American Pianist; b. January 22, 1953, Seoul, Korea.

1. Baker 7; Grove-AM; PAB-MI/2 (Bibliography).

C0242.
Ciccolini, **Aldo**. Italian Pianist; b. August 15, 1925, Naples.

1. Baker 7; DEU; Grove 6/4; PAB-MI/2 (Bibliography); Riemann 12.

2. CL 21/2; CK(KB) 3/5.

C0243.
Civil, **Alan**. English French-horn Player; b. June 13, 1929, Northampton.

1. Baker 7; Grove 6/4; PAB-MI/2 (Bibliography).

C0244.
Clapton, **Eric**. English Electric Guitarist; b. March 30, 1945, Ripley, Surrey.

1. Baker 7; DEU; JB; PAB-MI/2 (Bibliography).

4. Ballanti, Federico. Eric Clapton. Roma: Lato Side Editore, srl, 1982. 142 p., illus., discography.

   Pidgeon, John. Eric Clapton: a Biography. Bungay, Suffolk: The Chaucer Press Ltd, 1976 [revised edition London, 1985]. 144 p. + 8 plates, 13 illus., notes, groupography, discography.

   Turner, Steve. Conversations with Eric Clapton. London: Sphere Books Ltd., 1976. 116 p. + 12 plates, 53 illus., discography.

5. A0151.

C0245.
Clarke, **Herbert Lincoln**. American Cornetist; b. September 12, 1867, Woburn, Massachusetts; d. January 30, 1945, Long Beach, California.

1. Grove 6/4 (Bibliography); Grove-AM (Bibliography); PAB-MI/2 (Bibliography).

3. Clarke, Herbert Lincoln. How I Became a Cornetist: the Autobiography of a Cornet-Playing Pilgrim's Progress. St. Louis (MO): Jos. L. Huber, 1934. 74 p., portrait.

C0246.
Clarke, Kenny [Kenneth Spearman]. American Jazz Drummer; b. January 9, 1914, Pittsburgh, Pennsylvania; d. near Paris, France, January 26, 1985.

1. Baker 7; DEU; Grove 6/4 (Bibliography); Grove-AM (Bibliography - 11 entries); Grove-Jazz; JB; LJ; PAB-MI/2 (Bibliography); Riemann 12/ Supp. (Bibliography).

2. DB 30/8, 30/31.

C0247.
Clayton, Buck [Wilbur Dorsey]. American Jazz Trumpeter; b. November 12, 1911, Parsons, Kansas.

1. Baker 7; Grove-AM (Bibliography); Grove-Jazz; PAB-MI/2 (Bibliography).

2. DB 28/2, 31/13.

C0248.
Clement, Franz Joseph. Austrian Violinist; b. November 17, 1780, Vienna; d. November 3, 1842, Vienna.

1. Baker 7; DEU; Grove 6/4 (Bibliography); Mendel; MGG Supp. (Bibliography); Riemann 12 (Bibliography); Schmidl.

2. MQ 34/1.

4. Merk, M. Franz Joseph Clement (1780-1842). Ph.D. diss. University of Vienna, 1969.

C0249.
Clementi, Muzio. Italian Keyboardist and Pedagogue; b. January 23, 1752, Rome; d. March 10, 1832, Evesham, Worchestershire, England.

1. Baker 7 (Bibliography); DEU (Bibliography); Grove 6/4; Mendel; MGG (Bibliography); PAB-MI/2 (Bibliography); Riemann 12 (Bibliography) + Supp. (Bibliography); Schmidl (Bibliography); + Supp. (Bibliography).

3. Clementi, Muzio. Introduction to the Art of Playing on the Piano-forte: Containing the Elements of Music.... London: Clementi, Banger, Hyde, Collard & Davis, 1801.

4. Plantinga, Leon. Clementi: His Life and Music. London: Oxford University Press, 1977. xiii, 346 p., illus., 177-item bibliog., index.

5. A0014, A0023, A0051, B0020, B0050, C0984.3.

C0250.
Cliburn, Van [Harvey Lavan, Jr.]. American Pianist; b. July 12, 1934, Shreveport, LA.

1. Baker 7; DEU; Grove 6/4; Grove-AM; PAB-MI/2 (Bibliography); Riemann 12/Supp. (Bibliography).

2. CK(KB) 4/4; New York Times June 9, 1985.

4. Cahn, William. The Amazing Story of a New American Hero, Van Cliburn. New York: Published for Scholastic Book Services by the Ridge Press, 1959. 64 p., 55 illus.

Chasins, Abram with Villa Stiles. The Van Cliburn Legend. Garden City (NY): Doubleday & Company, Inc., 1959. 238 p., illus., index.

Khentova, Sof'ia Mikhailovna. Ven Klaibern. Moskva: Muzikal'noye izdatel'stvo, 1960. 102 p., illus.

Khentova, Sof'ia Mikhailovna. Ven Klaibern. Moskva: Muzyka, 1966. 106 p., illus., bibliographical footnotes.

5. B0130.

C0251.
Cochereau, Pierre. French Organist; b. July 9, 1924, St. Mandé, near Paris; d. March 6, 1984, Lyons.

1. Baker 7; DEU; Grove 6/4; PAB-MI/2 (Bibliography).

C0252.
Coenen, Franz. Dutch Violinist; b. December 26, 1826, Rotterdam; d. January 24, 1904, Leyden.

1. Baker 7; DEU; Fetis 2/Supp.; Grove 6/4 (Bibliography); Mendel; MGG/ Supp.; Schmidl.

C0253.
Cohen, Harriet. English Pianist; b. December 2, 1895, London; d. November 13, 1967, London.

1. Baker 7; DEU; Grove 6/4; PAB-MI/2 (Bibliography); Riemann 12.

3. Cohen, Harriet. A Bundle of Time: the Memoirs of Harriet Cohen. London: Faber and Faber, 1969. 330 p. + 16 plates, 38 illus., index.

Cohen, Harriet. Music's Handmaid. London: Faber and Faber Ltd, 1936. 173 p., index.

5. A0047.

C0254.
Cole, Cozy [William Randolph]. American Jazz Drummer; b. October 17, 1909, East Orange, New Jersey; d. January 29, 1981, Columbus, Ohio.

1. Baker 7; DEU; Grove-AM (Bibliography); Grove-Jazz; PAB-MI/2 (Bibliography).

2. DB 36/6.

CO255.
Coleman, Ornette. American Jazz Alto Saxophonist; b. March 9, 1930, Fort Worth, Texas.

1. Baker 7 (Bibliography); DEU (Bibliography); EdS/Supp.; Grove 6/4 (Bibliography) - 21 entries); Grove-AM (Bibliography - 26 entries); Grove-Jazz; JB (27 entries); JRRM; LJ; PAB-MI/2 (Bibliography); Riemann 12/Supp.

2. DB 27/15, 31/20, 32/8, 32/19, 32/26, 34/11, 36/26, 37/1, 40/19, 45/16, 48/7, 53/6, 54/8; HiFi/SR 5/2.

4. Spellman, A.B. Four Lives in the Bebop Business. New York: Pantheon Books, 1966 [2nd edition as Black Music, Four Lives, New York, 1970]. xiv, 241 p.

   Ornette Coleman, Cecil Taylor, Herbie Nichols and Jackie McLean.

5. A0159, B0048.

CO256.
Coltrane, John William. American Jazz Tenor Saxophonist; b. September 23, 1926, Hamlet, North Carolina; d. July 17, 1967, Huntington, Long Island, New York.

1. Baker 7; DEU (Bibliography); Grove 6/4 (Bibliography - 12 entries); Grove-AM (Bibliography - 18 entries); Grove-Jazz; JB (42 entries); JRRM (56 entries); LJ (13 entries); PAB-MI/2 (Bibliography); Riemann 12/Supp. (Bibliography).

2. DB 25/21, 27/20, 29/8, 32/26, 34/5, 34/18, 34/25, 38/14, 46/13 (Special Issue); Newsweek July 24, 1961.

4. Cole, Bill. John Coltrane. New York: Schirmer Books, 1976. vi, 264 p., 21 illus., notes, recording dates and personnel, 37 works cited, 225-item bibliography, index of names.

   Cole, William Shadrack. The Style of John Coltrane, 1955-1967. Ph.D. diss. Wesleyan University, 1975. 210. p., bibliography.

   Filtgen, Gerd and Michael Ausserbauer. John Coltrane: sein Leben, seine Musik, seine Schallplatten. Gauting-Buchendorf: OREOS Verlag GmbH, 1983. 220 p., illus., annotated discography, 20-item bibliography.

   Gelatt, Tim, comp. About John Coltrane: a Profile of His Life and Music. New York: New York Jazz Museum, 1974. 23 p., bibliography, discography.

   Gerber, Alain. Le cas Coltrane. Marseille: Editions Parenthèses, 1985. 157 p., 7 illus.

   Grey, De Sayles R. John Coltrane and His Attitude towards the Avant Garde in Jazz: an Ethnomusicological Study. Ph.D. diss. University of Pittsburgh.

Porter, Lewis R. John Coltrane's Music of 1960 through 1967: Jazz
Improvisation as Composition. Ph.D. diss. Brandeis University, 1983.
ix, 341 p., bibliography, discography.

Putschoegel, Gerd. John Coltrane: Untersuchungen zur Entwicklung
seiner improvisatorischen Gestaltungsmittel. Ph.D. diss. University
of Giessen.

Simpkins, Cuthbert Ormond. Coltrane: a Biography. New York: Herdon
House Publishers, 1975. 287 p. + 10 plates, 33 illus., chapter footnotes, appendices.

Thomas, J.C. Chasin' the Trane: the Music and Mystique of John
Coltrane. New York: Doubleday & Company, Inc., 1975. Reprint 1976.
252 p. + 8 plates, 24 illus., discography.

White III, Andrew Nathaniel. Trane 'n Me (a Semi-Autobiography): a
Treatise on the Music of John Coltrane. Washington (DC): Andrew's
Musical Enterprises, Inc., 1981. [iv], 55, [iii] p., discography.

5. A0159, B0048.

C0257.
Condon, Eddie [Albert Edwin]. American Jazz Banjoist/Guitarist; b.
November 16, 1905, Goodland, Indiana; d. August 4, 1973, New York City.

1. Baker 7; Grove-AM (Bibliography); Grove-Jazz; JB; JRRM; LJ; PAB-MI/2
   (Bibliography).

2. DB 23/25, 32/3; JJS 4/2; New Yorker April 28, 1945 and May 5, 1945.

3. Condon, Eddie. We Called It Music: a Generation of Jazz. New York:
   Henry Holt and Company, 1947. Reprint 1970. 341 p. + 4 plates, 20
   illus., index.

4. O'Neal, Hank. The Eddie Condon Scrapbook of Jazz. New York: St.
   Martin's Press, 1973. 288 p.

C0258.
Constantin, Louis. French Violinist; b. c.1585, Vexin district, near
Paris; d. October 25, 1657, Paris.

1. DEU; Fetis 2/2 + Supp.; Grove 6/4 (Bibliography); Mendel; Riemann 12
   (Bibliography); Schmidl.

4. Thoinan, Ernst [pseud. for A.E. Roquet]. Louis Constantin: roi des
   violons 1624-1657: notice biographique. Paris: J. Baur, Libraire-
   Editeur, 1878. 13 p.

C0259.
Cooper, Kenneth. American Harpsichordist; b. May 31, 1941, New York
City.

1. Baker 7; Grove-AM.

C0260.
Corea, Chick [Armando Anthony]. American Jazz Pianist; b. June 12, 1941, Chelsea, Massachusetts.

1. Baker 7; DEU; Grove-AM (Bibliography); Grove-Jazz; JB (11 entries); PAB-MI/2 (Bibliography); Riemann 12/Supp.

2. DB 36/7, 38/18, 40/9, 41/6, 43/17, 45/5, 46/5, 48/6, 53/1; HiFi/MusAm 29/2; CK(KB) 1/1, 4/2, 6/6, 9/7; KB 11/10.

C0261.
Corelli, Arcangelo. Italian Violinist; b. February 17, 1653, Fusignano, near Imola; d. January 8, 1713, Rome.

1. Baker 7 (Bibliography); DEU (Bibliography); Fetis 2/2; Grove 6/4 (Bibliography); Mendel; MGG (Bibliography); PAB-MI/2 (Bibliography); Riemann 12 (Bibliography) + Supp. (Bibliography); Schmidl + Supp. (Bibliography).

Slonimsky points out that "Corelli was famous as a virtuoso on the violin and may be regarded as the founder of modern violin technique; he systematized the art of proper bowing, and was one of the first to use double stops and chords on the violin." BAKER 7.

4. Stillings, Frank Stuart. Arcangelo Corelli. Ph.D. diss. University of Michigan, 1956. 356 p., bibliography.

5. A0093, B0020, B0050.

C0262.
Corigliano, John. American Violinist; b. August 28, 1901, New York City; d. September 1, 1975, Norfolk, Connecticut.

1. Baker 7; Grove-AM.

5. A0100.

C0263.
Cortot, Alfred Denis. French Pianist; b. September 26, 1877, Nyon, Switzerland; d. June 15, 1962, Lausanne, Switzerland.

1. Baker 7 (Bibliography); DEU (Bibliography); Grove 6/4 (Bibliography); MGG; PAB-MI/2 (Bibliography); Riemann 12 + Supp. (Bibliography); Schmidl + Supp.

His piano trio collaboration with Thibaud and Casals was legendary.

2. CL 3/5, 16/8; ML 16/2; PQ 127.

3. Cortot, Alfred. In Search of Chopin. Translated by Cyril and Rena Clarke. London: Peter Nevill Limited, 1951. 261 p., 8 illus., discography.

4. Gavoty, Bernard. Alfred Cortot. Genève: René Kister, 1953. 12 p. + 8 plates, 23 illus.

Gavoty, Bernard. Alfred Cortot. Paris: Buchet/Chastel Editions B/C, 1977. 316, [1] p. + 8 plates, 18 illus., discography.

Thieffry, Jeanne, ed. Alfred Cortot's Studies in Musical Interpretation. Translated by Robert Jaques. Foreword by Alfred Cortot. London: George G. Harrap & Co., Ltd., 1937. 378, [1] p., portrait, index of compositions.

5. A0008, A0048, B0028, B0041, B0042, B0061, B0080, D0012.

C0264.
Cossmann, Bernhard. German Cellist; b. May 17, 1822, Dessau; d. May 7, 1910, Frankfurt/M.

1. Baker 7; DEU; Fetis 2/2; Grove 6/4 (Bibliography); Mendel; MGG/Supp. (Bibliography); Riemann 12; Schmidl.

C0265.
Couperin, Armand-Louis. French Organist; b. February 25, 1727, Paris; d. February 2, 1789, Paris.

1. Baker 7; DEU; Fetis 2/2 + Supp.; Grove 6/4; Mendel; MGG; Riemann 12; Schmidl.

5. A0046.

   SEE: Bouvet, Charles. Calma (Chaumes-en-Brie) berceau des Couperin. Paris: Champion, 1927. 19 p., illus.

C0266.
Couperin, François le Grand. French Organist/Clavecinist; b. November 10, 1668, Paris; d. September 11, 1733, Paris.

1. Baker 7 (Bibliography); DEU (Bibliography); Fetis 2/2 + Supp.; Grove 6/4 (Bibliography); Mendel; MGG (Bibliography); PAB-MI/2 (Bibliography); Riemann 12 (Bibliography) + Supp. (Bibliography); Schmidl + Supp.

2. CL 7/4.

3. Couperin, François. L'Art de toucher le clavecin par Monsieur Couperin, organiste de roi.... Paris: l'auteur, 1716. 65 p. [1717 edition has 71 p.].

4. Tessier, André. Couperin: biographie critique. Paris: Henri Laurens, 1926. 126 p. + 2 plates, 12 illus., list of works, bibliography.

   Tiersot, Julien. Les Couperin. Paris: Félix Alcan, 1926. 216, [1] p., bibliography.

5. A0046.

C0267.
Courboin, Charles Marie. American Organist; b. April 2, 1884, Antwerp, Belgium; d. April 13, 1973, New York City.

1. Baker 7; Grove-AM.

C0268.
Cramer, Johann Baptist. German Pianist; b. February 24, 1771, Mannheim; d. April 16, 1858, London, England.

1. Baker 7 (Bibliography); DEU (Bibliography); Fetis 2/2; Grove 6/4 (Bibliography); Mendel; MGG (Bibliography); PAB-MI/2 (Bibliography); Riemann 12 (Bibliography) + Supp. (Bibliography); Schmidl.

3. Cramer, Johann Baptiste. Anweisung fuer das Piano-Forte, in welcher die Anfangsgruende der Musik deutlich erklaert...; nebst Lecktionen und Verspiele in den vorzueglichsten Dur- und Mol Toenen. Bonn: N. Simrock, c.1798. 47 p.

5. A0051.

C0269.
Cramer, Wilhelm. German Violinist, father of Johann; baptized June 2, 1746, Mannheim; d. October 5, 1799, London, England.

1. Baker 7; DEU; Fetis 2/2; PAB-MI/2 (Bibliography); Riemann 12 (Bibliography); Schmidl.

C0270.
Crawford, Jesse. American Theater Organist; b. December 2, 1895, Woodland, California; d. May 27, 1962, Sherman Oaks, California.

1. Grove-AM; PAB-MI/2 (Bibliography).

4. Landon, John W. Jesse Crawford: Poet of the Organ, Wizard of the Mighty Wurlitzer. Vestal (NY): The Vestal Press, 1974. xi, [i], 372 p., illus., 205-item bibliography, chapter notes, appendices including discography, index.

C0271.
Crossley, Paul Christopher Richard. English Pianist; b. May 17, 1944, Dewsbury, Yorkshire.

1. Baker 7; Grove 6/5; PAB-MI/2 (Bibliography).

C0272.
Crozier, Catharine. American Organist; b. January 18, 1914, Hobart, Oklahoma.

1. Baker 7; Grove 6/5; Grove-AM; PAB-MI/2 (Bibliography).

C0273.
Crusell, Bernhard Henrik. Finnish Clarinetist; b. October 15, 1775, Uusikanpunki, near Turku; d. July 28, 1838, Stockholm, Sweden.

1. Baker 7; DEU; Fetis 2/2; Grove 6/5 (Bibliography); Mendel; MGG/Supp. (Bibliography); Riemann 12 (Bibliography) + Supp. (Bibliography); Schmidl.

3. Grove 6/5 indicates that "his manuscript autobiography is in the Royal Library, Stockholm."

C0274.
Curzon, Clifford Michael. English Pianist; b. May 18, 1907, London: d. September 1, 1982, London.

1. Baker 7; DEU; Grove 6/5 (Bibliography); PAB-MI/2 (Bibliography); RIEMANN 12 + Supp.

2. GR 48/May; MM 27/6.

5. A0047, A0060, B0076.

   SEE: Culshaw, John. Putting the Record Straight: the Autobiography of John Culshaw. Edited posthumously by Erik Smith. New York: The Viking Press, 1981.

C0275.
Czerny, Carl. Austrian Pianist; b. February 20, 1791, Vienna; d. July 15, 1857, Vienna.

1. Baker 7; DEU (Bibliography); Fetis 2/2; Grove 6/5 (Bibliography); Mendel; MGG (Bibliography); PAB-MI/2 (Bibliography); Riemann 12 (Bibliography) + Supp. (Bibliography); Schmidl.

A student of Beethoven for three years, artists sought his expertise!

3. Czerny, Carl. Erinnerungen aus meinem Leben. MS. c.1842.

The MS is in the collection of the Gesellschaft der Musikfreunde in Vienna. A version of the MS was edited by Walter Kolneder in 1968: Erinnerungen aus meinem Leben. Strasbourg: Editions P.H. Heitz, 1968. 78 p. Partially published in MQ July/1956 and also in the Jahresbericht der Gesellschaft der Musikfreunde, Wien, 1870.

Czerny, Carl. On the Proper Performance of All Beethoven's Works for the Piano. Czerny's "Reminiscences of Beethoven" and Chapters II and III from Volume IV of the "Complete Theoretical and Practical Piano Forte School Op. 500". Vienna: Universal Edition, 1970. 119 p., port.

4. Steiger, H. Beitraege zu Karl Czernys Leben und Schaffen. Ph.D. diss. University of Munich, 1924.

Wehmeyer, Grete. Carl Czerny und die Einzelhaft am Klavier. Kassel: Baerenreiter-Verlag, 1983. 228 p., 98-item bibliography, index of names.

5. A0051, B0050.

C0276.
Czerny-Stefanska, Halina. Polish Pianist; b. December 31, 1922, Kraków.

1. Grove 6/5; MGG/Supp. (Bibliography); PAB-MI/2 (Bibliography); Riemann 12 + Supp.

4. Kydrynski, Lucjan with Wojciech Plewinski. Halina Czerny-Stefanska. Kraków: Polskie Wydawn. Muzyczne, 1963. 38 p., 28 illus.

C0277.
Cziffra, Gyoergy. Hungarian Pianist; b. September 5, 1921, Budapest.

1. Baker 7; DEU; Grove 6/5 (Bibliography); PAB-MI/2 (Bibliography); Riemann 12/Supp.

2. HiFiRev 3/2.

3. Cziffra, Gyoergy. Des canons et des fleurs. Translated by Gyoergy Cziffra, Jr. Paris: Editions Robert Laffont, 1977. 290, [3] p. + 4 plates, 17 illus.

5. B0042.

C0278.
Dameron, Tadd [Tadley Ewing]. American Jazz Pianist; b. February 21, 1917, Cleveland, Ohio; d. March 8, 1965, New York City.

1. Baker 7; DEU (Bibliography); Grove 6/5 (Bibliography); Grove-AM (Bibliography); Grove-Jazz; JB; JRRM; LJ; PAB-MI/2 (Bibliography).

C0279.
Da Motta, José Vianna. Portuguese Pianist; b. April 22, 1868, Isle St. Thomas, Portuguese Africa; d. May 31, 1948, Lisbon, Spain.

1. Baker 7 (Bibliography); Grove 6/5 (under Vianna da Motta - Bibliography); MGG (under Viana da Mota - Bibliography).

4. Anderson, Maria Josefina Abreu. Viana Da Mota interpretando os grandes músicos. Lisboa: Edição Da Autora, 1937. 195, [6] p., illus.

Branco, João de Freitas. Viana da Mota: uma contribuição para o estudo da sua personalidade e da sua obra. Lisboa: Fundacao Calouste Gulbenkian, 1972. 487 p., 41 illus., 73-item bibliography, periodicals, index of names.

Exposicão Comemorativa do Centenario de Vianna da Motta. Lisboa: Fundacão Calouste Gulbenkian, 1968. unpaginated [56 p.], 14 illus.

Lopes Graca, Fernando. Viana da Mota: subsidios para uma biografia, incluindo 22 cartas ao autor. Lisboa: Livraria Sa da Costa, 1949. 92, [3] p., 2 portraits. Edition of 500 copies.

Vianna Da Motta in Memoriam. Lisboa: Ramos, Alfonso & Moita, 1952. 207, [6] p., 20 illus. [edition of 500 copies].

5. SEE: Lopes Graca, Fernando. Reflexões sôbre a música. Lisboa: Seara Nova, 1941.

C0280.
Dancla, Arnaud. French Cellist; b. January 1, 1819, Bagnères-de-Bigorre; d. February 1, 1862, Bagnères-de-Bigorre.

1. Baker 7 (Bibliography); DEU (Bibliography); Fetis 2/2; Grove 6/5
   (Bibliography); Mendel; MGG; Riemann 12; Schmidl.

C0281.
Dancla, Jean-Baptiste-Charles. French Violinist, brother of **Arnaud**; b.
December 19, 1817. Bagnères-de-Bigorre; d. November 9, 1907, Tunis.

1. Baker 7 (Bibliography); DEU (Bibliography); Fetis 2/2 + Supp.; Grove
   6/5 (Bibliography); Mendel; MGG; PAB-MI/2 (Bibliography); Riemann 12;
   Schmidl.

3. Dancla, Charles. Notes & Souvenirs. 2. éd. rev./augm. [1st edition
   1891]. Paris: Le Bailly, O. Bornemann successeur, 1898. 173 p. + 1
   plate, portrait.

   Translated by Samuel Wolf as Notes and Souvenirs. Linthicum Heights
   (MD): Swand Publications, 1981. 83 p., portrait, list of works,
   translator's comments.

C0282.
Dancla, Leopold. French Violinist, brother of **Arnaud** and **Charles**; b.
June 1, 1823, Bagnères-de-Bigorre; d. April 29, 1895, Paris.

1. Baker 7 (Bibliography); DEU (Bibliography); Fetis 2/2; Grove 6/5
   (Bibliography); Mendel; MGG; Riemann 12; Schmidl.

C0283.
Dankworth, Johnny [John Philip William]. English Alto Saxophonist;
b. September 20, 1927, London.

1. Baker 7; Grove 6/5; Grove-Jazz; JB; LJ; PAB-MI/2 (Bibliography).

4. Collier, Graham, ed. Cleo & John: a Biography of the Dankworths.
   London: Quartet Books, 1976. 187 p.

C0284.
Dannreuther, Edward George. English Pianist; b. November 4, 1844, Strasbourg; d. February 12, 1905, London.

1. Baker 7 (Bibliography); DEU (Bibliography); EdS (Bibliography);
   Grove 6/5 (Bibliography); MGG (Bibliography); PAB-MI/2 (Bibliography); Riemann 12 + Supp. (Bibliography); Schmidl (Bibliography).

   His brother Gustav, (b. July 21, 1853, Cincinnati; d. December 19,
   1923, New York City), was a violinist.

5. SEE: Graves, Charles L. Post-Victorian Music with Other Studies and
   Sketches. Port Washington: Kennikat Press, 1971 [original 1911].

C0285.
Dauprat, Louis-François. French French-horn Player; b. May 24, 1781,
Paris; d. July 16, 1868, Paris.

1. Baker 7; DEU (Bibliography); Grove 6/5 (Bibliography); Mendel; MGG
   (Bibliography); Riemann 12; Schmidl.

C0286.
David, Ferdinand. German Violinist; b. January 19, 1810, Hamburg;
d. July 18, 1873, near Klosters, Switzerland.

1. Baker 7; DEU (Bibliography); Fetis 2/2 + Supp.; Grove 6/5 (Bibliography); Mendel; MGG (Bibliography); PAB-MI/2 (Bibliography); Riemann
12 (Bibliography) + Supp. (Bibliography); Schmidl.

A legendary teacher at the Leipzig Conservatory.

5. B0065.

C0287.
Davidov, Carl. Russian Cellist; b. March 15, 1838, Goldingen, Latvia;
d. February 26, 1889, Moscow.

1. Baker 7 (Bibliography); Fetis 2/Supp.; Grove 6/5 (Bibliography);
Mendel; MGG/Supp. (under Dawidow - Bibliography); Riemann 12 (under
Dawydow - Bibliography) + Supp. (Bibliography); Schmidl (under
Davidoff).

4. Hutor, Wassili. Carl Davidoff und seine Art das Violoncell zu
behandeln. Moskau: Privately Printed, 1899. 64, [1] p.

5. A0104.

C0288.
Davidovich, Bella. Russian Pianist; b. July 16, 1928, Baku.

1. Baker 7; Riemann 12/Supp. (under Dawidowitsch).

2. CL 22/6; HiFi/MusAm 29/9, 29/10, 33/2; CK(KB) 8/7.

5. A0075.

C0289.
Davies, Fanny. English Pianist; b. June 27, 1861, Guernsey; d. September
1, 1934, London.

1. Baker 7; Grove 6/5 (Bibliography); Schmidl/Supp.

2. RS 70-71.

5. B0056.

C0290.
Davis, Ivan. American Pianist; b. February 4, 1932, Electra, Texas.

1. Baker 7; Grove 6/5; Grove-AM; PAB-MI/2 (Bibliography).

2. CK(KB) 3/1.

C0291.
Davis, Miles [Dewey, III]. American Jazz Trumpeter; b. May 25, 1926,
Alton, Illinois.

1. Baker 7; DEU (Bibliography); Grove 6/5 (Bibliography); Grove-AM (Bibliography - 27 entries); Grove-Jazz; JB (69 entries); JRRM (106 entries); LJ; PAB-MI/2 (Bibliography); Riemann 12/Supp. (Bibliography).

2. DB 17/2, 25/5, 27/1, 29/23, 31/20, 32/21, 33/5, 34/7, 36/25, 37/17, 41/13, 47/9, 50/7, 50/8, 51/12; HiFi/MusAm 31/7; HiFi/SR 22/2; KB 13/10.

4. Carr, Ian. Miles Davis: a Biography. Foreword by Len Lyons. New York: William Morrow and Company, Inc., 1982. [iii], 310 p. + 8 plates, 34 illus., references, 65-item bibliography; musical examples, notes on repertoire, discography, index.

Chambers, Jack. Milestones I: the Music and Times of Miles Davis to 1960. Toronto: University of Toronto Press, 1983. xii, 345 p. + 5 plates, 15 illus., 185-item bibliography, index.

Chambers, Jack. Milestones II: the Music and Times of Miles Davis since 1960. Toronto: University of Toronto Press, 1983. [viii], 416 p. + 11 plates, 22 illus., references, 255-item bibliography, index.

Cole, Bill. Miles Davis: a Musical Biography. New York: William Morrow & Company, Inc., 1974. 256 p., recording sessions with the personnel, 318-item bibliography, transcriptions, index.

James, Michael. Miles Davis. London: Cassell & Company Ltd, 1961. 90 p.

Kerschbaumer, Franz. Miles Davis: stilkritische Untersuchungen zur musikalischen Entwicklung seines Personalstils. Graz: Akademische Druck- und Verlagsanstalt, 1978. 238 p., list of works, appendices, discography.

Based upon the author's 1976 Ph.D. diss. at the University of Graz.

Mortensen, Tore. Miles Davis den ny jazz: Miles Davis' musik i perioden 1969-1975. Aarhus: Privately Printed for the Author, 1977. vi, 155 p., discography, 19-item bibliography, musical examples, index of titles.

Nisenson, Eric. 'Round about Midnight: a Portrait of Miles Davis. New York: The Dial Press, 1982. xi, 244 p., illus., discography.

Weissmueller, Peter. Miles Davis: sein Leben, seine Musik, seine Schallplatten. Gauting-Buchendorf: OREOS Verlag, GmbH, 1984. 194 p., illus., annotated discography, 24-item bibliography.

5. A0001, A0029, B0048.

C0292.
Davison, Wild Bill [William Edward]. American Jazz Cornetist; b. January 5, 1906, Defiance, Ohio.

1. Baker 7; Grove-AM (Bibliog.); Grove-Jazz; JB; PAB-MI/2 (Bibliog.).

2. DB 25/19, 36/4.

C0293.
De Ahna, Heinrich Karl Hermann. Austrian Violinist; b. June 22, 1835, Vienna; d. November 1, 1892, Berlin, Germany.

1. Baker 7; DEU (under Ahna); Riemann 12 (under Ahna); Schmidl (under Ahna).

C0294.
De Franko, Buddy [Boniface Ferdinand Leonardo]. American Jazz Clarinetist; b. February 17, 1923, Camden, New Jersey.

1. Baker 7; Grove-AM (Bibliography); Grove-Jazz; PAB-MI/2 (Bibliography); Riemann 12/Supp. (Bibliography).

2. DB 26/2, 32/11, 33/8.

C0295.
Demessieux, Jeanne. French Organist; b. February 14, 1921, Montpellier; d. November 11, 1968, Paris.

1. Baker 7; DEU (Bibliography); Grove 6/5 (Bibliography); MGG + Supp. (Bibliography); PAB-MI/2 (Bibliography); Riemann 12 + Supp. (Bibliography).

4. Trieu-Colleney, Christiane. Jeanne Demessieux, une vie de luttes et de gloire. Avignon: Les Presses Universelles, 1977. 238 p. + 6 plates, chronology, discography.

C0296.
Demus, Joerg. Austrian Pianist; b. December 2, 1928, St. Polten.

1. Baker 7; DEU; Grove 6/5; PAB-MI/2 (Bibliography); Riemann 12 + Supp.

He is a noted accompanist of singers as well as a fine solo artist, and his collection of historic keyboard instruments is remarkable.

2. CL 6/1, 11/5.

5. A0008.

C0297.
Dengremont, Maurice. Brazilian Violinist; b. March 19, 1866, Rio de Janeiro, Brazil; d. September, 1893; Buenos Aires, Argentina.

1. Baker 7; Schmidl/Supp.

5. SEE: de Rezende, Carlos Penteado. Dois meninos prodígios de outrora em São Paulo. São Paulo: p.p., 1951. 60, [19] p., 9 illus.

C0298.
De Peyer, Gervase Alan. English Clarinetist; b. April 11, 1928, London.

1. Baker 7; Grove 6/5; PAB-MI/2 (Bibliography).

C0299.
Desmond, Paul [Paul Emil Breitenfeld]. American Jazz Alto Saxophonist;
b. November 25, 1924, San Francisco, CA; d. May 30, 1977, New York City.

1. Baker 7; DEU (Bibliography); Grove 6/5 (Bibliography); Grove-AM (Bibliography); Grove-Jazz; JB; LJ; PAB-MI/2 (Bibliography).

2. DB 29/26, 32/19; HiFi/MusAm 25/4.

5. B0048.

C0300.
Dessau, Bernhard. German Violinist; b. March 1, 1861, Hamburg; d. April
28, 1923, Berlin.

1. Baker 7; Riemann 12; Schmidl.

C0301.
De Vito, Gioconda. Italian Violinist; b. July 26, 1907, Martina Franca,
Lecce.

1. Baker 7; DEU; Grove 6/5; PAB-MI/2 (Bibliography); Riemann 12 + Supp.;
   Schmidl.

2. Strad Oct/1977.

C0302.
Dichter, Misha. American Pianist; b. September 27, 1945, Shanghai,
China.

1. Baker 7; Grove 6/5; Grove-AM; PAB-MI/2 (Bibliography).

   His wife, **Cipa** (b. May 20, 1944, Rio de Janeiro) is also a pianist.

2. CL 23/5; CK(KB) 3/3; PQ 92.

5. A0069, A0075.

C0303.
Dickenson, Vic[tor]. American Jazz Trombonist; b. August 6, 1906, Xenia,
Ohio.

1. Baker 7; Grove-AM (Bibliography); Grove-Jazz; PAB-MI/2 (Bibliography).

2. DB 31/31, 47/3.

C0304.
Diemer, Louis-Joseph. French Pianist; b. February 14, 1843, Paris;
d. December 21, 1919, Paris.

1. Baker 7; DEU (Bibliography); Fetis 2/Supp.; Grove 6/5 (Bibliography);
   MGG (Bibliography); PAB-MI/2 (Bibliography); Riemann 12; Schmidl.

5. A0028.

C0305.
Dieupart, Charles. French Violinist/Harpsichordist; b. c.1670;
d. c.1740, London, England.

1. Baker 7; DEU (Bibliography); Fetis 2/3; Grove 6/5 (Bibliography);
   Mendel; MGG (Bibliography); Riemann 12 + Supp. (Bibliography);
   Schmidl + Supp.

C0306.
Dilling, Mildred. American Harpist; b. February 23, 1894, Marion,
Indiana; d. December 30, 1982, New York City.

1. Baker 7; Grove-AM (Bibliography); Riemann 12/Supp.

2. New Yorker February 3, 1940.

C0307.
Diruta, Girolamo. Italian Organist; b. c.1554, Deruta, near Perugia;
d. after 1610.

1. Baker 7 (Bibliography); DEU; Fetis 2/3; Grove 6/5 (Bibliography);
   Mendel; MGG (Bibliography); Riemann 12 (Bibliography) + Supp.;
   Schmidl.

3. Diruta, Girolamo. Il transilvano dialogo sopra il vero modo di sonar
   organi, & istromenti da pena...Opera nuovamente ritrovata, uti-
   lissima, & necessaria a professori d'organo. Venezia: Allesandro
   Vincenti, 1593. In-fol., 36 f.

   Diruta, Girolamo. Seconda parte del Transilvano dialogo diviso in
   quattro libri del R.P. Girolamo Diruta perugino.... Venezia: Giacomo
   Vincenti, 1609. In-4, 26-36-12-25 p.

   These are the first comprehensive treatises which treated "the organ
   and its playing technique as distinct and separate from the clavier."
   BAKER 7.

C0308.
Dizi, François-Joseph. French Harpist; b. January 14, 1780, Namur;
d. November, 1847, Paris.

1. Baker 7; DEU; Fetis 2/3; Grove 6/5; Mendel; Riemann 12; Schmidl.

C0309.
Dobrzynski, Ignacy Feliks. Polish Pianist; b. February 15, 1807,
Romanov, Volhynia; d. October 10, 1867, Warsaw.

1. Baker 7; DEU (Bibliography); Fetis 2/3; Grove 6/5; Mendel; MGG/Supp.
   (Bibliography); PAB-MI/2 (Bibliography); Riemann 12 + Supp. (Bibliography); Schmidl.

C0310.
Dodds, Baby [Warren]. American Jazz Drummer; b. December 24, 1898, New
Orleans, Louisiana; d. February 14, 1959, Chicago, Illinois.

1. Baker 7 (duplicate entries!); DEU; Grove 6/5 (Bibliography); Grove-AM (Bibliography); Grove-Jazz; JB; JRRM; LJ; PAB-MI/2 (Bibliography); Riemann 12/Supp. (Bibliography).

2. DB 29/7.

3. Dodds, Warren. The Baby Dodds Story, as Told to Larry Garza. Los Angeles: Contemporary Press, 1959. 109 p., 20 illus., index.

5. A0029, A0031, A0034.

C0311.
Dodds, Johnny. American Jazz Clarinetist; b. April 12, 1892, New Orleans, Louisiana; d. August 8, 1940, Chicago, Illinois.

1. Baker 7; DEU; Grove 6/5 (Bibliography); Grove-AM (Bibliography); Grove-Jazz; JB; LJ; PAB-MI/2 (Bibliography); Riemann 12.

4. Lambert, George Edmund. Johnny Dodds. London: Cassell & Company Limited, 1961. 89, [1] p. + 2 plates, 4 illus., selected discography.

Riesco, José Francisco. El jazz classico y Johnny Dodds su rey sin corono. Santiago de Chile: Mueller, 1972. 352 p.

5. A0031.

C0312.
von Doehler, Theodor. Austrian Pianist; b. April 20, 1814, Naples, Italy; d. February 21, 1856, Florence, Italy.

1. Baker 7; DEU (Bibliography); Fetis 2/3; Grove 6/5; Mendel; PAB-MI/2 (under Dohler - Bibliography); Riemann 12; Schmidl.

C0313.
von Dohnanyi, Ernst. Hungarian Pianist; b. July 27, 1877, Pressburg; d. February 9, 1960, New York City.

1. Baker 7; DEU; EdS (Bibliography); Grove 6/5 (Bibliography); MGG; PAB-MI/2 (Bibliography); Riemann 12 (Bibliography) + Supp. (Bibliography); Schmidl + Supp.

3. von Dohnanyi, Ernst. Message to Posterity from Ernst von Dohnanyi. Translated by Ilona von Dohnanyi. Jacksonville (FL): H & W.B. Drew, 1960. 44 p.

4. Rueth, M.U. The Tallahasse Years of Ernst von Dohnanyi. M.A. thesis, Florida State University, 1962.

5. A0048.

C0314.
Dokshitcher, Timofey Alexandrovich. Soviet Trumpet Player; b. December 13, 1921, Nezhin.

1. Baker 7; Grove 6/5 (under Dokshitser - Bibliography).

C0315.
Doktor, Paul. American Violist; b. March 28, 1919, Vienna, Austria.

1. Baker 7; DEU; Grove 6/5; Grove-AM; PAB-MI/2 (Bibliography); Riemann 12 + Supp.

C0316.
Dolphy, Eric [Allen]. American Jazz Alto Saxophonist/Bass Clarinetist/ Flutist; b. June 20, 1928, Los Angeles, California; d. June 29, 1964, Berlin, West Germany.

1. DEU; Grove 6/5 (Bibliography); Grove-AM (Bibliography); Grove-Jazz; JB (13 entries); JRRM (10 entries); LJ; PAB-MI/2 (Bibliography); Riemann 12/Supp. (Bibliography).

2. DB 29/8, 31/24.

4. Simosko, Vladimir and Barry Tepperman. Eric Dolphy: a Musical Biography and Discography. Washington: Smithsonian Institution Press, 1974. Reprint 1979. ix, 132 p., 17 illus., annotated discography, composer credits, 39-item bibliography.

5. A0159.

C0317.
Domaniewski, Boleslaus Marian. Polish Pianist; b. July 16, 1857, Gronówek; d. September 11, 1925, Warsaw.

1. Baker 7; DEU; Grove 6/5 (Bibliography); Riemann 12; Schmidl.

C0318.
Domino, Fats [Antoine, Jr.]. American Jazz Pianist; b. February 26, 1928, New Orleans, Louisiana.

1. Baker 7; Grove-AM (Bibliography); PAB-MI/2 (Bibliography).

C0319.
Door, Anton. Austrian Pianist; b. June 20, 1833, Vienna; d. November 7, 1919, Vienna.

1. Baker 7; Riemann 12; Schmidl.

C0320.
Dorsey, Jimmy [James]. American Jazz Clarinetist/Alto Saxophonist; b. February 29, 1904, Shenandoah, PA; d. June 12, 1957, New York City.

1. Baker 7; DEU (Bibliography); Grove 6/5 (Bibliography); Grove-AM (Bibliography); Grove-Jazz; JB; JRRM; LJ; PAB-MI/2 (Bibliography); Riemann 12/Supp. (Bibliography).

4. Allen, Stuart S. The Fabulous Dorseys. London: Venture, 1947. 32 p.

Sanford, Herb. Tommy & Jimmy: the Dorsey Years. New Rochelle (NY): Arlington House Publishers, 1972. 305 p.

C0321.
Dorsey, Tommy [Thomas]. American Jazz Trombonist, brother of Jimmy; b.
November 19, 1905, Mahoney Plains, Pennsylvania; d. November 26, 1956,
Greenwich, Connecticut.

1. Baker 7; DEU (Bibliography); EdS; Grove 6/5 (Bibliography); Grove-AM
   (Bibliography); Grove-Jazz; JB; LJ; PAB-MI/2 (Bibliography).

2. DB 24/1.

5. SEE: Stuart S. Allen and Herb Sanford under Jimmy Dorsey (C0320.4).

C0322.
Dotzauer, Justus Johann Friedrich. German Cellist; b. June 20, 1783,
Haesselrieth, near Hildburghausen; d. March 6, 1860, Dresden.

1. Baker 7; DEU (Bibliography); Fetis 2/3; Grove 6/5 (Bibliography);
   Mendel; MGG (Bibliography); Riemann 12 + Supp. (Bibliography);
   Schmidl.

4. Eckhardt, J. Die Violoncellschulen von Justus Johann Dotzauer, F.A.
   Kummer, und Bernhard Romberg. Ph.D. diss. Cologne University, 1968.

5. A0104.

C0323.
Dotzauer, Karl Ludwig. German Cellist; b. December 7, 1811, Dresden;
d. July 1, 1897, Kassel.

1. Baker 7; DEU (Bibliography); Fetis 2/3; Mendel; MGG; Riemann 12.

C0324.
Downes, Ralph. English Organist; b. August 16, 1904, Derby.

1. Baker 7; Grove 6/5; PAB-MI/2 (Bibliography).

C0325.
Draghi, Giovanni Battista. Italian Harpsichordist/Organist; b. c.1640;
d. 1708, London, England.

1. Baker 7; DEU; Fetis 2/3; Grove 6/5 (Bibliography); MGG; Riemann 12
   + Supp. (Bibliography); Schmidl + Supp.

5. D0013 (Vol. 4).

C0326.
Dragonetti, Domenico Carlo Maria. Italian Double Bassist; b. April 7,
1763, Venice; d. April 16, 1846, London, England.

1. Baker 7; DEU (Bibliography); Fetis 2/3; Grove 6/5 (Bibliography);
   Mendel; MGG (Bibliography); PAB-MI/2 (Bibliography); Riemann 12
   (Bibliography) + Supp. (Bibliography); Schmidl.

4. Caffi, François. Biografia di Domenico Dragonetti. Venezia: Tipografico Veneziano, 1846. No copy located.

CO327.
Drdla, František Alois. Bohemian Violinist; b. November 28, 1868, Saar, Moravia; d. September 3, 1944, Gastein.

1. Baker 7; DEU; Grove 6/5 (Bibliography); MGG/Supp. (Bibliography); Riemann 12; Schmidl.

CO328.
Dresel, Otto. German Pianist; b. December 20, 1826, Geisenheim; d. July 26, 1890, Beverly, Massachusetts.

1. Baker 7; Fetis 2/Supp.; Grove-AM (Bibliography); Mendel; Riemann 12.

CO329.
Dreyschock, Alexander. Bohemian Pianist; b. October 15, 1818, Zack; d. April 1, 1869, Venice, Italy.

1. Baker 7; DEU; Fetis 2/3 + Supp.; Grove 6/5 (Bibliography); Mendel; MGG; PAB-MI/2 (Bibliography); Riemann 12; Schmidl.

CO330.
Dreyschock, Felix Raimund. Bohemian Violinist, brother of Alexander; b. August 20, 1824, Zack; d. February 6, 1869, Leipzig, Germany.

1. Baker 7; DEU; Fetis 2/3 + Supp.; Mendel; MGG; Riemann 12; Schmidl.

CO331.
Dreyschock, Felix. German Pianist, son of Raimund; b. December 27, 1860, Leipzig; d. August 1, 1906, Berlin.

1. Baker 7; DEU; MGG; Riemann 12.

CO332.
Drouet, Louis François-Philippe. French Flutist; b. April 14, 1792, Amsterdam, Holland; d. September 30, 1873, Bern, Switzerland.

1. Baker 7; DEU; Fetis 2/3 + Supp.; Grove 6/5; Mendel; MGG (Bibliography); Riemann 12; Schmidl.

At the age of sixteen he "was appointed solo flutist to King Louis of the Netherlands, and at 19 became solo flutist to Napoleon; after Napoleon's defeat, he played the flute with fine impartiality for King Louis XVIII." BAKER 7.

CO333.
Drozdov, Anatoly Nikolayevich. Russian Pianist; b. November 4, 1883, Saratov; d. September 10, 1950, Moscow.

1. Baker 7; DEU; Grove 6/5 (Bibliography); MGG/Supp.; Schmidl/Supp. (under Drosdov).

CO334.
Drozdowski, Jan [pseud. Jan Jordan]. Polish Pianist; b. February 2, 1857, Cracow; d. January 21, 1918, Cracow.

1. Baker 7; DEU (Bibliography); Grove 6/5 (Bibliography).

C0335.
Drucker, Stanley. American Clarinetist; b. February 4, 1929, Brooklyn,
New York.

1. Grove 6/5; Grove-AM; PAB-MI/2 (Bibliography).

C0336.
Drzewiecki, Zbigniew. Polish Pianist; b. April 8, 1890, Warsaw; d. April
11, 1971, Warsaw.

1. Grove 6/5; MGG (Bibliography); Riemann 12 + Supp.

4. Kisielewski, Stefan. Zbigniew Drzewiecki. Kraków: Polskie Wydawn,
   1976. 63 p., 36 illus., repertoire, discography.

C0337.
Duelon, Friedrich Ludwig. German Flutist; b. August 14, 1769, Oranienburg, near Potsdam; d. July 7, 1826, Wuerzburg.

1. Baker 7; Fetis 2/3; Grove 6/5; Mendel; MGG (Bibliography); Riemann
   12 (Bibliography) + Supp. (Bibliography); Schmidl.

3. Wieland, C.-M., ed. Duelons des blinden Floetenspielers Leben und
   Meinungen von ihm selbst bearbeitet. 2 vols. Zuerich, 1807-08.

C0338.
Dulcken, Luise. German Pianist; b. March 29, 1811, Hamburg; d. April 12,
1850, London, England.

1. Baker 7; Fetis 2/3 (under Dulken); Riemann 12; Schmidl.

C0339.
Dunham, Henry Morton. American Organist; b. July 29, 1853, Brockton,
Massachusetts; d. May 4, 1929, Brookline, Massachusetts.

1. Baker 7; Grove-AM (Bibliography); PAB-MI/2 (Bibliography).

3. Dunham, Henry Morton. The Life of a Musician Woven into a Strand of
   History of the New England Conservatory of Music. New York: Printed
   by Richmond Borough Publishing and Printing Company, 1931. 235 p., 26
   illus.

C0340.
Dunn, John. English Violinist; b. February 16, 1866, Hull; d. December
18, 1940, Harrogate.

1. Baker 7; DEU; MGG (Bibliography); Riemann 12; Schmidl/Supp.

C0341.
Dunn, John Petri. Scottish Pianist; b. October 26, 1878, Edinburgh;
d. February 4, 1931, Edinburgh.

1. Baker 7; Riemann 12 (Bibliography); Schmidl/Supp.

C0342.
Duport, Jean-Louis. French Cellist; b. October 4, 1749, Paris;
d. September 7, 1819, Paris.

1. Baker 7; DEU (Bibliography); Fetis 2/3; Grove 6/5 (Bibliography);
   Mendel; MGG (Bibliography); PAB-MI/2 (Bibliography); Riemann 12 +
   Supp. (Bibliography); Schmidl.

3. Duport, Jean-Louis. Essai sur le doigté du violoncelle et la conduite
   de l'archet avec une suite d'exercices. Paris: Pleyel, c.1813.

   "The foundation of modern cello playing." GROVE 6/5.

4. Kohlmorgen, Fritz. Die Brueder Duport und die Entwicklung der Violon-
   celltechnik von ihren Anfaengen bis zur Zeit Bernhard Rombergs. Ph.D.
   diss. University of Berlin, 1922. ii, 151 p., bibliography.

   Marx, Karl. Die Entwicklung des Violoncells und seiner Spieltechnik
   bis Jean-Louis Duport (1520-1820). Ph.D. diss. University of Saarbruecken, 1963.

5. A0104.

C0343.
DuPré, Jacqueline. English Cellist; b. January 26, 1945, Oxford;
d. October 19, 1987, London.

1. Baker 7; DEU; Grove 6/5; PAB-MI/2 (Bibliography).

2. GR 46/January; Strad Jan/1977, March/1984.

4. Wordsworth, William, ed. Jacqueline duPré: Impressions. New York:
   The Vanguard Press, 1983. 141, [3] p., 45 illus., honors, discography.

5. B0052.

C0344.
Dupré, Marcel. French Organist; b. May 3, 1886, Rouen; d. May 30, 1971,
Meudon, near Paris.

1. Baker 7 (Bibliography); DEU (Bibliography); Grove 6/5 (Bibliography);
   MGG (Bibliography) + Supp. (Bibliography); PAB-MI/2 (Bibliography);
   Riemann 12 + Supp. (Bibliography); Schmidl.

2. Musical Times 112 (1971).

4. Gavoty, Bernard. Marcel Dupré. Genève: René Kister, 1955. 29, [3] p.,
   25 illus., discography.

   Murray, Michael. Marcel Dupré: the Work of a Master Organist. Boston:
   Northeastern University Press, 1985. xxv, 259 p., 14 illus., discography, appendix, glossary, catalogue of works, select 67-item bibliography, index.

5. B0041, B0042.

C0345.
Durlet, Emmanuel. Belgian Pianist; b. October 11, 1893, Antwerp;
d. February 7, 1977, Antwerp.

1. Baker 7; DEU.

C0346.
Dushkin, Samuel. American Violinist; b. December 13, 1891, Suwalki,
Poland; d. June 24, 1976, New York City.

1. Baker 7; DEU; Grove 6/5 (Bibliography); Grove-AM (Bibliography);
   Riemann 12 + Supp. (Bibliography); Schmidl/Supp.

5. B0061.

C0347.
Duvernoy, Frédéric Nicolas. French French-horn Player; b. October 16,
1765, Montbéliard; d. July 19, 1838, Paris.

1. DEU; Fetis 2/3; Grove 6/5 (Bibliography); Mendel; MGG/Supp. (Bibliography); Riemann 12; Schmidl.

5. A0028.

C0348.
Eddy, Clarence Hiram. American Organist; b. June 23, 1851, Greenfield,
Massachusetts; d. January 10, 1937, Chicago, Illinois.

1. Baker 7; Grove 6/5; Grove-AM (Bibliography); Riemann 12; Schmidl.

3. A series of his reminiscences appeared in The Diapason (April 1932
   to May 1933).

C0349.
Egghard, Julius [pseud. of **Count von Hardegen**]. Austrian Pianist;
b. April 24, 1834, Vienna; d. March 23, 1867, Vienna.

1. Baker 7; Fetis 2/Supp.; Mendel; Riemann 12; Schmidl.

B0350.
Ehlers, Alice. American Harpsichordist; b. April 16, 1887, Vienna,
Austria.

1. Baker 7; Grove 6/6; Grove-AM; Riemann 12 + Supp.; Schmidl/Supp.

C0351.
Ehrlich, Karl Heinrich Alfred. Austrian Pianist; b. October 5, 1822,
Vienna; d. December 30, 1899, Berlin, Germany.

1. Baker 7 (Bibliography); DEU (Bibliography); Grove 6/6 (Bibliography);
   Mendel; MGG (Bibliography); Riemann 12 (Bibliography); Schmidl (Bibliography).

3. Ehrlich, Heinrich. Dreissig Jahre Kuenstlerleben. Berlin: Verlag Hugo Steinitz, 1893. 416, viii p., index of names.

CO352.
Eisenberg, Maurice. American Cellist; b. February 24, 1900, Koenigsberg, Germany; d. December 13, 1972, New York City.

1. Baker 7; DEU; Grove 6/6; Grove-AM; Riemann 12 + Supp. (Bibliography).

2. Strad Dec/1978.

3. Eisenberg, Maurice and M.B. Stanfield. Cello Playing of Today. Foreword by Pablo Casals. London: The Strad, 1957. xx, 147 p., 12 illus.

5. A0100.

CO353.
Ekier, Jan. Polish Pianist; b. August 29, 1913, Cracow.

1. Baker 7; Riemann 12 + Supp. (Bibliography).

CO354.
Eldridge, Roy "Little Jazz". American Jazz Trumpeter; b. January 30, 1911, Pittsburgh, Pennsylvania.

1. Baker 7; DEU; Grove 6/6 (Bibliography); Grove-AM (Bibliography); Grove-Jazz; JB; JRRM; LJ; PAB-MI/2 (Bibliography); Riemann 12/Supp. (Bibliography).

2. DB 23/19, 26/6.

CO355.
Ellegaard, France. Danish Pianist; b. October 10, 1912, Paris, France.

1. Baker 7; Riemann 12 + Supp.

CO356.
Eller, Louis. Austrian Violinist; b. June 9, 1820, Graz; d. July 12, 1862, Pau.

1. Baker 7; Fetis 2/3 + Supp.; Mendel; Riemann 12 (Bibliography); Schmidl/Supp.

CO357.
Ellington, Duke [Edward Kennedy]. American Jazz Pianist; b. April 29, 1899, Washington, D.C.; d. May 24, 1974, New York City.

1. Baker 7 (Bibliography); DEU (Bibliography); Grove 6/6 (Bibliography 31 entries); Grove-AM (Bibliography - 56 entries); Grove-Jazz; JB (79 entries); JRRM (68 entries); LJ; MGG/Supp. (Bibliography); PAB-MI/2 (Bibliography); Riemann 12 (Bibliography) + Supp. (Bibliography).

Ellington revolutionized jazz as a genre with extended improvisations, complex arrangements, and profound musicianship.

2. DB 23/26, 24/1, 29/12, 31/20, 31/24, 32/9, 32/21, 35/15, 35/25, 37/8, 39/2, 39/7, 40/4, 41/8; HiFi/MusAm 24/11; HiFi/MusRev 1/6; HiFi/SR 23/6; RS 29-30.

   NOTE: The Duke Ellington Society in New York City promotes concerts and other cultural events.

3. Ellington, Edward Kennedy. Music is My Mistress. Garden City (NY): Doubleday & Company, Inc., 1973. xv, 522 [1] p., illus., honors and awards, selected discography, compositions, 17-item bibliography.

   There is an index compiled by H.F. Huon (Melbourne, Australia: QED Corporation, 1980. 82 p.).

4. Connor, Donald Russell. 20 Years of the Duke, 1933-1955. Carnegie (PA): Pope's Records Unlimited, 1966. 12 p.

   Dance, Stanley. The World of Duke Ellington. New York: Charles Scribner's Sons, 1970. xiv, 311 p., illus., discography, chronology, index.

   Includes short sketches of twenty-six musicians with whom he worked.

   Ellington, Mercer with Stanley Dance. Duke Ellington in Person: an Intimate Memoir. Boston: Houghton Mifflin Company, 1978. xii, 236 p. + 12 plates, 42 illus., index.

   The Duke's son, Mercer (b. March 11, 1919), now leads the band.

   Gammond, Peter. Duke Ellington: His Life and Music. London: Phoenix House, 1958. xii, 255 p. + 8 plates, 40 illus., record guide.

   George, Don R. Sweet Man: the Real Duke Ellington. New York: G.P. Putnam's Sons, 1981. 272 p. + 4 plates, 13 illus., index.

   Gutman, Bill. Duke: the Musical Life of Duke Ellington. New York: Random House, Inc., 1977. 184, [1] p., 22 illus., index, discography.

   Jewell, Derek. Duke: a Portrait of Duke Ellington. New York: W.W. Norton & Company, Inc., 1977. 264 p., 33 illus., chronology, select discography and bibliography, index.

   Lambert, G.E. Duke Ellington. New York: A.S. Barnes and Company, Inc., 1961 [original London, 1959]. vi, 88 p. + 2 plates, 4 illus., selected discography, 7-item bibliography.

   Preston, Denis. Mood Indigo. Egham, Surrey: Citizen Press, 1946. 84 p.

   Ruland, Hans. Duke Ellington: sein Leben, seine Musik, seine Schall-platten. Gauting-Buchendorf: OREOS Verlag, 1983. 189, [1] p., illus., annotated discography, 16-item bibliography.

   de Trazegnies, Jean. Duke Ellington: Harlem Aristocrat of Jazz. Brussels: Hot Club de Belgique, 1946. 80 p.

Ulanov, Barry. Duke Ellington. New York: Creative Age Press, Inc.,
1946. Reprint 1975. x, 322 p. + 9 plates, 30 illus., discography,
index.

5. A0001, A0006, A0029, B0055, B0057.

C0358.
Ellis, Don[ald Johnson]. American Jazz Trumpeter; b. July 25, 1934, Los
Angeles, California; d. December 17, 1978, Hollywood, California.

1. Baker 7; Grove 6/6 (Bibliography); Grove-AM (Bibliography); Grove-
   Jazz; PAB-MI/2 (Bibliography); Riemann 12/Supp.

2. DB 30/1, 30/14, 33/13, 34/8, 37/8, 39/7, 41/2, 44/2.

5. SEE: Stuessy, Jr., Clarence Joseph. The Confluence of Jazz and
   Classical Music from 1950 to 1970. Ph.D. diss. University of
   Rochester, 1977. xviii, 512 p., illus., tables, musical
   examples, list of works, appendices, discography, bibliography.

C0359.
Elman, Mischa. American Violinist; b. January 20, 1891, Talnoy, Russia;
d. April 5, 1967, New York City.

1. Baker 7; DEU; Grove 6/6; Grove-AM (Bibliography); MGG/Supp. (Bibliography); PAB-MI/2 (Bibliography); Riemann 12 + Supp. (Bibliography);
   Schmidl.

2. Strad June/1967, July/1967, April/1987,

4. Carpenter, McDonnell. Mischa Elman and Joseph Szigeti: a Study of
   Their Art through Cheirology. New York: Vantage Press, Inc., 1955.
   xxiii, 27-48 p.

   Elman, Saul. Memoirs of Mischa Elman's Father. New York: Privately
   Printed for the Author, 1953. 201 p. + 3 plates, 8 illus.

5. A0100, A0115, A0132, A0142, B0010, B0037, B0053, B0089.

C0360.
Elvey, George Job. English Organist; b. March 27, 1816, Canterbury;
d. December 9, 1893, Windlesham, Surrey.

1. Baker 7; DEU; Fetis 2/Supp.; Grove 6/6; Mendel; MGG/Supp. (Bibliography); PAB-MI/2 (Bibliography); Riemann 12; Schmidl.

4. Elvey, Mary. Life and Reminiscences of George J. Elvey...Late
   Organist to H.M. Queen Victoria and Forty-Seven Years Organist of
   St. George's Chapel, Windsor. London: S. Low, Marston & Company,
   Limited, 1894. xv, [i], 347 p., 6 illus.

C0361.
Engel, Karl. Swiss Pianist; b. June 1, 1923, Birsfeld.

1. Baker 7; Riemann 12/Supp.

C0362.
Entremont, Philippe. French Pianist. French Pianist; b. June 6, 1934, Rheims.

1. Baker 7; DEU; Grove 6/6; PAB-MI/2 (Bibliography); Riemann 12/Supp.

2. CL 19/3; CK(KB) 4/9.

C0363.
Epstein, Julius. Austrian Pianist; b. August 7, 1832, Agram, Croatia; d. March 1, 1926, Vienna.

1. Baker 7; DEU; Mendel; MGG; Riemann 12 + Supp. (Bibliography); Schmidl.

4. Schuster, Heinrich Maria. Julius Epstein: ein Tonkuenstlerisches Charakterbild zu seinem 70. Geburtstag. Wien: Julius Karolus, 1902. 21, [2] p., portrait, list of works.

C0364.
Erdeli, Xenia Alexandrova. Russian Harpist; b. February 1878, Mirolyubovka, Ukraine; d. May 27, 1971, Moscow.

1. Grove 6/6

3. Erdeli, Kseniia Aleksandrovna. Arfa v moyey zhizni: memuari. Moskva: Muzika, 1967. 240 p. + 15 plates, illus.

4. V. Poltareva wrote a book about Erdeli's contributions to the Soviet school of harp playing (L'vov, 1959). No copy seen.

C0365.
Erdmann, Eduard Paul Ernst. Latvian Pianist; b. March 5, 1896, Tsezis (Wenden); d. June 21, 1958, Hamburg, Germany.

1. Baker 7; DEU; MGG + Supp.; Riemann 12 + Supp. (Bibliography); Schmidl.

2. RS 69.

4. Bitter, Christoph and M. Schloesser, eds. Begegnungen mit Eduard Erdmann [original: Eduard Erdmann: Erinnerungen seiner Freunde, Briefe und Aufzeichnungen. Darmstadt, 1967]. Meisenheim/Glan: Reprint by Anton Hain KG, 1972. 382 p., illus.

C0366.
Ernst, Heinrich Wilhelm. Moravian Violinist; b. May 6, 1814, Bruenn; d. October 8, 1865, Nice, France.

1. Baker 7; DEU (Bibliography); Fetis 2/3 + Supp.; Grove 6/6; Mendel; MGG/Supp. (Bibliography); PAB-MI/2 (Bibliography); Riemann 12 (Bibliography) + Supp. (Bibliography); Schmidl.

4. Heller, Amely. Heinrich Wilhelm Ernst im Urteile seiner Zeitgenossen. Wien: Selbstverlag, 1905 [original 1904]. 64 p., portrait, illus.

5. A0014

C0367.
Eschenbach, Christoph. German Pianist; b. February 20, 1940, Breslau.

1. Baker 7; DEU; Grove 6/6; PAB-MI/2 (Bibliography); Riemann 12/Supp.

C0368.
Essipova, Anna. Russian Pianist; b. February 13, 1851, St. Petersburg;
d. August 18, 1914, St. Petersburg.

1. Baker 7; DEU (Bibliography); PAB-MI/2 (Bibliography); Riemann 12
   (under Essipow) + Supp. (Bibliography); Schmidl (under Essipoff).

   Pupil and wife (1880-92) of **Leschetizky.** Prokofiev was her student.

4. Bertenson, Nikolai Vasil'evich. Anna Nikolaevna Essipova. Leningrad:
   Gos. musykal'noe izd-vo, 1960. 149 p., illus.

C0369.
Eto, Toshiya. Japanese Violinist; b. November 9, 1927, Tokyo.

1. Baker 7; Grove 6/6 (Bibliography); Riemann 12/Supp.

C0370.
Eulenstein, Charles. German Jews' Harpist; b. 1802, Heilbronn; d. 1890,
Styria.

1. Grove 6/6 (Bibliography); PAB-MI/2 (Bibliography).

3. Eulenstein, Charles. A Sketch of the Life of Charles Eulenstein, the
   Celebrated Performer on the Jews' Harp. London: James J. Welsh, 1833.
   69 p., portrait.

4. Roodenfels, Fanny. Eulenstein's musikalische Laufbahn. Stuttgart:
   Druck und Verlag von Strecker & Moser, 1892. xvi, 88 p.

C0371.
Evans, Bill [William John]. American Jazz Pianist; b. August 16, 1929,
Plainfield, New Jersey; d. September 15, 1980, New York City.

1. Baker 7; DEU (Bibliography); Grove 6/6 (Bibliography); Grove-AM
   (Bibliography); Grove-Jazz; JB; PAB-MI/2 (Bibliography); Riemann
   12/Supp.

   "...one of the most influential...of his generation." Grove-AM.

2. DB 27/25, 29/29, 31/28, 32/13, 43/5, 46/16, 48/11; HiFi/MusAm 18/12;
   HiFi/SR 11/1, 17/2, 29/6; CK(KB) 3/3, 6/6, 6/12.

4. Utterback, Joe. The Jazz Piano Style of Bill Evans. D.M.A. University of Kansas, 1979. vii, 104 p., musical examples, list of works,
   discography, bibliography.

5. A0035.

C0372.
Fachiri [née Arányi de Hunyadvar], **Adila**. British Violinist; b. February 26, 1886, Budapest, Hungary; d. December 15, 1962, Florence, Italy.

1. Baker 7; DEU (under Aranyi, d'); Grove 6/6; Riemann 12 + Supp.; Schmidl (under Aranyi).

5. SEE: Joseph Macleod under **Jelly d'Aranyi** (C0032.4).

C0373.
Falcinelli, Rolande. French Organist; b. February 18, 1920, Paris.

1. Baker 7; Riemann 12 + Supp. (Bibliography).

3. Falcinelli, Rolande. L'Orgue: cahiers et mémoires. Rolande Falcinelli et la classe d'orgue du Conservatoire. Paris: L'Orgus, 1981. 56 p., illus.

C0374.
Fantini, Girolamo. Italian Trumpeter; b. near Spoleto, c.1600 - ?.

1. DEU (Bibliography); Fetis 2/3; Grove 6/6 (Bibliography); Mendel; Riemann 12; Schmidl + Supp.

3. Fantini, Girolamo. Modo per imparare a sonare di tromba tanto di guerra quanto musicalmente in organo. Frankfurt: Daniel Watsch, 1638. 86 p. This is one of the earliest trumpet methods.

4. Eichborn, Hermann Ludwig. Girolamo Fantini: ein Virtuos des siebzehnten Jahrhunderts und seine Trompeten-Schule. Nashville (TN): The Brass Press, 1976. pp. 112-138 reprinted from Monatshefte fuer Musik-Gescgichte, 1890.

C0375.
Farnadi, Edith. Austrian Pianist; b. September 25, 1921, Budapest, Hungary.

1. Baker 7; Grove 6/6; Riemann 12 + Supp.

C0376.
Farnam, W[alter] Lynnwood. American Organist; b. January 13, 1885, Sutton, Quebec, Canada; d. November 23, 1930, New York City.

1. Baker 7; Grove 6/6; Grove-AM (Bibliography); PAB-MI/2 (Bibliography).

C0377.
Farrenc [née Dumont], **Jeanne-Louise**. French Pianist; b. May 31, 1804, Paris; d. September 15, 1875, Paris.

1. Baker 7; DEU; Fetis 2/3 + Supp.; Grove 6/6 (Bibliography); Mendel; MGG (Bibliography); Riemann 12; Schmidl.

"...a brilliant pianist, [she was] the only woman ever to hold a permanent position as an instrumentalist [at the Paris Conservatory] in the 19th century." Baker 7.

C0378.
Fay, Amy. American Pianist; b. May 21, 1844, Bayou Goula, Louisiana;
d. February 28, 1928, Watertown, Massachusetts.

1. Baker 7 (Bibliography); Grove-AM (Bibliography); PAB-MI/2 (Bibliography).

2. MQ April/1974.

3. Fay, Amy. Music-Study in Germany: from the Home Correspondence of
   Amy Fay. Chicago: Jansen, McClurg & Company, 1881. Reprint 1965/1979.
   348 p.

   There is a French translation (Paris, 1907) with an introduction by
   Vincent d'Indy.

4. McCarthy, S. Margaret and William, comp. & eds. More Letters of Amy
   Fay: the American Years, 1879-1916. Detroit: Information Coordinators, Inc., 1986. 168 p., 7 illus., index.

5. SEE: Neuls-Bates, Carol, ed. Women in Music: an Anthology of Source
   Readings from the Middle Ages to the Present. New York: Harper
   & Row, Publishers, 1982.

C0379.
Feinberg, Samuel. Russian Pianist; b. May 26, 1890, Odessa; d. October
22, 1962, Moscow.

1. Baker 7 (Bibliography); MGG/Supp. (Bibliography); Riemann 12 + Supp.
   (Bibliography); Schmidl.

C0380.
Ferguson, Maynard. Canadian Jazz Trumpeter; b. May 4, 1928, Montreal.

1. Baker 7; Grove-AM (Bibliography); Grove-Jazz; JB; PAB-MI/2 (Bibliography); Riemann 12 (Bibliography).

2. DB 23/20, 26/1, 27/20, 30/15, 39/7, 40/18, 42/11, 44/16, 47/7, 52/9.

C0381.
Fernández Bordas, Antonio. Spanish Violinist; b. January 12, 1870,
Orense; d. February 18, 1950, Madrid.

1. Baker 7; Riemann 12.

C0382.
Ferrari, Domenico. Italian Violinist; b. c.1722, Piacenza; d. 1780,
Paris, France.

1. Baker 7; DEU; Fetis 2/3; Grove 6/6 (Bibliography); Riemann 12 (Bibliography); Schmidl.

4. Kock, Virginia Downman. The Works of Domenico Ferrari (1722-1780).
   2 vols. Ph.D. diss. Tulane University, 1969. viii, 370 p.; vii,
   195 p., music, plates, tables, list of works, bibliography.

5. B0051.

C0383.
Ferras, Christian. French Violinist; b. June 17, 1933, Le Touquet-Paris-Plage; d. September 15, 1982, Paris.

1. Baker 7; DEU; Grove 6/6 (Bibliography); MGG; PAB-MI/2 (Bibliography); Riemann 12 + Supp.

C0384.
Festing, Michael Christian. English Violinist; b. c.1680, London; d. July 24, 1752, London.

1. Baker 7; DEU (Bibliography); Fetis 2/3; Grove 6/6 (Bibliography); PAB-MI/2 (Bibliography); Riemann 12 + Supp. (Bibliography); Schmidl.

C0385.
Feuermann, Emanuel. American Cellist; b. November 22, 1902, Kolomea, Galicia, Austria; d. May 25, 1942, New York City.

1. Baker 7; DEU; Grove 6/6; Grove-AM; PAB-MI/2 (Bibliography); Riemann 12 + Supp.; Schmidl/Supp.

2. Strad Sept/1972.

4. Itzkoff, Seymour W. Emanuel Feuermann, Virtuoso: a Biography. University (AL): The University of Alabama Press, 1979. 247 p., 26 illus., notes on interpretation by Emanuel Feuermann, discography by Fred Galland and Seymour Itzkoff, index.

   A member of two famous trios, first with Schnabel and Huberman and then with Rubinstein and Heifetz.

C0386.
Field, John. Irish Pianist; b. July 26, 1782, Dublin; d. January 23, 1857, Moscow, Russia.

1. Baker 7 (Bibliography); DEU (Bibliography); Fetis 2/3 + Supp. (Bibliography); Grove 6/6 (Bibliography - includes a section on "Piano Playing"); Mendel; MGG (Bibliography); PAB-MI/2 (Bibliography); Riemann 12 (Bibliography) + Supp. (Bibliography); Schmidl.

5. A0051, B0020, C0984.3.

C0387.
Filtsch, Károly. Hungarian Pianist; b. May 28, 1830. Szászebes; d. May 11, 1845, Venice, Italy.

1. Grove 6/6 (Bibliography).

4. Andrews, Irene Filtsch. About One Whom Chopin Loved: (Carl Filtsch). MS [Library of Congress ML 417.F45A6].

   "Contains photostat copies of newspaper articles, music, portraits, and 30 pages of text."

C0388.
Firkušný, Rudolf. Czechoslovakian Pianist; b. February 11, 1912,
Napajedla.

1. Baker 7; DEU; Grove 6/6; MGG/Supp. (Bibliography); PAB-MI/2 (BIbliography); Riemann 12 + Supp. (Bibliography); Schmidl.

2. CL 12/2, 23/2; HiFi/MusAm 32/11; CK(KB) 3/7; KB 13/6; PQ 139.

5. A0069, A0070, A0075.

C0389.
Fischer, Annie. Hungarian Pianist; b. July 5, 1914, Budapest.

1. Baker 7; DEU (Bibliography); Grove 6/6; MGG/Supp. (Bibliography);
   PAB-MI/2 (Bibliography); Riemann 12 + Supp.

2. HiFi/MusAm 32/10.

C0390.
Fischer, Edwin. Swiss Pianist; b. October 6, 1886, Basel; d. January 24,
1960, Zurich.

1. Baker 7; DEU Grove 6/6 (Bibliography); MGG; PAB-MI/2 (Bibliography);
   Riemann 12 + Supp. (Bibliography); Schmidl.

2. CL 26/8; RS 5, 6, 39.

3. Fischer, Edwin. Reflections on Music. London: Williams and Norgate,
   1951 [original Muenchen, 1949]. 47 p.

4. Gavoty, Bernard. Edwin Fischer. Genève: René Kister, 1954. 30, [2]
   p., 27 illus., discography.

   Haid, Hugo, ed. Dank an Edwin Fischer. Wiesbaden: F.A. Brockhaus,
   1962. 164 p., 33 illus., list of writings and compositions, discography, index.

5. A0008, B0080, B0129, D0012.

   SEE: Autobiography of Alfred Brendel (C0179.4).

   SEE: Dahms, Walter, ed. Der Musikus Almanach. Berlin-Steglitz:
        Panorama-Verlag, 1927.

C0391.
Fisk, Eliot Hamilton. American Guitarist; b. August 10, 1954, Philadelphia, Pennsylvania.

1. Baker 7; Grove-AM.

2. HiFi/MusAm 32/7.

C0392.
Fleisher, Leon. American Pianist; b. July 23, 1928, San Francisco, CA.

1. Baker 7; DEU; Grove 6/6; Grove-AM (Bibliography); PAB-MI/2 (Bibliography); Riemann 12/Supp.

2. CL 2/4, 25/8; HiFi/MusAm 33/4; NY Times Magazine September 12, 1982.

5. A0069, A0075.

C0393.
Flesch, Carl. Hungarian Violinist; b. October 9, 1873, Moson; d. November 14, 1944, Lucerne, Switzerland.

1. Baker 7; DEU (Bibliography); Grove 6/6 (Bibliography); MGG (Bibliography); PAB-MI/2 (Bibliography); Riemann 12 + Supp. (Bibliography); Schmidl + Supp. (Bibliography).

3. Flesch, Carl. The Memoirs of Carl Flesch. Translated by Hans Keller. New York: The Macmillan Company, 1958 [original London, 1957]. Reprint 1973 (limited edition of 500 copies from the Rockliff, London original with 4 new photographs)/1979. xiii, 393 p., 21 illus., 3 appendices, index.

Edited by Keller in collaboration with C.F. Flesch from the original German MS.

4. Brederode, Willem. Carl Flesch: een kleine biografische studie. Haarlem: De erven E.F. Bohn n.v., 1938. 64 p. + 4 plates, 10 illus.

5. B0028.

C0394.
Fleury, Louis François. French Flutist; b. May 24, 1878, Lyons; d. June 11, 1926, Paris.

1. Baker 7; DEU; Grove 6/6 (Bibliography); PAB-MI/2 (Bibliography); Riemann 12 + Supp.; Schmidl.

C0395.
Fodor, Eugene. American Violinist; b. March 5, 1950, Turkey Creek, Colorado.

1. Baker 7 (Bibliography); Grove-AM (Bibliography).

2. HiFi/MusAm 24/11; Strad Dec/1982.

C0396.
Foldes, Andor. Hungarian Pianist; b. December 21, 1913, Budapest.

1. Baker 7; DEU (Bibliography); Grove 6/6; MGG; PAB-MI/2 (Bibliography); Riemann 12 + Supp. (Bibliography).

2. HiFi/MusAm 21/1; MM 20/7.

4. Foldes, Lili. Two on a Continent. New York: E.P. Dutton & Company, 1947. 254 p.

von Lewinski, Wolf-Eberhard. Andor Foldes. Berlin: Rembrandt Verlag, 1970. 64 p., 34 illus.

C0397.
Foster, Pops [George Murphy]. American Jazz Double Bassist; b. May 18, 1892, McCall, Louisiana; d. October 30, 1969, San Francisco, California.

1. Grove-AM; Grove-Jazz; JB; JRRM; LJ; PAB-MI/2 (Bibliography).

3. Foster, Pops and Tom Stoddard. Pops Foster: the Autobiography of a New Orleans Jazzman. Introduction by Bertram Turetzky. Berkeley: University of California Press, 1971. xxii, 208 p. + 20 plates, 42 illus., chronology, selected discography, Foster discography 1924-1940, 12-item selected bibliography, index.

"...not a model of chronological accuracy... Grove-AM.

5. A0031.

C0398.
Foster, Sidney. American Pianist; b. May 23, 1917, Florence, South Carolina; d. February 7, 1977, Boston, Massachusetts.

1. Baker 7; Grove-AM (Bibliography); Riemann 12 (Bibliography).

C0399.
Fountain, Pete [Peter Dewey Fountain, Jr.]. American Jazz Clarinetist; b. July 3, 1930, New Orleans, Louisiana.

1. Baker 7; Grove-Jazz; JB; LJ; PAB-MI/2 (Bibliography).

2. DB 28/24, 52/1.

3. Fountain, Pete with Bill Neely. A Closer Walk: the Pete Fountain Story. Chicago: Regnery, 1972. viii, 202 p. + 12 plates, 48 illus., list of record albums.

C0400.
Fournier, Pierre Léon Marie. French Cellist; b. June 24, 1906, Paris; d. January 8, 1986, Paris.

1. Baker 7; DEU; Grove 6/6; MGG/Supp.; Riemann 12 + Supp.

4. Gavoty, Bernard. Pierre Fournier. Genève: René Kister, 1955. 27, [5] p., 25 illus., discography.

5. B0041, B0110.

C0401.
Fox, Roy. American Cornetist; b. October 25, 1901, Denver, Colorado.

1. Grove 6/6 (Bibliography); JB; LJ; PAB-MI/2 (Bibliography).

3. Fox, Roy. Hollywood, Mayfair, and All That Jazz: the Roy Fox Story. London: Frewin, 1975. 248 p., illus.

C0402.
Fox, Virgil Keel. American Organist; b. May 3, 1912, Princeton, Illinois; d. October 25, 1980, Palm Beach, Florida.

1. Baker 7; Grove 6/6 (Bibliography); Grove-AM (Bibliography); PAB-MI/2 (Bibliography); Riemann 12/Supp.

2. HiFi 13/8; CK(KB) 2/6, 5/3.

C0403.
Fradkin, Fredric. American Violinist; b. April 2, 1892, Troy, New York; d. October 3, 1963, New York City.

1. Baker 7; Grove-AM.

C0404.
Fraenzl, Ferdinand. German Violinist, son of Ignaz; b. May 20, 1770, Schwetzingen; d. October 27, 1833, Mannheim.

1. Baker 7 (Bibliography); Grove 6/6 (Bibliography); Mendel; MGG (Bibliography); Riemann 12 (Bibliographhy) + Supp. (Bibliography); Schmidl.

C0405.
Fraenzl, Ignaz. German Violinist; b. June 3, 1736, Mannheim; d. September 3, 1811, Mannheim.

1. Baker 7 (Bibliography); Grove 6/6 (Bibliography); Mendel; MGG (Bibliography); Riemann 12 (Bibliography) + Supp.; Schmidl.

C0406.
Frager, Malcolm. American Pianist; b. January 15, 1935, St. Louis, MO.

1. Baker 7; Grove 6/6; Grove-AM (Bibliography); PAB-MI/2 (Bibliography); Riemann 12.

2. CL 9/9; HiFi 10/12; PQ 97.

C0407.
Francescatti, Zino. French Violinist; b. August 9, 1902, Marseilles.

1. Baker 7; DEU (Bibliography); Grove 6/6; MGG/Supp.; PAB-MI/2 (Bibliography); Riemann 12.

2. Strad March/1986, Aug/1987.

5. A0100, A0132.

C0408.
Franchomme, Auguste-Joseph. French Cellist; b. April 10, 1808, Lille; d. January 21, 1884, Paris.

1. Baker 7; DEU (Bibliography); Fetis 2/3; Grove 6/6 (Bibliography); Mendel; MGG (Bibliography); PAB-MI/2 (Bibliography); Riemann 12 (Bibliography) + Supp. (Bibliography); Schmidl.

5. A0104.

C0409.
Franci, Rinaldo. Italian Violinist; b. 1854, Siena; d. January 2, 1907,
Siena.

1. Schmidl.

4. Proveddi, Arrigo. Il violinista Sienese Rinaldo Franci. Siena: Tip.
Editrice S. Bernardino, 1910. 107 p., portrait.

C0410.
Franck, Eduard. German Pianist; b. October 5, 1817, Breslau; d. December
1, 1893, Berlin.

1. Baker 7; DEU; Grove 6/6 (Bibliography); Mendel; MGG (Bibliography);
PAB-MI/2 (Bibliography); Riemann 12; Schmidl.

His son, **Richard** (b. January 3, 1858, Cologne; d. January 22, 1938,
Heidelberg), was also a pianist. He wrote Musikalische und unmusi-
kalische Erinnerungen (Heidelberg, 1928), a copy of which I have
been unable to locate.

C0411.
François, Samson. French Pianist; b. May 18, 1924, Frankfurt/M, Germany;
d. October 22, 1970, Paris.

1. Baker 7; DEU; Grove 6/16 (under Samson-François); Riemann 12 + Supp.
(Bibliography).

4. Gavoty, Bernard. Samson Francois. Genève: René Kister, 1955. 30 p.,
24 illus., recordings.

Spycket, Jérôme. Scarbo: le roman de Samson François. Lausanne: Van
De Velde/Payot, 1985. 238, [1] p., 43 illus., discography, repertoire.

5. B0041.

C0412.
Frank, Claude. American Pianist; b. December 24, 1925, Nuremberg,
Germany.

1. Baker 7; Grove 6/6; Grove-AM; PAB-MI/2 (Bibliography); Riemann 12/
Supp.

2. CL 22/1.

5. A0070.

C0413.
Franko, Sam. American Violinist; b. January 20, 1857, New Orleans,
Louisiana; d. May 6, 1937, New York City.

1. Baker 7; DEU; Grove-AM; PAB-MI/2 (Bibliography); Riemann 12.

3. Franko, Sam. <u>Chords and Dischords: Memoirs and Musings of an American Musician</u>. New York: The Viking Press, Inc., 1938. [vi], 186 p., 18 illus., published works, index.

An early advocate of native-born American musicians.

C0414.
Fraser, Norman. English Pianist; b. November 26, 1904, Valparaiso, Chile.

1. Baker 7; DEU; PAB-MI/2 (Bibliography); Riemann 12 + Supp. (Bibliography).

C0415.
Freeman, Bud [Lawrence]. American Jazz Tenor Saxophonist; b. April 13, 1906, Chicago, Illinois.

1. DEU; Grove 6/6 (Bibliography); Grove-AM (Bibliography); Grove-Jazz; JB; LJ; PAB-MI/2 (Bibliography).

2. DB 38/13.

3. Freeman Lawrence. <u>If You Know of a Better Life Please Tell Me</u>. Dublin: Basehall Eaves, 1976. 61 p.

Freeman, Lawrence. <u>You Don't Look Like a Musician</u>. Detroit: Belcamp Publishing, 1974. viii, 125 p., index.

5. A0159.

C0416.
Freire, Nelson. Brazilian Pianist; b. October 18, 1944, Boa Esperanza.

1. Baker 7; Grove 6/6; PAB-MI/2 (Bibliography); Riemann/Supp.

2. CL 16/1.

C0417.
Frey, Emil. Swiss Pianist; b. April 8, 1889, Baden, Aargau; d. May 20, 1946, Zurich.

1. Baker 7; DEU; Grove 6/6; MGG; Riemann 12 + Supp.; Schmidl/Supp.

C0418.
Frey, Walter. Swiss Pianist, brother of Emil; b. January 26, 1898, Basel.

1. Baker 7; DEU; Grove 6/6; MGG; Riemann 12 + Supp.

2. CL 24/3.

C0419.
Fried, Miriam. Romanian Violinist; b. September 9, 1946, Satu Mare.

1. Baker 7; Grove 6/6 (Bibliography); PAB-MI/2 (Bibliography).

2. HiFi/MusAm 27/7; Strad June/1972, Oct/1985.

C0420.
Friedberg, Carl. German Pianist; b. September 18, 1872, Bingen; d. September 8, 1955, Merano, Italy.

1. Baker 7; DEU (Bibliography); Riemann 12 + Supp. (Bibliography); Schmidl.

4. Smith, Julia Frances. <u>Master Pianist: the Career and Teaching of Carl Friedberg</u>. Foreword by Dame Myra Hess. New York: Philosophical Library, 1963. xviii, 183 p., 13 illus., compositions, discography, list of pupils, notes, index.

Ethel Leginska and Elly Ney are among his famous pupils.

C0421.
Friedheim, Arthur. American Pianist; b. October 26, 1859, St. Petersburg, Russia (of German Parents); d. October 19, 1932, New York City.

1. Baker 7; DEU; Grove 6/6; PAB-MI/2 (Bibliography); Riemann 12; Schmidl/Supp.

3. Friedheim, Arthur. <u>Life and Liszt: the Recollections of a Concert Pianist</u>. Edited by Theodore L. Bullock. New York: Taplinger Publishing Co., 1961/R1986. viii, 335 p. + 4 plates, illus., index.

C0422.
Friedman, Erick. American Violinist; b. August 16, 1939, Newark, NJ.

1. Baker 7; Grove-AM (Bibliography); PAB-MI/2 (Bibliography); Riemann 12.

2. HiFi 12/2.

5. A0048, A0115.

C0423.
Friedman, Ignaz. Polish Pianist; b. February 14, 1882, Podgorez, near Cracow; d. January 26, 1948, Sydney, Australia.

1. Baker 7; DEU; Grove 6/6 (Bibliography); MGG/Supp. (Bibliography); PAB-MI/2 (Bibliography); Riemann 12 + Supp.; Schmidl + Supp.

4. Heiles, W.H. <u>Rhythmic Nuance in Chopin's Performance Recorded by Moritz Rosenthal, Ignaz Friedman and I.J. Paderewski</u>. Ph.D. diss. University of Illinois, 1964.

C0424.
Friskin, James. American Pianist; b. March 3, 1886, Glasgow, Scotland; d. March 16, 1967, New York City.

1. Baker 7; Grove 6/6; Grove-AM; PAB-MI/2 (Bibliography); Riemann 12 + Supp.; Schmidl.

C0425.
Frugoni, Orazio. Swiss Pianist; b. January 28, 1921, Davos.

1. Baker 7; Grove 6/6; Grove-AM; PAB-MI/2 (Bibliography).

2. HiFi 4/3.

C0426.
Fuchs, Carl. German Cellist; b. June 3, 1865, Offenbach/M.; d. June 9, 1951, Manchester, England.

1. DEU; Riemann 12; Schmidl/Supp.

3. Fuchs, Carl. <u>Musical and Other Recollections of Carl Fuchs</u>...
Translation, by the author's wife, of <u>Erinnerungen eines Offen-</u>
<u>bacher Cellisten</u>. Manchester: Sherratt and Hughes, 1937. 131, [1]
p., 24 illus., index.

This is a revision with additional material from Fuchs' articles
published in the <u>Manchester Evening News</u>.

C0427.
Fuchs, Joseph. American Violinist; b. April 26, 1900, New York City.

1. Baker 7; Grove 6/7; Grove-AM (Bibliography).

5. A0100, A0115.

C0428.
Fuchs, Lillian. American Violist, sister of **Joseph**; b. November 18, 1903, New York City.

1. Baker 7; Grove 6/7; Grove-AM (Bibliography); PAB-MI/2 (Bibliography);
Riemann 12/Supp.

2. Strad Jan/1986.

C0429.
Fuller, Albert. American Harpsichordist; b. July 21, 1926, Washington, D.C.

1. Baker 7; DEU; Grove-AM; PAB-MI/2 (Bibliography); Riemann 12.

C0430.
Gabrilowitsch, Ossip. Russian Pianist; b. February 7, 1878, St. Petersburg; d. September 14, 1936, Detroit, Michigan.

1. Baker 7; DEU; Grove 6/7; Grove-AM (Bibliography); MGG; PAB-MI/2 (Bibliography); Riemann 12.

4. Clemens, Clara. <u>My Husband Gabrilowitsch</u>. New York: Harper & Brothers
Publishers, 1938. Reprint 1979. 351 p., 13 illus., index.

5. B0028, B0061, B0089.

SEE: Volpe, Marie. Marie Volpe for "Music for Miami": an Autobiography. Miami: Hurricane House Publishers, Inc., 1967.

C0431.
Galamian, Ivan Alexander. American Violinist; b. February 5, 1903, Tabriz, Persia; d. April 14, 1981, New York City.

1. Baker 7; Grove 6/7; Grove-AM (Bibliography); Riemann 12/Supp.

5. A0100, B0027.

C0432.
Gallico, Paolo. American Pianist; b. May 13, 1868, Trieste; d. July 6, 1955, New York City.

1. Baker 7; DEU; Grove 6/7; Grove-AM; Riemann 12; Schmidl.

C0433.
Galston, Gottfried. American Pianist; b. August 31, 1879, Vienna, Austria; d. April 2, 1950, St. Louis, Missouri.

1. Baker 7; PAB-MI/2 (Bibliography); Riemann 12; Schmidl/Supp.

4. Bayne, Pauline Shaw. The Gottfried Galston Music Collection and the Galston-Busoni Archive. Knoxville (TN): The University of Tennessee Library, 1978. 297 p., 18 illus.

C0434.
Galway, James. Irish Flutist; b. December 8, 1939, Belfast.

1. Baker 7; DEU; Grove 6/7 (Bibliography); PAB-MI/2 (Bibliography).

2. GR 58/November; HiFi/SR 43/4.

3. Galway, James. An Autobiography. London: Chappell & Company, Limited, 1978. 181 p. + 4 plates, 16 illus.

5. B0027.

C0435.
Ganz, Wilhelm. German Pianist; b. November 6, 1833, Mainz; d. September 12, 1914, London, England.

1. Baker 7; DEU (Bibliography); Grove 6/7 (Bibliography); Riemann 12. (Bibliography).

3. Ganz, Wilhelm. Memories of a Musician: Remeniscences of Seventy Years of Musical Life. London: John Murray, 1913. xv, 357 p., 19 illus., index.

C0436.
Garbousova, Raya. American Cellist; b. October 10, 1905, Tiflis, Russia.

1. Baker 7; DEU; Grove 6/7; Grove-AM; Riemann 12 + Supp. (under Garbuzova).

C0437.
Garner, Erroll [Lewis]. American Jazz Pianist; b. June 15, 1921,
Pittsburgh, Pennsylvania; d. January 2, 1977, Los Angeles, California.

1. Baker 7; DEU (Bibliography); Grove 6/7 (Bibliography); Grove-AM (Bibliography - 10 entries); Grove-Jazz; JB; JRRM; PAB-MI/2 (Bibliography); Riemann 12.

2. DB 23/16, 24/22, 29/27, 34/21, 37/21; JJS 6/1.

4. Doran, James M. Erroll Garner: the Most Happy Piano. Metuchen (NJ):
   The Scarecrow Press, 1985. xv, 481 p., chronology, discography, filmography, 39-item selected bibliography, index.

   This is the third title in Studies in Jazz, an important series,
   from the Institute of Jazz Studies at Rutgers University, New Jersey.

C0438.
Gaviniès, Pierre. French Violinist; b. May 11, 1728, Bordeaux;
d. September 8, 1800, Paris.

1. Baker 7; DEU (Bibliography); Fetis 2/3; Grove 6/7 (Bibliography);
   Mendel; MGG (Bibliography); Riemann 12 (Bibliography); Schmidl
   (Bibliography).

4. Ginter, Anthony Francis. The Sonatas of Pierre Gaviniès. Ph.D. diss.
   Ohio State University, 1976. xi, 374 p., tables, musical examples,
   appendices, bibliography.

C0439.
Gazzelloni, Severino. Italian Flutist; b. January 5, 1919, Roccasecca,
Frosinone.

1. Baker 7; DEU (Bibliography); Grove 6/7; MGG/Supp.; PAB-MI/2 (Bibliography); Riemann 12/Supp.

3. Gazzelloni, Severino and Emilia Granzotto. Il flauto d'oro. Torino:
   ERI Edizione Rai, 1984. 155, [2] p.

   Gazzelloni, Severino. Gazzelloni su Severino Gazzelloni. Roma: Magma,
   1977. 138, [1] p., 24 illus.

C0440.
Gebhard, Heinrich. American Pianist; b. July 25, 1878, Sobernheim, Germany; d. May 5, 1963, North Arlington, New Jersey.

1. Baker 7; DEU.

C0441.
Gehot, Jean or **Joseph.** Belgian Violinist; b. April 8, 1756, Brussels;
d. c.1820 in America.

1. Baker 7; DEU (Bibliography); Fetis 2/3; Grove 6/7 (Bibliography);
   Grove-AM (Bibliography); Mendel; MGG (Bibliography); Riemann 12.

3. Gehot, Joseph. The Art of Bowing on the Violin, Calculated for the Practice and Improvement of Juvenile Performers. London: G. Goulding, c.1790. 9 p.

C0442.
Gelber, Bruno-Leonardo. Argentine Pianist; b. March 19, 1941, Buenos Aires.

1. Baker 7; Riemann 12/Supp.

5. A0060.

C0443.
Geminiani, Francesco Saverio. Italian Violinist; baptized December 5, 1687, Lucca; d. September 17, 1762, Dublin, Ireland.

1. Baker 7; DEU (Bibliography); Fetis 2/3; Grove 6/7 (Bibliography); Mendel; MGG (Bibliography); PAB-MI/2 (Bibliography); Riemann 12 (Bibliography) + Supp. (Bibliography); Schmidl (Bibliography) + Supp. (Bibliography).

   Baker 7 includes a good account of the erroneous attribution of The Art of Playing the Violin (London, 1730) to Geminiani.

3. Geminiani, Francesco. Rules for Playing in a True Taste on the Violin, German Flute, Violoncello, and Harpsichord.... London, n.p., c.1746. 19 p.

4. Betti, Adolfo. La vita e l'arte di Francesco Geminiani. Lucca: G. Giusti, 1933. 20 p., portrait.

5. B0020.

C0444.
Gendron, Maurice. French Cellist; b. December 26, 1920, Nice.

1. Baker 7; DEU; Grove 6/7 (Bibliography); MGG/Supp.; PAB-MI/2 (Bibliography); Riemann 12 + Supp.

2. Strad Oct/1985.

C0445.
Gérardy, Jean. Belgian Cellist; b. December 6, 1877, Spa; d. July 4, 1929, Spa.

1. Baker 7; Grove 6/7 (Bibliography); Schmidl.

5. B0053.

C0446.
Germani, Fernando. Italian Organist; b. April 5, 1906, Rome.

1. Baker 7; DEU; Grove 6/7; MGG; PAB-MI/2 (Bibliography); Riemann 12 + Supp.; Schmidl/Supp.

C0447.
Gerster, Ottmar. German Violinist; b. June 29, 1897, Braunfels;
d. August 31, 1969, Leipzig.

1. Baker 7; DEU; Grove 6/7; MGG + Supp. (Bibliography); PAB-MI/2 (Bibliography); Riemann 12 + Supp. (Bibliography); Schmidl.

C0448.
Getz, Stan [Stanley]. American Jazz Tenor Saxophonist; b. February 2,
1927, Philadelphia, Pennsylvania.

1. Baker 7; DEU; Grove 6/7 (Bibliography); Grove-AM (Bibliography);
   Grove-Jazz; JB (10 entries); LJ; PAB-MI/2 (Bibliography); Riemann
   12/Supp. (Bibliography).

   "...one of the supremely melodious improvisers in modern jazz..."
   Grove-AM.

2. DB 24/4, 27/8, 30/5, 32/11, 33/10, 33/11, 38/10, 43/14, 45/1;
   HiFiRev 2/4; HiFi/SR 30/3.

4. Astrup, Arne. The Stan Getz Discography. Texarkana (TX): J.L.
   Atkins, 1979. 119 p.

   Walker, Malcolm. Stan Getz: a Discography 1944-1955. London: p.p.,
   1957, 20 p.

5. A0035, A0159.

C0449.
Geyer, Stefi. Swiss Violinist; b. January 28, 1888, Budapest, Hungary;
d. December 11, 1956, Zurich.

1. Baker 7; Grove 6/7 (Bibliography); Riemann 12/Supp.

C0450.
van den Gheyn, Matthias. Flemish Organist/Carillonist; b. April 7, 1721,
Tirlemont, Brabant; d. June 22, 1785, Louvain.

1. Baker 7; DEU; MGG (Bibliography); Riemann 12 (under van den Gheyn);
   Schmidl + Supp.

4. van Elewyck, Xavier. Matthias van den Gheyn, le plus grand organiste
   et carillonneur belge du XVIIIe siècle.... Paris: Librairie de P.
   Lethielleux, 1862. 79, [1] p.

C0451.
Ghiglia, Oscar. Italian Guitarist; b. August 13, 1938, Livorno.

1. Baker 7; Grove 6/7; PAB-MI/2 (Bibliography).

C0452.
Ghitalla, Armando. American Trumpeter; b. June 1, 1925, Alfa, Illinois.

1. Baker 7; Grove 6/7; Grove-AM.

C0453.
de'Giardini, Felice. Italian Violinist; b. April 12, 1716, Turin;
d. June 8, 1796, Moscow, Russia.

1. Baker 7 (Bibliography); DEU (Bibliography); Fetis 2/3; Grove 6/7
   (Bibliography); Mendel; MGG (Bibliography); PAB-MI/2 (Bibliography);
   Riemann 12 (Bibliography) + Supp. (Bibliography); Schmidl + Supp.

4. McVeigh, Simon. The Violinist in London's Concert Life, 1750-1784:
   Felice de'Giardini and His Contemporaries. Ph.D. diss. Hertford
   College, Oxford University, 1980.

5. D0011 (Vol. 6).

C0454.
Gieseking, Walter. German Pianist; b. November 5, 1895, Lyons, France;
d. October 26, 1956, London, England.

1. Baker 7; DEU; Grove 6/7 (Bibliography); MGG; PAB-MI/2 (Bibliography);
   Riemann 12 (Bibliography) + Supp. (Bibliography); Schmidl/Supp.

2. CL 25/9; RS 6, 12.

3. Gieseking, Walter. So wurde Ich Pianist. Wiesbaden: F.A. Brockhaus,
   1963. 147 p., 35 illus., index.

4. Gavoty, Bernard. Walter Gieseking. Genève: René Kister, 1955. 29,
   [3] p., 23 illus., recordings.

   Laaff, Ernst. Walter Gieseking zum Gedaechtnis: Ansprache gehalten
   in der Gedenkfeier der Stadt Wiesbaden am 4. November 1956. Wiesbaden: Stadtverwaltung, 1956. 20 p., portrait.

5. A0008, A0048, B0041, B0042, B0044, B0061, B0080, B0129.

C0455.
Giesen, Hubert. German Pianist/Accompanist; b. January 13, 1898,
Cornelimuenster, near Aachen.

1. Riemann 12 + Supp.

3. Giesen, Hubert. Am Fluegel Hubert Giesen: meine Lebenserinnerungen.
   Frankfurt am Main: S. Fischer Verlag, 1972. 300, [2] p. + 6 plates,
   28 illus., discography by Ute Mayer, index.

C0456.
Gigout, Eugène. French Organist; b. March 23, 1844, Nancy; d. December
9, 1925, Paris.

1. Baker 7; DEU; Fetis 2/Supp.; Grove 6/7 (Bibliography); MGG (Bibliography); PAB-MI/2 (Bibliography); Riemann 12 (Bibliography); Schmidl.

C0457.
Gilbert, Kenneth. Canadian Harpsichordist/Organist; b. December 16,
1931, Montreal.

1. Baker 7; Grove 6/7; PAB-MI/2 (Bibliography).

C0458.
Gilels, Emil Grigor'yevich. Soviet Pianist; b. October 19, 1916, Odessa;
d. October 14, 1985, Moscow.

1. Baker 7 (Bibliography); DEU (Bibliography); Grove 6/7 (Bibliography);
   MGG/Supp. (Bibliography); PAB-MI/2 (Bibliography); Riemann 12 + Supp.
   (Bibliography).

2. GR 57/June; RS 80.

4. Khentova, Sof'ia Mikhailovna. Emil' Gilel's. Moskva: Gos. musykal'noe
   izd-vo, 1959. 181 p., illus.

   2nd edition (Moskva: Muzika, 1967). 277 p., illus., bibliographical
   footnotes.

5. A0060, A0069, A0091.

C0459.
Gillespie, Dizzy [John Birks]. American Jazz Trumpeter; b. October 21,
1917, Cheraw, South Carolina.

1. Baker 7; DEU (Bibliography); EdS (Bibliography); Grove 6/7 (Bibliography); Grove-AM (Bibliography - 20 entries); Grove-Jazz; JB (27
   entries); JRRM (28 entries); LJ; PAB-MI/2 (Bibliography); Riemann 12
   + Supp. (Bibliography).

2. DB 25/2, 27/13, 32/13, 33/8, 39/9, 40/14, 45/8, 53/1; HiFi/MusAm
   26/1; MQ 59/4.

3. Gillespie, Dizzy with Al Fraser. to BE, or not...to Bop: Memoirs.
   Garden City (NY): Doubleday & Company, Inc., 1979. xix, 552 p. + 24
   plates, 94 illus., chronology, selected discography, filmorgraphy,
   index.

4. Goetze, Werner. Dizzy Gillespie: ein Portraet. Wetzlar: Pegasus
   Verlag, 1960. 48 p., + 8 plates, 15 illus., discography, 8-item
   bibliography.

   Horricks, Raymond. Dizzy Gillespie and the Be-Bop Revolution. New
   York: Hippocrene Books Inc, 1984. 95 p., illus., selected discography by Tony Middleton, 10-item bibliography.

   James, Michael. Dizzy Gillespie. London: Cassell and Company Limited,
   1959. 89 p., illus., discography.

5. A0001, A0006, A0025, A0029.

C0460.
Gil-Marchex, Henri. French Pianist; b. December 16, 1894, St. Georges
d'Espéranee (Isère); d. November 22, 1970, Paris.

1. Baker 7; Riemann 12 + Supp. (Bibliography).

C0461.
Gimpel, Bronislaw. American Violinist; b. January 29, 1911, Lemberg
(Lwow), Austria; d. May 1, 1979, Los Angeles, California.

1. Baker 7; DEU; Grove 6/7; Grove-AM (Bibliography); Riemann 12 + Supp.

2. Strad Dec/1976.

C0462.
Gimpel, Jacob. American Pianist, brother of Bronislaw; b. April 16,
1906, Lemberg (Lwow), Austria.

1. Baker 7; PAB-MI/2 (Bibliography); Riemann/Supp.

C0463.
Gingold, Josef. American Violinist; b. October 28, 1909, Brest-Litovsk,
Russia.

1. Baker 7; Grove 6/7; Grove-AM (Bibliography); PAB-MI/2 (Bibliography).

2. Strad March/1983.

3. An autobiography exists in MS.

C0464.
Giornovichi, Giovanni Mane [Jarnowick]. Italian Violinist; b. c.1735,
Raguso or Palermo; d. November 23, 1804, St. Petersburg, Russia,

1. Baker 7 (Bibliography); DEU (under Jarnovič); Fetis 2/4 (under
   Jarnowick); Grove 6/7 (Bibliography); Riemann 12 (under Jarnowick -
   Bibliography) + Supp. (Bibliography); Schmidl.

4. Nunamaker, Norman Kurt. The Virtuoso Violin Concerto before Paganini:
   the Concertos of Lolli, Giornovichi, and Waldemar (1750-1815). Ph.D.
   diss. Indiana University, 1968. vii, 258 p., illus., tables, music.

5. B0092.

C0465.
Gitlis, Ivry. Israeli Violinist; b. August 22, 1922, Haifa.

1. Baker 7; DEU; Grove 6/7; PAB-MI/2 (Bibliography); Riemann 12/Supp.

3. Gitlis, Ivry. L'Ame et la corde. Paris: Editions Robert Laffont,
   1980. 284, [1] p. + 4 plates, 16 illus.

C0466.
Giuliani, Mauro Giuseppe Sergio Pantaleo. Italian Guitarist; b. July 27,
1781, Bisceglie, near Bari; d. May 8, 1829, Naples.

1. Baker 7 (Bibliography); DEU (Bibliography); Fetis 2/4; Grove 6/7
   (Bibliography); Mendel; MGG/Supp. (Bibliography); PAB-MI/2 (Bibliog-
   raphy); Riemann 12 (Bibliography) + Supp. (Bibliography); Schmidl +
   Supp.

4. Heck, Thomas F. The Birth of the Classic Guitar and Its Cultivation in Vienna, Reflected in the Career and Compositions of Mauro Giuliani (d. 1829). 2 vols. Ph.D. diss. Yale University, 1970. x, 286 p., 8-part comprehensive research bibliography; xiv, 218 p. + 60 p. music, thematic catalogue, appendices, bibliography.

C0467.
Gleason, Harold. American Organist; b. April 26, 1892, Jefferson, Ohio; d. June 27, 1980, La Jolla, California.

1. Baker 7; Grove-AM; PAB-MI/2 (Bibliography).

C0468.
Goddard, Arabella. English Pianist; b. January 12, 1836, St.-Servan, near Saint-Malo, France; d. April 6, 1922, Boulogne, France.

1. Baker 7; Grove 6/7; Mendel; PAB-MI/2 (Bibliography); Riemann 12 (under James William Davison); Schmidl.

C0469.
Godowsky, Leopold. American Pianist; b. February 13, 1870, Soshly, near Vilna, Poland; d. November 21, 1938, New York City.

1. Baker 7 (Bibliography); DEU (Bibliography); Grove 6/7 (Bibliography); Grove-AM (Bibliography); MGG (Bibliography); PAB-MI/2 (Bibliography); Riemann 12 (Bibliography) + Supp. (Bibliography); Schmidl.

2. HiFi/SR 10/2.

5. B0028.

There is a special collection of materials relating to the life and career of Godowsky in the Library of Congress. "...one of the out-standing masters of the piano..." Baker 7.

SEE: Godowsky, Dagmar. First Person Plural: the Lives of Dagmar Godowsky. New York: The Viking Press, 1958.

C0470.
Goldberg, Johann Gottlieb. German Organist/Harpsichordist; baptized March 14, 1727, Danzig; d. April 13, 1756, Dresden.

1. Baker 7; DEU; Fetis 2/4; Grove 6/7 (Bibliography); Mendel; MGG (Bibliography); PAB-MI/2 (Bibliography); Riemann 12 (Bibliography) + Supp. (Bibliography); Schmidl.

4. Dadder, Ernst A. Johann Gottlieb Goldberg: Leben und Werke. Ph.D. diss. University of Bonn, 1923.

C0471.
Goldberg, Szymon. American Violinist; b. June 1. 1901, Wloclawek, Poland.

1. Baker 7; DEU; Grove 6/7 (Bibliography); Grove-AM (Bibliography); MGG/Supp.; PAB-MI/2 (Bibliography); Riemann 12 + Supp.

4. Gavoty, Bernard. Szymon Goldberg. Genève: René Kister, 1960. 30,
   [3] p., 22 illus., discography.

C0472.
Goldsand, Robert. American Pianist; b. March 17, 1911, Vienna, Austria.

1. Baker 7; Grove 6/7; Grove-AM; PAB-MI/2 (Bibliography); Riemann 12.

C0473.
Goldschmidt, Otto Moritz David. German Pianist; b. August 21, 1829,
Hamburg; d. February 24, 1907, London, England.

1. Baker 7; DEU (Bibliography); Fetis 2/4; Grove 6/7 (Bibliography);
   MGG (Bibliography); Riemann 12; Schmidl.

5. SEE: Cowden, Robert H. under Charles-Auguste de Bériot (C0116.4).
      NOTE: entries under Jenny Lind.

C0474.
Goldstein, Mikhail. Soviet Violinist; b. November 8, 1917, Odessa.

1. Baker 7; Riemann 12/Supp.

3. Goldstein, Mikhail Emanulilovich. Zapiski muzykania. Frankfurt/M.:
   p.p., n.d. 141 p., portrait.

C0475.
Goode, Richard. American Pianist; b. June 1, 1943, New York City.

1. Baker 7; Grove 6/7; Grove-AM.

2. HiFi/MusAm 31/10.

C0476.
Goodman, Benny [Benjamin David]. American Clarinetist; b. May 30, 1909,
Chicago, Illinois; d. June 13, 1986, New York City.

1. Baker 7; DEU (Bibliography); Grove 6/7 (Bibliography); Grove-AM (Bibliography - 13 entries); Grove-Jazz; JB (35 entries); JRRM (29
   entries); LJ; MGG/Supp. (Bibliography); PAB-MI/2 (Bibliography);
   Riemann 12 + Supp. (Bibliography).

2. DB 23/3-5, 29/11, 31/9, 31/20, 33/15, 35/5, 37/21, 44/19, 45/11,
   49/9; HiFi/SR 47/2.

3. Goodman, Benny with Irving Kolodin. The Kingdom of Swing. New York:
   Stackpole, 1939. Reprint 1961. 265 p., 5 illus.

4. Connor, D. Russell and Warren W.B.G. Hicks. Benny Goodman: a Bio-
   Discography of Benny Goodman. New Rochelle (NY): Arlington House
   Publishers, 1969. 691 p., 2 recordings.

   Connor, D. Russell. The Record of a Legend - Benny Goodman. New York:
   Let's Dance Corporation, 1984. 382 p., illus., index.

5. A0006, B0087.

C0477.
Goodman, Isador. South African Pianist; b. May 27, 1909, Capetown.
                                        d. December 2, 1982, Capetown.
1. Grove 6/7.

4. Goodman, Virginia. Isador Goodman, a Life in Music. Sydney: William
   Collins Pty Ltd, 1983. 215 p. + 8 plates, 28 illus., index.

C0478.
Goodson, Katharine. English Pianist; b. June 18, 1872, Watford, Hertfordshire; d. April 14, 1958, London.

1. Baker 7; Riemann 12; Schmidl/Supp.

C0479.
Goossens, Leon Jean. English Oboist; b. June 12, 1897, Liverpool.

1. Baker 7; DEU; Grove 6/7; PAB-MI/2 (Bibliography); Riemann 12 + Supp.
   (Bibliography).

4. Wynne, Barry. Music in the Wind: the Story of Leon Goossens and His
   Triumph over a Shattering Accident. London: Souvenir Press Ltd.,
   1967. vii, 119 p. + 6 plates, 23 illus.

C0480.
Gordon, Dexter Keith. American Jazz Tenor Saxophonist; b. February 27,
1923, Los Angeles, California.

1. Baker 7; DEU; Grove-AM (Bibliography); Grove-Jazz; JB; JRRM; LJ;
   PAB-MI/2 (Bibliography).

2. DB 28/23, 36/11, 39/12, 44/3.

5. A0035, A0159.

C0481.
Gordon, Jacques. American Violinist; b. March 7, 1899, Odessa, Russia;
d. September 15, 1948, Hartford, Connecticut.

1. Baker 7; Grove-AM; Riemann 12.

C0482.
Gorodnitzki, Sasha. American Pianist; b. May 24, 1905, Kiev, Ukraine,
Russia; d. April 4, 1986, New York City.

1. Baker 7; Grove-AM (Bibliography).

C0483.
Gottschalk, Louis Moreau. American Pianist; b. May 8, 1829, New Orleans,
Louisiana; d. December 18, 1869, Rio de Janeiro, Brazil.

1. Baker 7 (Bibliography); DEU (Bibliography); Fetis 2/Supp. (Bibliography); Grove 6/7 (Bibliography); Grove-AM (Bibliography); Mendel;

MGG (Bibliography); PAB-MI/2 (Bibliography); Riemann 12 (Bibliography) + Supp. (Bibliography); Schmidl.

"...acknowledged as one of the most important 19th-century American musicians." Grove-AM.

2. HiFi/SR 21/3; MQ 6/2, 18/1, 31/3, 33/3.

3. Gottschalk, Louis Moreau. Notes of a Pianist during His Professional Tours in the United States, Canada, the Antilles, and South America. Edited by Clara Gottschalk. Translated by Robert E. Peterson. Philadelphia: J.B. Lippincott & Co., 1881. xxxi, 480 p., portrait.

There is an edited edition with explanatory notes by Jeanne Behrand (New York, 1964).

4. Arpin, P. Biographie L.M. Gottschalk, pianiste Américain. New York: Imprimerie du Courrier des Etas-Unis, 1853. 64 p., list of works.

Doyle, John G. Louis Moreau Gottschalk 1829-1869: a Bibliographical Study and Catalog of Works. Detroit: Information Coordinators [published for the College Music Society], 1982. x, 386 p., catalog of compositions, index to recorded compositions, index.

Hensel, Octavia [pseud. for Mary Alice Ives Seymour]. Life and Letters of Louis Moreau Gottschalk. Boston: Oliver Ditson, 1870. 213 p.

Lang, Francisco Curt. Vida y muerte de Louis Moreau Gottschalk en Rio de Janeiro (1869). Mendoza: Universidad Nacional de Cuyo, 1951. 286, [6] p., illus.

Loggins, Vernon. Where the World Ends: the Life of Louis Moreau Gottschalk. Baton Rouge: Louisiana State University Press, 1958. xii, 273 p., bibliographical notes, index.

Korf, William E. The Orchestral Music of Louis Moreau Gottschalk. Stroudsburg: Sun Presse, 1983. iii, 162 p., 131-item bibliography, notes, discography.

Rubin, L. Gottschalk in Cuba. Ph.D. diss. Columbia University, 1974. 223 p., bibliography.

5. A0014, A0016, A0023, A0051.

C0484.
Gould, Glenn Herbert. Canadian Pianist; b. September 25, 1932, Toronto; d. October 4, 1982, Toronto.

1. Baker 7; DEU (Bibliography); Grove 6/7 (Bibliography); PAB-MI/2 (Bibliography); Riemann 12 + Supp. (Bibliography).

2. GR 50/February; HiFi/MusAm 17/11, 20/6, 24/2, 33/1, 33/2; HiFi/SR 10/6, 12/4; CK(KB) 6/8, 9/2; PQ 79, 85, 87, 94, 105, 110, 115, 120, 135.

3. Gould, Glenn. _Variations by Himself and His Friends_. Edited by John McGreevy. Foreword by Herbert von Karajan. Toronto: Doubleday Canada Limited, 1983. 319 p., 45 illus., notes on contributors, 51-item bibliography, published compositions, discography, filmography, radio documentaries.

4. Cott, Jonathan. _Conversations with Glenn Gould_. Boston: Little, Brown and Company, 1984. 159 p., 19 illus., discography, private tapes, radio and TV programs, filmography.

   Payzant, Geoffrey. _Glenn Gould Music & Mind_. Toronto: Van Norstrand Reinhold Ltd., 1978. xiii, 192 p. + 16 plates, 22 illus., notes, 45-item bibliography, published compositions, filmography, discography, index.

5. A0033, A0060, A0069, B0055.

   SEE: Lipman, Samuel. _The House of Music: Art in an Era of Institutions_. Boston: David R. Godine, Publisher, 1984.

C0485.
Graffman, Gary. American Pianist; b. October 14, 1928, New York City.

1. Baker 7; Grove 6/7; Grove-AM; PAB-MI/2 (Bibliography); Riemann 12/ Supp.

2. CL 21/6, 25/6; CK(KB) 4/12.

3. Graffman, Gary. _I Really Should Be Practicing_. Garden City (NY): Doubleday & Company, Inc., 1981. x, 350 p., illus., index of names.

5. B0058.

C0486.
Grandjany, Marcel [Georges Lucien]. American Harpist; b. September 3, 1891, Paris, France; d. February 24, 1975, New York City.

1. Baker 7; DEU; Grove 6/7; Grove-AM; MGG/Supp. (Bibliography); PAB-MI/2 (Bibliography); Riemann 12 + Supp.

4. Ingelfield, Ruth K. _Marcel Grandjany: Concert Harpist, Composer, and Teacher_. Washington: University Press of America, 1977. vi, 119 p., 26 illus.

C0487.
Grappelli, Stéphane. French Jazz Violinist; b. January 26, 1908, Paris.

1. Baker 7; DEU (under Grapelly); Grove 6/7; Grove-Jazz; JB; PAB-MI/2 (Bibliography); Riemann 12/Supp.

2. DB 48/4, 48/5; Strad Nov/1979.

4. Horricks, Raymond. _Stephane Grappelli or the Violin with Wings: a Profile_. Tunbridge Wells (Kent): Midas Books, 1983. 134 p., 45 illus., discography by Tony Middleton, index of names.

5.   A0004.

C0488.
Graudan, Nicolai. American Cellist; b. September 5, 1896, Libau, Russia;
d. August 9, 1964, Moscow.

1. Baker 7; DEU; Grove 6/7; Grove-AM.

C0489.
de Greef, Arthur. Belgian Pianist; b. October 10, 1862, Louvain; d.
August 29, 1940, Brussels.

1. Baker 7 (Bibliography); DEU (Bibliography); Grove 6/5 (under De
   Greef - Bibliography); Riemann 12 (under De Greef); Schmidl (under
   De Greef).

2. RS 29-30.

5. B0028.

C0490.
Greenhouse, Bernard. American Cellist; b. January 3, 1916, Newark, NJ.

1. Baker 7; Grove 6/7; Grove-AM; Riemann 12/Supp.

2. Strad Sept/1987.

C0491.
Gregoir, Jacques Mathieu Joseph. Belgian Pianist; b. January 19, 1817,
Antwerp; d. October 29, 1876, Brussels.

1. Baker 7; DEU; Fetis 2/Supp.; Grove 6/7; Riemann 12; Schmidl.

C0492.
Grimm, Karl Konstantin Ludwig. German Harpist; b. February 17, 1820,
Berlin; d. May 23, 1882, Berlin.

1. Baker 7; Fetis 2/Supp.; Grove 6/7 (Bibliography).

C0493.
de Groot, Cor[nelis Wilhelmus]. Dutch Pianist; b. July 7, 1914.

1. Baker 7; DEU; MGG/Supp. (Bibliography); Riemann 12 + Supp. (Bibliography).

C0494.
Gruemmer, Paul. German Cellist; b. February 26, 1879, Gera; d. October
30, 1965, Zug, Switzerland.

1. Baker 7; DEU; Grove 6/7 (Bibliography); MGG/Supp. (Bibliography);
   Riemann 12; Schmidl/Supp.

3. Gruemmer, Paul. Begegungen aus dem Leben eines Violoncellisten.
   Muenchen, 1963. No copy located.

C0495.
Gruenberg, Erich. English Violinist; b. October 12, 1924, Vienna.

1. Baker 7; Grove 6/7 (Bibliography).

2. Strad May/1975, May/1984.

C0496.
Gruenfeld, Alfred. Austrian Pianist; b. July 4, 1852, Prague; d. January 4, 1924, Vienna.

1. Baker 7; Riemann 12; Schmidl + Supp.

C0497.
Gruenfeld, Heinrich. Austrian Cellist, brother of **Alfred**; b. April 21, 1855, Prague; d. August 26, 1931, Berlin, Germany.

1. Baker 7; Riemann 12.

3. Gruenfeld, Heinrich. In Dur und Moll: Begegnungen und Erlebnisse aus Fuenfzig Jahren. Geleitwort von Gerhart Hauptmann. Leipzig: Grethlein & Co., 1923. 279, [3] p., 9 illus., index of names.

C0498.
Gruetzmacher, Friedrich Wilhelm Ludwig. German Cellist; b. March 1, 1832, Dessau; d. February 23, 1903, Dresden.

1. Baker 7; DEU; Fetis 2/Supp.; Grove 6/7 (Bibliography); Mendel; MGG; Riemann 12 + Supp. (Bibliography); Schmidl.

2. Strad Nov/1978.

4. Luetzen, Ludolf. Die Violoncell-Transkriptionen Friedrich Gruetzmachers: Untersuchungen zur Transkription in Sicht und Handhabung der 2. Haelfte des 19. Jahrhunderts. Regensburg: Gustav Bosse Verlag, 1974. [iv], 260 p., 107-item bibliography.

5. A0104.

C0499.
Grumiaux, Arthur. Belgian Violinist; b. March 21, 1921, Villers-Perwin; d. October 16, 1986, Brussels.

1. Baker 7; DEU; Grove 6/7; MGG; PAB-MI/2 (Bibliography); Riemann 12.

2. GR 48/January.

5. A0008.

C0500.
Grunenwald, Jean-Jacques. French Organist; b. February 2, 1911, Cran-Gevrier, near Annecy; d. December 19, 1982, Paris.

1. Baker 7; DEU (Bibliography); Grove 6/7; MGG (Bibliography); PAB-MI/2 (Bibliography); Riemann 12 (Bibliography) + Supp. (Bibliography).

5. SEE: Machabey, Armand. Portraits de trente musiciens francais. Paris: Richard-Masse Editeurs, 1949. 169, [7] p., 31 portraits.

C0501.
Guénin, Marie Alexandre. French Violinist; b. February 20, 1744, Maubeuge; d. January 22, 1835, Etampes.

1. Baker 7; DEU (Bibliography); Fetis 2/4; Grove 6/7 (Bibliography); Mendel; MGG (Bibliography); Riemann 12 + Supp. (Bibliography); Schmidl.

C0502.
Guillemain, Louis Gabriel. French Violinist; b. November 7, 1705, Paris; d. October 1, 1770, Paris.

1. Baker 7; DEU (Bibliography); Fetis 2/4 + Supp.; Grove 6/7 (Bibliography); MGG (Bibliography); Riemann 12 (Bibliography) + Supp. (Bibliography).

There is important material in the Archives des Yvelines.

C0503.
Guillon, Jean. French Organist; b. April 4, 1930, Angers.

1. Baker 7; Grove 6/7; PAB-MI/2 (Bibliography).

C0504.
Guilmant, Félix Alexandre. French Organist; b. March 12, 1837, Boulogne; d. March 29, 1911, Meudon, near Paris.

1. Baker 7 (Bibliography); DEU (Bibliography); Fetis 2/Supp.; Grove 6/7 (Bibliography); MGG (Bibliography); PAB-MI/2 (Bibliography); Riemann 12 (Bibliography) + Supp. (Bibliography); Schmidl

5. SEE: D'Indy, Vincent. La schola cantorum en 1925. Paris: Librairie Bloud et Gay, 1927.

C0505.
Gulda, Friedrich. Austrian Pianist; b. May 16, 1930, Vienna.

1. Baker 7; DEU (Bibliography); Grove 6/7 (Bibliography); Grove-Jazz; JB (10 entries); MGG; PAB-MI/2 (Bibliography); Riemann 12 + Supp. (Bibliography).

2. DB 30/13.

4. Geitel, Klaus. Fragen an Friedrich Gulda: Anmerkungen zu Musik und Gesellschaft. Berlin: Rembrandt Verlag, 1973. 53 p., 12 illus., chronology, discography.

Jantsch, Erich. Friedrich Gulda: die Verantwortung des Interpreten. Wien: Josef Weinberger, 1953. 60 p. + 1 plate, 4 illus., sources of reviews, discography, chronology.

5. A0008.

C0506.
Gulli, Franco. Italian Violinist; b. September 1, 1926, Trieste.

1. Baker 7; DEU; Grove 6/7; PAB-MI/2 (Bibliography); Riemann 12/Supp.

2. Strad Aug/1985.

C0507.
Gumpert, Friedrich Adolf. German French-horn Player; b. April 27, 1841, Lichtenau; d. December 31, 1906, Leipzig.

1. Baker 7; Grove 6/7 (under Gumbert); Schmidl (under Gumbert).

C0508.
Gusikoff, Michel. American Violinist; b. May 15, 1893, New York City; d. July 10, 1978, New York City.

1. Baker 7; Grove-AM; PAB-MI/2 (Bibliography).

His great-grandfather, **Michal Jozef Guzikov** (b. September 14, 1806, Szklow, Poland; d. October 21, 1937, Aachen, Germany), was a virtuoso performer on the Xylophone.

C0509.
Gutmann, Adolph. German Pianist; b. January 12, 1819, Heidelberg; d. October 27, 1882, Spezia.

1. Baker 7; Fetis 2/4; Mendel; PAB-MI/2 (Bibliography); Schmidl.

C0510.
Haas, Monique. French Pianist; b. October 20, 1906, Paris.

1. Baker 7; DEU; Grove 6/8; PAB-MI/2 (Bibliography); Riemann 12 + Supp.

C0511.
Haas, Werner. German Pianist; b. March 3, 1931, Stuttgart; d. October 13, 1976, Nancy, France.

1. Baker 7; DEU; Riemann 12/Supp.

C0512.
Haberbier, Ernst. German Pianist; b. October 5, 1813, Koenigsberg; d. March 12, 1869, Bergen, Norway.

1. Baker 7; Fetis 2/4 + Supp.; Mendel; Schmidl.

C0513.
Hackett, Bobby [Robert Leo]. American Jazz Cornetist/Guitarist; b. January 31, 1915, Providence, Rhode Island; d, June 7, 1976, West Chatham, Massachusetts.

1. Baker 7; Grove-AM (Bibliography); Grove-Jazz; LJ; PAB-MI/2 (Bibliography).

2. DB 18/3, 24/3.

5. SEE: Balliett, Whitney. <u>Alec Wilder and His Friends</u>. Boston: Houghton
     Mifflin Company, 1974.

C0514.
Haebler, Ingrid. Austrian Pianist; b. June 20, 1926, Vienna.

1. Baker 7; Grove 6/8; PAB-MI/2 (Bibliography); Riemann 12 + Supp.

C0515.
Haendel, Ida. British Violinist; b. December 15, 1924, Chelm, Poland.

1. Baker 7; Grove 6/8; PAB-MI/2 (Bibliography); Riemann 12/Supp.

3. Haendel, Ida. <u>Woman with Violin: an Autobiography</u>. London: Victor
     Gollancz Ltd, 1970. 334 p., 11 illus., index.

C0516.
Haig, Al [Allan Warren]. American Jazz Pianist; b. July 22, 1924,
Newark, New Jersey; d. November 16, 1982, New York City.

1. Baker 7; DEU (Bibliography); Grove 6/8 (Bibliography); Grove-AM (Bib-
     liography - 11 entries); Grove-Jazz; PAB-MI/2 (Bibliography).

C0517.
Halič, Carl. Czechoslovakian Violinist; b. February 1, 1859, Hohenelbe,
Bohemia; d. December 21, 1909, Berlin, Germany.

1. Baker 7; DEU; Grove 6/8 (Bibliography); Riemann 12; Schmidl.

C0518.
Hall, Elsie [Maud Stanley]. South African Pianist; b. June 22, 1877;
Toowoomba, Queensland; d. June 27, 1976, Cape Town.

1. Grove 6/8 (Bibliography).

3. Hall, Elsie. <u>The Good Die Young: the Autobiography of Elsie Hall</u>.
     Cape Town: Constantia Publishers, 1969. 106 p. + 5 plates, 15 illus.

C0519.
Hall, Marie [Mary Paulina]. English Violinist; b. April 8, 1884, Newcastle upon Tyne; d. November 11, 1956, Cheltenham.

1. Baker 7 (Bibliography); Grove 6/8; Riemann 12; Schmidl/Supp.

5. B0053.

C0520.
Hambourg, Mark. British Pianist; b. June 12, 1879, Bogutchar, Russia;
d. August 26, 1960, Cambridge, England.

1. Baker 7; DEU; Grove 6/8 (Bibliography); MGG/Supp. (Bibliography);
     PAB-MI/2 (Bibliography); Riemann 12; Schmidl/Supp.

3. Hambourg, Mark. <u>From Piano to Forte: a Thousand and One Notes</u>.
     London: Cassell and Company Ltd, 1931. 310, [1] p., 16 illus., index.

Hambourg, Mark. How to Play the Piano. Philadelphia: Theodore Presser Company, 1922. viii, [i], 122 p., illus.

Hambourg, Mark. The Eighth Octave: Tones and Semi-Tones Concerning Piano-Playing, the Savage Club, and Myself. London: Williams and Norgate Ltd., 1951. 164 p., 9 illus., index.

5. A0047, B0028, B0053.

C0521.
Hamm, Adolf. Swiss Organist; b. March 9, 1882, Strasbourg; d. October 15, 1938, Basel.

1. Baker 7; Riemann 12.

4. Sacher, Paul, ed. Adolf Hamm 1882-1938, Organist am Muenster zu Basel: Erinnerungsschrift. Basel: Holbein-Verlag, 1942. 391 p., 7 illus., list of concerts, list of works,

C0522.
Hampton, Lionel. American Jazz Vibraphonist; b. April 12, 1909, Louisville, Kentucky.

1. Baker 7; DEU (Bibliography); EdS (Bibliography); Grove 6/8 (Bibliography); Grove-AM (Bibliography); Grove-Jazz; JB (11 entries); JRRM; PAB-MI/2 (Bibliography); Riemann 12 + Supp. (Bibliography).

A pioneer who brought the vibraphone into the mainstream of jazz.

2. DB 26/7, 29/10, 32/9, 39/8, 45/14.

5. A0001, A0006.

C0523.
Hancock, Herbie [Herbert Jeffrey]. American Jazz Pianist; b. April 12, 1940, Chicago, Illinois.

1. Baker 7; DEU; Grove-AM (Bibliography); Grove-Jazz; JB; JRRM; PAB-MI/2 (Bibliography).

2. DB 32/22, 36/9, 38/2, 40/10, 41/17, 44/15, 46/10, 49/9, 53/7; HiFi/MusAm 27/9; CK(KB) 3/11, 6/3, 9/2.

C0524.
Harasiewicz, Adam. Polish Pianist; b. July 1, 1932, Chodziez.

1. Baker 7; DEU; Riemann 12/Supp.

C0525.
Harich-Schneider, Eta. German Harpsichordist; b. November 16, 1897, Oranienburg, Berlin.

1. DEU; Grove 6/8 (Bibliography); MGG/Supp. (Bibliography); PAB-MI/2 (Bibliography); Riemann 12 (Bibliography) + Supp. (Bibliography).

3. Harich-Schneider, Eta. Charaktera und Katastrophen: Augenzeugen-berichte einer reisenden Musikerin. Frankfurt/M.: Verlag Ullstein GmbH, 1978. 483, [1] p. + 4 plates, 21 illus., index of names.

C0526.
Harrell, Lynn. American Cellist; b. January 30, 1944, New York City.

1. Baker 7; Grove 6/8; Grove-AM (Bibliography); PAB-MI/2 (Bibliography).

He became first cellist of the Cleveland Orchestra at age twenty-one!

2. Strad May/1978, Nov/1986.

C0527.
Harrison, Beatrice. English Cellist; b. December 9, 1892, Roorke, India; d. March 10, 1965, Smallfield, Surrey.

1. Baker 7; Grove 6/8 (Bibliography).

Her sister, Mary (b. March, 1891, Roorke, India; d. June 8, 1959, South Nutfield, Surrey), was a violinist.

3. Harrison, Beatrice. The Cello and the Nightingales: the Autobiography of Beatrice Harrison. Edited by Patricia Cleveland-Peck. London: John Murray (Publishers) Ltd., 1985. 176 p. + 6 plates, 26 illus., discography, index.

C0528.
Harrison, Hazel Lucile. American Pianist; b. May 12, 1883, La Porte, Indiana; d. April 28, 1969, Washington, D.C.

1. Grove-AM (Bibliography); PAB-MI/2 (Bibliography).

4. Cazort, Jean E. and Constance Tibbs Hobson. Born to Play: the Life and Career of Hazel Harrison. Westport (CT): Greenwood Press, 1983. xviii, 171 p., 12 illus., chronology, notes, 22-item bibliography, index.

C0529.
Harrison, Sidney. English Pianist; b. May 4, 1903, London.

1. Grove 6/8 (Bibliography); PAB-MI/2 (Bibliography).

3. Harrison, Sidney. Teacher Never Told Me. London: Elek Books Limited, 1961. 200 p.

C0530.
Harth, Sidney. American Violinist; b. October 5, 1929, Cleveland, Ohio.

1. Baker 7; Grove 6/8; Grove-AM (Bibliography); PAB-MI/2 (Bibliography); Riemann 12/Supp.

C0531.
Hartmann, Arthur. American Violinist; b. July 23, 1881, Maté Szalka, Hungary; d. March 30, 1956, New York City.

1. Baker 7; Grove-AM (Bibliography); PAB-MI/2 (Bibliography); Schmidl/
   Supp.

C0532.
Haskil, Clara. Romanian Pianist; b. January 7, 1895, Bucharest;
d. December 7, 1960, Brussels, Belgium.

1. Baker 7; DEU; Grove 6/8 (Bibliography); MGG/Supp.; PAB-MI/2 (Bibliography); Riemann 12 + Supp. (Bibliography).

2. RS 63-64.

4. Gavoty, Bernard. Clara Haskil. Genève: René Kister, 1962. 32 p., 30
   illus., discography.

   Spycket, Jérôme. Clara Haskil. Préface by Herbert von Karajan.
   Lausanne: Editions Payot, 1975. 280, [3] p. + 13 plates, 63 illus.,
   discography, repertoire.

   Wolfensberger, Rita. Clara Haskil. Bern: Alfred Scherz Verlag, 1961.
   168, [1] p. + 7 plates, 7 illus., discography, index of names.

   Contributors include Pierre Fournier, Ferenc Fricsay, Rafael Kubelik,
   Igor Markevitch, and Peter Rybar.

5. B0080.

C0533.
Haupt, Karl August. German Organist; b. August 25, 1810, Kuhnau,
Silesia; d. July 4, 1891, Berlin.

1. Baker 7; DEU; Fetis 2/4; Mendel; Riemann 12; Schmidl.

C0534.
Hauschka, Vincenz. Bohemian Cellist; b. January 21, 1766, Mies, Bohemia;
d. September 13, 1840, Vienna, Austria.

1. Baker 7; DEU (under Houška - Bibliography); Fetis 2/4; Mendel; MGG
   (Bibliography); Riemann 12 (Bibliography).

3. His MS autobiography (1826) is in the library of the Gesellschaft der
   Musikfreunde in Vienna. It was edited by J. Peschek and published in
   the Festschrift der Bergstadt Mies (Mies, 1931).

C0535.
Hauser, Miska. Austrian Violinist; b. 1822, Pressburg (Bratislava);
d. December 8, 1887, Vienna.

1. Baker 7; DEU; Fetis 2/Supp.; Mendel; MGG (Bibliography); Riemann 12
   (Bibliography); Schmidl.

3. Hauser, Miska. Aus dem Wanderbuche eines Oesterreichischen Virtuosen:
   Briefe aus Californien, Suedamerika und Australien. Compiled and
   Edited by Sigmund Hauser. Leipzig: Friedr. Ludw. Herbig, 1859. viii,
   239 p.

Translated by Eric Benson, Donald Peet Cobb, and Horatio F. Stoll, Jr. as Letters of Miska Hauser (San Francisco: WPA History of Music in San Francisco, Volume 3, May, 1939).

5. B0070.

C0536.
Hausmann, Robert. German Cellist; b. August 13, 1852, Rottleberode, Harz; d. January 18, 1909, Vienna, Austria.

1. Baker 7; Grove 6/8; Riemann 12; Schmidl.

He inherited his uncle's 1724 Stradivarius known as "The Hausmann".

C0537.
Havemann, Gustav. German Violinist; b. March 15, 1882, Guestrow; d. January 2, 1960, Schoeneiche, near Berlin.

1. Baker 7; DEU; MGG/Supp.; Riemann 12 + Supp. (Bibliography); Schmidl/ Supp.

C0538.
Hawes, Hampton. American Jazz Pianist; b. November 13, 1928, Los Angeles, California; d. May 19, 1977, Los Angeles.

1. Grove-Jazz; JB; LJ; PAB-MI/2 (Bibliography).

2. DB 24/15, 33/21, 35/21, 39/17.

3. Hawes, Hampton and Don Asher. Raise Up off Me. New York: Coward, McCann & Geoghegan, Inc., 1974. 179 p.

C0539.
Hawkins, Coleman Randolph. American Jazz Tenor Saxophonist; b. November 21, 1904, St. Joseph, Missouri; d. May 19, 1969, New York City.

1. Baker 7; DEU (Bibliography); EdS (Bibliography); Grove 6/8 (Bibliography); Grove-AM (Bibliography - 16 entries); Grove-Jazz; JB (13 entries); JRRM (12 entries); LJ; Riemann 12 + Supp. (Bibliography).

2. DB 23/23, 30/1, 33/10, 34/20, 35/3.

4. James, Burnett. Coleman Hawkins. New York: Hippocrene Books Inc., 1984. 93 p., illus., selected discography by Tony Middleton, 4-item bibliography.

McCarthy, Albert J. Coleman Hawkins. London: Cassell & Company Ltd, 1963. 89 p.

5. A0159.

C0540.
Haynes, Roy Owen. American Jazz Drummer; b. March 13, 1926, Roxbury, Massachusetts.

1. Baker 7; Grove-AM (Bibliography); Grove-Jazz; PAB-MI/2 (Bibliography).

2. DB 17/24, 29/7, 33/25, 47/2.

C0541.
Heifetz, Jascha. American Violinist; b. February 2, 1901, Vilna, Lithuania; d. December 10, 1987, Los Angeles, California.

1. Baker 7; DEU; Grove 6/8 (Bibliography); Grove-AM (Bibliography); MGG; PAB-MI/2 (Bibliography); Riemann 12 + Supp. (Bibliography); Schmidl.

He is a fabulous artist of extraordinary musical and technical gifts.

2. Grand Baton 12 (1975); HiFi/MusAm 25/8; HiFi/SR 36/2; Strad Feb/1986 (Special Issue); Saturday Review April 24, 1971.

3. There is a special collection of materials by and about Heifetz at the Library of Congress, Washington, D.C.

4. Axelrod, Herbert R., comp. & ed. Heifetz. Neptune City (NJ): Paganiniana Publications, 1976. 506 p., illus., discography by John Anthony Maltese, index.

Contributions by Henry Roth, John A. Maltese, and Constance Hope as well as quotations from interviews with Heifetz are included. The artist filed a seven and a half million dollar lawsuit against both Axelrod and the publisher.

Taylor, Deems. Jascha Heifetz: Biographical Notes, with a Reference to "Music School", His First Motion Picture for Samuel Goldwyn. New York: United Artists Corp., 1939. 16 p., portrait.

Weschler-Vered, Artur. Jascha Heifetz. London: Robert Hale, 1986. 240 p. + 16 plates, 38 illus., discography, 44-item bibliography; references, index.

5. A0008, A0100, A0115, A0132, A0142, B0012, B0030, B0037, B0039, B0045, B0055, B0061, B0086, B0089, B0109, D0012.

C0542.
Heinemeyer, Ernst Wilhelm. German Flutist; b. February 25, 1827, Hannover; d. February 12, 1869, Vienna, Austria.

1. Baker 7; Fetis 2/Supp.; Mendel (under his father, Christian); Riemann 12; Schmidl.

C0543.
Heitmann, Fritz. German Organist; b. May 9, 1891, Ochsenwerder, near Hamburg; d. September 7, 1953, Berlin.

1. Grove 6/8; MGG/Supp.; Riemann 12.

4. Voge, Richard, ed. Fritz Heitmann: das Leben eines Deutschen Organisten. Berlin: Verlag Merseburger, 1963. 167 p., 2 illus.

C0544.
Hekking, Anton. Dutch Cellist; b. September 7, 1856, The Hague;
d. November 18, 1935, Berlin, Germany.

1. Baker 7; DEU; MGG (Bibliography); Riemann 12; Schmidl.

C0545.
Hekking, Gérard Prosper. French Cellist; b. August 22, 1879, Nancy;
d. June 5, 1942, Paris.

1. Baker 7; DEU; MGG (Bibliography); Riemann 12; Schmidl/Supp.

C0546.
Heller, Stephen. Hungarian Pianist; b. May 15, 1813, Pest; d. January
14, 1888, Paris, France.

1. Baker 7 (Bibliography); DEU (Bibliography); Fetis 2/4 + Supp.; Grove
   6/8 (Bibliography); Mendel; MGG (Bibliography); PAB-MI/2 (Bibliography); Riemann 12 (Bibliography) + Supp. (Bibliography); Schmidl.

2. MQ 21/4.

4. Barbedette, M.H. Stephen Heller, sa vie et ses oeuvres. Paris: Maho,
   1876.

   Booth, Ronald Earl, Jr. The Life and Music of Stephen Heller. Ph.D.
   diss. University of Iowa, 1969. 248 p., bibliography.

   Eigeldinger, Jean-Jacques, ed. Stephen Heller: lettres d'un musicien
   romantique à Paris. Paris: Flammarion, 1981. 338 p., 18 illus., Bibliography, index of names, index of music.

   Mueller-Kersten, Ursula. Stephen Heller, ein Klaviermeister der
   Romantik: biographische und stilkritische Studien. Frankfurt am Main:
   Verlag Peter Lang GmbH, 1986. 558 p., index of names, general index,
   bibliography, iconography.

C0547.
Hellmesberger, Georg, Jr. Austrian Violinist; b. January 27, 1830,
Vienna; d. November 12, 1852, Hannover, Germany.

1. Baker 7; DEU; Fetis 2/4; Grove 6/8 (Bibliography); Mendel; MGG (Bibliography); PAB-MI/2 (Bibliography); Riemann 12; Schmidl.

4. Barthlme, Anton. Von alten Hellmesberger: komische Aussprueche und
   Anekdoten. Wien: Verlagsbuchhandlung Carl Konegen, 1908. x, [i], 98,
   [1] p., portrait.

   Prosl, Robert Maria. Die Hellmesberger: Hundert Jahre aus dem Leben
   einer Wiener Musikerfamilie. Wien: Gerlach & Wiedling, 1947. 128,
   [32] p., 32 illus., notes, index of names, list of illustrations.

C0548.
Hellmesberger, Joseph, Sr. Austrian Violinist, brother of George, Jr.;
b. November 3, 1828, Vienna; d. October 24, 1893, Vienna.

1. Baker 7; DEU; Fetis 2/4 + Supp.; Grove 6/8 (Bibliography); Mendel;
   MGG (Bibliography); PAB-MI/2 (Bibliography); Riemann 12 + Supp.
   (Bibliography); Schmidl.

5. B0037.

   SEE: Barthlme, Anton under Georg Hellmesberger, Jr. (C0547.4)

   SEE: Prosl, Robert Maria under Georg Hellmesberger, Jr. (C0547.4).

C0549.
Hemke, Frederik LeRoy. American Saxophonist; b. July 11, 1935,
Milwaukee, Wsiconsin.

1. Baker 7; Grove-AM.

C0550.
Hendrix, Jimi [James Marshall]. American Rock Guitarist; b. November 27,
1942, Seattle, Washington; d. September 18, 1970, London, England.

1. Baker 7 (Bibliography); DEU (Bibliography); Grove-AM (Bibliography);
   PAB-MI/2 (Bibliography); Riemann 12/Supp.

2. DB 35/7, 49/10.

C0551.
Hennes, Therese. German Pianist; b. 1861, Wiesbaden.

1. Mendel.

   Her father, Aloys (b. September 8, 1827, Aachen; d. June 8, 1889,
   Berlin), was a pianist and successful pedagogue. "His daughter,
   Therese, was a child prodigy, who made an exceptionally successful
   tour in England in 1877." Baker 7.

4. Hennes, Aloys. Therese Hennes and Her Musical Education: a Biographical Sketch. Translated by H. Mannheimer. London: Samuel Tinsley,
   1877. vi, 162 p., portrait.

C0552.
von Henselt, Georg Martin Adolph. German Pianist; b. May 9, 1814,
Schwabach, Bavaria; d. October 10, 1889, Warmbrunn, Silesia.

1. Baker 7 (Bibliography); DEU (Bibliography); Fetis 2/4; Grove 6/8
   (Bibliography); Mendel; MGG (Bibliography); Riemann 12 (Bibliography) + Supp. (Bibliography); Schmidl.

5. A0063, B0021, C0984.3.

   SEE: La Mara [pseud. for Ida Maria Lipsius]. Musikalische Studien-
        koepfe. Leipzig: Breitkopf & Haertel, 1868-82. vol. 3 of 5.

C0553.
Herman, Woody [Woodrow Charles]. American Clarinetist; b. May 16, 1913,
Milwaukee, Wisconsin; d. October 29, 1987, Los Angeles, California.

1. Baker 7; DEU (Bibliography); Grove 6/8 (Bibliography); Grove-AM (Bibliography - 13 entries); Grove-Jazz; JB; LJ; PAB-MI/2 (Bibliography); Riemann 12 + Supp. (Bibliography).

2. DB 17/22, 24/14, 25/8, 28/9, 30/10, 35/8, 37/8, 38/17, 41/7, 43/18, 53/11; HiFi/SR 5/4.

C0554.
Hermstedt, Johann Simon. German Clarinetist; b. December 29, 1778, Langensalza; d. August 10, 1846, Sondershausen.

1. Baker 7; DEU (Bibliography); Fetis 2/4; Grove 6/8 (Bibliography); Mendel; MGG (Bibliography); Riemann 12 (Bibliography); Schmidl.

5. SEE: Spohr, Ludwig. Ludwig Spohr's Autobiography. 2 vols. London: Reeves and Turner, 1878 [original published posthumously as Ludwig Spohrs Selbstbiographie. Kassel, 1860/61].

C0555.
Herseth, Adolph. American Trumpeter; b. July 25, 1921, Lake Park, Minnesota.

1. Baker 7; Grove 6/8; Grove-AM (Bibliography).

C0556.
Herz, Henri. Austrian Pianist; b. January 6, 1803, Vienna; d. January 5, 1888, Paris, France.

1. Baker 7; DEU; Fetis 2/4 + Supp.; Grove 6/8 (Bibliography); Mendel; MGG (Bibliography); PAB-MI/2 (Bibliography); Riemann 12 + Supp. (Bibliography); Schmidl.

3. Herz, Henri. Mes voyages en Amérique. Paris: A. Faure, 1866. 328 p. + 2 plates, illus.

This is a reprint of his letters/reports to the Moniteur Universal.

5. A0014, A0016, B0070, B0102.

C0557.
Hess, Myra. English Pianist; b. February 25, 1890, London; d. November 25, 1965, London.

1. Baker 7; DEU (Bibliography); Grove 6/8; PAB-MI/2 (Bibliography); Riemann 12 (Bibliography).

2. RS 24.

4. Lassimonne, Denise, comp. Myra Hess, by Her Friends. Edited by Howard Ferguson. London: Hamish Hamilton Ltd., 1966. xi, 119 p. + 12 plates, 15 illus., discography.

McKenna, Marian Cecilia. Myra Hess: a Portrait. London: Hamish Hamilton Ltd., 1976. xii, 319 p. + 8 plates, 24 illus., discography, notes, index.

5. A0047, B0044.

C0558.
Hess, Willy. German Violinist; b. July 14, 1859, Mannheim; d. February 17, 1939, Berlin.

1. Baker 7 (Bibliography); DEU (Bibliography); Grove (Bibliography); Riemann 12 + Supp (Bibliography); Schmidl/Supp.

C0559.
Hesse-Bukowska, Barbara. Polish Pianist; b. June 1, 1930, Lodz.

1. Baker 7; PAB-MI/2 (Bibliography); Riemann 12/Supp.

C0560.
Higginbotham, J.C. American Jazz Trombonist; b. May 11, 1906, Social Circle, Georgia; d. May 26, 1973, New York City.

1. Baker 7; DEU; Grove-AM (Bibliography); Grove-Jazz; JB; LJ; PAB-MI/2 (Bibliography).

2. DB 8/6, 26/1, 31/3.

C0561.
Hilsberg, Alexander. American Violinist; b. April 24, 1897, Warsaw, Poland; d. August 10, 1961, Camden, Maine.

1. Baker 7 (Bibliography); Grove-AM (Bibliography).

5. A0100.

C0562.
Hinderas [Henderson], Natalie. American Pianist; b. June 15, 1927, Oberlin, Ohio; d. July 22, 1987, Philadelphia, Pennsylvania.

1. Baker 7; Grove-AM (Bibliography); PAB-MI/2 (Bibliography).

2. CK(KB) 3/8.

C0563.
Hines, Earl [Kenneth] "Fatha". American Jazz Pianist; b. December 28, 1905, Duquesne, Pennsylvania; d. April 22, 1983, Oakland, California.

1. Baker 7; DEU (Bibliography); Grove 6/8 (Bibliography); Grove-AM (Bibliography); Grove-Jazz; JB; JRRM; LJ; PAB-MI/2 (Bibliography); Riemann 12 + Supp. (Bibliography).

2. DB 25/22, 30/10, 30/13, 32/18, 46/10; HiFi/SR 32/1, 44/2; CK(KB) 3/11, 8/4.

4. Dance, Stanley. The World of Earl Hines. New York: Charles Scribner's Sons, 1977. ix, 324 p., 145 illus., appendix, chronology, 27-item bibliography, discography, index.

5. A0004, A0006, B0054.

C0564.
Hirt, Al[ois Maxwell]. American Jazz Trumpeter; b. November 7, 1922, New Orleans, Louisiana.

1. Baker 7; Grove-AM (Bibliography); Grove-Jazz; PAB-MI/2 (Bibliography).

2. DB 28/14, 36/18.

C0565.
Hirt, Franz Josef. Swiss Pianist; b. February 7, 1899, Lucerne.

1. Baker 7; Grove 6/8 (Bibliography); PAB-MI/2 (Bibliography); Riemann 12 + Supp.

C0566.
Hirt, Fritz. Swiss Violinist; b. August 9, 1888, Lucerne; d. January 5, 1970, Chigny-sur-Morges.

1. Baker 7; DEU; Riemann 12 + Supp.

C0567.
Hodges, Edward. English Organist; b. July 20, 1796, Bristol; d. September 1, 1867, Clifton.

1. Baker 7 (Bibliography); Fetis 2/Supp.; Grove 6/8 (Bibliography); Grove-AM (Bibliography); Mendel; PAB-MI/2 (Bibliography); Riemann 12; Schmidl/Supp.

4. Hodges, Faustina H. <u>Edward Hodges...Organist of the Churches of St. James...Organist and Director in Trinity Parrish, New York, 1839-1859</u>. New York: G.P. Putnam's Sons, 1896. Reprint 1970. xviii, 302 p., 31 illus.

C0568.
Hodges [Hodge], Johnny or **"Rabbitt"** [John Cornelius]. American Jazz Alto/Soprano Saxophonist; b. July 25, 1906, Cambridge, Massachusetts; d. May 11, 1970, New York City.

1. Baker 7; DEU (Bibliography); Grove 6/8; Grove-AM (Bibliography); Grove-Jazz; JB; PAB-MI/2 (Bibliography); Riemann 12 + Supp. (Bibliography).

2. DB 33/24.

5. A0159.

SEE: Autobiography of **Duke Ellington** (C0357.3).

SEE: Jewell, Derek under **Duke Ellington** (C0357.4).

Hodges played with Ellington's band from 1928 to 1951 rejoining him in 1955 after attempting his own band and septet.

C0569.
Hoelscher, Ludwig. German Cellist; b. August 23, 1907, Solingen.

1. Baker 7 (Bibliography); DEU (Bibliography); Riemann 12 (Bibliography) + Supp. (Bibliography).

4. von Lewinski, Wolf-Eberhard. Ludwig Hoelscher zum 75. Geburtstag. Tutzing: Verlegt bei Hans Schneider, 1967. 78, [2] p. + 11 plates, 39 illus., list of premieres.

   Valentin, Erich. Cello, das Instrument und sein Meister Ludwig Hoelscher. Pfullingen: Verlag Guenther Neske, 1955. 191 p. + 9 plates, 15 illus.

C0570.
Hoffman, Richard. English Pianist; b. May 24, 1831, Manchester; d. August 17, 1909, Mt. Kisco, New York.

1. Baker 7; Grove 6/8 (Bibliography); Grove-AM (Bibliography); Riemann 12.

3. Hoffman, Richard. Some Musical Recollections of Fifty Years...with a Biographical Sketch by His Wife. New York: Charles Scribner's Sons, 1910. Reprint 1976. viii, 108 p. + plates, illus.

C0571.
Hofmann, Josef. American Pianist; b. January 20, 1876, Podgorze, near Cracow, Poland; d. February 16, 1957, Los Angeles, California.

1. Baker 7; DEU (Bibliography); Grove 6/8 (Bibliography); Grove-AM (Bibliography); MGG; PAB-MI/2 (Bibliography); Riemann 12 + Supp (Bibliography); Schmidl + Supp.

2. HiFi 5/7; HiFi/SR 27/6; RS 3, 32.

3. Hofmann, Josef. Piano Playing with Piano Questions Answered. Philadelphia: Theodore Presser Co., 1920 [original 1915]. xiii, 183 p., portrait, index of questions, index.

   Piano Playing (New York: McClure) was first published in 1908, and Piano Questions Answered (New York: Doubleday) appeared in 1909. Hofmann also composed under the pseudonym of Michel Dvorsky. "At the peak of his career, he came to be regarded as one of the greatest pianists of the century." Baker 7.

4. Graydon, Nell S. and Margaret D. Sizemore. The Amazing Marriage of Marie Eustis and Josef Hofmann. Columbia (SC): University of South Carolina Press, 1965. ix, 216 p. + 6 plates, 25 illus., notes and sources, index.

   Husarik, S. Josef Hofmann (1876-1957): the Composer and Pianist, with an Analysis of Available Reproductions of His Performances. Ph.D. diss. University of Iowa, 1983.

5. A0053, B0001, B0008, B0030, B0037, B0089, B0108, B0109.

SEE: Campa, Gustavo E. Críticas musicales. Paris: Libreria Paul
   Ollendorff, 1911.

C0572.
Hollaender, Gustav. German Violinist; b. February 15, 1855, Loebschuetz,
Silesia; d. December 4, 1915, Berlin.

1. Baker 7; DEU; Grove 6/8 (Bibliography); MGG (Bibliography); Riemann
   12; Schmidl.

C0573.
Hollander, Lorin. American Pianist; b. July 19, 1944, New York City.

1. Baker 7; Grove-AM; PAB-MI/2 (Bibliography); Riemann 12/Supp.

2. CK(KB) 5/7; KB 10/4.

C0574.
Holliger, Heinz. Swiss Oboist; b. May 21, 1939, Langenthal.

1. Baker 7; DEU; Grove 6/8 (Bibliography); MGG/Supp. (Bibliography);
   PAB-MI/2 (Bibliography); Riemann 12/Supp. (Bibliography).

5. B0110.

C0575.
Hollins, Alfred. English Pianist; b. September 11, 1865, Hull; d. May
17, 1942, Edinburgh.

1. Baker 7; PAB-MI/2 (Bibliography).

3. Hollins, Alfred. A Blind Musician Looks Back: an Autobiography.
   Edinburgh: William Blackwood & Sons Ltd., 1936. xiii, 278 p.,
   portrait, index.

C0576.
Holmes, Alfred. English Violinist; b. November 9, 1837, London; d. March
4, 1876, Paris, France.

1. Baker 7; DEU; Fetis 2/Supp.; Grove 6/8; Mendel; Riemann 12; Schmidl.

C0577.
Holmes, Henry. English Violinist, brother of Alfred; b. November 7,
1839, London; d. December 9, 1905, San Francisco, California.

1. Baker 7; DEU; Fetis 2/Supp.; Grove 6/8; PAB-M/2 (Bibliography);
   Riemann 12.

C0578.
Holst, Henry. Danish Violinist; b. July 25, 1899, Copenhagen.

1. Baker 7; Grove 6/8 (Bibliography); PAB-MI/2 (Bibliography); Riemann
   12 + Supp.

He was concertmaster of the Berlin Philharmonic from 1923 to 1931.

C0579.
Holy, Alfred. Portuguese Harpist; b. August 5, 1866, Oporto; d. May 8, 1948, Vienna, Austria.

1. Baker 7; Grove 6/8 (Bibliography); Riemann 12; Schmidl/Supp.

C0580.
Honegger, Henri. Swiss Cellist; b. June 10, 1904, Geneva.

1. Baker 7; PAB-MI/2 (Bibliography); Riemann 12.

C0581.
Hopekirk, Helen. Scottish Pianist; b. May 20, 1856, Edinburgh; d. November 19, 1945, Cambridge, Massachusetts.

1. Baker 7; Grove-AM; Riemann 12; Schmidl.

4. Hall, Constance Huntington, comp. Helen Hopekirk, 1856-1945. Cambridge (MA): p.p., 1954. 41 p., repertoire, performances, compositions, pupils.

C0582.
Horák, Josef. Czechoslovakian Bass Clarinetist; b. March 24, 1931, Znojmo.

1. Baker 7; Grove 6/8 (Bibliography); PAB-MI/2 (Bibliography).

4. Steinmetz, Karel. Josef Horák: Paganini der Bassklarinette. Lucerne, 1971. No copy located.

C0583.
Horowitz, Vladimir. American Pianist; b. October 1, 1904, Berdichev, Russia.

1. Baker 7 (Bibliography); DEU (Bibliography); Grove 6/8 (Bibliography); Grove-AM (Bibliography); MGG/Supp. (Bibliography); PAB-MI/2 (Bibliography); Riemann 12 + Supp. (Bibliography); Schmidl/Supp.

   Horowitz earned "...the reputation of a piano virtuoso of the highest caliber, so that his very name became synonymous with pianistic greatness...his concerts sold out without fail whenever and wherever he chose to play...his performances of works by Chopin, Liszt, Tchaikovsky, and Rachmaninoff are incomparable." Baker 7.

2. CL 17/3, 18/7, 25/2, 25/6; HiFi 7/10; HiFi/MusAm 15/10, 23/7, 28/1, 28/6; CK(KB) 2/1, 9/3; MM 23/12; PQ 90, 107, 121.

4. Plaskin, Glenn. Horowitz: a Biography of Vladimir Horowitz. New York: William Morrow and Company, Inc., 1983. 607 p., 63 illus., source notes, discography by Robert McAlear, repertoire, index.

5. A0008, A0033, A0060, A0069, B0012, B0027, B0030, B0044, B0055, B0108, B0109, D0012.

   SEE: Lipman, Samuel under Glenn Gould (C0484.5).

C0584.
Horszowski, Mieczyslaw. American Pianist; b. June 23, 1892, Lemberg
(Lwow), Poland.

1. Baker 7; DEU; Grove 6/8 (Bibliography); Grove-AM (Bibliography);
   PAB-MI/2 (Bibliography); Riemann 12/Supp.; Schmidl/Supp.

2. CK(KB) 9/4; Mus/Am 70/17, 80/13.

C0585.
Hřimalý, Johann. Czechoslovakian Violinist; b. April 13, 1844, Pilsen;
d. January 24, 1915, Moscow, Russia.

1. Baker 7; DEU; Grove 6/8 (Bibliography); Riemann 12; Schmidl.

C0586.
Hubay, Jenoe. Hungarian Violinist; b. September 15, 1858, Budapest;
d. March 12, 1937, Vienna, Austria.

1. Baker 7; DEU; Grove 6/8; MGG (Bibliography); PAB-MI/2 (Bibliography);
   Riemann 12 + Supp. (Bibliography); Schmidl + Supp.

4. Haraszti, Emil, ed. Hubay Jenoe: élete es munkaí. Budapest: Singer
   Es Wolfner Kiadása, 1913 [limited edition of 200 copies]. 206, [1]
   p., illus., list of compositions, 23-item bibliography.

C0587.
Hubbard, Freddie [Frederick De Wayne]. American Jazz Trumpeter; b. April
7, 1938, Indianapolis, Indiana.

1. Baker 7; DEU; Grove-AM (Bibliography); Grove-Jazz; JB; JRRM; PAB-MI/2
   (Bibliography).

2. DB 29/2, 33/24, 39/20, 41/2, 45/12, 48/11.

5. A0032.

C0588.
Huberman, Bronislaw. Polish Violinist; b. December 19, 1882, Czes-
tochowa; d. June 15, 1947, Corsier-sur-Vevey, Switzerland.

1. Baker 7 (Bibliography); DEU (Bibliography); Grove 6/8 (Bibliography);
   MGG (Bibliography); PAB-MI/2 (Bibliography); Riemann 12 + Supp.;
   Schmidl + Supp.

2. ML 2/2; Strad Dec/1982.

3. Huberman, Bronislaw. Aus der Werkstatt des Virtuosen. Leipzig: Hugo
   Heller & Cie., 1912. 61 p., 2 portraits.

   Reprinted in translation as Z Warsztatu Wirtuoza (Katowice: Katow-
   ickie Zaklady Graficzne, 1964). Also Linthicum Heights (MD), 1986.

   Huberman, Bronislaw. Vaterland Europa. Berlin: Verlag fuer Kultur-
   politik G.M.B.H., 1932. 89 p., portrait.

4. Ibbeken, Ida, comp. An Orchestra Is Born: the Founding of the Pales-
tine Orchestra as Reflected in Bronislaw Huberman's Letters,
Speeches, and Articles, Compiled from the Huberman Archives. Tel-
Aviv: Yachdev, United Publishers Co., Ltd., 1969. 88 [English], 81
[Hebrew], [12] p., illus.

Ibbeken, Ida, comp. The Listener Speaks: 55 Years of Letters from the
Audience to Bronislaw Huberman. Israel: Ramoth Hashawin, 1961. vi,
129, [2] p., portrait.

5. A0142, B0020, B0037.

SEE: Autobiography of Carl Flesch (C0393.3).

C0589.
Huenten, Franz. German Pianist; b. December 26, 1793, Coblenz; d. February 22, 1878, Coblenz.

1. Baker 7; Fetis 2/4; Grove 6/8 (Bibliography); Mendel; MGG (Bibliography); Riemann 12 + Supp. (Bibliography); Schmidl.

4. Zoellner, Gerd. Franz Huenten: sein Leben und sein Werk. Cologne:
Beitrag zur rheinischen Musikgeschichte, 1959. 317 p.

C0590.
Hughes, Edwin. American Pianist; b. August 15, 1884, Washington, D.C.;
d. July 17, 1965, New York City.

1. Baker 7; Grove-AM; PAB-MI/2 (Bibliography); Riemann 12.

2. MQ 1/4, 11/3.

C0591.
Hummel, Johann Nepomuk. German Pianist; b. November 14, 1778, Pressburg;
d. October 17, 1837, Weimar.

1. Baker 7 (Bibliography); DEU (Bibliography); Fetis 2/4; Grove 6/8
(Bibliography); Mendel; MGG (Bibliography); PAB-MI/2 (Bibliography);
Riemann 12 (Bibliography) + Supp. (Bibliography); Schmidl.

2. CL 14/3; MQ 56/2, 59/1.

3. Hummel, Johann Nepomuk. Ausfuehrliche theoretisch-practische
Anweisung zum Piano-Forte-Spiel, vom ersten Elementar-Unterrichte
an bis zur vollkommensten Ausbildung. Wien: Verlag von Tobias
Haslinger, Musikverleger, 1828. 440 p., portrait.

"...an elaborate instruction book and one of the first to give a
sensible method of fingering." Baker 7.

4. Meyer, Walter. Johann Nepomuk Hummel als Klavier-komponist. Ph.D.
diss. University of Kiel, 1922. 62 p.

Mitchell, Francis Humphries. The Piano Concertos of Johann Nepomuk
Hummel. Ph.D. diss. Northwestern University, 1957. 264 p.

Sachs, Joel. Kapellmeister Hummel in England and France. Detroit: Information Coordinators, Inc., 1977 [based upon his Ph.D. diss. Columbia University, 1968]. 153 p., 157-item bibliography, biographical glossary and index.

5. A0014, A0051, C0984.3.

   SEE: Spohr, Ludwig. Louis Spohrs Selbstbiographie. 2 vols. Kassel, 1860/61 [London: Reeves & Turner, 1878].

C0592.
Hurford, Peter John. English Organist; b. November 22, 1930, Minehead, Somerset.

1. Baker 7; Grove 6/8; PAB-MI/2 (Bibliography).

2. GR 47.

C0593.
Hurwitz, Emanuel. English Violinist; b. May 7, 1919, London.

1. Baker 7; Grove 6/8 (Bibliography); PAB-MI/2 (Bibliography).

2. Strad April/1977, Aug/1979.

C0594.
Hutcheson, Ernest. American Pianist; b. July 20, 1871, Melbourne, Australia; d. February 9, 1951, New York City.

1. Baker 7; Grove 6/8; Grove-AM; PAB-MI/2 (Bibliography); Riemann 12 + Supp.; Schmidl.

3. Hutcheson, Ernest. The Literature of the Piano: a Guide for Amateur and Student. 2nd rev. ed. New York: Alfred A. Knopf, 1949 [original 1948]. viii, 3-374, xxxv p., bibliography, index.

5. B0061.

   SEE: Moresby, Isabelle. Australia Makes Music. Melbourne: Longmans, Green and Co., 1948.

C0595.
Igumnov, Konstantin. Russian Pianist; b. May 1, 1873, Lebedyan, near Tambov; d. March 24, 1948, Moscow.

1. Baker 7; DEU (Bibliography); Grove 6/9 (Bibliography); Riemann 12 + Supp. (Bibliography).

C0596.
Istomin, Eugene. American Pianist; b. November 26, 1925, New York City.

1. Baker 7; DEU; Grove 6/9; Grove-AM (Bibliography); PAB-MI/2 (Bibliography); Riemann 12/Supp.

2. HiFi/MusAm 20/4.

5. B0058.

C0597.
Iturbi, José. Spanish Pianist; b. November 28, 1895, Valencia; d. June 28, 1980, Hollywood, California.

1. Baker 7; DEU; Grove 6/9; Grove-AM; PAB-MI/2 (Bibliography); Riemann 12; Schmidl/Supp.

5. B0086.

C0598.
Jackson, Milt or Bags [Milton]. American Jazz Vibraphonist; b. January 1, 1923, Detroit, Michigan.

1. Baker 7; DEU (Bibliography); Grove 6/9 (Bibliography); Grove-AM (Bibliography - 11 entries); Grove-Jazz; JB; LJ; PAB-MI/2 (Bibliography).

2. DB 25/24, 28/14, 29/2, 42/9.

4. Wilbraham, Roy J. Milt Jackson: a Discography and Biography Including Records Made with the Modern Jazz Quartet. London: Frognal Bookshop, 1968. No copy located.

The Modern Jazz Quartet synthesized "cool" and "classical" jazz.

5. A0032.

C0599.
Jacob, Benjamin. English Organist; b. May 15, 1778, London; d. August 24, 1829, London.

1. Baker 7; DEU (Bibliography); Grove 6/9 (Bibliography); Mendel; MGG (Bibliography); PAB-MI/2 (Bibliography); Riemann 12 (Bibliography); Schmidl.

2. MQ 21/2.

4. Anon. Statement of the Facts Relating to the Expulsion of Mr. [Benjamin] Jacob from the Organ of Surrey Chapel.... London: p.p., 1825. 36 p.

Wesley, S. Letters of Samuel Wesley to Mr. Jacobs,...Relating to the Introduction into This Country of the Works of John Sebastian Bach. London: Partridge & Co., 1875. Reprint 1957. 50 p.

C0600.
Jaëll, Alfred. French Pianist; b. March 5, 1832, Trieste; d. February 27, 1882, Paris.

1. Baker 7; DEU; Fetis 2/4 + Supp.; Grove 6/9; Mendel; MGG; PAB-MI/2 (Bibliography); Riemann 12 + Supp.; Schmidl.

5. A0028, B0112.

C0601.
Jaëll-Trautmann, Marie. French Pianist, wife of Alfred; b. August 17, 1846, Steinseltz, Alsace; d. February 4, 1925, Paris.

1. Baker 7; DEU (Bibliography); Fetis 2/Supp.; Grove 6/9 (Bibliography); Mendel; MGG (Bibliography); Riemann 12 (Bibliography) + Supp. (Bibliography); Schmidl.

4. Kiener, Hélène. Marie Jaëll, 1846-1925: problèmes d'esthétique et de pédagogie musicales. Paris: Flammarion Editeur, 1952. 210 p. + 2 plates, 4 illus.

C0602.
James, Harry [Haag]. American Jazz Trumpeter; b. March 15, 1916, Albany, Georgia; d. July 5, 1983, Las Vegas, Nevada.

1. Baker 7; DEU (Bibliography); EdS; Grove-AM (Bibliography); Grove-Jazz; JB; IJ; PAB-MI/2 (Bibliography); Riemann 12/Supp. (Bibliography).

2. DB 18/4, 25/2, 32/9.

4. Stacy, Frank. Harry James' Pin-up Life Story. New York: Arco Publishing Co., 1944. 32 p.

5. B0087.

C0603.
Janigro, Antonio. Italian Cellist; b. January 21, 1918, Milan.

1. Baker 7; DEU; Grove 6/9; PAB-MI/2 (Bibliography); Riemann 12 + Supp. (Bibliography).

4. Gavoty, Bernard. Antonio Janigro. Genève: René Kister, 1962. 30, [2] p., 26 illus., discography.

C0604.
Janis [Yanks abbreviated from Yankelevitch], Byron. American Pianist; b. March 24, 1928, McKeesport, Pennsylvania.

1. Baker 7 (Bibliography); Grove 6/9; Grove-AM (Bibliography); PAB-MI/2 (Bibliography); Riemann/Supp. (Bibliography).

2. CL 2/3.

5. A0069.

C0605.
Jarrett, Keith. American Jazz Pianist; b. May 8, 1945, Allentown, PA.

1. Baker 7; DEU; Grove-AM (Bibliography); Grove-Jazz; PAB-MI/2 (Bibliography); Riemann 12/Supp.

2. DB 39/1, 41/17, 51/6; CK(KB) 2/3, 5/9, 7/4; KB 11/3, 12/9.

C0606.
Jedliczka, Ernst. Russian Pianist; b. June 5, 1855, Poltava; d. August
3, 1904, Berlin, Germany.

1. Baker 7; Riemann 12; Schmidl/Supp.

C0607.
Jehin-Prume, Françoise. Belgian Violinist; b. April 18, 1839, Spa;
d. May 29, 1899, Montreal, Canada.

1. Baker 7; Grove 6/9; Riemann 12; Schmidl.

There is an extensive entry in Encyclopedia of Music in Canada.
Toronto: University of Toronto Press, 1981.

4. Anon. [Jehin-Prume, Jules]. Une vie d'artiste. Montreal, c.1900.

C0608.
Jenson [Lockington], Dylana Ruth. American Violinist; b. May 14, 1961,
Los Angeles, California.

1. Baker 7; Grove-AM (Bibliography).

C0609.
Joachim, Joseph. German Violinist; b. June 28, 1831, Kittsee, near
Pressburg; d. August 15, 1907, Berlin.

1. Baker 7 (Bibliography); DEU (Bibliography); Fetis 2/4 + Supp.; Grove
   6/9 (Bibliography); Mendel; MGG (Bibliography); PAB-MI/2 (Bibliography); Riemann 12 (Bibliography) + Supp. (Bibliography); Schmidl.

2. Strad Sept/1978.

3. Bickley, Nora, ed. and trans. Letters from and to Joseph Joachim.
   London: Macmillan and Co., Limited, 1914. Reprint 1972. xiii, 470 p.,
   portrait, index.

   Moser, Andreas, comp. and ed. Briefe von und an Joseph Joachim. 3
   vols. (1842-1857; 1858-1968; 1869-1907). Berlin: Verlegt von Julius
   Bard, 1911/12/13. xii, 476 p., 9 illus.; viii, 478 p., 7 illus.;
   vi, 546 p., 9 illus., index to the three volumes.

4. Breitburg, Iulia Abramovna. Iozef Ioakhim: pedagog i ispoluitel'.
   Moskva: Muzyka, 1966. 114 p., portrait, bibliographical footnotes.

   Fuller-Maitland, J.A. Joseph Joachim. London: John Lane: The Bodley
   Head, 1905. vi, [iii], 63 p., 71 illus.

   Kohut, Adolph. Josef Joachim: ein Lebens- und Kuenstlerbild. Berlin:
   A. Glas Musikalienhandlung, 1891. [ii], 96 p., portrait.

   Moser, Andreas. Joseph Joachim: ein Lebensbild. Berlin: B. Behr,
   1898. viii, 301 p., portrait. 2nd revised and enlarged ed. Berlin:
   Verlag der Deutschen Brahms Gesellschaft, m.b.H., 1908/10. 2 vols.
   (1831-56) xii, 225 p., portrait; (1856-1907) 401 p., portrait, index.

Stoll, Barrett. Joseph Joachim: Violinist, Pedagogue, and Composer. Ph.D. diss. University of Iowa, 1978. 383 p., bibliography.

Storck, Karl. Joseph Joachim: eine Studie. Leipzig: Hermann Seemann Nachfolger, n.d. [1902]. 41 p., portrait.

Tua, Teresa. Joachim - ricordi e note. Roma: Nuova Antologia, 1907. 47 p., 5 illus.

5. A0035, A0093, B0008, B0020, B0035, B0037, B0065, B0083, B0102, B0109.

C0610.
Johannesen, Grant. American Pianist; b. July 30, 1921, Salt Lake City, Utah.

1. Baker 7; Grove-AM (Bibliography); PAB-MI/2 (Bibliography); Riemann 12/Supp.

2. CL 18/8; CK(KB) 7/6; HiFi/MusAm 26/11; PQ 106.

C0611.
Johansen, Gunnar. American Pianist; b. January 21, 1906, Copenhagen, Denmark.

1. Baker 7; Grove-AM (Bibliography); PAB-MI/2 (Bibliography).

2. CL 8/4, 26/10; HiFi/MusAm 26/11.

C0612.
Johnson, Bunk [William Geary]. American Jazz Trumpeter; b. December 27, 1879, New Orleans, Louisiana; d. July 7, 1949, New Iberia, Louisiana.

1. Baker 7; Grove 6/9 (Bibliography); Grove-AM (Bibliography - 11 entries); Grove-Jazz; JB (12 entries); JRRM (20 entries); LJ; PAB-MI/2 (Bibliography).

4. Sonnier, Austin M., Jr. Willie Geary 'Bunk' Johnson: the New Iberia Years. New York: Crescendo Publishing Co., 1977. 81 p. + 3 plates, illus., discography.

5. A0031.

C0613.
Johnson, James P[rice]. American Jazz Pianist; b. February 1, 1891, Brunswick, New Jersey; d. November 17, 1955, New York City.

1. Baker 7; DEU (Bibliography); Grove 6/9 (Bibliography); Grove-AM (Bibliography - 12 entries); Grove-Jazz; LJ; PAB-MI/2 (Bibliography).

4. Brown, Scott E. & Robert Hilbert. James P. Johnson: a Case of Mistaken Identity published with A James P. Johnson Discography 1917-1950. Metuchen (NJ): The Scarecrow Press, 1982. viii, 500 p., notes, list of compositions, 260-item bibliography, index; discography (pp. 325-478), index of titles, index of names.

Brown's Ph.D. diss. at Yale University (1982) was titled, A Case of Mistaken Identity: the Life and Music of James P. Johnson.

5. A0031, B0054.

C0614.
Johnson, J.J. [James Louis]. American Jazz Trombonist; b. January 22, 1924, Indianapolis, Indiana.

1. Baker 7; DEU (Bibliography); Grove 6/9 (Bibliography); Grove-AM (Bibliography - 13 entries); Grove-Jazz; JRRM; LJ; PAB-MI/2 (Bibliography); Riemann 12/Supp. (Bibliography).

   J.J. was a seminal figure of the bop era.

2. DB 28/10, 31/3, 32/2, 37/11.

4. Fini, Francesco. The Jay Jay Johnson Complete Discography. Imola: Galeati, 1962. 26 p.

C0615.
Jones, Elvin Ray. American Jazz Drummer; b. September 9, 1927, Pontiac, Michigan.

1. Baker 7; DEU; Grove 6/9 (Bibliography); Grove-AM (Bibliography); Grove-Jazz; JB; JRRM; LJ; PAB-MI/2 (Bibliography); Riemann 12/Supp.

2. DB 30/8, 33/6, 33/16, 36/6, 36/20, 39/5, 40/18, 44/10, 44/21; JJS 4/1, 4/2, 5/1.

C0616.
Jones, Geraint. Welsh Organist/Harpsichordist; b. May 16, 1917, Porth.

1. Baker 7; DEU; Grove 6/9; PAB-MI/2 (Bibliography); Riemann 12/Supp.

C0617.
Jones, Jo[nathan]. American Jazz Drummer; b. October 7, 1911, Chicago, Illinois; d. September 3, 1985, New York City.

1. Baker 7; DEU; Grove 6/9; Grove-AM (Bibliography); Grove-Jazz; JRRM; PAB-MI/2 (Bibliography).

2. DB 25/13, 32/7, 38/6.

5. A0092.

C0618.
Jones, Philly Joe [Joseph Rudolf]. American Jazz Drummer; b. July 15, 1923, Philadelphia, Pennsylvania; d. August 30, 1985, Philadelphia.

1. Baker 7; Grove-AM (Bibliography); Grove-Jazz; JB; JRRM; PAB-MI/2 (Bibliography).

2. DB 26/5, 43/15.

C0619.
Jones, Quincy Delight, Jr. American Jazz Trumpeter; b. March 14, 1933,
Chicago, Illinois.

1. Baker 7; DEU; Grove-AM (Bibliography); Grove-Jazz; JB; JRRM; PAB-MI/2
   (Bibliography); Riemann 12/Supp.

2. DB 27/3, 37/23, 42/17, 52/4.

4. Horricks, Raymond. Quincy Jones. New York: Hippocrene Books Inc.,
   1985. 127 p. + 4 plates, 15 illus., selected discography by Tony
   Middleton.

C0620.
Jones, Thad[eus Joseph]. American Jazz Trumpeter; b. March 28, 1923,
Pontiac, Michigan; d. August 20, 1986, Copenhagen, Denmark.

1. Baker 7; Grove-Jazz; JB; JRRM; PAB-MI/2 (Bibliography).

2. DB 30/11, 35/4, 37/8, 39/14, 40/13, 52/8.

C0621.
Joseffy, Rafael. American Pianist; b. July 3, 1852, Hunfalu, Hungary;
d. June 25, 1915, New York City.

1. Baker 7; Grove 6/9 (Bibliography); Grove-AM (Bibliography); PAB-MI/2
   (Bibliography); Riemann 12 (Bibliography); Schmidl.

2. MQ 2/3.

C0622.
Kalichstein, Joseph. Israeli Pianist; b. January 15, 1946, Tel Aviv.

1. Baker 7; Grove-AM; PAB-MI/2 (Bibliography).

2. CK(KB) 6/6.

C0623.
Kalish, Gilbert. American Pianist; b. July 2, 1935, Brooklyn, New York.

1. Baker 7; Grove-AM.

C0624.
Kalkbrenner, Friedrich Wilhelm Michael. German Pianist; b. between
November 2 and 8, 1785, near Kassel; d. June 10, 1849, Deuil, Siene-
et-Oise, France.

1. Baker 7 (Bibliography); DEU (Bibliography); Fetis 2/4; Grove 6/9
   (Bibliography); Mendel; MGG (Bibliography); PAB-MI/2 (Bibliography);
   Riemann 12 (Bibliography); Schmidl.

3. Kalkbrenner, Friedrich. Méthode pour apprendre le pianoforte à l'aide
   du guide-mains, contenant les principes de musique, un système complet de doigter, la classification des auteurs a étudier.... Paris:
   Pleyel, 1831.

4. Dumes, Carles. Notice biographique sur la vie et sur les travaux de Frédéric Guillaume Michel Kalkbrenner. Paris: Aux bureaux de la Renotamée, 1842. 24 p.

Nautsch, Hans. Friedrich Kalkbrenner: Wirkung und Werk. Hamburg: Verlag der Musikalienhandlung Karl Dieter Wagner, 1983. xi, 255 p., list of compositions, 109-item bibliography.

5. A0014.

C0625.
Kaminski, Joseph. Israeli Violinist; b. November 17, 1903, Odessa, Russia; d. October 14, 1972, Gedera, Israel.

1. Baker 7; DEU (Bibliography); Grove 6/9 (Bibliography); Riemann 12/ Supp.

C0626.
Kaminsky, Max. American Jazz Trumpeter; b. September 7, 1908, Brockton, Massachusetts.

1. Grove-Jazz; JB; LJ; PAB-MI/2 (Bibliography).

3. Kaminsky, Max with V.E. Hughes. My Life in Jazz. New York: Harper & Row, Publishers, Incorporated, 1963. 242 p. + 4 plates, 19 illus., index.

C0627.
Kapell, William. American Pianist; b. September 20, 1922, New York City; d. October 29, 1953, King's Mountain, near San Francisco, California.

1. Baker 7; Grove 6/9; Grove-AM; PAB-MI/2 (Bibliography).

C0628.
Karr, Gary Michael. American Double Bassist; b. November 20, 1941, Los Angeles, California.

1. Baker 7; Grove 6/9; Grove-AM; PAB-MI/2 (Bibliography).

2. MM 14/6, 27/3; Strad Jan/1984.

C0629.
Kastner, Alfred. American Harpist; b. March 10, 1870, Vienna, Austria; d. May 24, 1948, Hollywood, California.

1. Baker 7; Grove 6/9 (Bibliography); Grove-AM (Bibliography); Riemann 12; Schmidl.

C0630.
Katchen, Julius. American Pianist; b. August 15, 1926, Long Branch, New York; d. April 29, 1969, Paris, France.

1. Baker 7; DEU (Bibliography); Grove 6/9; Grove-AM; Riemann 12 + Supp.

2. GR 47/June; HiFi 12/12; HiFi/MusAm 19/9.

C0631.
Kates, Stephen. American Cellist; b. May 7, 1943, New York City.

1. Baker 7; Grove-AM; PAB-MI/2 (Bibliography); Riemann 12/Supp.

2. Strad Oct/1986.

C0632.
Katin, Peter. English Pianist; b. November 14, 1930, London.

1. Baker 7; Grove 6/9; PAB-MI/2 (Bibliography).

C0633.
Katz, Mindru. Israeli Pianist; b. June 3, 1925, Bucharest, Romania;
d. January 30, 1978, Istanbul, Turkey.

1. Baker 7; Grove 6/9; PAB-MI/2 (Bibliography).

C0634.
Kee, Piet. Dutch Organist; b. August 30, 1927, Zaandam.

1. Baker 7; DEU; Grove 6/9; MGG; PAB-MI/2 (Bibliography); Riemann 12/
   Supp.

C0635.
Kehr, [Heinz-] Gunter. German Violinist; b. March 16, 1920, Darmstadt.

1. Baker 7; Riemann 12 + Supp. (Bibliography).

3. Kehr, Heinz-Gunter. Untersuchungen zur Violintechnik um die Wende des
   18. Jahrhunderts: ein Beitrag zur Entwicklungsgeschichte des Violinspiels. Ph.D. diss. University of Cologne, 1941. iii, 231 p.

C0636.
Kell, Reginald Clifford. English Clarinetist; b. June 8, 1906, York;
d. August 5, 1981, Frankfort, Kentucky.

1. Baker 7; Grove 6/9 (Bibliography); PAB-MI/2 (Bibliography).

C0637.
Kellermann, Berthold. German Pianist; b. March 5, 1853, Nuremberg;
d. June 6, 1926, Munich.

1. DEU; Riemann 12; Schmidl/Supp.

3. Kellermann, Berthold. Erinnerungen: ein Kuenstlerleben. Leipzig:
   Eugen Rentsch Verlag, 1932. 238 p. + 2 plates, index of names.

C0638.
Kempff, Wilhelm. German Pianist; b. November 25, 1895, Juterborg.

1. Baker 7; DEU (Bibliography); Grove 6/9 (Bibliography); MGG (Bibliography); PAB-MI/2 (Bibliography); Riemann 12 + Supp. (Bibliography);
   Schmidl + Supp.

Kempff is a major interpreter of the Romantic repertoire.

2. RS 9.

3. Kempff, Wilhelm. Unter dem Zimbelstern: das Werden eines Musikers. Stuttgart: Engelhornverlag Adolf Spemann, 1951. Reprint as Unter dem Zimbelstern: Jugenderinnerungen eines Pianisten (Laaber: Laaber-Verlag, 1978). 282 p., portrait.

Kempff, Wilhelm. Was Ich hoerte, was Ich sah: Reisebilder eines Pianisten. Muenchen: R. Piper & Co. Verlag, 1981. 179 p., 27 illus.

4. Gavoty, Bernard. Wilhelm Kempff. Genève: René Kister, 1954. 30 p., illus.

5. A0008, A0060, B0041, B0042, B0110.

C0639.
Kentner, Louis Philip. British Pianist; b. July 19, 1905, Karwin, Silesia (now Karvina, Czechoslovakia); d. September 21, 1987.

1. Baker 7; DEU; Grove 6/9; PAB-MI/2 (Bibliography); Riemann 12.

5. A0047.

C0640.
Keppard, Freddie. American Jazz Cornetist; b. February 15, 1889, New Orleans, Louisiana; d. July 15, 1933, Chicago, Illinois.

1. Baker 7; DEU (Bibliography); Grove 6/9 (Bibliography); Grove-AM (Bibliography); Grove-Jazz; PAB-MI/2 (Bibliography); Riemann 12 + Supp. (Bibliography).

5. A0031.

C0641.
Kessler, Joseph Christoph. German Pianist; b. August 26, 1800, Augsburg; d. January 14, 1872, Vienna, Austria.

1. Baker 7; Fetis 2/5; Mendel; Riemann 12; Schmidl.

4. Pyllemann, Fr. "Mitteilung persoenlicher Aufzeichnungen Kristoph Kessler." Allgemeine Musikalische Zeitung 7/12 (1872).

C0642.
Khandoshkin, Ivan. Russian Violinist; b. 1747; d. March 28, 1804, St. Petersburg.

1. Baker 7 (Bibliography); DEU (Bibliography); Grove 6/10 (Bibliography); PAB-MI/2 (Bibliography).

4. Mischakoff, Anne. The String Music of Ivan Evstaf'evich Khandoshkin (1747-1804): a Stylistic and Historical Analysis. D.M.A. diss. University of Illinois, 1978. 268 p.

C0643.
Kilenyi, Edward, Jr. American Pianist; b. May 7, 1911, Philadelphia, PA.

1. Baker 7; Grove-AM (Bibliography); PAB-MI/2 (Bibliography).

C0644.
Kincaid, William. American Flutist; b. April 26, 1895, Minneapolis, Minnesota; d. March 27, 1967, Philadelphia, Pennsylvania.

1. Baker 7; Grove 6/10; Grove-AM; PAB-MI/2 (Bibliography).

C0645.
Kindler, Hans. American Cellist; b. January 8, 1892, Rotterdam, Holland; d. August 30, 1949, Watch Hill, Rhode Island.

1. Baker 7; Grove-AM (Bibliography); PAB-MI/2 (Bibliography); Riemann 12 + Supp.

C0646.
King, Oliver A. English Pianist; b. July 6, 1855, London; d. August 23, 1923, London.

1. Baker 7; DEU; Riemann 12; Schmidl.

C0647.
Kipnis, Igor. American Harpsichordist; b. September 27, 1930, Berlin, Germany.

1. Baker 7 (Bibliography); DEU; Grove 6/10; Grove-AM; PAB-MI/2 (Bibliography); Riemann 12/Supp.

2. CL 14/8, 23/8; CK(KB) 4/1; KB 10/8.

C0648.
Kirby, John. American Jazz Double Bassist; b. December 31, 1908, Baltimore, Maryland; d. June 14, 1952, Los Angeles, California.

1. Baker 7; DEU; Grove-AM (Bibliography); Grove-Jazz; JRRM; PAB-MI/2 (Bibliography).

2. DB 34/12.

C0649.
Kirk, Andy [Andrew Dewey]. American Jazz Saxophonist; b. May 28, 1898, Newport, Kentucky.

1. Baker 7; Grove 6/10 (Bibliography); Grove-AM (Bibliography); Grove-Jazz; PAB-MI/2 (Bibliography).

C0650.
Kirk, Roland T. [Rahsaan]. American Jazz Tenor Saxophonist; b. August 7, 1936, Columbus, Ohio; d. December 5, 1977, Bloomington, Indiana.

1. Baker 7; DEU; Grove-AM (Bibliography); Grove-Jazz; PAB-MI/2 (Bibliography); Riemann 12/Supp.

2. DB 27/16, 30/12, 34/10, 41/14.

C0651.
Kirkpatrick, John. American Pianist; b. March 18, 1905, New York City.

1. Baker 7; DEU; Grove 6/10; Grove-AM.

"His signal achievement was the first performance of the 'Concord Sonata' by Charles Ives, which he gave in N.Y. on Jan. 20, 1939, playing it from memory...[critical for]...the public recognition of Ives." Baker 7.

C0652.
Kirkpatrick, Ralph Leonard. American Harpsichordist; b. June 10, 1911, Leonminster, Massachusetts; d. April 13, 1984, Guilford, Connecticut.

1. Baker 7 (Bibliography); DEU (Bibliography); Grove 6/10; Grove-AM (Bibliography); MGG; PAB-MI/2 (Bibliography); Riemann 12 + Supp.

3. Kirkpatrick, Ralph. Early Years. New York: Peter Lang, 1985. 128 p. + 6 plates, 11 illus.

5. B0110.

C0653.
Kirshbaum, Ralph Henry. American Cellist; b. March 4, 1946, Denton, TX.

1. Baker 7; Grove 6/10; Grove-AM.

2. Strad March/1987.

C0654.
Kjellstroem, Sven. Swedish Violinist; b. March 30, 1875, Lulea; d. December 5, 1950, Stockholm.

1. Baker 7; DEU; MGG (Bibliography); Riemann 12/Supp.

C0655.
Klengel, Julius. German Cellist; b. September 24, 1859, Leipzig; d. October 27, 1933, Leipzig.

1. Baker 7; DEU; Grove 6/10; MGG (Bibliography); PAB-MI/2 (Bibliography); Riemann 12; Schmidl.

5. A0104.

C0656.
Klien, Walter. Austrian Pianist; b. November 27, 1928, Graz.

1. Baker 7; Grove 6/10; Riemann 12/Supp.

2. CL 20/4.

C0657.
Klimov, Valery. Soviet Violinist; b. October 16, 1931, Kiev.

1. Baker 7; Grove 6/10; Riemann 12/Supp.

C0658.
Klindworth, Karl. German Pianist; b. September 25, 1830, Hannover;
d. July 27, 1916, Stolpe, near Potsdam.

1. Baker 7; DEU (Bibliography); Grove 6/10; Mendel; MGG (Bibliography);
   PAB-MI/2 (Bibliography); Riemann 12 (Bibliography) + Supp. (Bibliography); Schmidl.

C0659.
Klosé, Hyacinthe-Eléonore. French Clarinetist; b. October 11, 1808,
Corfu; d. August 29, 1880, Paris.

1. Baker 7; DEU; Fetis 2/5 + Supp.; Grove 6/10 (Bibliography); Mendel;
   PAB-MI/2 (Bibliography); Riemann 12 (Bibliography); Schmidl.

C0660.
Kneisel, Franz. German-American Violinist; b. June 26, 1865, Bucharest,
Romania; d. March 26, 1926, New York City.

1. Baker 7; Grove-AM (Bibliography); PAB-MI/2 (Bibliography); Riemann
   12 + Supp. (Bibliography); Schmidl.

He played a key role in the development of American musical taste.

4. Danek, V.B. A Historical Study of the Kneisel Quartet. DMEd diss.
   Indiana University, 1962.

   Rice, Edwin T. Franz Kneisel, January 26th, 1865-March 26th, 1926:
   Commemorative Address.... New York: p.p., 1936. 4 p. + 1 plate.

   White, Elise Fellows. Memorial to Dr. Franz Kneisel, March 30, 1926.
   1 vol. MS of portraits, press clippings, programs. In the Library
   of Congress.

5. SEE: Aldrich, Richard. Musical Discourse. New York, 1928.

   SEE: Foote, Arthur. An Autobiography. Norwood (MA), 1946.

   SEE: Howe, M.A. DeWolfe. The Boston Symphony Orchestra: an Historical
       Sketch. Boston, 1914.

C0661.
Knorr, Julius. German Pianist; b. September 22, 1807, Leipzig; d. June
17, 1861, Leipzig.

1. Baker 7; DEU (Bibliography); Fetis 2/5; Mendel; MGG (Bibliography);
   Riemann 12; Schmidl.

C0662.
Koch, Caspar Petrus. American Organist; b. November 25, 1872, Carnap,
Germany; d. April 3, 1970, Pittsburgh, Pennsylvania.

1. Baker 7; Grove-AM.

C0663.
Kochanski, Paul. Polish Violinist; b. September 14, 1887, Odessa, Russia; d. January 12, 1934, New York City.

1. Baker 7; DEU; Grove 6/10 (Bibliography); Grove-AM (Bibliography); PAB-MI/2 (Bibliography); Riemann 12 + Supp. (Bibliography); Schmidl/ Supp.

2. Strad Sept/1987.

5. B0061.

C0664.
Kocián, Jaroslav. Czechoslovakian Violinist; b. February 22, 1883, Ustí nad Ordicí; d. March 9, 1950, Prague.

1. Baker 7; DEU (Bibliography); Grove 6/10 (Bibliography); MGG (Bibliography); Riemann 12 + Supp. (Bibliography); Schmidl.

3. Kocián, Jaroslav. Sborník stati a vzpomínek. Praha: Státní Nakladatelstvi krásné literatury, hudby a umění, 1953. 225 p., 22 illus., index.

4. Slajs, Antonin. Jaroslav Kocián. Pardubice: Krajsky dum osvety, 1958. 75, [4] p., 6 illus., list of concerts.

C0665.
Kocsis, Zoltán. Hungarian Pianist; b. May 30, 1952, Budapest.

1. Baker 7; Grove 6/10; PAB-MI/2 (Bibliography).

C0666.
Koczalski, Raoul Armand George. Polish Pianist; b. January 3, 1884, Warsaw; d. November 24, 1948, Poznan.

1. Baker 7; DEU (Bibliography); Grove 6/10; MGG (Bibliography); Riemann 12 (Bibliography); Schmidl + Supp.

C0667.
Koehler, Ernesto. Italian Flutist; b. December 4, 1849, Modena; d. May 17, 1907, St. Petersburg, Russia.

1. Baker 7; Riemann 12 (Bibliography); Schmidl.

C0668.
Kogan, Leonid Borisovich. Soviet Violinist; b. November 14, 1924, Dnepropetrovsk; d. December 17, 1982, Mytishcha.

1. Baker 7 (Bibliography); DEU (Bibliography); Grove 6/10 (Bibliography); MGG/Supp. (Bibliography); PAB-MI/2 (Bibliography); Riemann 12/Supp. (Bibliography).

"His playing exemplified the finest qualities of the Russian School: an emotionally romantic elan and melodious filigree of technical detail." Baker 7.

2. Strad April/1983.

4. Grigor'ev, Vladimir Iur'evich. _Leonid Kogan_. Moskva: Muzyka, 1975.
   175, [1] p. + 8 plates, 12 illus., discography, 28-item bibliography.

5. B0071.

C0669.
Kolisch, Rudolf. American Violinist; b. July 20, 1896, Klamm, Austria;
d. August 1, 1978, Watertown, Massachusetts.

1. Baker 7; DEU (Bibliography); Grove 6/10 (Bibliography); Grove-AM
   (Bibliography); Riemann 12 + Supp. (Bibliography).

C0670.
Konitz, Lee. American Jazz Alto Saxophonist; b. October 13, 1927,
Chicago, Illinois.

1. Baker 7; DEU (Bibliography); Grove 6/10 (Bibliography); Grove-AM
   (Bibliography - 10 entries); Grove-Jazz; JB; JRRM; LJ; PAB-MI/2
   (Bibliography); Riemann 12 + Supp. (Bibliography).

2. DB 25/10, 31/29, 35/14, 38/4, 47/1.

C0671.
Kontarsky, Aloys. German Pianist; b. May 14, 1931, Iserlohn, Westphalia.

1. Baker 7; DEU; Grove 6/10 (Bibliography); PAB-MI/2 (Bibliography);
   Riemann 12/Supp.

   His brothers, Alfons (b. October 9, 1932) and Bernhard (b. April 26,
   1937), are also concert pianists.

C0672.
de Kontski, Apollinaire. Polish Violinist; b. October 23, 1825, Cracow;
d. June 29, 1879, Warsaw.

1. Baker 7; DEU (under Katski - Bibliography); Fetis 2/5; Grove 6/9
   (under Katski - Bibliography); Mendel; Riemann 12 + Supp. (Bibliography); Schmidl.

   His brother, Antoine, was a well known pianist/student of John Field.

C0673.
Kosleck, Julius. German Trumpeter/Cornetist; b. December 3, 1825,
Neugard; d. November 5, 1904, Berlin.

1. Baker 7; Grove 6/10 (Bibliography); Mendel; PAB-MI/2 (Bibliography);
   Riemann 12 (Bibliography); Schmidl.

C0674.
Kotek, Eduard Joseph. Russian Violinist; b. October 25, 1855, Kamenetz-
Podolsk; d. January 4, 1885, Davos, Switzerland.

1. Baker 7; Grove 6/10; Schmidl.

C0675.
Kraft, Walter Wilhelm Johann. German Organist; b. June 9, 1905, Cologne;
d. May 9, 1977, Anversa [according to DEU].

1. Baker 7; DEU (Bibliography); Grove 6/10; MGG (Bibliography); Riemann
   12 + Supp. (Bibliography); Schmidl/Supp.

C0676.
Kraft, William. American Percussionist; b. September 6, 1923, Chicago,
Illinois.

1. Baker 7 (Bibliography); Grove-AM; PAB-MI/2 (Bibliography); Riemann
   12/Supp.

C0677.
Krasner, Louis. American Violinist; b. June 21, 1903, Cherkassy, Russia.

1. Baker 7; Grove 6/10; Grove-AM; PAB-MI/2 (Bibliography).

2. Strad April/1986.

C0678.
Kraus, H.J. Detlef. German Pianist; b. November 30, 1919, Hamburg.

1. Baker 7; PAB-MI/2 (Bibliography); Riemann 12/Supp.

2. CL 22/10.

C0679.
Kraus, Lili. Hungarian Pianist; b. April 3, 1905, Budapest; d. April 3,
1986, Asheville, North Carolina.

1. Baker 7 (Bibliography); Grove 6/10; Grove-AM (Bibliography); PAB-
   MI/2 (Bibliography).

2. CL 7/6, 10/4-5, 19/7; HiFi/SR 34/2; CK(KB) 9/10; PQ 136.

5. A0069.

C0680.
Krebbers, Herman Albertus. Dutch Violinist; b. June 18, 1923, Hengelo.

1. Grove 6/10; PAB-MI/2 (Bibliography); Riemann 12 + Supp.

4. van Verre, Tony. Herman Krebbers: Portret van een Kunstenaar. Amsterdam: Meulenholl Nederland bv, 1981. 133, [3] p., 33 illus., discography.

C0681.
Kreisler, Fritz. American Violinist; b. February 2, 1875, Vienna,
Austria; d. January 29, 1962, New York City.

1. Baker 7; DEU (Bibliography); Grove 6/10 (Bibliography); Grove-AM
   (Bibliography); MGG; PAB-MI/2 (Bibliography); Riemann 12 (Bibliography) + Supp. (Bibliography); Schmidl + Supp.

2. HiFi 12/5; Strad March/1975, July/1978, Sept/1986, Jan/1987 (Special Issue).

3. Kreisler, Fritz. Four Weeks in the Trenches: the War Story of a Violinist. Boston: Houghton Mifflin Company, 1915. vii, [ii], 85, [1] p., 8 illus.

   There is a special collection of materials by and about Kreisler at the Library of Congress in Washington, D.C.

4. Lochner, Louis Paul. Fritz Kreisler. New York: The Macmillan Company, 1950. Reprint 1977. xx, 455 p. + 6 plates, 6 illus., compositions, discography, 270-item bibliography, index.

   Pincherle, Marc. Fritz Kreisler. Genève: René Kister, 1956. 30, [2] p., 25 illus., discography.

   Yampol'sky, Izrail' Markovich. Frits Kreysler: zhizn' i tvorchestvo. Moskva: Muzyka, 1975. 158, [2] p. + 8 plates, discography, bibliography.

5. A0008, A0033, A0100, A0115, A0132, B0001, B0028, B0030, B0035, B0037, B0039, B0045, B0053, B0083, B0089, B0092, B0098, B0109.

   SEE: Downes, Irene, ed. Olin Downes on Music: a Selection of His Writings during the Half-century 1906-1955. New York, 1957.

C0682.
Kremer, Gidon. Soviet Violinist; b. February 27, 1947, Riga, Latvia.

1. Baker 7; DEU; PAB-MI/2 (Bibliography).

2. Strad Oct/1984.

4. von Lewinski, Wolf-Eberhard. Gidon Kremer: Interviews-Tatsachen-Meinungen. Mainz: B. Schotts Soehne, 1982. 152, [1] p., illus., discography.

C0683.
Kreutzer, Leonid. Russian Pianist; b. March 13, 1884, St. Petersburg; d. October 30, 1953, Tokyo, Japan.

1. Baker 7; DEU; MGG (Bibliography); Riemann 12.

C0684.
Kreutzer, Rodolphe. French Violinist; b. November 16, 1766, Versailles; d. January 6, 1831, Geneva, Switzerland.

1. Baker 7 (Bibliography); DEU; Fetis 2/5 + Supp.; Grove 6/10; Mendel; MGG (Bibliography); PAB-MI/2 (Bibliography); Riemann 12 (Bibliography) + Supp. (Bibliography); Schmidl.

4. Hardy, Joseph. Rodolphe Kreutzer: sa jeunesse a Versailles 1766-1789. Paris: Librairie Fischbacher, 1910. 70 p., portrait.

Williams, Michael D. The Violin Concertos of Rodolphe Kreutzer. D.Ed. diss. University of Indiana, 1973.

C0685.
Krupa, Gene. American Jazz Drummer; b. January 15, 1909, Chicago, Illinois; d. October 16, 1973, Yonkers, New York.

1. Baker 7; DEU; Grove 6/10; Grove-AM (Bibliography); Grove-Jazz; JB; JRRM; LJ; PAB-MI/2 (Bibliography); Riemann 12 + Supp. (Bibliography).

2. DB 25/6, 29/7, 32/25, 40/20, 41/5; HiFi/MusAm 24/3.

4. Edwards, Ernie, George Hall and Bill Korst. Gene Krupa and His Orchestra. 1938-1951. Whittier (CA): Jazz Discographies Unlimited, 1968. 36 p.

   Shaw, Arnold. Gene Krupa's Pin-up Life Story. New York: Arco Publishing Co., 1945. 32 p.

5. A0001, A0092.

C0686.
Kubelik Jan. Czechoslovakian (naturalized Hungarian) Violinist; b. July 5, 1880, Michle, near Prague; d. December 5, 1940, Prague.

1. Baker 7 (Bibliography); DEU (Bibliography); Grove 6/10 (Bibliography); MGG (Bibliography); PAB-MI/2 (Bibliography); Riemann 12 + Supp. (Bibliography); Schmidl.

4. Cápová-Richterová, Blazena Ladislava. Ve stínu velikého mistra: hrst vzpomínek na mistra Jana Kubelíka. Toronto: Edice "Nový domov," 1970. 127 p., 21 illus.

   Vratislavský, Jan. Jan Kubelík. Praha: Supraphon, 1978. 78, [2] p. + 6 plates, phonodisk, discography, bibliography.

5. A0142, B0010, B0024, B0035, B0053, B0098, B0109.

   SEE: Kuehle, Gustav. Kuenstler-Album: eine Sammlung von Bildern und Biographien beruehmter Kuenstler und Kuenstlerinnen der Gegenwart auf der Gebiete der Musik. Band I. Leipzig, n.d.

C0687.
Kuhe, Wilhelm. Bohemian Pianist; b. December 10, 1823, Prague; d. October 9, 1912, London, England.

1. Baker 7; Fetis 2/5 + Supp.; Grove 6/10; Mendel; PAB-MI/2 (Bibliography); Schmidl.

3. Kuhe, Wilhelm. My Musical Recollections. London: Richard Bentley and Son, 1896. xxviii, [i], 394 p., 17 illus., index.

C0688.
Kulenkampff, Georg. German Violinist; b. January 23, 1898, Bremen; d. October 4, 1948, Schaffhausen.

1. Baker 7; DEU (Bibliography); Grove 6/10; MGG/Supp.; Riemann 12.

5. B0080, B0129.

C0689.
Kyriakou, Rena. Greek Pianist; b. February 25, 1918, Iraklion.

1. Baker 7; Grove 6/10.

C0690.
Labarre, Théodore-Francois-Joseph. French Harpist; b. March 5, 1805,
Paris; d. March 9, 1870, Paris.

1. Baker 7; DEU; Fetis 2/5 + Supp.; Grove 6/10 (Bibliography); Mendel;
   MGG (Bibliography); Riemann 12; Schmidl.

5. SEE: Méreaux, Amédée under Charles-Auguste de Bériot (C0115.4).

   SEE: Rensch, R. The Harp: Its History, Technique and Repertoire.
   London, 1969.

C0691.
Lachmund, Carl Valentine. American Pianist; b. March 27, 1857, Boone-
ville, Missouri; d. February 20, 1928, Yonkers, New York.

1. Baker 7; PAB-MI/2 (Bibliography).

3. Lachmund, Carl Valentine. Mein Leben mit Franz Liszt: aus dem Tage-
   buch einer Liszt-Schuelers. Eschwege: G.E. Schroeder-Verlag, 1970.
   316 p., 66 illus., Liszt's pupils 1878-1885.

C0692.
Laidlaw, Anna Robena. English Pianist; b. April 30, 1819, Bretton, Yorkshire; d. May 29, 1901, London.

1. Baker 7; Mendel; Riemann 12 (Bibliography); Schmidl.

C0693.
Lalewicz, Georg. Russian Pianist; b. August 21, 1875, Suwalki, Poland;
d. December 1, 1951, Buenos Aires, Argentina.

1. Baker 7; Riemann 12/Supp.; Schmidl.

C0694.
Lamond, Frederic Archibald. Scottish Pianist; b. January 28, 1868,
Glasgow; d. February 21, 1948, Stirling.

1. Baker 7; DEU (Bibliography); Grove 6/10; Riemann 12 (Bibliography);
   Schmidl.

2. RS 65.

3. Lamond, Frederic. The Memoirs of Frederic Lamond. Foreword by Ernest
   Newman. Glasgow: William Maclellan, 1949. 130 p. + 4 plates, 8 illus.

5. A0048, B0028, B0056, B0129.

C0695.
Landowska, Wanda. American Harpsichordist; b. July 5, 1879, Warsaw,
Poland; d. August 16, 1959, Lakeville, Connecticut.

1. Baker 7 (Bibliography); DEU (Bibliography); Grove 6/10
(Bibliography);
    Grove-AM (Bibliography); MGG (Bibliography); PAB-MI/2 (Bibliography);
    Riemann 12 (Bibliography) + Supp. (Bibliography); Schmidl.

2. CL 19/2; HiFi 10/10, 14/12; HiFi/SR 21/4; RS 13, 15-16.

3. Landowska, Wanda. Music of the Past. New York: Alfred A. Knopf, Inc.,
    1924. v, [ii], 185 p., 4 illus., index of names.

    Restout, Denise, comp. and ed. Landowska on Music. New York: Stein
    and Day / Publishers, 1964. 434 p. + 8 plates, 26 illus., discog-
    raphy, index.

4. Anon. Wanda Landowska: pianiste & claveciniste. Paris: Des éditions
    de la Société musicale, 1905. 15 p., 3 illus.

    Gavoty, Bernard. Wanda Landowska. Genève: René Kister, 1957. 30,
    [2] p., 23 illus., discography, compositions.

5. A0033, A0048, B0041, B0042, B0044, B0092, D0012.

    SEE: Gelatt, Roland. Music Makers: Some Outstanding Musical Per-
    formers of Our Day. New York: Alfred A. Knopf, 1953.

    SEE: LePage, Janet Weiner. Women Composers, Conductors, and Musicians
    of the Twentieth Century: Selected Biographies. 2 vols. Metuchen
    (NJ): Scarecrow Press, 1980/83. vol. 1.

C0696.
Lang, Eddie [Salvatore Massaro]. American Jazz Guitarist; b. October 25,
1902, Philadelphia, Pennsylvania; d. March 26, 1933, New York City.

1. Baker 7; DEU; Grove 6/10 (Bibliography); Grove-AM (Bibliography);
    Grove-Jazz; JB; LJ; PAB-MI/2 (Bibliography).

5. A0108, A0143, B0054.

C0697.
Lanzetti, Salvatore. Italian Cellist; b. c.1710, Naples; d. c.1780,
Turin.

1. Baker 7; DEU (under Lancetti); Fetis 2/5; Grove 6/10 (Bibliography);
    Mendel; MGG (Bibliography); Riemann 12 (Bibliography); Schmidl.

3. One of the earliest virtuosos on the cello, Lanzetti was known to
    have written Principes de doigter pour le violoncelle dans tous les
    tons (Amsterdam: Hummel) sometime before 1770. Not cited in RISM
    BVI/1. No copy located.

C0698.
Laredo [y Unzueta], Jaime Eduardo. Bolivian Violinist; b. June 7, 1941, Cochabamba.

1. Baker 7; DEU; Grove 6/10; Grove-AM (Bibliography); PAB-MI/2 (Bibliography); Riemann 12/Supp.

His first wife was the American pianist, Ruth Meckler (C0798).

4. Anon. Jaime Laredo: homenaje. Cochabamba: Universidad Mayor de San Simon, 1959. 66 p.

C0699.
Laretei, Kaebi Alma. Swedish Pianist; b. July 14, 1922, Tartu, Dorpat.

1. Riemann 12/Supp.

2. PQ 55.

3. Laretei, Kaebi. En bit jord: beraettelse. Stockholm: Bonniers Boktryckeri, 1976. 258, [4] p.

Laretei, Kaebi. Vem spelar jag foer? Stockholm: Albert Bonniers Foerlag, 1970. 136, [1] p.

C0700.
La Rocca, Nick [Dominick James]. American Jazz Cornetist; b. April 11, 1889, New Orleans, Louisiana; d. February 22, 1961, New Orleans.

1. Baker 7; DEU; Grove-Jazz; PAB-MI/2 (Bibliography); Riemann 12 + Supp. (Bibliography).

His memorabilia are presently housed at Tulane University.

4. Brunn, H.O. The Story of the Original Dixieland Jazz Band. Baton Rouge (LA): Louisiana State University Press, 1960. xx, 268 p. + 8 plates, 11 illus., 9 tables, index.

Lange, Horst Heinz. Nick La Rocca: ein Portraet. Wetzlar: Pegasus Verlag, 1960. 48 p. + 8 plates, 16 illus., discography.

C0701.
de Larrocha [y de la Calle], Alicia. Spanish Pianist; b. May 23, 1923, Barcelona.

1. Baker 7; Grove 6/10 (Bibliography); PAB-MI/2 (under De Larrocha - Bibliography); Riemann 12 (Bibliography).

2. CL 10/1, 21/4; GR 51/October, 64/November; HiFi/MusAm 17/12, 28/8; HiFi/SR 24/5, 44/3; CK(KB) 5/4; MM 28/2.

5. A0069, A0070, B0058.

SEE: "Monsalvat" reprints under Claudio Arrau (C0039.5).

C0702.
Laskine, Lily. French Harpist; b. August 31, 1893, Paris.

1. Baker 7; DEU; Grove 6/10.

C0703.
Lateiner, Jacob. American Pianist; b. May 31, 1928, Havana, Cuba.

1. Baker 7; Grove 6/10; Grove-AM; PAB-MI/2 (Bibliography).

C0704.
Laub, Ferdinand. Austrian Violinist; b. January 19, 1832, Prague;
d. March 18, 1875, Gries, near Bozen, Tyrol.

1. Baker 7; DEU (Bibliography); Fetis 2/5 + Supp.; Grove 6/10 (Bibliography); Mendel; MGG (Bibliography); Riemann 12 (Bibliography) +
   Supp.; Schmidl.

C0705.
Lautenbacher, Susanne. German Violinist; b. April 19, 1932, Augsburg.

1. Baker 7; Riemann 12/Supp.

C0706.
Lavigne, Antoine-Joseph. French Oboist; b. March 23, 1816, Besancon;
d. August 1, 1886, Manchester, England.

1. Baker 7; Fetis 2/5.

C0707.
Lebègue, Nicolas-Antoine. French Organist; b. 1631, Laon; d. July 6,
1702, Paris.

1. Baker 7; DEU (Bibliography); Fetis 2/1 (under Bègue); Grove 6/10
   (Bibliography); Mendel (under Begue); MGG (Bibliography); Riemann 12
   (Bibliography) + Supp. (Bibliography); Schmidl + Supp.

3. DEU mentions an MS: Méthode pour toucher l'orgue. Paris? 1676.

4. Dufourcq, Norbert. Nicolas Lebègue (1631-1702): organiste de la
   Chapelle royale, organiste de Saint-Merry de Paris. Etude biographique, suivie de nouveaux documents inédits relatifs à l'orgue français
   au XVIIe siècle. Paris: Picard e Cie., 1954. 217, [2] p. + 16 plates,
   discography, 59-item bibliography, index of names.

C0708.
Lebrun, Jean. French French-horn Player; b. April 6, 1759, Lyons; d.
c.1809, Paris.

1. Baker 7; DEU (Bibliography); Grove 6/10 (Bibliography); Mendel; MGG
   (Bibliography); Riemann 12; Schmidl.

C0709.
Lebrun, Ludwig August. German Oboist; baptized May 2, 1752, Mannheim;
d. December 16, 1790, Berlin.

1. Baker 7; DEU; Fetis 2/5; Grove 6/10 (Bibliography); Mendel; MGG (Bibliography); Riemann 12; Schmidl.

C0710.
Leclair, Jean Marie [l'aîné]. French Violinist; b. May 10, 1697, Lyons; d. October 22, 1764, Paris.

1. Baker 7 (Bibliography); DEU (Bibliography); Fetis 2/5 + Supp.; Grove 6/10 (Bibliography); Mendel (under Claire); MGG (Bibliography); PAB-MI/2 (Bibliography); Riemann 12 (Bibliography) + Supp. (Bibliography); Schmidl + Supp.

2. MQ 50/4.

4. Zaslaw, Neal A. Materials for the Life and Works of Jean-Marie Leclair L'aîné. Ph.D. diss. Columbia University, 1970. 526 p.

5. A0131, B0051.

C0711.
Lee, Sebastian. German Cellist; b. December 24, 1805, Hamburg; d. January 4, 1887, Hamburg.

1. Baker 7; DEU; Fetis 2/5; Grove 6/10; Mendel; Riemann 12; Schmidl.

5. A0104.

C0712.
Lefèvre, Jean Xavier. French Clarinetist; b. March 6, 1763, Lausanne; d. November 9, 1829, Paris.

1. Baker 7; DEU (Bibliography); Fetis 2/5; Grove 6/10 (Bibliography); Mendel; MGG/Supp. (Bibliography); Riemann 12 (Bibliography) + Supp. (Bibliography); Schmidl.

4. Youngs, Lowell Vere. Jean Xavier Lefèvre: His Contributions to the Clarinet and Clarinet Playing. D.M.A. diss. Catholic University, 1970. iv, 166 p., plates, musical examples, bibliography.

C0713.
Leginska [Liggins], Ethel. English Pianist; b. April 13, 1886, Hull; d. February 26, 1970, Los Angeles, California.

1. Baker 7; DEU; Grove-AM (Bibliography); PAB-MI/2; Riemann 12; Schmidl.

C0714.
Lemare, Edwin Henry. American Organist; b. September 9, 1865, Ventnor, Isle of Wright, England; d. September 24, 1934, Los Angeles, California.

1. Baker 7; DEU; Grove-AM; PAB-MI/2 (Bibliography); Riemann 12; Schmidl + Supp.

3. Lemare, Edwin Henry. Organs I Have Met: the Autobiography of Edwin H. Lemare, 1866-1934...with Reminiscences by His Wife.... Los Angeles: The Schoolcraft Co., 1956. ix, 122 p., 16 illus., works.

C0715.
Léonard, Hubert. Belgian Violinist; b. April 7, 1819, Bellaire, near
Liège; d. May 6, 1890, Paris, France.

1. Baker 7; Deu (Bibliography); Fetis 2/5 + Supp.; Grove 6/10 (Bibliography); Mendel; MGG (Bibliography); Riemann 12 + Supp.; Schmidl.

5. A0093.

   SEE: Imbert, Hugues. Médaillons contemporains. Paris: Librairie
   Fischbacher, 1902.

C0716.
Leonhardt, Gustav Maria. Dutch Organist/Harpsichordist; b. May 30, 1928,
's Graveland.

1. Baker 7; DEU; Grove 6/10; PAB-MI/2 (Bibliography); Riemann 12/Supp.
   (Bibliography).

2. CL 18/3; HiFi/MusAm 29/3.

5. B0014.

C0717.
Le Roy, René. French Flutist; b. March 4, 1898, Maisons-Laffitte, near
Paris.

1. Baker 7; DEU; Riemann 12/Supp.

5. A0161.

C0718.
Leschetizky, Theodor. Austrian Pianist; b. June 22, 1830, Lancut,
Austrian Poland; d. November 14, 1915, Dresden, Germany.

1. Baker 7; DEU (under Leszetycki - Bibliography); Fetis 2/Supp; Grove
   6/10 (Bibliography); MGG (Bibliography); PAB-MI/2 (Bibliography);
   Riemann 12 (Bibliography) + Supp. (Bibliography).

   He was the teacher of Gabrilowitsch, Paderewski, and Schnabel!

2. ML 35/3; RS 18.

4. Hullah, Annette. Theodor Leschetizky. London: John Lane, the Bodley
   Head, 1906. 85 p., 9 illus.

   Newcomb, Ethel. Leschetizky as I Knew Him. New York: D. Appleton and
   Company, 1921. Reprint 1967 [has a 127-item bibliography by Frederick
   Freedman and Philip Solomita]. viii, 295 p. + 1 plate.

   Potocka, Angèle. Theodore Leschetizky: an Intimate Study of the Man
   and the Musician. Translated by Genevieve Seymour Lincoln. New York:
   The Century Company, 1903. xii, [i], 307 p., 13 illus.

5. A0047, A0058, B0035, B0037.

C0719.
Levant, Oscar. American Pianist; b. December 27, 1906, Pittsburgh, Pennsylvania; d. August 14, 1972, Beverly Hills, California.

1. Baker 7; DEU; Grove 6/10; Grove-AM; PAB-MI/2 (Bibliography); Riemann 12 + Supp.

3. Levant, Oscar. A Smattering of Ignorance. New York: Doubleday, Doran & Co., Inc., 1940. xi, 267 p.

Levant, Oscar. The Memoirs of an Amnesiac. New York: G.P. Putnam's Sons, 1965. 320 p.

Levant, Oscar. The Unimportance of Being Oscar. New York: G.P. Putnam's Sons, 1968. 255 p. + 7 plates, 66 illus., index.

C0720.
Levitzki, Mischa. Russian Pianist; b. May 25, 1898, Kremenchug; d. January 2, 1941, Avon-by-the-Sea, New Jersey.

1. Baker 7; DEU; Grove-AM (Bibliography); PAB-MI/2 (Bibliography); Riemann 12; Schmidl/Supp.

5. B0061.

C0721.
Lévy, Lazare. French Pianist; b. January 18, 1882, Brussels, Belgium; d. September 20, 1964, Paris.

1. Baker 7; DEU; Riemann 12/Supp.; Schmidl/Supp.

C0722.
Lewenthal, Raymond. American Pianist; b. August 29, 1926, San Antonio, Texas.

1. Baker 7; Grove 6/10; Grove-AM; PAB-MI/2 (Bibliography); Riemann/Supp.

2. CL 9/4; HiFi/SR 15/5.

C0723.
Lewis [Zeno], George [Lewis Francis]. American Jazz Clarinetist; b. July 13, 1900, New Orleans, Louisiana; d. December 31, 1968, New Orleans.

1. DEU; Grove 6/10 (Bibliography); Grove-AM (Bibliography); Grove-Jazz; JB; LJ; PAB-MI/2 (Bibliography).

2. DB 30/24.

4. Bethell, Tom. George Lewis: a Jazzman from New Orleans. Berkeley: University of California Press, 1977. [iii], 387 p., illus., discography, notes, 247-item bibliography, index.

McCarthy, Albert J. George Lewis: a Biography, Record Survey and Discography. London: National Jazz Federation, 1958. 16 p.

Stewart, Jay Allison [pseud. for Dorothy Tate]. Call Him George. London: P. Davies, 1961. 286 p. [Reprint New York, 1969. 303, [1] p., 6 illus.].

5. A0031, A0035.

C0724.
Lewis, John Aaron. American Jazz Pianist; b. May 3, 1920, La Grange, IL.

1. Baker 7; DEU (Bibliography); Grove 6/10 (Bibliography); Grove-AM (Bibliography - 20 entries); Grove-Jazz; JB; LJ; PAB-MI/2 (Bibliography).

2. DB 23/3, 24/4, 26/3; HiFi 10/10; CK(KB) 3/4; JJS 4/1.

5. A0001.

SEE: Stuessy, Jr., Clarence under Don Ellis (C0358.5).

C0725.
Lewis, Lux [Meade Anderson]. American Jazz Pianist; b. September 4, 1905, Chicago, Illinois; d. June 7, 1964, Minneapolis, Minnesota.

1. Baker 7; DEU; Grove 6/10 (Bibliography); Grove-AM (Bibliography); Grove-Jazz; LJ.

2. DB 26/4.

C0726.
Leygraf, Hans. Swedish Pianist; b. September 7, 1920, Stockholm.

1. Baker 7; DEU; PAB-MI/2 (Bibliography); Riemann 12 + Supp.

C0727.
Lhévinne, Josef. Russian Pianist; b. December 13, 1874, Orel; d. December 2, 1944, New York City.

1. Baker 7; DEU (Bibliography); Grove 6/10; Grove-AM (Bibliography); PAB-MI/2 (Bibliography); Riemann 12 + Supp.; Schmidl.

He and Rosina established a major studio at the Julliard Graduate School in New York City.

2. CL 20/10; RS 44.

4. Wallace, Robert Kimball. A Century of Music Making: the Lives of Josef and Rosina Lhevinne. Bloomington: Indiana University Press, 1976. xi, 350 p. + 9 plates, 39 illus., notes, 50-item bibliography, discography, filmography, index.

A revision and expansion of Kimball's 1972 Columbia University Ph.D. dissertation, The Life and Times of Josef and Rosina Lhévinne: the Middle Years, 1904-1937.

5. A0048, B0028, B0061, B0108, D0012.

C0728.
Lhévinne, Rosina [née Bessi]. Russian Pianist, wife of Josef; b. March 28, 1880, Kiev; d. November 9, 1976, Glendale, California.

1. Baker 7; DEU; Grove 6/10; Grove-AM (Bibliography); PAB-MI/2 (Bibliography); Riemann 12/Supp.

She was one of the finest pedagogues of her generation.

2. CL 4/2, 16/1; PQ 128; RS 44.

5. B0058.

SEE: Wallace, Robert K. under Josef Lhévinne (C0727.4).

C0729.
Liberace, (Walter) [Wladzin Valentino]. American Pianist; b. May 16, 1919, West Allis, Wisconsin; d. February 4, 1987, Palm Springs, CA.

1. Baker 7 (Bibliography); Grove-AM (Bibliography); PAB-MI/2 (Bibliography).

2. HiFi/SR 26/5; CK(KB) 4/1.

3. Liberace. Liberace: an Autobiography. New York: G.P. Putnam's Sons, 1973. 316 p. + 16 plates, 45 illus.

Liberace. The Things I Love. Edited by Tony Palmer. New York: Grosset & Dunlap, Publishers, 1976. 222, [1] p., illus.

4. Anon. "Liberace: Complete Life Story." Liberace Magazine, vol. 1, no. 1. New York: Ideal Publishing Corp., 1956. 74 p., illus.

Anon. The Wonderful Private World of Liberace. New York: Harper & Row, Publishers, 1986. 222, [1] p., illus.

Guild, Leo. The Loves of Liberace. New York: Avon Publications, 1956. 160 p., illus.

C0730.
Libert, Henri. French Organist; b. December 15, 1869, Paris; d. January 14, 1937, Paris.

1. Baker 7; DEU; Riemann 12 + Supp. (Bibliography); Schmidl + Supp.

C0731.
Lie [Lie-Nissen], Erika. Norwegian Pianist; b. January 17, 1845, Kongsvinger; d. October 27, 1903, Christiania.

1. Baker 7; Mendel.

C0732.
Liebling, Emil. American Pianist; b. April 12, 1851, Pless, Silesia; d. January 20, 1914, Chicago, Illinois.

1. Baker 7; DEU; Grove-AM; PAB-MI/2 (Bibliography).

3. Liebling, Emil. As Others See Us: a Faithful Record of Mr. Emil
   Liebling's Concert Experiences during the Concert Season of 1893–
   94. Chicago: Printed for Private Distribution, 1894. xliii p.

C0733.
Liebling, Georg [pseud. for André Myrot]. American Pianist; b. January
22, 1865, Berlin, Germany; d. February 7, 1946, New York City.

1. Baker 7; DEU; Riemann 12; Schmidl.

4. Braun, Gottfried. Hofpianist Georg Liebling: Biographie. Berlin:
   Verlag der Buchhandlung Franz Barschall, n.d. c.1895. 17, [1] p.

C0734.
Lill, John Richard. English Pianist; b. March 17, 1944, London.

1. Baker 7; Grove 6/10; PAB-MI/2 (Bibliography).

2. GR 56/January.

C0735.
Linde, Hans-Martin. German Flutist; b. May 24, 1930, Werne, near
Dortmund.

1. Baker 7; DEU; Grove 6/10; PAB-MI/2 (Bibliography); Riemann 12/Supp.
   (Bibliography).

C0736.
Lipatti, Dinu. Romanian Pianist; b. April 1, 1917, Bucharest; d. December 2, 1950, Chene-Bourg, near Geneva, Switzerland.

1. Baker 7; DEU (Bibliography); Grove 6/11 (Bibliography); MGG (Bibliography); PAB-MI/2 (Bibliography); Riemann 12 (Bibliography) + Supp.
   (Bibliography).

2. GR 28; RS 15.

4. Anon. 1970: in memoriam Dinu Lipatti, 1917–1950. Genève: Editions
   Labor et Fides, 1970. 127, [2] p., illus, discography, compositions.

   Originally published in 1952 as Hommage à Dinu Lipatti (93 p. + 13
   plates, 21 illus., discography, compositions).

   Lipatti, Anna. La vie du pianiste Dinu Lipatti: écrite par sa mère.
   Paris: La Colombe, 1954. 92, [1] p. + 8 plates, 20 illus., discography, compositions.

   Reprint (?): Dinu Lipatti: la douleur de ma vie. Genève: Perret-
   Gentil, 1967. 93 p. + 4 plates, 10 illus., discography, compositions.

   Tanasescu, Dragos. Dinu Lipatti: Monografie. Bucureşti: Editura muzicala a uniunii compozitorilor, 1971. 224 p. + 6 plates, illus., discography, compositions, 83-item bibliography.

Tanasescu, Dragos. Lipatti. Bucharest: Meridiane Publishing House, 1965. 98 p., illus., discography.

5. B0080; D0012.

C0737.
Lipinsky, Karol Józef. Polish Violinist; b. October 30, 1790, Radzyn; d. December 16, 1861, near Lwow.

1. Baker 7; DEU (Bibliography); Fetis 2/5; Grove 6/11; Mendel; MGG (Bibliography); Riemann 12 (Bibliography) + Supp. (Bibliography); Schmidl.

4. Powroiniak, Józef. Karol Lipínski. Kraków: Polskie Wydawnictwo Muzyczne, 1970. 259, [1] p., 39 illus., 16-item bibliography.

C0738.
List, Eugene. American Pianist; b. July 6, 1918, Philadelphia, PA.

1. Baker 7; Grove 6/11; Grove-AM (Bibliography); PAB-MI/2 (Bibliography); Riemann 12 + Supp.

2. CL 18/5.

C0739.
Listemann, Bernhard Friedrich Wilhelm. American Violinist; b. August 28, 1841, Schlotheim, Germany; d. February 11, 1917, Chicago, Illinois.

1. Baker 7; DEU; Grove-AM (Bibliography); Mendel; PAB-MI/2 (Bibliography); Riemann 12; Schmidl + Supp.

C0740.
Liszt, Franz [Ferencz]. Hungarian Pianist; b. October 22, 1811, Raiding, near Oedenburg; d. July 31, 1886, Bayreuth, Germany.

1. Baker 7 (Bibliography); DEU (Bibliography); Fetis 2/5 + Supp.; Grove 6/11 (Bibliography); Mendel; MGG (Bibliography); PAB-MI/2 (Bibliography); Riemann 12 (Bibliography) + Supp. (Bibliography); Schmidl + Supp.

2. CL 6/4; MM 13/2; PQ 89 (Special Issue).

3. His extensive correspondence, much of it as yet unpublished, is in the Liszt Museum in Weimar. Lina Ramann edited the Gesammelte Schriften (Leipzig, 6 vols., 1800-1883), and Julius Kapp published a Register zu Liszts Gesammelten Schriften in 1909.

Souvenirs d'un pianiste: réponse aux souvenirs d'une Cosaque. Paris: Lachaud et Burdin, 1874. 255 p.

Sometimes erroneously attributed to Liszt.

4. Dobiey, Herbert. Die Klaviertechnick des jungen Franz Liszt. Ph.D. diss. Berlin University, 1932. 47 p.

Goodman, Alfred. Liszts amerikanische Schueler. Ph.D. diss. Technical University of Berlin, 1972. 172 p., illus., bibliography.

Landau, Hela. Die Neuerungen der Klaviertechnik bei Franz Liszt. Ph.D. diss. University of Vienna, 1933.

Machnek, Elsie. The Pedagogy of Franz Liszt. Ph.D. diss. Northwestern University, 1965. 244 p., bibliography.

Perényi, Eleanor. Liszt: the Artist as Romantic Hero. Boston: Little, Brown and Company, 1974. x, i, 466 p. + 16 plates, 16 illus., 179-item bibliography, notes, index.

Reis, Pedro Batalha. Liszt na sua passagem por Lisboa em 1845. Lisboa: Edicões De Sassetti & Ca, 1945. 172, [3] p., 32 illus., index.

Ruesch, Walter. Franz Liszts Années de Pèlerinage: Beitraege zur Geschichte seines Persoenlichkeit und seines Stiles. Ph.D. diss. University of Zurich, 1934. 63 p.

Siloti, Alexander Il'yich. Moy vospominaniya o Franz Liste. St. Petersburg, 1911 [Edinburgh, 1913. Reprint 1986]. No copy located.

Steinberg, Arne. Franz Liszt's Approach to Piano Playing. D.M.A. University of Maryland, 1971. 263 p.

Stradal, August. Erinnerungen an Franz Liszt. Bern: Verlag Paul Haupt, 1929. 173 p. + 2 plates, illus.

Stradal was a piano student of Liszt in 1884.

Streletzki, Anton. Personal Recollections of Chats with Liszt. London: E. Donajowski, n.d. c.1893. 23 p.

Walker, Alan. Franz Liszt: the Virtuoso Years 1811-1847. New York: Alfred A. Knopf, Inc., 1983. xxiii, 481 p., 23 illus., catalogue of concert works ???-item bibliography, source list, index.

Walker's Prologue, "Liszt and the Literature", is most helpful.

5. A0014, A0023, A0033, A0035, A0047, A0051, A0063, B0011, B0020, B0035, B0065, B0083, B0109, B0128, C0694.3, C0984.3.

SEE: Autobiography of Alfred Brendel (C0179.3).

SEE: Entries under José Vianna Da Motta, a student of Liszt. (C0279).

SEE: Autobiography of Arthur Friedheim (C0421.3).

SEE: Hueffer, Francis. Half a Century of Music in England 1837-1887: Essays towards a History. London: Chapman and Hall Ltd., 1889.

SEE: Newman, Ernest. The Life of Richard Wagner. vol. 4. New York: Alfred A, Knopf, 1946.

SEE: Roës, Paul. Music, the Mystery and the Reality. Translated by
Edna Dean McGray. Chevy Chase (MD): E&M Publishing, 1978.

SEE: Wagner, Richard. My Life. New York: Tudor Publishing Company,
1936 [original 1911].

C0741.
Llobet, Miguel. Catalan Guitarist; b. October 18, 1875, Barcelona;
d. February 22, 1938, Barcelona.

1. Baker 7; DEU; Grove 6/11; Riemann 12; Schmidl + Supp.

C0742.
Lloyd-Webber, Julian. English Cellist; b. April 14, 1951, London.

1. Baker 7; PAB-MI/2 (Bibliography).

3. Lloyd-Webber, Julian. Travels with My Cello. London: Pavilion Books
Limited, 1984. 129 p. + 4 plates, 15 illus., discography, index.

C0743.
Locatelli, Pietro. Italian Violinist; b. September 3, 1695, Bergamo;
d. March 30, 1764, Amsterdam, Holland.

1. Baker 7 (Bibliography); DEU (Bibliography); Fetis 2/5; Grove 6/11
(Bibliography); Mendel; MGG (Bibliography) + Supp.; PAB-MI/2 (Bib-
liography); Riemann 12 (Bibliography) + Supp. (Bibliography);
Schmidl + Supp.

4. Calmeyer, John Hendrick. The Life, Times, and Works of Antonio
Pietro Locatelli. Ph.D. diss. University of North Carolina, 1969.
vi, 465 p., illus., list of works, bibliography.

C0744.
Loeillet, Jean-Baptiste. French Harpsichordist; b. November 18, 1680,
Ghent, Belgium; d. July 19, 1730, London, England.

1. Baker 7 (Bibliography); DEU (Bibliography); Fetis 2/5; Grove 6/11
(Bibliography); Mendel; MGG (Bibliography); PAB-MI/2 (Bibliography);
Riemann 12 (Bibliography) + Supp. (Bibliography); Schmidl + Supp.

C0745.
Loesser, Arthur. American Pianist; b. August 26, 1894, New York City;
d. January 4, 1969, Cleveland, Ohio.

1. Baker 7; Grove-AM.

2. CL 26/9.

C0746.
Loevensohn, Marix. Belgian Cellist; b. March 31, 1880, Courtrai;
d. April 24, 1943, Montauban, France.

1. Baker 7; Riemann 12 + Supp. (Bibliography).

C0747.
Lolli, Antonio. Italian Violinist; b. c.1730, Bergamo; d. August 10, 1802, Palermo.

1. Baker 7 (Bibliography); DEU (Bibliography); Fetis 2/5; Grove 6/11 (Bibliography); Mendel; MGG (Bibliography); Riemann 12 (Bibliography) + Supp. (Bibliography); Schmidl.

2. MQ 56.

4. de Rangoni, Giovanni Battista. Saggio sul gusto della musica col carattere dei tre celebri sonatori de violino, i signori Nardini, Lolli e Pugnani. Livorno: Tommaso Masi e compagni, 1790. vii, 91 p.

C0748.
Long, Marguerite [Marie Charlotte]. French Pianist; b. November 13, 1874, Nîmes; d. February 13, 1966, Paris.

1. Baker 7 (Bibliography); DEU (Bibliography); Grove 6/11; Riemann 12 + Supp. (Bibliography).

3. Long, Marguerite. Au piano avec Maurice Ravel. Paris: Julliard, 1971. 186, [1] p. + 4 plates, 10 illus.

She wrote similar books on Debussy (1960) and Fauré (1963).

4. Khentova, Sof'ia Mikhailovna. Margarita Long. Moskva: Gos. musykal' noe izd-vo, 1961. 103 p., illus., bibliographical footnotes.

Weill, Janine. Marguerite Long: une vie fascinante. Paris: Julliard, 1969. 246 p. + 2 plates, 11 illus.

C0749.
Longy, Gustave Georges Léopold, French Oboist; b. August 29, 1868, Abbeville; d. March 29, 1930, Mareuil (Dordogne).

1. Baker 7; Grove-AM (Bibliography).

The Boston Public Library has a collection of materials on Longy.

C0750.
de Lorenzo, Leonardo. American Flutist; b. August 29, 1875, Viggiano, Italy; d. July 27, 1962, Santa Barbara, California.

1. Baker 7; DEU; Schmidl (double entry).

3. de Lorenzo, Leonardo. My Complete Story of the Flute: the Instrument, the Performer, the Music. New York: The Citadel Press, 1951. xvi, 493, [32] p., 35 illus. Also listed as A0903.

C0751.
Loriod, Yvonne. French Pianist; b. January 20, 1924, Houilles, Seine-et-Oise.

1. Baker 7; DEU; Grove 6/11; PAB-MI/2 (Bibliography); Riemann 12 + Supp.

C0752.
Lowenthal, Jerome Nathaniel. American Pianist; b. February 11, 1932,
Philadelphia, Pennsylvania.

1. Baker 7; Grove-AM.

C0753.
Loyonnet, Paul. French Pianist; b. May 13, 1889, Paris.

1. Encyclopedia of Music in Canada (Bibliography); PAB-MI/2 (Bibliography).

3. Loyonnet, Paul. Paradoxes sur le pianiste. Ottawa: Les Editions
   Leméac Inc., 1981. 195 p.

4. Allard, Ghyslaine. La technique pianistique de Paul Loyonnet. thesis.
   University of Montreal, 1962.

C0754.
Luboshutz [Luboshits], Léa. Russian Violinist; b. February 22, 1885,
Odessa; d. March 18, 1965, Philadelphia, Pennsylvania.

1. Baker 7; DEU; Grove-AM; PAB-MI/2 (Bibliography); Riemann 12.

C0755.
Luca, Sergiu. Israeli Violinist; b. April 4, 1943, Bucharest, Romania.

1. Baker 7; Grove 6/11; Grove-AM.

C0756.
Luebeck, Ernst. Dutch Pianist; b. August 24, 1829, The Hague;
d. September 17, 1876, Paris, France.

1. Baker 7; DEU; Mendel; Riemann 12; Schmidl.

C0757.
Lupu, Radu. Romanian Pianist; b. November 30, 1945, Galati.

1. Baker 7; DEU; Grove 6/11; PAB-MI/2 (Bibliography).

2. CL 5/6, 20/5, 24/6.

C0758.
Luvisi, Lee. American Pianist; b. December 12, 1937, Louisville,
Kentucky.

1. Baker 7; Grove-AM; PAB-MI/2 (Bibliography); Riemann 12/Supp.

C0759.
Lympany [Johnstone], Moura. English Pianist; b. August 18, 1916,
Saltash.

1. Baker 7; DEU; Grove 6/11 (Bibliography); PAB-MI/2 (Bibliography);
   Riemann 12 + Supp.

C0760.
Lyttelton, Humphrey. English Jazz Trumpeter; b. May 23, 1921, Eton, Bucks.

1. Grove 6/11; Grove-Jazz; JB; JRRM; LJ; PAB-MI/2 (Bibliography).

3. Lyttelton, Humphrey. I Play as I Please: the Memoirs of an Old Etonian Trumpeter. London: MacGibbon & Kee, 1954. 200 p., illus.

Lyttelton, Humphrey. Second Chorus. London: MacGibbon & Kee, 1958. 198 p. + 6 plates, 18 illus., discography.

Lyttelton, Humphrey. Take It from the Top: an Autobiographical Scrapbook. London: Robson Books Ltd, 1975. 164 p. + 4 plates, illus.

"...a collection of anecdotal portraits of jazz players." Grove 6.

Lyttelton, Humphrey. Why No Beethoven. London: Robson Books Ltd, 1984. 176 p., illus.

C0761.
Ma, Yo-Yo. Chinese Cellist; b. October 7, 1955, Paris, France.

1. Baker 7; DEU; Grove-AM (Bibliography).

2. GR 62/June; Strad May/1984.

5. B0027.

C0762.
Magaloff, Nikita. Swiss Pianist; b. February 21, 1912, St. Petersburg, Russia.

1. Baker 7; Grove 6/11; PAB-MI/2 (Bibliography); Riemann 12 + Supp.

5. B0110.

C0763.
Majeske, Daniel Harold. American Violinist; b. September 17, 1932, Detroit, Michigan.

1. Baker 7; Grove-AM.

C0764.
Malcuzynski, Witold. Polish Pianist; b. August 10, 1914, Warsaw, Poland; d. July 17, 1977, Palma, Majorca.

1. Baker 7; DEU (Bibliography); Grove 6/11 (Bibliography); PAB-MI/2 (Bibliography); Riemann 12 + Supp. (Bibliography).

4. Gavoty, Bernard. Witold Malcuzynski. Genève: René Kister, 1957. 27, [5] p., 23 illus., recordings.

5. B0041.

C0765.
Malgoire, Jean-Claude. French Oboist; b. November 25, 1940, Avignon.

1. Baker 7; DEU; Grove 6/11; PAB-MI/2 (Bibliography).

2. GR 54/May.

C0766.
Malkin, Joseph. American Cellist; b. September 24, 1879, Propoisk, near Odessa, Russia; d. September 1, 1969, New York City.

1. Baker 7; DEU; Grove-AM; PAB-MI/2 (Bibliography); Riemann 12 + Supp.

C0767.
Mana-Zucca [Zuckermann, Augusta]. American Pianist; b. December 25, 1887, New York City; d. March 8, 1981, Miami Beach, Florida.

1. Baker 7; DEU; Grove 6/11; Grove-AM; PAB-MI/2 (Bibliography).

Her MS memoirs and papers are at the University of Miami.

C0768.
Mandel, Alan. American Pianist; b. July 17, 1935, New York City.

1. Baker 7; PAB-MI/2 (Bibliography).

2. HiFi/SR 23/6.

C0769.
Manen, Juan. Spanish Violinist; b. March 14, 1883, Barcelona; d. June 26, 1971, Barcelona.

1. Baker 7; DEU; Grove 6/11; Riemann 12 + Supp.; Schmidl.

3. Manen, Juan. _Mes experiencias_. 3 vols. Barcelona: Editorial Juventud, S.A., 1944/1964/1970. 280 p. + 8 plates, 19 illus.; 191 p., 4 illus.; 262, [9] p., compositions, publications.

   The volumes are subtitled: _El nino prodigioso_, _El joven artista_, and _Trabajar, sufrir, avanzar: variaciones sin tema_.

C0770.
Mangione, Chuck [Charles Frank]. American Jazz Trumpeter/Flugelhornist; b. November 29, 1940, Rochester, New York.

1. Baker 7; Grove-AM (Bibliography); Grove-Jazz; JB; PAB-MI/2 (Bibliography).

2. DB 38/20, 40/10, 42/9, 45/6.

C0771.
Mann, Herbie. American Jazz Flutist; b. April 16, 1930, New York City.

1. Baker 7; Grove-Jazz; JB; PAB-MI/2 (Bibliography).

2. DB 23/17, 25/3, 31/24, 35/24, 37/25, 41/16, 47/12.

C0772.
Manone, Wingy [Joseph]. American Jazz Trumpeter; b. February 13, 1904, New Orleans, Louisiana; d. July 9, 1982, Las Vegas, Nevada.

1. Grove-Jazz; JB; LJ; PAB-MI/2 (Bibliography).

2. DB 25/23, 33/7.

3. Manone, Wingy. Trumpet on the Wing. Foreword by Bing Crosby. Garden City (NY): Doubleday & Co., Inc., 1948. 256 p. + 4 plates, 9 illus., discography.

C0773.
Marchal, André-Louis. French Organist; b. February 6, 1894, Paris.

1. Baker 7; DEU (Bibliogaphy); Grove 6/11; PAB-MI/2 (Bibliography); Riemann 12 + Supp. (Bibliography).

C0774.
Marchand, Louis. French Organist/Harpsichordist; b. February 2, 1669, Lyons; d. February 17, 1732, Paris.

1. Baker 7 (Bibliography); DEU; Fetis 2/5; Grove 6/11 (Bibliography); Mendel; MGG (Bibliography); PAB-MI/2 (Bibliography); Riemann 12 (Bibliography) + Supp. (Bibliography); Schmidl.

5. BO050.

C0775.
Marcovici, Silvia. Romanian Violinist; b. January 30, 1952, Bacau.

1. Baker 7; PAB-MI/2 (Bibliography); Riemann 12/Supp.

C0776.
Maréchal, Maurice. French Cellist; b. October 3, 1892, Dijon; d. April 19, 1964, Paris.

1. Baker 7; DEU; Riemann 12; Schmidl + Supp.

4. Ginzburg, Lev Solomonovich. Moris Mareshal. Moskva: Muzika, 1972. 176 p. + 9 plates., illus., bibliographical references.

C0777.
Marks, Alan. American Pianist; b. May 14, 1949, Chicago, Illinois.

1. Baker 7; Grove-AM; PAB-MI/2 (Bibliography).

C0778.
Marlowe [Sapira], Sylvia. American Harpsichordist; b. September 26, 1908, New York City; d. December 11, 1981, New York City.

1. Baker 7; Grove 6/11; Grove-AM (Bibliography); PAB-MI/2 (Bibliography).

2. HiFi/MusAm 32/6.

C0779.
Marsalis, Wynton. American Trumpeter; b. October 18, 1961, New Orleans, Louisiana.

1. Baker 7; Grove-AM; Grove-Jazz.

2. DB 49/1, 49/12, 51/7, 54/11.

5. A0035.

C0780.
Marsik, Martin Pierre Joseph. Belgian Violinist; b. March 9, 1848, Liège; d. October 21, 1924, Paris, France.

1. Baker 7; DEU (Bibliography); Grove 6/11 (Bibliography); PAB-MI/2 (Bibliography); Riemann 12 + Supp. (Bibliography); Schmidl.

C0781.
Marteau, Henri. Swedish Violinist; b. March 31, 1874, Reims, France; d. October 3, 1934, Lichtenberg, Bavaria.

1. Baker 7; DEU (Bibliography); Grove 6/11 (Bibliography); PAB-MI/2 (Bibliography); Riemann 12; Schmidl.

4. Marteau, Blanche. Henri Marteau: Siegeszug einer Geige. Tutzing: Verlegt bei Hans Schneider, 1971. 648 p. + 12 plates, illus., index of names.

   Weiss, Guenther and Hermann Muellich. Mitteilungen des Hauses Marteau in Lichtenberg/Ofr. Tutzing: Verlegt bei Hans Schneider, 1982. 101 p., illus.

C0782.
Martins, João Carlos. Brazilian Pianist; b. June 25, 1940, São Paulo.

1. Baker 7; Riemann 12/Supp.

2. CK(KB) 7/8.

C0783.
Mason, William. American Pianist; b. January 24, 1829, Boston, Massachusetts; d. July 14, 1908, Boston.

1. Baker 7 (Bibliography); DEU (Bibliography); Grove 6/11 (Bibliography); Grove-AM (Bibliography); PAB-MI/2 (Bibliography); Riemann 12; Schmidl.

3. Mason, William. Memories of a Musical Life. New York: The Century Co., 1901. Reprint 1970. xii, 306 p., 13 illus., index.

4. Graber, Kenneth G. The Life and Works of William Mason (1829-1908). Ph.D. diss. Univeristy of Iowa, 1976. xiv, 358 p., illus., tables, musical examples, list of works, appendices, bibliography.

C0784.
Massart, Lambert-Joseph. Belgian Violinist; b. July 19, 1811, Liège;
d. February 13, 1892, Paris, France.

1. Baker 7; DEU; Fetis 2/6 + Supp.; Grove 6/11; MGG (Bibliography);
Riemann 12; Schmidl.

C0785.
Masselos, William. American Pianist; b. August 11, 1920, Niagara Falls,
New York.

1. Baker 7; Grove 6/11; Grove-AM.

2. CL 24/1.

C0786.
Matteis, Nicola. Italian Violinist; b. Naples(?); d. c.1714, London(?).

1. Baker 7; DEU; Fetis 2/6 (under Mattheis); Grove 6/11 (Bibliography);
MGG (Bibliography); Riemann 12 (Bibliography) + Supp. (Bibliography); Schmidl + Supp.

2. MQ 28/2, 46/1.

3. Matteis, Nicola. The False Consonances of Musick or Instructions for
the Playing a True Base upon the Guitarre, with Choice Examples and
cleare Directions to Enable Any Man in a Short Time to Play All
Musicall Ayres. London: J. Carr, 1682 [original, in Italian, London,
c. 1680]. 96 p.

4. Proctor, G.A. The Works of Nicola Matteis, Sr.. Ph.D. diss. University of Rochester, 1960.

5. D0011 (Vol. 10).

C0787.
Matthaei, Karl. Swiss Organist; b. April 23, 1897, Olten; d. February 8,
1960, Winterthur.

1. Baker 7; DEU; Grove 6/11 (Bibliography); Riemann 12 + Supp. (Bibliography); Schmidl/Supp.

C0788.
Matthay, Tobias Augustus. English Pianist; b. February 19, 1858, London;
d. December 14, 1945, High Marley, near Haslemere, Surrey.

1. Baker 7 (Bibliography); DEU (Bibliography); Grove 6/11 (Bibliography); MGG/Supp. (Bibliography); PAB-MI/2 (Bibliography); Riemann
12 + Supp. (Bibliography); Schmidl + Supp.

Internationally acclaimed as a teacher and writer (author of nineteen
books on pedagogy and interpretation), Matthay's influence in piano
circles remains formidable.

2. CL 21/3; PQ 134; RS 5, 24.

4. Matthay, Jessie Henderson. The Life and Works of Tobias Matthay. London: Boosey & Hawkes, Ltd., 1945. xiii, 113 p. + 22 plates, 22 illus., list of educational works.

C0789.
Matthews, Denis James. English Pianist; b. February 27, 1919, Coventry.

1. Baker 7; DEU; Grove 6/11; PAB-MI/2 (Bibliography); Riemann 12 + Supp.

3. Matthews, Denis. In Pursuit of Music. London: Victor Gollancz Ltd, 1966. 189 p., index.

C0790.
Maugars, André. French Bass Violist; b. c.1580; d. c.1645.

1. DEU (Bibliography); Fetis 2/6 + Supp.; Grove 6/11 (Bibliography); MGG (Bibliography); Riemann 12 (Bibliography) + Supp.; Schmidl + Supp.

4. Roquet, Antoine-Ernest [pseud. for Ernest Thoinan]. Maugars, célèbre joueur de viole, musicien du Cardinal de Richelieu...: sa biographie. Paris: A. Claudin, Libraire-Editeur, 1865. 43 p.

C0791.
Maurer, Ludwig Wilhelm. German Violinist; b. February 8, 1789, Potsdam; d. October 25, 1878, St. Petersburg, Russia.

1. Baker 7; DEU (Bibliography); Fetis 2/6 + Supp.; Grove 6/11 (Bibliography); Mendel; MGG (Bibliography); Riemann 12; Schmidl.

C0792.
Mayseder, Joseph. Austrian Violinist; b. October 26, 1789, Vienna; d. November 21, 1863, Vienna.

1. Baker 7; Fetis 2/6; Grove 6/11 (Bibliography); Mendel; MGG (Bibliography); PAB-MI/2 (Bibliography); Riemann 12 (Bibliography) + Supp. (Bibliography); Schmidl.

4. Hellsberg, Eugen. Joseph Mayseder (1789-1863). 2 vols. Ph.D. diss. University of Vienna, 1955. 176 p.; 193 p., thematic catalogue, bibliography.

C0793.
Mazas, Jacques-Féréol. French Violinist; b. September 23, 1782, Lavaur (Tarn); d. August 25, 1849, Bordeaux.

1. Baker 7; DEU (Bibliography); Fetis 2/6; Grove 6/11 (Bibliography); Mendel; MGG (Bibliography); PAB-MI/2 (Bibliography); Riemann 12 (Bibliography); Schmidl.

C0794.
McDonald, Susan. American Harpist; b. May 26, 1935, Rock Island, IL.

1. Baker 7; Grove 6/11; PAB-MI/2 (Bibliography).

C0795.
McLaughlin, John. British Guitarist; b. January 4, 1942, Yorkshire.

1. Baker 7; Grove-AM (Bibliography); Grove-Jazz; JB (11 entries); PAB-MI/2 (Bibliography).

2. DB 41/11, 45/12, 49/4, 52/3.

5. A0108.

C0796.
McPartland, Jimmy [James]. American Jazz Trumpeter; b. March 15, 1907, Chicago, Illinois.

1. Baker 7; Grove-Jazz; LJ; PAB-MI/2 (Bibliography).

2. DB 24/24, 26/7.

5. A0025.

C0797.
McPartland [née Turner], Margaret Marian. English Jazz Pianist; b. March 20, 1920, Windsor.

1. Baker 7; Grove-AM (Bibliog.); Grove-Jazz; JB; LJ; PAB-MI/2 (Bibliog.)

2. DB 24/18, 26/6, 30/27; HiFi/MusAm 19/1; CK(KB) 2/1, 3/12, 7/2.

C0798.
Mead, Olive. American Violinist; b. November 22, 1874, Cambridge, Massachusetts; d. February 27, 1946, Cambridge.

1. Grove-AM (Bibliography). See also MusAm 5/25, 15/19.

C0799.
Mehegan, John. American Jazz Pianist; b. June 6, 1916, Hartford, Connecticut; d. April 3, 1984, New Canaan, Connecticut.

1. Baker 7; Grove-Jazz; JB; JRRM; PAB-MI/2 (Bibliography).

C0800.
Menges, Isolde Marie. English Violinist; b. May 16, 1893, Hove; d. January 13, 1976, Richmond, Surrey.

1. Baker 7; Grove 6/12; PAB-MI/2 (Bibliography); Riemann 12.

C0801.
Menter, Joseph. German Cellist; b. January 23, 1808, Teisbach, Bavaria; d. April 18, 1856, Munich.

1. Baker 7; Fetis 2/6; Riemann 12 + Supp.; Schmidl.

C0802.
Menter, Sophie. German Pianist, daughter of **Joseph**; b. July 29, 1846, Munich; d. February 23, 1918, Munich.

1. Baker 7; Mendel; PAB—MI/2 (Bibliography); Riemann 12; Schmidl.

C0803.
Menuhin, Yehudi. American Violinist; b. April 22, 1916, New York City.

1. Baker 7; Grove 6/12; Grove-AM (Bibliography); MGG (Bibliography); PAB—MI/2 (Bibliography); Riemann 12 + Supp. (Bibliography); Schmidl/ Supp.

2. GR 53/April; HiFi/MusAm 16/4; RS 48; Strad Feb/1976.

3. Menuhin, Yehudi. The Compleat Violinist: Thoughts, Exercises, Reflections of an Itinerant Violinist. Edited by Christopher Hope. New York: Summit Books, 1986. x, 148 p., illus.

   Mehuhin, Yehudi. Theme and Variations. New York: Stein and Day, Publishers, 1972. xiv, 192 p. + 4 plates, 13 illus., index.

   Menuhin, Yehudi. Unfinished Journey. London: Macdonald and Janes Publishers Limited, 1977. xvii, 393 p. + 24 plates, 68 illus., index.

4. Anon. Virtuoso: the Menuhin Issue. Waverly (PA): The Virtuoso Concert Society, 1964. 71, [1] p., illus.

   Daniels, Robin. Conversations with Menuhin. Foreword by Lawrence Durrell. New York: St. Martin's Press, 1979. 188, [4] p., illus., index.

   Fenby, Eric. Menuhin's House of Music: an Impression of the Yehudi Menuhin School at Stoke d'Abernon Surrey England. Foreword by Yehudi Menuhin. New York: Praeger Publishers, 1969. 140 p., illus.

   Gavoty, Bernard. Yehudi Menuhin et Georges Enesco. Genève: René Kister, 1955. 29, [3] p., 27 illus., recordings.

   Jocelyn, Edith Frances. Music Festivals with Yehudi Menuhin: a Series of Letters 1958/1959. London: W. Paxton & Co., Ltd., 1959. unpaginated [94 p.].

   Magidoff, Robert. Yehudi Menuhin: the Story of the Man and the Musician. Garden City (NY): Doubleday and Company, 1955. 319 p. + 8 plates, 39 illus., recordings, index. [2nd edition with additional chapters by Henry Raynor. London: Hale, 1973. 350 p. + 12 plates, illus., recordings, index].

   Menuhin, Diana. Life with Yehudi: Fiddler's Moll. Foreword by Yehudi Menuhin. New York: St. Martin's Press, 1984. xii, [ii], 237 p. + 4 plates, 16 illus., index.

   Rolfe, Lionel Menuhin. The Mehuhins: a Family Odyssey. San Francisco: Panjandrum/Aris Books, 1978. xvii, 21-251, [5] p., illus., index.

   Schultz, Klaus, ed. Yehudi Menuhin und das Berliner Philharmonische Orchester. Berlin: Sonderheft der Philharmonischen Blaetter, 1979. 78 p., illus., discography.

Spingel, Hans Otto. Yehudi Menuhin. Berlin: Rembrandt Verlag, 1964. 61 p., 34 illus., discography.

Wenzl, Oldrich. Yehudi Menuhin. Praha: Mladá Fronta, 1964. 48, [2] p., poems.

Wymer, Norman. Yehudi Menuhin. London: Phoenix House, 1961. 107 p., 14 illus., index.

5. A0008, A0100, A0132, A0142, B0030, B0039, B0041, B0045, B0058, B0070, B0081, B0092, B0110, B0130, D0012.

C0804.
von Meyer [de Meyer], Leopold. German Pianist; b. December 20, 1816, Baden, near Vienna; d. March 5, 1883, Dresden.

1. Baker 7; Fetis 2/6; Mendel; Schmidl.

3. de Meyer, Leopold. The Biography of Leopold de Meyer, Imperial and Royal Court Pianist, by Diploma, to Their Majesties the Emperors of Austria and Russia. London: Printed by Palmer and Clayton, 1845. 32 p., 4 illus.

C0805.
Meyer, Waldemar Julius. German Violinist; b. February 4, 1853, Berlin; d. December 30, 1940. Unterschoenau, Berchtesgarden.

1. Riemann 12.

3. Meyer, Waldemar Julius. Aus einem Kuenstlerleben. Berlin: Verlag von Georg Stilke, 1925. 112 p., 24 illus.

C0806.
Mezzrow, Mezz [Milton Mesirow]. American Jazz Clarinetist; b. November 9, 1899, Chicago, Illinois; d. August 5, 1972, Paris, France.

1. Grove-AM (Bibliography); Grove-Jazz; PAB-MI/2 (Bibliography); JB (11 entries); JRRM; LJ; Riemann 12 + Supp. (Bibliography).

Important primarily for the recording sessions he organized.

2. DB 31/32, 35/11.

3. Mezzrow, Milton and Bernard Wolfe. Really the Blues. New York: Random House, Inc., 1946. 388 p., glossary, index.

4. Panassié, Hugues. Quand Mezzrow enregistre: histoire des disques de Milton Mezzrow et Tommy Ladnier. Preface by Milton Mezzrow. Paris: Robert Laffont, 1952. 158, [3] p.

5. A0001.

C0807.
Michelangeli, Arturo Benedetti. Italian Pianist; b. January 5, 1920, Brescia.

1. Baker 7; Grove 6/12 (Bibliography); PAB-MI/2 (Bibliography); Riemann 12 (under Benedetti Michelangeli).

2. MM 21/10.

5. A0060, B0042.

C0808.
Middelschulte, Wilhelm. German Organist; b. April 3, 1863, Werne, near Dortmund; d. May 4, 1943, Werne.

1. Baker 7; MGG/Supp. (Bibliography); PAB-MI/2 (Bibliography); Riemann 12; Schmidl.

2. MQ 14/2.

C0809.
Mikhasoff, Ivar Emilan. American Pianist; b. March 8, 1944, Albany, NY.

1. Baker 7; Grove-AM; PAB-MI/2 (Bibliography).

2. HiFi/MusAm 32/12, 33/7.

C0810.
Miller, Robert. American Pianist; b. December 5, 1930, New York City; d. November 30, 1981, Bronxville, New York.

1. Baker 7; Grove-AM (Bibiography); PAB-MI/2 (Bibliography).

C0811.
Milstein, Nathan Mironovich. American Violinist; b. December 31, 1904, Odessa, Russia.

1. Baker 7; Grove 6/12 (Bibliography); Grove-AM (Bibliography); MGG/ Supp. (Bibliography); PAB-MI/2 (Bibliography); Riemann 12 + Supp. (Bibliography).

2. GR 52/April; HiFi/MusAm 27/11; Strad July-August/1976.

4. Gavoty, Bernard. <u>Nathan Milstein</u>. Geneve: Rene Kister, 1956. 30, [2] p., 24 illus., recordings.

5. A0100, A0115, A0132, B0030.

SEE: Autobiography of **Gregor Piatigorsky** (C0909.3).

C0812.
Mingus, Charles. American Jazz Double Bassist; b. April 22, 1922, Nogales, Arizona; d. January 5, 1979, Cuernavaca, Mexico.

1. Baker 7; Grove 6/12 (Bibliography); Grove-AM (Bibliography); Grove-Jazz; JB (22 entries); JRRM; LJ; PAB-MI/2 (Bibliography); Riemann 12 + Supp. (Bibliography).
                                                            HiFi/SR 13/6; JJS 5/2.
2. DB 23/1, 27/15, 27/17, 38/10, 39/9, 42/4, 45/1, 45/20, 46/15.

3. Mingus, Charles. Beneath the Underdog: His World as Composed by Mingus. Edited by Nel King. New York: Alfred A. Knopf, 1971. 366 p.

4. Lindenmaier, H.L. and H.J. Salewski. The Man Who Never Sleeps: the Charles Mingus Discography 1945-1978. Freiburg, 1983. No copy seen.

Luzzi, Mario. Charles Mingus. Roma: Lato Side Editori srl, 1983. 200, [7] p., illus., discography.

Priestly, Brian. Mingus: a Critical Biography. London: Quartet Books Limited, 1982. xii, 308 p. + 8 plates, 25 illus., musical examples, 71-item discography, references, index.

Weber, Horst and Gerd Filtgen. Charles Mingus: sein Leben, sein Musik, seine Schallplatten. Mingus in Europa Volume 1. Gauting-Buchendorf: OREOS Verlag, 1984. 178, [6] p., illus., discography, 27-item bibliography.

Wilbraham, Roy J. Charles Mingus: a Biography and Discography. London: p.p., 1967. 33 p.

5. B0048.

C0813.
Mischakoff [Fischberg], Mischa. American Violinist; b. April 3, 1895, Proskurov, Russia; d. February 1, 1981, Petoskey, Michigan.

1. Baker 7; Grove 6/12; Grove-AM (Bibliography).

5. A0100.

C0814.
Moiseiwitsch [Moyseivich], Benno. British Pianist; b. February 22, 1890; Odessa, Russia; d. April 9, 1963, London.

1. Baker 7; Grove 6/12; PAB-MI/2 (Bibliography); Riemann 12 + Supp.

2. HiFi/SR 8/5.

4. Moiseiwitsch, Maurice. Moiseiwitsch, Biography of a Concert Pianist. London: Frederick Miller Ltd., 1965. 198, [1] p., 15 illus., index.

5. A0047, A0048.

C0815.
Molitor, Alois Franz Simon Joseph. Austrian Guitarist; b. November 3, 1766, Neckarsulm, Wuertemberg; d. February 21, 1848, Vienna.

1. Riemann 12, Schmidl + Supp.

4. Zuth, Josef. Simon Molitor und die Wiener Gitarristik (um 1800). Wien: Anton Goll, 1920. 85, [2] p. + 9 plates, bibliography, works.

5. A0129.

C0816.
de Monasterio, Jesús. Spanish Violinist; b. March 21, 1836, Potes, near
Santander; d. September 28, 1903, Casar del Periedo.

1. Baker 7; Fetis 2/6 + Supp.; Grove 6/12 (Bibliography); Schmidl.

C0817.
Monk, Thelonious "Sphere". American Jazz Pianist. b. October 10, 1918,
Rocky Mount, North Carolina; d. February 17, 1982, Weehawken, NJ.

1. Baker 7; EdS/Supp.; Grove 6/12 (Bibliography); Grove-AM (Bibliography - 19 entries); Grove-Jazz; JB; JRRM; LJ; PAB-MI/2 (Bibliography); Riemann 12 + Supp. (Bibliography).

2. DB 23/15, 25/22, 30/27, 31/22, 32/12, 51/1; CK(KB) 8/7.
                         Time Magazine February 28, 1964.
5. B0048.

C0818.
Montgomery, Little Brother [Eurreal Wilford]. American Blues/Jazz
Pianist; b. April 18, 1906, Kentwood, Louisiana; d. September 6, 1985,
Chicago, Illinois.

1. Grove-AM (Bibliography); Grove-Jazz; JB; LJ; PAB-MI/2 (Bibliography).

2. CK(KB) 3/4.

4. Zur Heide, Karl Gert. Deep South Piano: the Story of Little Brother
   Montgomery. London: Studio Vista, 1970. 107, [5] p., 37 illus., discography, index.

   Includes a valuable biographical "Who's Who" section.

C0819.
Montgomery, Wes. American Jazz Guitarist; b. March 6, 1925, Indianapolis, Indiana; d. June 15, 1968, Indianapolis.

1. Baker 7; Grove-AM (Bibliography); Grove-Jazz; JRRM; PAB-MI/2 (Bibliography).

2. DB 35/13.

5. A0108, A0143.

C0820.
Montoya, Carlos Garcia. American Flamenco Guitarist; b. December 13,
1903, Madrid, Spain.

1. Baker 7; PAB-MI/2 (Bibliography); Riemann 12/Supp.

C0821.
Moodie, Alma. Australian Violinist; b. September 12, 1900, Brisbane;
d. March 7, 1943, Frankfurt, Germany.

1. Baker 7; Riemann 12.

C0822.
Moore, Gerald. English Pianist/Accompanist; b. July 30, 1899, Watford;
d. March 13, 1987, Buckinghamshire.

1. Baker 7; Grove 6/12; MGG/Supp. (Bibliography); PAB-MI/2 (Bibliography); Riemann 12 + Supp. (Bibliography).

   As one of the greatest accompanists, "...he attained the foremost
   rank and a well-nigh legendary fame." Baker 7.

2. CL 6/2; GR 47/July, 50/April; HiFi/SR 19/4.

3. Moore, Gerald. Am I Too Loud: a Musical Autobiography. New York: The
   Macmillan Company, 1962. viii, [vii], 288 p., 12 illus.

   Moore, Gerald. Farewell Recital: Further Memoirs. New York: Taplinger
   Publishing Company, 1978. [v], 178 p. + 4 plates, 13 illus., index.

   Moore, Gerald. Further-Moore: Interludes in an Accompanist's Life.
   London, 1983. No copy located.

   Moore, Gerald. The Unashamed Accompanist. New York: The Macmillan
   Company, 1956 [original 1944]. ix, 84 p.

5. B0052.

C0823.
Moravec, Ivan. Czechoslovakian Pianist; b. November 9, 1930, Prague.

1. Baker 7; Grove 6/12 (Bibliography); Riemann 12/Supp.

2. CL 9/2, 24/2; CK(KB) 9/1; PQ 98.

C0824.
Mori, Nicolas. English Violinist; b. January 24, 1796, London; d. June
14, 1839, London.

1. Baker 7; Grove 6/12 (Bibliography).

4. Duffin, E.W. Particulars of the Illness and Death of the Late Mr.
   Mori, the Violinist. London: Wilson & Son, 1839. 20 p.

C0825.
Morini[-Siracusano], Erica [Erika]. American Violinist; b. January 5,
1904, Vienna, Austria.

1. Baker 7; Grove 6/12; Grove-AM (Bibliography); PAB-MI/2 (Bibliography); Riemann 12.

5. A0100.

C0826.
Morton, Jelly Roll [Ferdinand Joseph La Menthe]. American Jazz Pianist;
b. September 20, 1885, New Orleans, Louisiana; d. July 10, 1941, Los
Angeles, California.

1. Baker 7; Grove 6/12 (Bibliography); Grove-AM (Bibliography - 27 entries); Grove-Jazz; JB (20 entries); JRRM; LJ; PAB-MI/2 (Bibliography); Riemann 12 + Supp. (Bibliography).

   He ranks "...alongside Ellington and Monk as one of the most important composer-pianists in jazz history." Grove 6/12.

2. DB 5/1.

4. Cusack, T. Jelly Roll Morton: an Essay in Discography. London: Cassell & Company, Limited, 1952. 40 p.

   Davies, John R.T. and Laurie Wright. Morton's Music. New Orleans (LA): Storyville Publications, 1968. 38 p.

   Lomax, Alan. Mister Jelly Roll: the Fortunes of Jelly Roll Morton, New Orleans Creole and "Inventor of Jazz". New York: Duell, Sloane & Pearce, 1950. 318 p., illus. [2nd edition Berkeley: University of California Press, 1973].

C0827.
Moscheles, Ignaz. German Pianist; b. May 23, 1794, Prague, Czechoslovakia; d. March 10, 1870, Leipzig.

1. Baker 7 (Bibliography); Grove 6/12 (Bibliography); MGG (Bibliography); PAB-MI/2 (Bibliography); Riemann 12 + Supp. (Bibliography).

3. Moscheles, Felix, ed. Fragments of an Autobiography. New York: Harper & Brothers, Publishers, 1899. viii, 364 p., 3 illus.

4. Engel, Hans. Die Entwicklung des Deutschen Klavierkonzertes von Mozart bis Liszt. Ph.D. diss. University of Munich, 1924 [Leipzig: Breitkopf und Haertel, 1927. 271 p.].

   Gresham, Carolyn Denton. Ignaz Moscheles: an Illustrious Musician in the Nineteenth Century. Ph.D. diss. University of Rochester, 1980. 384 p.

   Heussner, I. Ignaz Moscheles in seinen Klavier-Sonaten, Kammermusikwerken, und Konzerten. Ph.D. diss. University of Marburg, 1963.

   Moscheles, Charlotte. Aus Moscheles Leben. 2 vols. Leipzig, 1872. Translated by A.D. Coleridge. New York: H. Holt and Company, 1873. xviii, 434 p., illus.

   Moscheles [Charlotte], ed. Recent Music and Musicians as Described in the Diaries and Correspondence of Ignatz Moscheles. Translated by A.D. Coleridge. New York: Henry Holt and Company, 1874. Reprint 1970. xviii, 434 p., catalogue of compositions, index of names.

5. A0014, A0023, A0047, A0051, B0020, B0050, B0065, C0984.3.

   SEE: Mereaux, Amédée under Charles-Auguste de Bériot (C0116.4).

   SEE: Cowden, Robert H. under Hans von Buelow (C0193.5).

C0828.
Moszkowski, Moritz. German Pianist; b. August 23, 1854, Breslau;
d. March 4, 1925, Paris, France.

1. Baker 7; Fetis 2/Supp.; Grove 6/12 (Bibliography); MGG (Bibliography); PAB-MI/2 (Bibliography); Riemann 12 (Bibliography) + Supp.
   (Bibliography); Schmidl.

C0829.
Moten, Bennie [Benjamin]. American Jazz Pianist; b. November 13, 1894,
Kansas City, Kansas; d. April 2, 1935, Kansas City.

1. Baker 7; Grove 6/12 (Bibliography); Grove-AM (Bibliography); Grove-
   Jazz; LJ; PAB- MI/2 (Bibliography).

C0830.
Moyse, Marcel Joseph. French Flutist; b. May 17, 1889, Saint-Amour,
Jura; d. November 1, 1984, Brattleboro, Vermont.

1. Baker 7; Grove 6/12.

C0831.
Muehlfeld, Richard Bernhard Hermann. German Clarinetist; b. February 28,
1856, Salzungen; d. June 1, 1907, Meiningen.

1. Baker 7; Grove 6/12 (Bibliography); MGG (Bibliography); PAB-MI/2
   (under Muhlfeld - Bibliography); Riemann 12; Schmidl.

C0832.
Mule, Marcel. French Saxophonist; b. June 24, 1901, Aube.

1. Baker 7; Riemann 12/Supp.

4. Rosseau, Eugene. Marcel Mule: His Life and the Saxophone. Shell Lake
   (WI): Etoile Music, Incorporated, 1982. ix, 154 p., 30 illus., list
   of students, discography, index.

C0833.
Mulligan Gerry [Gerald Joseph]. American Jazz Saxophonist; b. June 4,
1927, New York City.

1. Baker 7; EdS/Supp.; Grove 6/12 (Bibliography); Grove-AM (Bibliography - 10 entries); Grove-Jazz; JB; LJ; PAB-MI/2 (Bibliography);
   Riemann 12 + Supp. (Bibliography).

2. DB 23/15, 25/5, 27/11, 27/12, 28/9, 30/2, 31/10, 41/17, 43/13, 46/11.

4. Morgan, Alun and Raymond Horricks. Gerry Mulligan: a Biography,
   Appreciation, Record Survey and Discography. London: National Jazz
   Federation, 1958. 16 p.

5. A0159, B0048.

C0834.
Munn, Mary Elizabeth. Canadian Pianist; b. June 28, 1909, Montreal.

1. Encyclopédia of Music in Canada (Bibliography).

4. Mackenzie, Nadine. La lumière dans la nuit: la vie de Mary Munn....
Québec: Editions Naaman, 1984. 74, [1] p., 10 illus.

C0835.
Murphy, Turk [Melvin E.]. American Jazz Trombonist; b. December 16,
1915, Palmero, California; d. May 30, 1987, San Francisco.

1. Baker 7; Grove-AM (Bibliography); Grove-Jazz; JRRM; PAB-MI/2 (Bibliography).

4. Goggin, J. Turk Murphy: Just for the Record. San Francisco, 1982.
No copy located.

C0836.
Musin, Ovide. Belgian Violinist; b. September 22, 1854, Nandrin, near
Liège; d. November 24, 1929, Brooklyn, New York.

1. Baker 7 (Bibliography); Grove-AM (Bibliography); PAB-MI/2 (Bibliography); Riemann 12/Supp.; Schmidl.

3. Musin, Ovide. My Memories: a Half-Century of Adventures and Experiences. New York: Musin Publishing Co., 1920. xiii, 298 p., 21
illus., index.

5. A0093.

C0837.
Nachez, Tivadar [Theodor Naschitz]. Hungarian Violinist; b. May 1, 1859,
Budapest; d. May 29, 1930, Lausanne, Switzerland.

1. Baker 7; Riemann 12; Schmidl.

C0838.
Nadermann, Jean François Joseph. French Harpist; b. 1781, Paris; d.
April 2, 1835, Paris.

1. Baker 7; Fetis 2/6; Grove 6/13 (Bibliography); Mendel; MGG (Bibliography); Riemann 12; Schmidl.

C0839.
Nardini, Pietro. Italian Violinist; b. April 12, 1722, Livorno; d. May
7, 1793, Livorno.

1. Baker 7 (Bibliography); Fetis 2/6 + Supp.; Grove 6/13 (Bibliography);
Mendel; MGG (Bibliography); PAB-MI/2 (Bibliography); Riemann 12 (Bibliography) + Supp. (Bibliography); Schmidl + Supp.

A pupil of Tartini, his playing was highly praised by none other than
Leopold Mozart.

4. Leone, Raimondo. Elogio di Pietro Nardini celebratissimo professor di
violono, fatto dall'abate Raimondo Leone di Pienza. Firenze: Gaetano
Cambiagi, 1793. 44 p.

Pfaefflin, Klara. Pietro Nardini: seine Werke und sein Leben. Ein Beitrag zur Erforschung vorklassischer Instrumentalmusik. Ph.D. diss. University of Tuebingen, 1935 [Wolfenbuettel: Kallmeyer, 1936]. 95, xx p., bibliography.

5. A0131, B0020.

C0840.
Nat, Yves. French Pianist; b. December 28, 1890, Béziers; d. August 31, 1956, Paris.

1. Baker 7; Grove 6/13 (Bibliography); MGG; Riemann 12 + Supp. (Bibliography); Schmidl/Supp.

C0841.
Navarra, André Nicolas. French Cellist; b. October 13, 1911, Biarritz; d. July 31, 1988, Siena, Italy.

1. Baker 7; Grove 6/13; PAB-MI/2 (Bibliography); Riemann 12 + Supp. (Bibliography).

C0842.
Navarro, Fats [Theodore]. American Jazz Trumpeter. b. September 24, 1923, Key West, Florida; d. July 7, 1950, New York City.

1. Baker 7; Grove 6/13 (Bibliography); Grove-AM (Bibliography); Grove-Jazz; JB; JRRM; PAB-MI/2 (Bibliography); Riemann 12 + Supp. (Bibliography).

2. DB 33/2, 37/4; New Yorker June 12, 1978.

C0843.
Nelsova [Katznelson], Zara. American Cellist; b. December 23, 1918, Winnipeg, Canada.

1. Baker 7; Grove 6/13; Grove-AM; PAB-MI/2 (Bibliog.); Riemann 12/Supp.

2. Strad Oct/1978, May/1979.

C0844.
Neruda [Lady Hallé], Wilma Maria Francisca. Czechoslovakian Violinist; b. March 21, 1839, Bruenn; d. April 15, 1911, Berlin, Germany.

1. Baker 7 (Bibliography); Fetis 2/Supp.; Grove 6/13 (Bibliography); MGG (Bibliography); Riemann 12 + Supp. (Bibliography); Schmidl.

C0845.
Neuhaus, Heinrich. Russian Pianist; b. April 12, 1888, Elizavetgrad; d. October 10, 1964, Moscow.

1. Baker 7 (Bibliography); Grove 6/13 (Bibliography); Riemann 12 + Supp. (Bibliography).

3. Riemann 12/Supp. mentions Awtobiografitscheskije sapiski. Moscow, 1974.

C0846.
Neveu, Ginette. French Violinist; b. August 11, 1919, Paris; d. October 28, 1949, Azores Islands.

1. Baker 7; Grove 6/13; MGG (Bibliography); Riemann 12/Supp.

2. GR 58/September; Strad Sept/1980; RS 7.

4. Ronze-Neveu, Marie Jeanne. Ginette Neveu: la fulgurante carrière d'une grande artiste. Paris: Pierre Horay, 1952. 157, [3] p. + 2 plates, 4 illus.

   The English translation (London: Rockliff, 1957) by Joyce Kemp includes a foreword by Sir John Barbirolli, additional illustrations and an index.

5. A0008.

C0847.
Newman, Anthony. American Harpsichordist/Pianist/Organist; b. May 12, 1941, Los Angeles, California.

1. Baker 7 (Bibliography); Grove-AM; PAB-MI/2 (Bibliography).

2. CK(KB) 3/4; HiFi/MusAm 22/4.

C0848.
Ney, Elly. German Pianist; b. September 27, 1882, Duesseldorf; d. March 31, 1968, Tutzing, near Munich.

1. Baker 7; Grove 6/13 (Bibliography); MGG (Bibliography); Riemann 12 + Supp. (Bibliography).

3. Ney, Elly with Josef Magnus Wehner. Ein Leben fuer die Musik. Darmstadt: Franz Schneekluth, 1952. 318, [2] p. + 8 plates, 22 illus. 2nd edition: Erinnerungen und Betrachtungen: mein Leben aus der Musik. Aschaffenburg: Paul Pattloch Verlag, 1957. 386, [1] p., 27 illus., list of conductors.

   Ney, Elly. Briefwechsel mit Willem van Hoogstraten. vol. 1 (1910–1926). Edited by Barbara Lischke. Tutzing: Verlegt bei Hans Schneider, 1970. 333, [1] p., index of names.

   Ney was the wife of the Dutch conductor from 1911 to 1927.

4. Herzfeld, Friedrich. Elly Ney. Genève: René Kister, 1962. 30, [2] p., 22 illus., recordings.

   van Hoogstraten, Eleonore, ed. Worte des Dankes an Elly Ney. Tutzing: Verlegt bei Hans Schneider, 1968. 82, [1] p. + 9 plates, 9 illus., discography, index of names.

   Maurina, Zenta. Begegnung mit Elly Ney: eine Danksagung. Memmingen: Maximilian Dietrich Verlag, 1956. 95 p. + 6 plates, 6 illus.

von Pidoll, Carl. Elly Ney: Gedanken ueber ein Kuenstlertum. Leipzig: Helingsche Verlagsanstalt, 1942. 176 p.

Schindler, Heinrich. Elly Ney. Muenchen: Verlag Guenther Olzog, 1957. 39, [1] p., 10 illus.

Valentin, Erich. Elly Ney: Symbol einer Generation. Muenchen: Verlegt bei Walter Ricke, 1962. 22, [1] p., 7 illus.

Vogel, Heinrich. Aus den Tagebuechern von Elly Ney. Tutzing: Verlegt bei Hans Schneider, 1979. 162 p., index of names.

5. B0061, B0129.

C0849.
Nicastro, Oscar. Uruguayan Cellist; b. March 24, 1894, Montevideo; d. June 22, 1971, Montevideo.

1. Riemann 12/Supp. (Bibliography); Schmidl.

4. Xavier de Salas, M. Oscar Nicastro y su arte excepcional. Santiago: Talleres S. Vicente, 1939. 78 p. + 2 plates, 2 portraits, works.

C0850.
Nichols, Red [Ernest Loring]. American Jazz Cornetist; b. May 8, 1905, Ogden, Utah; d. June 28, 1965, Las Vegas, Nevada.

1. Baker 7 (double entry - Bibliography); Grove 6/13 (Bibliography); Grove-AM (Bibliography); Grove-Jazz; JB; JRRM; LJ; PAB-MI/2 (Bibliography).

2. DB 26/14.

4. Johnson, Grady. The Five Pennies: the Biography of Jazz Band Leader, Red Nichols, Containing a Novelization of Dena Pictures' Paramount Release...The Five Pennies. New York: Dell Pub. Co., 1959. 191 p.

Lange, Horst Heinz. Loring 'Red' Nichols: ein Portraet. Wetzlar: Pegasus Verlag, 1960. 48 p. + 8 plates, 16 illus., discography.

C0851.
Nicolet, Aurèle. Swiss Flutist; b. January 22, 1926, Neuchâtel.

1. Baker 7; Grove 6/13 (Bibliography); MGG/Supp.; PAB-MI/2 (Bibliography); Riemann 12 + Supp.

5. A0162.

C0852.
Nikolayev, Leonid Vladimirovich. Russian Pianist; b. August 13, 1878, Kiev; d. October 11, 1942, Tashkent.

1. Baker 7 (Bibliography); Grove 6/13 (Bibliography); MGG (under Nikolajew - Bibliography); Riemann 12 (under Nikolajew) + Supp. (Bibliography); Schmidl (under Nikolajew).

C0853.
Nikolayeva, Tatiana Petrovna. Soviet Pianist; b. May 4, 1924, Bezhitz.

1. Baker 7; Grove 6/13 (Bibliography); Riemann 12/Supp. (under Niko-
   lajewa). ͬ

C0854.
Noone, Jimmie. American Jazz Clarinetist; b. April 23, 1895, Cut-Off,
Louisiana; d. April 19, 1944, Los Angeles, California.

1. Baker 7; Grove 6/13 (Bibliography); Grove-AM (Bibliography); Grove-
   Jazz; JB; JRRM; PAB-MI/2; Riemann 12.

C0855.
Norvo, Red [Kenneth Norville]. American Jazz Xylophonist/Vibraphonist;
b. March 31, 1908, Beardstown, Illinois.

1. Baker 7; Grove 6/13 (Bibliography); Grove-AM (Bibliog. - 10 entries);
   Grove-Jazz; JB; JRRM; PAB-MI/2; Riemann 12 + Supp. (Bibliog.).

2. DB 25/11, 34/18, 44/18.

5. A0004.

C0856.
Novães, Guiomar. Brazilian Pianist; b. February 28, 1895, São João da
Bõa Vista; d. March 7, 1979, São Paulo.

1. Baker 7; Grove 6/13; PAB-MI/2 (Bibliography); Riemann 12 + Supp.

2. CL 10/9; HiFi 8/5.

5. B0061, B0089.

C0857.
Nyiregyházi, Erwin. American Pianist; b. January 19, 1903, Budapest,
Hungary; d. April 13, 1987, Los Angeles, California.

1. Baker 7; Grove 6/13 (Bibliography); Grove-AM (Bibliography); Riemann
   12; Schmidl.

2. CL 18/1; HiFi/SR 41/1; PQ 117.

4. Révész, Géza. The Psychology of a Musical Prodigy. New York: Harcourt, Brace & Company, Inc., 1925 [original Leipzig, 1916?].
   ix, 180 p.

C0858.
Oborin, Lev Nikolayevich. Soviet Pianist; b. September 11, 1907, Moscow;
d. January 5, 1974, Moscow.

1. Baker 7; Grove 6/13 (Bibliography); Riemann 12 + Supp. (Bibliography).

He was renowned as an excellent teacher at the Moscow Conservatory.

4. Khentova, Sof'ia Mikhailovna. <u>Lev Oborin</u>. Moscow: Muzyka, 1964.
   201 p., illus., bibliographical footnotes.

C0859.
Odnoposoff, Adolfo. Argentine Cellist; b. February 22, 1917, Buenos
Aires.

1. Baker 7; PAB-MI/2 (Bibliography); Riemann 12/Supp.

C0860.
Odnoposoff, Ricardo. Argentine Violinist, brother of Adolfo; b. February 24, 1914, Buenos Aires.

1. Baker 7; Grove 6/13 (Bibliography); Riemann 12 + Supp. (Bibliography).

C0861.
Ogdon, John Andrew Howard. English Pianist; b. January 27, 1937, Manchester.

1. Baker 7; Grove 6/13 (Bibliography); PAB-MI/2 (Bibliography); Riemann
   12/Supp.

2. GR 49/July; MM 16/8.

4. Ogdon, Brenda Lucas and Michael Kerr. <u>Virtuoso: the Story of John
   Ogdon</u>. London: Hamish Hamilton, 1981. x, 293 p. + 4 plates, 13
   illus., index.

C0862.
Ohlsson, Garrick Olof. American Pianist; b. April 3, 1948, Bronxville,
New York.

1. Baker 7; Grove 6/13; Grove-AM (Bibliography); PAB-MI/2 (Bibliography); Riemann 12/Supp.

2. CL 13/9; HiFi/SR 38/2; CK(KB) 3/11, 6/9; PQ 99.

5. A0069, A0070.

C0863.
Oistrakh, David. Soviet Violinist; b. September 30, 1908, Odessa;
d. October 24, 1974, Amsterdam, Holland.

1. Baker 7 (Bibliography); Grove 6/13 (Bibliography); MGG (Bibliography) + Supp.; PAB-MI/2 (Bibliography); Riemann 12 + Supp. (Bibliography).

   He fused "a phenomenal technique [with] stylistic fidelity to works
   by different composers of different historical periods." <u>Baker 7</u>.

2. GR 50/March; HiFi 5/2; HiFi/SR 24/1; Strad Oct/1984.

4. Bronin, V. <u>David Oistrakh</u>. Moskva: Gos. musykal'noe izd-vo, 1954.
   47 p., illus.

Grinberg, M. David Oistrakh. Moskva: Muzyka, 1963. 34 p., illus.

IAmpol'skii, Izrail' Markovich. David Oistrakh. Moskva: Muzyka, 1964. 130 p., illus., bibliographical footnotes.

IUzefovich, Viktor Aronovich. David Oistrakh. Moskva: Sov. kompozitor, 1978. 351 p., illus., discography.

Jurik, Marian. David Oistrach. Praha: Supraphon, 1977. 66 p. + 12 plates, illus, phonodisk, discography, bibliography.

Jusefovich, Viktor and David Oistrakh. Conversations with David Oistrakh. Translated by Nicholas de Pfeiffer [from the 1977 German edition]. London: Cassell & Company Limited, 1979. 248 p., illus., index of names.

Markiz, L. David Oistrakh. Moskva: Muzyka, 1977. 24 p., illus.

Nabering, Dirk. David und Igor Oistrach. Berlin: Rembrandt Verlag, 1968. 62 p., 32 illus.

Richter, Evelyn and Ernst Krause. David Oistrach: ein Arbeitsportraet fotografiert von Evelyn Richter. Berlin: Henschelverlag Kunst und Gesellschaft, 1973. 171 p., illus., chronology, discography.

Soroker, Yakov. David Oistrakh. Jerusalem: LEXICON Publishing House, 1982. 183 p. + 7 plates, 21 illus., chronology, students, bibliography includes 79 titles by Oistrakh and 38 titles about him, discography, index.

5. A0008, A0132, B0042, B0071.

C0864.
Oistrakh, Igor Davidovich. Soviet Violinist, son of David; b. April 27, 1931, Odessa.

1. Baker 7; Grove 6/13; PAB-MI/2 (Bibliography); Riemann 12 + Supp. (Bibliography).

2. Strad Oct/1984.

5. SEE: Nabering, Dirk under David Oistrakh (C0863.4).

C0865.
Oliveira, Elmar. American Violinist; b. June 8, 1950, Waterbury, CT.

1. Baker 7; Grove-AM (Bibliography); PAB-MI/2 (Bibliography).

2. HiFi/MusAm 30/12.

C0866.
Oliver, King [Joseph]. American Jazz Cornetist; b. May 11, 1885, near Abend, Louisiana; d. April 8, 1938, Savannah, Georgia.

1. Baker 7 (Bibliography); Grove 6/13 (Bibliography); Grove-AM (Bibliography - 10 entries); Grove-Jazz; JB; JRRM (21 entries); LJ; PAB-MI/2 (Bibliography); Riemann 12 + Supp. (Bibliography).

2. JJS 3/2.

4. Allen, Walter C. and Brian A.L. Rust. King Joe Oliver. Belleville (NJ): W.C. Allen [mimeo], n.d. [1955]. 162 p.

Allen, Walter C. and Brian A.L. Rust. King Joe Oliver. London: Sidgwick and Jackson Limited, 1958. xii, 224 p., 5 illus., discography, 33-item bibliography, appendix.

Williams, Martin T. King Oliver. London: Cassell & Company Limited, 1960. 89, [1] p. + 2 plates, 5 illus., discography.

5. A0004, A0029, A0031.

C0867.
Olof, Theo. Dutch Violinist; b. May 5, 1924, Bonn, Germany.

1. Grove 6/13; PAB-MI/2 (Bibliography); Riemann 12 + Supp.

3. Olof, Theo. Daar sta je dan. Den Haag: Daamen N.V., 1958. 124 p. + 8 plates, 18 illus.

Olof, Theo. Daar sta je dan opnieuw. Nieuwkoop: Heuff, 1973. 129 p.

Olof, Theo. Divertimento van en over Theo Olof. Den Haag: Bert Bakker-Daammen NV, 1968. 208 p., illus.

C0868.
Ondříček, František. Czechoslovakian Violinist; b. April 29, 1857, Prague; d. April 12, 1922, Milan, Italy.

1. Baker 7 (Bibliography); Grove 6/13 (Bibliography); MGG (Bibliography); PAB-MI/2 (Bibliography); Riemann 12 (Bibliography) + Supp. (Bibliography); Schmidl (under Ondriczek).

4. Sich, Bohuslav. František Ondříček: Český houslista. Praha: Edition Supraphon, 1970. 384, [2] p. + 12 plates, 60 illus., compositions, discography, repertoire, bibliography, index.

C0869.
Oppens, Ursula. American Pianist; b. February 2, 1944, New York City.

1. Baker 7; Grove-AM; PAB-MI/2 (Bibliography).

2. CL 26/4; DB 47/1; HiFi/MusAm 26/7; CK(KB) 4/10.

C0870.
Orlov, Nicolai Andreyevich. Russian Pianist; b. February 26, 1892, Elets; d. May 31, 1964, Grantown-on-Spey, Scotland.

1. Baker 7; Grove 6/13; Riemann 12 (under Orlow) + Supp.

C0871.
Ornstein, Leo. American Pianist; b. December 11, 1892, Kremenchug,
Russia.

1. Baker 7 (Bibliography); Grove 6/13; PAB-MI/2 (Bibliography); Riemann
   12 (Bibliography) + Supp.; Schmidl.

2. MQ 4/2.

4. Martens, Frederick H. Leo Ornstein: the Man, His Ideas, His Work.
   New York: Breitkopf & Haertel, Inc., 1918. 89 p., illus.

5. SEE: Van Vechten, Carl. Music and Bad Manners. New York: Alfred A.
   Knopf, Inc., 1916.

C0872.
Orozco, Rafael. Spanish Pianist; b. January 24, 1946, Córdoba.

1. Baker 7; Grove 6/13; PAB-MI/2 (Bibliography).

C0873.
Orsi, Romeo. Italian Clarinetist; b. October 18, 1843, Como; d. June 11,
1918, Milan.

1. Baker 7; Riemann 12/Supp.; Schmidl.

C0874.
Ortiz, Cristina. Brazilian Pianist; b. April 17, 1950, Bahia.

1. Baker 7; PAB-MI/2 (Bibliography); Riemann 12/Supp.

2. CL 8/9.

C0875.
Ory, Kid [Edward]. American Jazz Trombonist; b. December 25, 1886, La
Place, Louisiana; d. January 23, 1973, Honolulu, Hawaii.

1. Baker 7; Grove 6/13 (Bibliography); Grove-AM (Bibliography); Grove-
   Jazz; JB; JRRM; LJ; PAB-MI/2 (Bibliography); Riemann 12 + Supp. (Bibliography).

2. DB 26/1.

5. A0001, A0031.

C0876.
de Pachmann, Vladimir. Russian Pianist; b. July 27, 1848, Odessa;
d. January 6, 1933, Rome, Italy.

1. Baker 7 (Bibliography); Grove 6/14 (Bibliography); PAB-MI/2 (Bibliography); Riemann 12 (Bibliography) + Supp. (Bibliography); Schmidl.

2. HiFi/MusAm 19/7; RS 3.

5. A0048, B0053.

SEE: Buffen, Frederick F. Musical Celebrities: Second Series. London: Chapman & Hall, Limited, 1893.

SEE: Symons, Arthur. Plays, Acting and Music: a Book of Theory. London: Constable & Company Ltd, 1909.

C0877.
Paderewski, Ignacy Jan. Polish Pianist; b. November 18, 1860, Kurylowka, Podolia (Russian Poland); d. June 29, 1941, New York City.

1. Baker 7 (Bibliography); Grove 6/14 (Bibliography); Grove-AM (Bibliography); MGG (Bibliography); PAB-MI/2 (Bibliography); Riemann 12 (Bibliography) + Supp. (Bibliography); Schmidl.

   A larger than life figure, "Paderewski eclipsed even Caruso as an idol of the masses...in 1919 he was named prime minister of the Polish Republic, the first musician to occupy such a post in any country at any period.... His position in the world of the performing arts remains undiminished by the later achievements of younger men and women pianists." Baker 7.

2. CL 21/6; HiFi/SR 19/4; RS 10.

3. Paderewski, Ignace Jan and Mary Lawton. The Paderewski Memoirs. New York: Charles Scribner's Sons, 1938. Reprint 1980. x, 404 p. + 21 plates, 41 illus., index.

4. Annales Paderewski. Morges (Switzerland): La Société Paderewski. No. 1 (October, 1979. 32 p., 5 illus.) to No. 10 (May, 1987).

   Baughan, Edward Algernon. Ignaz Jan Paderewski. London: John Lane, The Bodley Head, 1908. 92 p. + 10 plates, 10 illus.

   Baumgartner, André. La vérité sur le prétendu drame Paderewski: documents et témoignages. Genève: Editions de la Cité, 1948. 154, [4] p., illus.

   Duleba, Wladyslaw. Ignacy Jan Paderewski: Mala kronika zycia pianisty i kompozytora. Warszawa: Polskie Wydawnictwo Muzyczne, 1960. 141 p., illus., compositions, repertoire.

   Finck, Henry T. Paderewski and His Art. New York: Whittingham & Atherton, 1895. 43 p., illus.

   Fuchss, Werner. Paderewski: reflets de sa vie. Genève: S.A. Tribune de Genève, 1981. 276, [2] p., illus., 22-item bibliography, index of names.

   Giron, Simone. Le Drame Paderewski. Genève: Editions de L'Epée, 1948. 173, [8] p., 9 illus.

   Gronowicz, Antoni. Paderewski: Pianist and Patriot. Translated by Jessie McEwen. Edinburgh: Thomas Nelson and Sons, 1943. 216 p., illus., index.

Halski, Czeslaw. Ignacy Jan Paderewski: dzieje wielkiego Polaka i wielkeigo Europejczyka. Londyn: Stowarzyszenie Polskich Kombatantów Gryf Publications Ltd, 1964. 100 p. + 4 plates, 8 illus., works, 106-item bibliography.

Kellogg, Charlotte. Paderewski. New York: The Viking Press, 1956. 224 p., index.

Landau, Rom. Ignace Paderewski: Musician and Statesman. New York: Thomas Y. Crowell Company Publishers, 1934. Reprint 1976. xiii, 314 p., 42-item annotated bibliography, index.

Lipmann, Eric. Paderewski l'idole des années folles. n.p. Editions Balland, n.d. 341, [1] p., 21-item bibliography.

Nossig, Alfred. I.J. Paderewski. Leipzig: Hermann Seemann Nachfolger, 1901. 29, [4] p., illus.

Opienski, Henryk. I.J. Paderewski: esquisse de sa vie et de son oeuvre. Lausanne: Editions Spes, 1948. 148 p. + 10 plates, illus., works, index of names.

Phillips, Charles. Paderewski: the Story of a Modern Immortal. New York: The Macmillan Company, 1933. Reprint 1978. xx, 563 p., 4 illus., works, recordings, index.

Piber, Andrzej. Droga do slawy: Ignacy Paderewski w latach 1860-1902. Warszawa: Panstwowy Instytut Wydawniczy, 1982. 677, [1] p. + 20 plates, 47 illus., notes, 3 indices.

Strakacz, Aniela. Paderewski as I Knew Him: from the Diary of Aniela Strakacz. Translated by Halina Chybowska. New Brunswick (NJ): Rutgers University Press, 1949. [iv], 338 p. + 7 plates, 24 illus., index.

Zamoyski, Adam. Paderewski. New York: Atheneum, 1982. xii, 289 p. + 8 plates, 44 illus., works, repertoire, notes, 253-item bibliography, index.

5. A0033, A0047, A0051, B0008, B0010, B0020, B0035, B0039, B0053, B0056, B0083, B0089, B0098, B0105, B0109.

   SEE: Armstrong, William. The Romantic World of Music. New York: E.P. Dutton & Company, 1922.

   SEE: Buffen, Frederick F. under Vladimir de Pachmann (C0876.5).

   SEE: Finck, Henry T. My Adventures in the Golden Age of Music. New York: Funk & Wagnalls Company, 1926.

   Music editor of the New York Evening Post (1881-1924).

   SEE: Finck, Henry T. Success in Music and How It Is Won. New York: Charles Scribner's Sons, 1909.

   SEE: Heiles, W.H. under Ignaz Friedman (C0423.4).

SEE: McMillan, Mary Lee and Ruth Dorval Jones. My Helenka. Durham (NC): N.C. Moore Publishing Company, 1972.

SEE: Symons, Arthur under Vladimir de Pachmann (C0876.5).

C0878.
Paganini, Niccolò. Italian Violinist; b. October 27, 1782, Genoa; d. May 27, 1840, Nice, France.

1. Baker 7 (Bibliography); Fetis 2/6 + Supp.; Grove 6/14 (Bibliography); Mendel; MGG (Bibliography); PAB-MI/2 (Bibliography); Riemann 12 (Bibliography) + Supp. (Bibliography); Schmidl (Bibliography) + Supp. (Bibliography).

2. ML 42/4; MQ 16/1, 39/1; Strad May/1977, Dec/1977, July/1978, June/1979, June/1980, Oct/1982.

4. Aarvig, Christian Andreas. Paganini-legenden: En analogi. Kobenhavn: Wilhelm Hansens Musikforlag, 1935. 102, [1] p., illus., chronology, list of compositions.

Anders, G.E. Nicolo Paganini: sa vie, sa personne et quelques mots sur son secret. Paris: Chez Delaunay, 1831. 42 p. The English translation appeared as Biographical Sketch of Nicolo Paganini.... (London: S. Robinson, 1831. 45 p.), and there is a Russian version, Nikolai Paganini ego zhisn'.... (St. Petersburg: Tipografia Meditsinekago, 1831. 65 p.).

Armando, Walter, G. Paganini: eine Biographie. Hamburg: Ruetten & Loening Verlag, 1960. 382, [2] p. + 16 plates, 33 illus.

van Berkel, Cor. Paganini. Haarlem: Gottmer, 1948. 207 p. + 22 plates, illus., chronology, 35-item bibliography.

Berri, Pietro. Gli autografi Paganiniani di Novara. Novara: Tipografia Pietro Riva & C., 1964. 12 p., 4 illus.

Berri, Pietro. Paganini: documenti e testimonianze. Genova: Sigla effe, 1962. 189 p., 40 illus., notes, index of names.

Berri, Pietro. Paganini: la vita e le opere. Milano: Bompiani, 1982. 576, [7] p. + 8 plates, 16 illus., chronology, catalogue of works, discography, 45-item essential bibliography, genealogy.

Betti, Ferruccio. Paganini e Parma: tutti i rapporti di Paganini con Parma sua "novella" patria adottiva, con descrizione della villa di Gaione e del suo sepolcro alla "Villetta". Parma: Scuola Tipografia Benedettina, 1961. 121, [4] p., 17 illus.

Bruni, Oreste. Niccolò Paganini, celebre violinista genovese. Firenze: Tipografia Galletti e Cocci, 1873. 147, [2] p. 2nd edition, revised and expanded, 1903.

Casini, Claudio. Paganini. Milano: Electa Editrice, 1982. 142 p., illus., 31-item bibliography, index of names.

Castiglioni, Vittore. Paganini: Biografia. Roma: La Pilotta Editrice, 1982. 221 p. + 8 plates, illus., works, 68-item bibliography.

Codignola, Arturo, ed. Paginiana. Milano: Edizioni Luigi Alfieri [for the Civico Istituto Colombiano, Genoa], 1953. 89, [1] p. + 9 plates, illus., bibliography.

Codignola, Arturo, ed. Paganini intimo. Genova: Edito a Cura del Municipio Di Genova, 1935. 691 p., 23 illus., appendix of letters, list of compositions, index of names, general index.

Codignola, Mario. Arte e magia di Nicolò Paganini. Milano: Piccola Biblioteca Ricordi, 1959. 106, [1] p., 14-item bibliography, index of names.

Conestabile, Giovanni Carlo. Vita di Niccolò Paganini da Genova. Perugia: Tipografia di Vincenzo Bartelli, 1851. 317 p., portrait. Revised and annotated by Federico Mompellio, Milano: Società editrice Dante Alighieri, 1936. vii, 646 p., illus., appendix of works, 241-item bibliography.

de Courcy, Geraldine I. Chronology of Nicolo Paganini's Life. Chronologie von Nicolo Paganinis Leben. German translation by Hans Dunnebeil. Wiesbaden: Rud. Erdmann, Musikverlag, 1961. 80, [1] p. + 4 plates, 10 illus.

de Courcy, Geraldine I. Paganini, the Genovese. 2 vols. Norman: University of Oklahoma Press, 1957. Reprint 1977. xv, 423 p., 8 illus.; vii, 431 p., 2 illus., genealogy, works, iconography, 565-item bibliography, index.

Volune one covers the period 1782-1831; volume two, 1832-1840.

Day, Lillian. Paganini of Genoa. New York: The Macaulay Company, 1929. Reprint (?) 1966. xii, 318 p., 32 illus., necrology, works, 49-item bibliography; index.

Escudier, Léon. Aus dem Leben Paganini's. Translation of Vie anecdotique de Paganini (Paris, 1856). Leipzig: J.A. Bergson-Sonenberg, 1862. 102 p. [published with Escudier's portrait of Malibran].

Fayolle, François Joseph Marie. Paganini et Bériot, ou Avis aux jeunes artistes qui se destinent à l'enseignement du violin. Paris: Chez M. Legouest, Editeur, 1831. 67, [4] p.

Fetis, Francois Joseph. Notice biographique sur Niccolo Paganini, suivie de l'ánalyse de ses ouvrages et précédée d'une esquisse de l'histoire du violon. Paris: Chez Schonenberger, Editeur, 1851. 95 p. 2nd edition translated by Wellington Guernsey as Biographical Notice of Nicolo Paganini. with an Analysis of His Compositions, and a Sketch of the History of the Violin (London: Schott & Co., 1876). Reprint 1976. 90 p., illus.

Flodin, Robert Wendell. The Meaning of Paganini. San Francisco: Morgan Printing Company, 1953. 19 p., 19-item bibliography.

Gatto, Giuseppe, ed. Paganini: Rivista del Comune anno 56 (1976). Genova: Industrie Grafiche Editoriali, 1976. 142 p., illus.

Harrys, Georg. Paganini in seinem Reisewagen und Zimmer, in seinen redseligen Stunden, in gesellschaftlichen Zirkeln und seinen Concerten. Braunschweig: Verlag von Friedr. Vieweg, 1830. xii, 68 p.

Compiled from Harrys' travel journals and diaries. The Library of Congress copy has thirty-four additional pages of press notices and comments regarding Paganini's death.

IAmpol'skii, Izrail Markovich. Nikkolo Paganini: zhizn i tvorchestvo. Moskva: Muzika, 1968. 448 p., illus., bibliography.

Ianegie, Ion. Paganini: omul si opera. Bucureşti: Editura Muzicala a Uniunii Compozitorilor din R.P.R., 1964 [original 1962]. 281, [2] p. + 14 plates, 49 illus., list of works, 116-item bibliography.

Istel, Edgar. Niccolo Paganini. Leipzig: Druck und Verlag von Breitkopf & Haertel, 1919. 60 p., portrait, bibliography.

Kapp, Julius. Paganini: eine Biographie. Berlin: Verlegt bei Schuster und Loeffler, 1913. Reprint 1969. xi, [ii], 167, 36, [4] p., 60 illus., published and unpublished works, bibliography.

Kendall, Alan. Paganini: a Biography. London: Chappell & Company Limited, 1982. 160 p. + 4 plates, 17 illus., list of works, index.

Lancelotti, Mario A. Cautro ensayos sobre Nicolás Paganini. Buenos Aires: Libreria Huemul, 1945. 132, [1] p. + 3 plates, illus., bibliographical footnotes.

L'Héritier, Louis François. Notice sur le célèbre violinist Nicolo Paganini. Paris: E. Guyot, Editeur, 1830. 66 p., portrait. Translated as Some Account of the Celebrated Violinist, Nicolo Paganini. London: Baldwin and Co., 1830 [with additional notes and 2 plates].

Neill, Edward. Nicolò Paganini: la vita attraverso le opere i documenti e le immagini. Genova: Casa di Risparmio di Genova e Imperia, 1978. 439, [4] p., illus., annotated catalogue of works, 270-item bibliography.

Neill, Edward. Paganini epistolario. Edizione speciale per il Commune di Genova. Genova: Siag Editore, 1984. 318 p., 16-item bibliography, index of names.

Némethy, Ferenc. Paganini, a "Sátán hegeduese": halálának százéves fordulójára irta. Budapest: Rózsavoelgyi és társa, 1940. 181, [2] p., 12 illus., compositions, index.

Ormcy, Imre. Niccolò Paganini életének krónikája. Budapest: Zenemukiado, 1966. 114, [2] p., works.

Pal'min, Aleksandr Georgievich. Nikkolo Paganini. Leningrad: Muzyka, 1968. 88 p., illus.

Pizzetti, Ildebrando. Niccolò Paganini. Torino: Edizioni Arione, 1940. 36 p. + 8 plates, 28 illus.

Podenzani, Nino. Il romanzo di Niccolò Paganini. Milano: Casa Editrice Ceschina, 1940. 420, [1] p.

Polko, Elise. Nicolo Paganini und die Geigenbauer. Leipzig: Bernhard Schlicke, 1876. 228, [1] p., portrait.

Powrozniak, Józef. Paganini. Kraków: Polskie Wydawnictwo Muzyczne, 1972. 224, [1] p., 33 illus., 30-item bibliography, works, index of names.

Prod'Homme, Jacques Gabriel. Paganini. Paris: Henri Laurens, Editeur, 1907. 126, [2] p., 13 illus., works, 27-item bibliography. Translation by Alice Mattullath (New York: C. Fischer 1911). Reprint 1976.

Pulver, Jeffrey. Paganini, the Romantic Virtuoso. London: H. Joseph, Limited, 1936. Reprint 1970 with a new bibliography compiled by Frederick Freedman. 328 p., portrait, 7-item bibliography, index.

Salvaneschi, Nino. Un violino, 23 donne e il diavolo: la vita ardente di Niccolò Paganini. Milano: Edizioni Corbaccio, 1938. 286 p.

Salzedo, S. L. Paganini's Secret at Last. London: Nicholson & Watson, 1946. 39 p., 2 illus., 28-item bibliography.

Sartorelli, Fausto. L'uomo violine: Paganini. Roma: Edizioni Abete, 1981. 121 p. + 28 plates, 30 illus.

de Saussine, Renée. Paganini le magicien. Préface by Jacques Thibaud. Paris: Gallimard, 1938. Reprint 1950. 252 p., bibliography, works. Translated by Marjorie Lawrence as Paganini (London: Hutchinson, 1953). Reprint 1970.

Schottly, Julius Max. Paganini's Leben und Treiben als Kuenstler und als Mensch: mit unpartheiischer beruecksichtigung der Meinungen seiner Anhaenger und Gegner. Prag: J.G. Calve'sche Buchhandlung, 1830. Reprint 1974. x, [ii], 410, [9] p. + folding plate, portrait.

Sheppard, Leslie and Herbert R. Axelrod. Paganini. Neptune City (NJ): Paganiniana Publications, Inc., 1979. 703 p., illus., discography, Library of Congress Paganini Collection, index.

Spivacke, Harold. Paganiana. Washington (DC): U.S. Government Printing Office, 1945. 19 p. + 6 plates, 14 illus. [The previous entry has a similar listing of the collection in Washington, D.C.].

Spronk, Johannes Engelbertus Wilhelmus. Bijdrage tot de biografie van Nicolo Paganini. Gorinchem: J. Noorduijn en Zoon N.V., 1965. 117 p., 22 illus., 108 item bibliography. [Ph.D. diss. University of Leiden].

Stratton, Stephen Samuel. Nicolo Paganini: His Life and Work. New York: Charles Scribner's Sons, 1907. Reprint 1971. iv, 205 p. + 27 plates, 27 illus., 53-item bibliography.

Sugden, John. Niccolo Paganini: Supreme Violinist or Devil's Fiddler? Neptune City (NJ): Paganiniana Publications, Inc., 1980. 168, [2] p., 47 illus., 111-item bibliography, discography, index.

Tibaldi Chiesa, Mary. Paganini: la vita e l'opera. Milano: Garazanti, 1944. 484, [2] p. + 18 plates, 32 illus., bibliography.

Tonazzi, Bruno. Paganini a Trieste. 2nd enlarged edition. Padova: Edizioni G. Zanibon, n.d., 54 p., 3 illus., index of names.

Valensi, Théodore. Paganini, 1784-1840. Nice: Les E.L.F. et Jacques Dervyl, 1950. 248 p. + 6 plates, 6 illus.

Vernarelli, Gerardo. Nicolò Paganini nei disegni di un impressionista contemporaneo. Roma: Fernando Gerra, 1940. 15, xv p. + 24 plates, 24 illus.

Vyborny, Zdenek. Paganini v Karlovych Varech. Plzen: Krajské Naklada-telstvi, 1961. 77, [18] p., 13 illus., 37-item bibliography.

5. A0014, A0016, A0023, A0033, A0036, A0093, B0011, B0020, B0024, B0035, B0037, B0050, B0083, B0092, B0102, B0109.

SEE: Haweis, H.R. My Musical Life. London: Longmans, Green, and Co., 1896.

SEE: Kinsky, Georg. "Paganini's musikalischer Nachlass" in Musikhis-torisches Museum von Wilhelm Heyer in Koeln, IV (Leipzig, 1916), 402-47.

SEE: Phipson, T.L. under Giovanni Bottesini (C0170.5).

C0879.
Page, Hot Lips [Oran Thaddeus]. American Jazz Trumpeter; b. January 27, 1908, Dallas, Texas; d. November 5, 1954, New York City.

1. Baker 7; Grove-AM (Bibliography); Grove-Jazz; LJ; PAB-MI/2 (Bibliog-raphy).

C0880.
Parish-Alvars, Elias. English Harpist; b. February 28, 1808, Teignmouth; d. January 25, 1849, Vienna, Austria.

1. Baker 7; Fetis 2/6; Grove 6/14; Mendel; MGG (Bibliography); Riemann 12 + Supp. (Bibliography); Schmidl.

C0881.
Parker Charlie, Bird, Yardbird [Charles, Jr.]. American Jazz Alto/Tenor Saxophonist; b. August 29, 1920, Kansas City, Kansas; d. March 12, 1955, New York City.

1. Baker 7 (Bibliography); EdS; Grove 6/14 (Bibliography) - 29 entries); Grove-AM (Bibliography - 51 entries); Grove-Jazz; JB (46 entries); JRRM (31 entries); LJ (24 entries); PAB/MI-2 (Bibliography); Riemann 12 (Bibliography) + Supp. (Bibliography).

2. DB 16/17, 22/8, 31/20, 32/6 (Special Issue); 37/7, 41/19, 47/8; HiFi/ MusAm 23/2, 35/3; JJS 1/1, 2/1, 2/2, 5/2; MQ 52/3, 59/4.

4. Davis, Nathan Tate. Charlie Parker's Kansas City Environment and Its Effect on His Later Life. Ph.D. diss. Wesleyan University, 1974. 279 p., bibliography.

Harrison, Max. Charlie Parker. London: Cassell & Company Limited, 1960. 86, [1] p. + 2 Plates, 4 illus., discography.

Hirschmann, T. Untersuchungen zu den Kompositionen von Charlie Parker. Ph.D. diss. University of Mainz, 1982.

Owens, Thomas. Charlie Parker: Techniques of Improvisation. 2 vols. Ph.D. diss. UCLA, 1974. 385 p.; 478 p., transcriptions, bibliography.

Priestly, Brian. Charlie Parker. New York: Hippocrene Books, Inc., 1984. 96 p., 11 illus., discography, 9-item bibliography.

Reisner, Robert George. Bird: the Legend of Charlie Parker. New York: The Citadel Press, 1962. Reprint 1975. 256 p., illus., chronology, discography by Erik Wiedemann.

Russell, Ross. Bird Lives: the High Life and Hard Times of Charlie Parker. New York: Charterhouse, 1973. x, 404 p. + 8 plates, 32 illus., 28-item select bibliography, discography, index.

Schmidt, Siegfried. Charlie Parker: ein Portraet. Wetzlar: Pegasus Verlag, 1959. 48 p. + 8 plates, 16 illus., discography.

5. A0001, A0026, A0029, A0159.

SEE: Fayenz, Franco. Il nuovo jazz degli anni '40. Roma: Lato Side Editori, 1982. 124, [19] p., 21 illus., discographies.

Lester Young, Charlie Parker, and Lennie Tristano.

C0882.
Parlow, Kathleen. Canadian Violinist; b. September 20, 1890, Calgary; d. August 19, 1963, Oakville, Ontario.

1. Baker 7; Grove 6/14 (Bibliography); PAB-MI/2 (Bibliography); Riemann 12/Supp. (Bibliography); Schmidl/Supp.

4. French [née Parlow], Maida. Kathleen Parlow: a Portrait. Toronto: Ryerson Press, 1967. vii, [i], 167 p. + 4 plates, 20 illus., index.

C0883.
Parnas, Leslie. American Cellist; b. November 11, 1931, St. Louis, MO.

1. Baker 7; Grove-AM; PAB-MI/2 (Bibliography); Riemann 12/Supp.

2. Strad Nov/1987.

C0884.
Parratt, Walter. English Organist; b. February 10, 1841, Huddersfield;
d. March 27, 1924, Windsor.

1. Baker 7 (Bibliography); Grove 6/14 (Bibliography); PAB-MI/2 (Bibliography); MGG (Bibliography).

4. Tovey, Donald Francis. Walter Parratt, Master of the Music. London:
Oxford University Press, 1941. 183, [1] p., index.

C0885.
Patorni-Casadesus, Regina. French Clavecinist; b. July 7, 1886, Paris;
d. August 28, 1961, Paris.

1. DEU; EdS; MGG (Bibliography).

3. Patorni-Casadesus, Regina. Souvenirs d'une claveciniste: ma famille
Casadesus. Paris: La Ruche Ouvrière, 1962. 228, [1] p., illus.

C0886.
Pattison, John Nelson. American Pianist; b. October 22, 1845, Niagara
Falls, New York; d. July 27, 1905, New York City.

1. Baker 7; PAB-MI/2 (Bibliography); Schmidl/Supp.

4. Cromwell, George Reed. Memoir of J.N. Pattison, the Great Pianist and
Composer. New York: Press of Torrey Bros., 1868. 16 p.

C0887.
Pauer, Ernst. Austrian Pianist; b. December 21, 1826, Vienna; d. May 9,
1905, Jugenheim, near Darmstadt, Germany.

1. Baker 7; Fetis 2/6 + Supp; Grove 6/14; Mendel; PAB-MI/2 (Bibliography); Riemann 12; Schmidl.

3. Pauer, Ernst. A Dictionary of Pianists and Composers for the Pianoforte, with an Appendix of Manufacturers of the Instrument. London:
Novello, Ewer and Co., 1895. v, 159 p.

An extremely valuable source for obscure artists.

Pauer, Ernst. The Art of Pianoforte-playing. London: Novello and
Company, Limited, 1877. 88 p. + folding plate.

C0888.
Pauer, Max. English Pianist, son of Ernst; b. October 31, 1866, London;
d. May 12, 1945, Jugenheim, near Darmstadt, Germany.

1. Baker 7; Grove 6/14; MGG (Bibliography); Riemann 12; Schmidl.

3. Pauer, Max. Unser seltsames Ich: Lebensschau eines Kuenstlers. Stuttgart: J. Engelhorns Nachf. Adolf Spemann, 1942. 119, [1] p.

C0889.
Pauk, Gyoergy. British Pianist; b. October 26, 1936, Budapest, Hungary.

1. Baker 7; Grove 6/14 (Bibliography); PAB-MI/2 (Bibliography).

C0890.
Peinemann, Edith. German Violinist; b. March 3, 1937, Mainz.

1. Baker 7; Grove 6/14 (Bibliography); PAB-MI/2 (Bibliography); Riemann 12 + Supp.

5. B0110.

C0891.
Pelissier, Victor. French French-horn Player; b. c.1740–50, Paris?; d. c.1820, New Jersey?

1. Baker 7 (Bibliography); Grove 6/14 (Bibliography); Grove-AM (Bibliography); PAB-MI/2 (Bibliography).

C0892.
Pembaur, Joseph, Jr. Austrian Pianist; b. April 20, 1875, Innsbruck; d. October 12, 1950, Munich, Germany.

1. Baker 7; MGG (Bibliography); Riemann 12 (Bibliography).

4. Graef, Otto A. and Karl Ude. Josef Pembaur: ein Bekenntnis seiner Freunde [65th birthday]. Meunchen: Tukan-Verlag, n.d. [1940]. 72 p.

   Werner, Christine. Josef Pembaur zum 60. Geburtstag. Burg: August Hopfer Verlag, 1935. 16, [1], 2 portraits.

C0893.
Pennario, Leonard. American Pianist; b. July 9, 1924, Buffalo, New York.

1. Baker 7; Grove 6/14; Grove-AM (Bibliography); PAB-MI/2 (Bibliography); Riemann 12/Supp. (Bibliography).

2. CL 3/6; CK(KB) 5/2; PQ 82.

C0894.
Pepper, Art[hur Edward, Jr,]. American Jazz Alto Saxophonist; b. September 1, 1925, Gardena, California; d. June 15, 1982, Los Angeles, CA.

1. Baker 7; Grove 6/14 (Bibliography); Grove-AM (Bibliography); Grove-Jazz; JB; LJ; PAB-MI/2 (Bibliography).

2. DB 23/19, 25/1, 31/22, 40/4, 42/11, 46/18.

3. Pepper, Art and Laurie. Straight Life: the Story of Art Pepper. New York: Schirmer Books, 1979. xxii, 516, [1] p. + 16 plates, 45 illus., discography by Todd Selbert, index.

C0895.
Perabo, Johann Ernst. American Pianist; b. November 14, 1845, Wiesbaden, Germany; d. October 29, 1920, Boston, Massachusetts.

1. Baker 7; Grove 6/14; Grove-AM; PAB-MI/2 (Bibliography).

C0896.
Perahia, Murray. American Pianist; b. April 19, 1947, New York City.

1. Baker 7; Grove 6/14; Grove-AM (Bibliography); PAB-MI/2 (Bibliography).

2. CL 20/7, 24/6, 26/5; GR 52/February, 60/June, 64/May; CK(KB) 8/4.

C0897.
Perlemuter, Vlado. French Pianist; b. May 26, 1904, Kaunas, Lithuania.

1. Baker 7; Grove 6/14; PAB-MI/2 (Bibliography); Riemann 12/Supp.

2. CL 21/3; GR 57/July.

C0898.
Perlman, Itzhak. American Violinist; b. August 31, 1945, Tel Aviv, Israel.

1. Baker 7 (Bibliography); Grove 6/14 (Bibliography); Grove-AM (Bibliography); PAB-MI/2 (Bibliography); Riemann 12/Supp.

2. GR 50/June, 59/September; HiFi/MusAm 29/8; Newsweek April 14, 1980; Strad April/1976.

5. B0027, B0052.

B0899.
Persinger, Louis. American Violinist; b. February 11, 1887, Rochester, Illinois; d. December 31, 1966, New York City.

1. Baker 7; Grove 6/14 (Bibliography); Grove-AM (Bibliography); PAB-MI/2 (Bibliography); Riemann 12 + Supp. (Bibliography).

5. A0100.

SEE: Autobiography of **Yehudi Menuhin** (C0803.3).

SEE: Magidoff, Robert under **Yehudi Menuhin** (C0803.4).

C0900.
Peterson, Oscar [Emmanuel]. Canadian Jazz Pianist; b. August 15, 1925, Montreal.

1. Baker 7; Grove 6/14 (Bibliography); Grove-AM (Bibliography); Grove-Jazz; JB; LJ; PAB-MI/2 (Bibliography); Riemann 12 + Supp. (Bibliography).

"...one of the finest jazz pianists of the day." Baker 7.

2. DB 24/12, 26/22, 32/13; HiFi/MusAm 25/2; CK(KB) 4/3, 6/12, 9/10.

4. Palmer, Richard. Oscar Peterson. Tunbridge Wells (Kent): Spellmount Ltd, 1984. 93 p., 7 illus., notes, discography.

C0901.
Petri, Egon. American Pianist; b. March 23, 1881, Hannover, Germany;
d. May 27, 1962, Berkeley, California.

1. Baker 7; Grove 6/14 (Bibliography); Grove-AM (Bibliography); PAB-MI/2
   (Bibliography); Riemann 12 + Supp. (Bibliography); Schmidl.

2. RS 39.

5. SEE: Hull, Anne. Vignettes. n.p.: Tipografia Peres, n.d. [1972].
   Privately printed in an edition of 100 copies, Vignettes includes Petri and Harry Partch, the composer.

C0902.
Petschnikoff, Alexander. Russian Violinist; b. January 1, 1873, Jelez;
d. November 3, 1949, Buenos Aires, Argentina.

1. Riemann 12 (under Petschnikow); Schmidl (under Petchnikoff).

4. Petschnikoff, Lili. The World at Our Feet. New York: Vantage Press,
   1968. 221 p. + 6 plates, 12 illus.

C0903.
Pettiford, Oscar. American Jazz Double Bassist; b. September 30, 1922,
Okmulgee, Oklahoma; d. September 8, 1960, Copenhagen, Denmark.

1. Baker 7; Grove-AM (Bibliography); Grove-Jazz; JB; JRRM; LJ; PAB-MI/2
   (Bibliography); Riemann 12 + Supp. (Bibliography).

2. DB 17/26, 33/11.

5. SEE: Barnet, Charlie with Stanley Dance. Those Swinging Years: the
   Autobiography of Charlie Barnet. Baton Rouge (LA): Louisiana
   State University Press, 1984. xvii, 225 p., 47 illus., players,
   arrangers, singers, films, select discography, index.

C0904.
Pfannstiehl, Bernhard. German Organist; b. December 18, 1861, Schmal-
kalden; d. October 21, 1940, Freiberg.

1.Baker 7 (Bibliography); Riemann 12 (Bibliography) + Supp. (Bibliography); Schmidl.

C0905.
Pfundt, Ernst Gotthold Benjamin. German Timpanist; b. June 17, 1806,
Dommitzsch, near Torgau; d. December 7, 1871, Leipzig.

1. Baker 7; Mendel (under Pfund); Riemann 12; Schmidl.

C0906.
Philipp, Isidor. French Pianist; b. September 2, 1863, Budapest,
Hungary; d. February 20, 1958, Paris.

1. Baker 7; Grove 6/14 (Bibliography); Grove-AM (Bibliography); PAB-MI/2
   (Bibliography); Riemann 12 + Supp.; Schmidl + Supp.

"In 1977 the American Liszt Society established the Isidor Philipp Archive and Memorial Library at the University of Louisville School of Music." Grove-AM.

2. MQ 21/4, 29/3; PQ 88; RS 1/8.

3. Philipp, Isidor. La Technique de Liszt. 2 vols. Paris, 1932. No copy located.

C0907.
Phillips, Harvey Gene. American Tuba Player; b. December 2, 1929, Aurora, Missouri.

1. Baker 7; Grove 6/14; Grove-AM; PAB-MI/2 (Bibliography).

2. New Yorker December 15, 1975.

C0908.
Piastro, Michel [Mishel]. American Violinist; b. July 1, 1891, Kerch, Crimea, Russia; d. April 10, 1970, New York City.

1. Baker 7; Grove-AM; Riemann 12 + Supp.

C0909.
Piatigorsky, Gregor. American Cellist; b. April 17, 1903, Ekaterinoslav, Russia; d. August 6, 1976, Los Angeles, California.

1. Baker 7; Grove 6/14 (Bibliography); Grove-AM (Bibliography); MGG/ Supp. (Bibliography); PAB-MI/2 (Bibliography); Riemann 12 + Supp.; Schmidl/Supp.

   "...a leading cellist of his generation." Grove-AM.

2. HiFi 11/2; HiFi/MusAm 26/11; Strad Oct/1976.

3. Piatigorsky, Gregor. Cellist. Garden City (NY): Doubleday & Company, Inc., 1965. Reprint 1976. viii, 273 p. + 6 plates, 27 illus., index. The German edition (Tuebingen: Wunderlich, 1968) translated by Else Winter includes a discography.

5. A0100, B0030.

   SEE: Newton, Ivor. At the Piano: the World of an Accompanist. London: Hamish Hamilton Limited, 1966.

   SEE: Rosenberg, Deena and Bernard. The Music Makers. New York: Columbia University Press, 1979.

C0910.
Piatti, Alfredo Carlo. Italian Cellist; b. January 8, 1822, Borgo Canale, near Bergamo; d. July 18, 1908, Crocetto di Mozzo.

1. Baker 7; Fetis 2/7 + Supp.; Grove 6/14 (Bibliography); Mendel; MGG (Bibliography); PAB-MI/2 (Bibliography); Riemann 12 (Bibliography) + Supp. (Bibliography); Schmidl.

"...in the cello world [he] occupied a position of artistry and au-
thority comparable with that of Joachim among violinists." Baker 7.

4. Latham, Morton. Alfredo Piatti: a Sketch. London: W.E. Hill and Sons,
1901. 122 p., portrait.

5. A0104.

C0911.
Pixis, Johann Peter. German Pianist; b. February 10, 1788, Mannheim;
d. December 22, 1874, Baden-Baden.

1. Baker 7 (Bibliography); Fetis 2/7; Grove 6/14 (Bibliography); Mendel;
MGG (Bibliography); PAB-MI/2 (Bibliography); Riemann 12 (Bibliography); Schmidl.

C0912.
Planté, Francis. French Pianist; b. March 2, 1839, Orthez, Basses-
Pyrénées; d. December 19, 1934, St. Avit, near Mont-de-Marsan.

1. Baker 7; Fetis/2 Supp.; Grove 6/14 (Bibliography); PAB-MI/2 (Bibliography); Riemann 12 (Bibliography); Schmidl + Supp.

4. Comettant, Oscar. Francis Planté: Portrait musical a la plume. Paris:
Huget et Cie, Editeurs, 1874. 35 p., portrait.

Lenoir, Auguste. Francis Planté, doyen des pianistes. Hossegor:
Librairie D. Chabas, Editeur, 1931. viii, 230, [3] p. + 5 plates,
5 illus.

5. A0028, B0083, B0112.

C0913.
Pollack, Ben. American Jazz Drummer; b. June 22, 1903, Chicago,
Illinois; d. June 7, 1971, Palm Springs, California.

1. Baker 7; Grove-AM (Bibliography); Grove-Jazz; JB; JRRM.

C0914.
Pollini, Maurizio. Italian Pianist; b. January 5, 1942, Milan.

1. Baker 7; Grove 6/15; PAB-MI/2 (Bibliography); Riemann 12/Supp.

2. GR 52/May.

5. A0060.

SEE: Meyer-Josten, Juergen under Daniel Barenboim (C0071.5).

C0915.
Pommier, Jean-Bernard. French Pianist; b. August 17, 1944, Bézier.

1. Baker 7; Grove 6/15; PAB-MI/2 (Bibliography).

5. A0060.

C0916.
Ponti, Michael. American Pianist; b. October 29, 1937, Freiburg, Germany.

1. Baker 7; Riemann/Supp.

C0917.
Ponty, Jean-Luc. French Jazz Violinist; b. September 29, 1942, Arran-ches, Normandy.

1. Baker 7; Grove 6/15; Grove-Jazz; JB; PAB-MI/2 (Bibliography); Riemann 12/Supp. (Bibliography).

2. DB 33/22, 40/14, 42/20, 44/20, 51/1; HiFi/SR 28/3.

C0918.
Popper, David. Czechoslovakian Cellist; b. December 9, 1843, Prague; d. August 7, 1913, Baden, near Vienna, Austria.

1. Baker 7; Fetis 2/Supp.; Grove 6/15 (Bibliography); Mendel; Riemann 12; Schmidl.

4. De'ak, Stephen. David Popper. Neptune City (NJ): Paganiniana Publi-cations, Inc., 1980. 317 p., illus., publications, index.

C0919.
Porro, Pierre Jean. French Guitarist; b. 1750, Béziers; d. May 31, 1831, Montmoreney.

1. Baker 7 (Bibliography); Fetis 2/7; Grove 6/15 (Bibliography); MGG (Bibliography); Riemann 12; Schmidl + Supp.

5. A0129.

C0920.
Posselt, Ruth. American Violinist; b. September 6, 1914, Medford, MA.

1. Baker 7; Grove-AM.

C0921.
Postnikova, Viktoria. Soviet Pianist; b. January 12, 1944, Moscow.

1. Baker 7; Grove 6/15; PAB-MI/2 (Bibliography).

C0922.
Potter, Philip Cipriani. English Pianist; b. October 2, 1792, London; d. September 26, 1871, London.

1. Baker 7 (Bibliography); Fetis 2/7 + Supp.; Grove 6/15 (Bibliography); Mendel; MGG (Bibliography); PAB-MI/2 (Bibliography); Riemann 12 (Bibliography) + Supp.; Schmidl.

4. Peter, Philip Henry. The Life and Work of Cipriani Potter (1792-1871). 2 vols. Ph.D. diss. Northwestern University, 1972. xiii, 284 p.; 355 p., plates, thematic catalogue, bibliography.

C0923.
Poulet, Gérard. French Violinist; b. August 12, 1938, Bayonne.

1. Baker 7; PAB-MI/2 (Bibliography); Riemann 12/Supp.

C0924.
Powell, Bud [Earl]. American Jazz Pianist; b. September 27, 1924, New York City; d. August 1, 1966, New York City.

1. Baker 7; Grove 6/15 (Bibliography); Grove-AM (Bibliography - 11 entries); Grove-Jazz; JB; JRRM; LJ; PAB-MI/2 (Bibliography); Riemann 12/Supp. (Bibliography).

2. DB 18/12, 29/29, 31/28, 33/19, 33/21; KB 10/6.

C0925.
Powell, Maud. American Violinist; b. August 22, 1868, Peru, Illinois; d. January 8, 1920, Uniontown, Pennsylvania.

1. Baker 7; Grove-AM (Bibliography); PAB-MI/2 (Bibliography); Schmidl.

2. Strad Aug/1980, Nov/1987.

4. Shaffer, Karen A. and Neva Garner Greenwood. Maud Powell: Pioneer American Violinist. Ames: Iowa State University Press, 1988. xx, 530 p. + 16 plates, 122 illus., appendices, discography, notes, index.

C0926.
Preston, Simon John. English Organist; b. August 4, 1938, Bournemouth.

1. Baker 7; Grove 6/15; PAB-MI/2 (Bibliography).

C0927.
Příhoda, Váša. Czechoslovakian Violinist; b. August 22, 1900, Vodnany; d. July 26, 1960, Vienna, Austria.

1. Baker 7; Grove 6/15 (Bibliography); MGG (Bibliography); Riemann 12 + Supp. (Bibliography); Schmidl.

4. Vratislavsky, Jan. Váša Příhoda. Praha: Supraphon, 1970. 69, [2] p. + 8 plates, illus., list of works, discography, bibliography, record.

5. B0024.

C0928.
Prill, Emil. German Flutist; b. May 10, 1867, Stettin; d. February 28, 1940, Berlin.

1. Baker 7; Riemann 12, Schmidl.

C0929.
Prill, Karl. German Violinist, brother of Emil; b. October 22, 1864, Berlin; d. August 18, 1931, Vienna, Austria.

1. Baker 7; Riemann 12; Schmidl.

C0930.
Prima, Louis. American Jazz Trumpeter; b. December 7, 1911, New Orleans, Louisiana; d. August 24, 1978, New Orleans.

1. Baker 7; Grove-Jazz; JB; PAB-MI/2 (Bibliography).

C0931.
Primrose, William. Scottish Violist; b. August 23, 1903, Glasgow; d. May 1, 1982, Provo, Utah.

1. Baker 7; Grove 6/15; Grove-AM; PAB-MI/2 (Bibliography); Riemann 12 + Supp.

Eugène Ysaÿe suggested that he take up the viola; brilliant advice.

3. Primrose, William. Walk on the North Side: Memoirs of a Violist. Provo (Utah): Brigham Young University Press, 1978. xiii, 237 p., illus., discography by François de Beaumont, index.

5. A0100, D0012.

C0932.
Prudent, Emile [Racine Gauthier]. French Pianist; b. February 3, 1817, Angoulême; d. May 13, 1863, Paris.

1. Baker 7; Fetis 2/7; Grove 6/15; Mendel; MGG/Supp. (Bibliography); Schmidl.

C0933.
Pryor, Arthur Willard. American Trombonist; b. September 22, 1870, St. Joseph, Missouri; d. June 18, 1942, Long Branch, New Jersey.

1. Baker 7 (Bibliography); Grove-AM (Bibliography); PAB-MI/2 (Bibliography).

4. Frizane, D.E. Arthur Pryor (1870-1942): American Trombonist, Band-Master, Composer. Ph.D. diss. University of Kansas, 1984.

5. SEE: Schwartz, H.W. Bands of America. Garden City (NY): Doubleday & Company, Inc., 1957.

C0934.
Pugnani, Giulio Gaetano. Italian Violinist; b. November 27, 1731, Turin; d. July 15, 1798, Turin.

1. Baker 7 (Bibliography); Fetis 2/7; Grove 6/15 (Bibliography); Mendel; MGG (Bibliography); PAB-MI/2 (Bibliography); Riemann 12 (Bibliography) + Supp. (Bibliography); Schmidl + Supp.

5. B0020, B0051, D0011 (Vol. 12).

SEE: McVeigh, Simon under Felice de'Giardini (C0453.4).

SEE: de Rangoni, Giovanni under Antonio Lolli (C0747.4).

C0935.
Pugno, Stéphane Raoul. French Pianist; b. June 23, 1852, Montrouge, Seine; d. January 3, 1914, Moscow, Russia.

1. Baker 7; Grove 6/15 (Bibliography); MGG; PAB-MI/2 (Bibliography); Riemann 12; Schmidl.

2. RS 3.

5. B0028, B0056, B0083, B0105.

SEE: Imbert, Hugues under Hubert Leonard (C0715.5).

C0936.
Puppo, Giuseppe. Italian Violinist; b. June 12, 1749, Lucca; d. April 19, 1827, Florence.

1. Baker 7; Fetis 2/7; Grove 6/15 (Bibliography); Mendel; MGG (Bibliography); Schmidl.

C0937.
Puyana, Rafael. Colombian Harpsichordist; b. October 14, 1931, Bogotá.

1. Baker 7; Grove 6/15; Riemann 12.

2. HiFi 12/10.

C0938.
Quantz, Johann Joachim. German Flutist; b. January 30, 1697, Oberscheden, Hannover; d. July 12, 1773, Potsdam.

1. Baker 7; Fetis 2/7; Grove 6/15 (Bibliography); Mendel; MGG (Bibliography); PAB-MI/2 (Bibliography); Riemann 12 (Bibliography) + Supp. (Bibliography); Schmidl.

3. His autobiography is in: Marpurg, Friedrich Wilhelm. Historisch-kritische Beytraege zur Aufnahme der Musik. Berlin: J.J. Schuetzens Witwe [-G.A. Lange], 1754-1778. Vol. 1, 1755; reprinted in Willi Kahl, Selbstbiographien deutscher Musiker des XVIII. Jahrhunderts, Koeln, 1948.

3. Quantz, Johann Joachim. Versuch einer Anweisung, die Floete traversiere zu spielen; mit verschiedenen, zur Befoerderung des guten Geschmackes in der praktischen Musik dienlichen Anmerkungen begleitet, und mit Exempeln erlaeutert. Berlin: Johann Friedrich Voss, 1752. 334 p., xxiv plates.

4. Raskin, Adolf Heinrich. Johann Joachim Quantz: sein Leben und seine Kompositionen. Ph.D. diss. University of Cologne, 1923. 211 p.

5. SEE: Helm, Everett. Music at the Court of Frederick the Great. Norman: University of Oklahoma Press, 1960.

SEE: Nettl, Paul under Franz Benda (C0105.3).

C0939.
Quiroga, Manuel. Spanish Violinist; b. April 15, 1890, Pontevedra; d. April 19, 1961, Pontevedra.

1. Baker 7; Riemann 12, Schmidl.

C0940.
Rabin, Michael. American Violinist; b. May 2, 1936, New York City; d. January 19, 1972, New York City.

1. Baker 7; Grove-AM (Bibliography); PAB-MI/2 (Bibliography); Riemann 12/Supp.

2. Strad May/1986.

C0941.
Rabinof, Benno. American Violinist; b. October 11, 1910, New York City; d. July 2, 1975, Brevard, North Carolina.

1. Baker 7; Grove-AM (Bibliography); Riemann 12/Supp.

C0942.
Rachmaninoff, Sergei Vasil'yevich. Russian Pianist [He became an American citizen shortly before his death]; b. April 1, 1873, Oneg, district of Novgorod; d. March 28, 1943, Beverly Hills, California.

1. Baker 7 (Bibliography); EdS (Bibliography); Grove 6/15 (under Rakhmaninov - Bibliography); Grove-AM (Bibliography); MGG (under Rachmaninow - Bibliography); PAB-MI/2 (Bibliography); Riemann 12 (Bibliography) + Supp. (Bibliography); Schmidl (under Rachmaninow).

2. CL 12/7 (Centennial Issue); HiFi/MusAm 24/1, 28/6; HiFiRev 3/4; HiFi/SR 30/5; MQ 13/3, 30/1, 30/2.

3. Rachmaninoff, Sergei. Rachmaninoff's Recollections Told to Oskar von Riesemann. Translated from the MS by Dolly Rutherford. New York: The Macmillan Company, 1934. [xviii], 15-272 p., 13 illus., list of compositions, index.

4. Bazanow, Milolai. Rachmaninow. Warszawa: Panstwowy Instytut Wydawniczy, 1972. 446, [2] p. + 20 plates, 29 illus., list of compositions, 16-item bibliography, index.

Culshaw, John. Rachmaninov: the Man and His Music. New York: Oxford University Press, 1950. 174, [16] p., illus., bibliography, index.

Lyle, Watson. Rachmaninoff: a Biography. London: William Reeves Bookseller Limited, n.d. [1938]. xii, 2-247 p., list of compositions, annotated discography, index.

Norris, Geoffrey. Rakhmaninov. London: J.M. Dent & Sons Ltd, 1976. xi, 211 p. + 4 plates, 8 illus., calendar, works, personalia, 21-item bibliography, index.

Palmieri, Robert. Sergei Vasil'evich Rachmaninoff: a Guide to Research. New York: Garland Publishing, Inc., 1985. xvii, 335 p. + 12 plates, discography, 375-item bibliography, references, author index, index of proper names, index of compositions, subject index.

Seroff, Victor I. Rachmaninoff. New York: Simon and Schuster, Inc., 1950. xiv, [12], 269 p., 21 illus., works, bibliography, index.

5. A0047, A0048, A0053, B0086, B0089, B0109, D0012.

C0943.
Ramin, Guenther. German Organist; b. October 15, 1898, Karlsruhe; d. February 27, 1956, Leipzig.

1. Baker 7 (Bibliography); Grove 6/15 (Bibliography); MGG (Bibliography); Riemann 12 (Bibliography) + Supp. (Bibliography); Schmidl/ Supp.

4. Hanke, Wolfgang. Guenther Ramin. Berlin: Union-Verlag, 1969. 31 p., 12 illus., chronology, bibliography, discography.

Hasse, Elisabeth (Ramin). Erinnerungen an Guenther Ramin. Berlin: Verlag Meresburger, 1958. 64 p., portrait.

Ramin, Charlotte. Guenther Ramin: ein Lebensbericht. Freiburg i. br.: Atlantis Verlag, 1958. 183, [1] p., 8 illus., list of works, discog.

5. B0080.

C0944.
Rampal, Jean-Pierre Louis. French Flutist; b. January 7, 1922, Marseilles.

1. Baker 7; Grove 6/15; MGG/Supp.; PAB-MI/2; Riemann 12 + Supp.

2. HiFi/MusAm 15/5.

5. SEE: Monsalvat reprints under Claudio Arrau (C0039.5).

C0945.
Ránki, Dezsoe. Hungarian Pianist; b. September 8, 1951, Budapest.

1. Baker 7; Grove 6/15; PAB-MI/2 (Bibliography).

C0946.
Rappoldi-Kahrer, Laura. Austrian Pianist; b. January 14, 1853, Mistelbach, near Vienna; d. August 2, 1925, Dresden, Germany.

1. Baker 7; Grove 6/15 (Bibliography); Mendel; Riemann 12.

Her husband, Eduard Rappoldi (b. February 21, 1831, Vienna; d. May 16, 1903, Dresden), was a fine chamber music violinist.

3. Rappoldi-Kahrer, Laura. Memorien von Laura Rappoldi-Kahrer, im auftrage von Elisabeth Nitzsche.... Dresden: Im eigenen Verlag von Elisabeth Neitzsche, 1929. 126 p., 7 illus.

C0947.
Rascher, Sigurd Manfred. American Saxophonist; b. May 15, 1907, Elberfeld [now Wuppertal], Germany.

1. Baker 7; Grove 6/15; Grove-AM; PAB-MI/2 (Bibliography).

C0948.
Reinhardt, Django [Jean Baptiste]. Belgian Jazz Guitarist; b. January 23, 1910, Liberchies; d. May 16, 1953, Fontainbleau, France.

1. Baker 7; Grove 6/15 (Bibliography); Grove-Jazz; PAB-MI/2 (Bibliography); Riemann 12 + Supp. (Bibliography).

2. DB 33/14, 43/4; HiFiRev 1/11.

4. Delaunay, Charles. Django Reinhardt. Translated by Michael James. London: Cassell and Company, Limited, 1961. 247 p., illus., discography. The French edition (Paris: Le Terrain vague, 1968) includes a filmography.

   Schulz-Koehn, Dietrich. Django Reinhardt: ein Portraet. Wetzler: Pegasus Verlag, 1960. 48 p., illus., discography.

5. A0001, A0108.

C0949.
Reinken [Reincken], Johann Adam. Dutch Organist; b. April 26, 1623; d. November 24, 1722, Hamburg, Germany.

1. Baker 7 (Bibliography); Fetis 2/7 (under Reincke); Grove 6/15 (Bibliography); Mendel; MGG (Bibliography); PAB-MI/2 (Bibliography); Riemann 12 (Bibliography) + Supp. (Bibliography); Schmidl.

C0950.
Reisenauer, Alfred. German Pianist; b. November 1, 1863, Koenigsberg; d. October 3, 1907, Libau, Latvia.

1. Baker 7; Grove 6/15 (Bibliography); MGG (Bibliography); Riemann 12; Schmidl.

4. Schwerin, Josephine. Erinnerungen an Alfred Reisenauer. Koenigsberg: Graefe & Unzer Verlag, 1909. 63 p., portrait.

C0951.
Reisenberg, Nadia. American Pianist; b. July 14, 1904, Vilna, Russia; d. June 10, 1983, New York City.

1. Baker 7; Grove-AM (Bibliography).

4. Sherman, Robert and Alexander Sherman. Nadia Reisenberg: a Musician's Scrapbook. Foreword by Gary Graffman. College Park (MD): International Piano Archives at the University of Maryland, 1986. 192 p., illus.

C0952.
Reményi [né Hoffman], **Ede** [Eduard]. Hungarian Violinist; b. January 17, 1828, Mislolc; d. May 15, 1898, San Francisco, California.

1. Baker 7 (Bibliography); Fetis 2/Supp.; Grove 6/15 (Bibliography); Mendel; MGG (Bibliography); Riemann 12 (Bibliography) + Supp. (Bibliography); Schmidl.

Some original materials are in the New York Public Library.

4. Kelley, Gwendolyn Dunlevey and George P. Upton. Edouard Remenyi, Musician, Literateur, and Man: an Appreciation, with Sketches of His Life and Artistic Career, by Friends and Contemporaries, to Which are Added Critical Reviews of His Playing and Selections from His Literary Papers and Correspondence. Chicago: A.C. McClurg & Co., 1906. xi, 9-255 p. + 8 plates, index.

5. B0035.

C0953.
Rémusat, Jean. French Flutist; b. May 11, 1815, Bordeau; d. September 1, 1880, Shanghai, China.

1. Baker 7; Fetis 2/7 (under Remuzat) + Supp.; Mendel (under Remuzat); Schmidl.

C0954.
Renié, Henriette. French Harpist; b. September 18, 1875 Paris; d. March 1, 1956, Paris.

1. Baker 7; Riemann 12/Supp.; Schmidl.

5. B0096.

C0955.
Reynolds, Verne. American French-horn Player; b. July 18, 1926, Lyons, Kansas.

1. Baker 7; PAB-MI/2 (Bibliography); Riemann 12/Supp.

C0956.
Ricci, Ruggiero. American Violinist; b. July 24, 1918, San Francisco, CA

1. Baker 7; Grove 6/15 (Bibliography); Grove-AM (Bibliography); PAB-MI/2 (Bibliography); Riemann 12 + Supp.

2. HiFi 12/5; Strad March/1977, Oct/1982.

5. A0100, B0070.

C0957.
Rich, Buddy [Bernard]. American Jazz Drummer; b. June 30, 1917, Brooklyn, New York.

1. Baker 7; Grove 6/15; Grove-AM; Grove-Jazz; JB; LJ; PAB-MI/2.

2. DB 27/12, 27/13, 33/6, 34/8, 34/25, 36/6, 37/2, 37/6, 41/7, 45/3, 45/4.

4. Balliett, Whitney. Super Drummer: a Profile of Buddy Rich. Indianapolis (IN): The Bobbs-Merrill Company, 1968. 128 p., illus.

5. A0004.

C0958.
Richter, Sviatoslav Teofilovich. Soviet Pianist; b. March 20, 1915, Zhitomir.

1. Baker 7; Grove 6/15; MGG/Supp. (Bibliography); PAB-MI/2 (Bibliography); Riemann 12/Supp. (Bibliography).

"...among the outstanding pianists of the 20th century." Grove 7.

2. HiFi 8/10, 12/10; HiFi/SR 5/4; RS 84.

4. Del'son, Viktor Yul'evich. Sviatoslav Rikhter. Moskva: Muzika, 1960. 25 p., illus.

Del'son, Viktor Yul'evich. Sviatoslav Richter. Bucuresti: Editura Muzicala a Uniunii Compozitorilor din R.P., 1962. 144, [3] p. + 8 plates, 16 illus. Translated from the Russian edition (Moskva: Gos. musykal'noe izd-vo, 1961).

Egert, Georg. Svjatoslav Richter. Berlin: Rembrandt Verlag, 1966. 31 p. + 15 plates, 26 illus.

Jurík, Marián. Svjatoslav Richter. Praha: Supraphon, 1974. 50 p. + 7 plates, illus., phonodisk, discography, bibliography.

5. A0060, A0091, B0042, B0055, B0071.

C0959.
Richter-Haaser, Hans. German Pianist; b. January 6, 1912, Dresden; d. December 16, 1980, Dresden.

1. Baker 7; Grove 6/15; PAB-MI/2 (Bibliography); Riemann 12 + Supp.

C0960.
Ries, Ferdinand. German Pianist; b. November 28, 1784, Bonn; d. January 13, 1838, Frankfurt/M.

1. Baker 7 (Bibliography); Fetis 2/7; Grove 6/16 (Bibliography); Mendel; MGG (Bibliography); PAB-MI/2 (Bibliography); Riemann 12 (Bibliography) + Supp. (Bibliography); Schmidl.

4. Ueberfeldt, Ludwig. Ferdinand Ries' Jugendentwicklung. Ph.D. diss. University of Bonn, 1915. viii, 63 p.

C0961.
Rinck, Johann Christian Heinrich. German Organist; b. February 18, 1770, Elgersburg; d. August 7, 1846, Darmstadt.

1. Baker 7; Fetis 2/7 (under Rink - Bibliography); Grove 6/16 (Bibliography); Mendel; MGG (Bibliography); Riemann 12 (Bibliography) + Supp. (Bibliography); Schmidl.

3. Rinck, Johann Christian Heinrich. Selbstbiographie. Breslau: bei G. P. Uderholz, 1833. [iv], 26 p., list of compositions.

His library is now in the collection at Yale University.

C0962.
Risler, Joseph Edouard. French Pianist; b. February 23, 1973, Baden-Baden; d. July 22, 1929, Paris.

1. Baker 7; Riemann 12; Schmidl.

4. Anon. Edouard Risler. Paris: A. Dandelot, 1902. 52 p., portrait.

5. B0105.

C0963.
Ritter, Hermann. German Violist; b. September 16, 1849, Wismar, Mecklenburg; d. January 22, 1926, Wuerzburg.

1. Baker 7; Fetis 2/Supp.; Grove 6/16; MGG (Bibliography); Riemann 12; Schmidl.

C0964.
Rivé-King, Julie. American Pianist; b. October 30, 1854, Cincinnati, Ohio; d. July 24, 1937, Indianapolis, Indiana.

1. Baker 7 (Bibliography); Grove-AM (Bibliography); PAB-MI/2 (Bibliography); Riemann 12; Schmidl.

C0965.
Roach, Max[well]. American Jazz Drummer; b. January 10, 1925, New York City.

1. Baker 7; Grove 6/16; Grove-AM (Bibliography - 10 entries); Grove-Jazz; JB; JRRM; LJ; PAB-MI/2; Riemann 12 + Supp. (Bibliography).

2. DB 16/10, 25/6, 28/7, 32/7, 33/6, 35/6, 39/5, 45/18, 47/4, 52/10.

C0966.
Robison, Paula Judith. American Flutist; b. June 8, 1941, Nashville, TN.

1. Baker 7; Grove 6/16; Grove-AM (Bibliography).

C0967.
Rode, Jacques-Pierre Joseph. French Violinist; b. February 16, 1774, Bordeaux; d. November 25, 1830, Châuteau-Bourbon, near Damazan.

1. Baker 7; Fetis 2/7 + Supp.; Grove 6/16 (Bibliography); Mendel; MGG (Bibliography); PAB-MI/2 (Bibliography); Riemann 12 (Bibliography) + Supp. (Bibliography); Schmidl.

2. Strad April/1979.

4. Ahlgrimm, Johann. Jacques-Pierre Rode. Ph.D. diss. University of
Vienna, 1929.

Pougin, Arthur. Notice sur Rode violiniste français. Paris: Pottier
de Lalaine, Editeur, 1874. 64 p.

C0968.
Roesgen-Champion, Marguerite. Swiss Harpsichordist; b. January 25, 1894,
Geneva; d. June 30, 1976, Paris, France.

1. Baker 7; Riemann 12 + Supp. (Bibliography); Schmidl/Supp.

C0969.
Rogé, Pascal. French Pianist; b. April 6, 1951, Paris.

1. Baker 7; Grove 6/16; PAB-MI/2 (Bibliography).

C0970.
Rogers, Shorty [Milton Rajonsky]. American Jazz Trumpeter; b. April 14,
1924, Great Barrington, Massachusetts.

1. Baker 7; Grove 6/16; Grove-AM (Bibliography); Grove-Jazz; PAB-MI/2
(Bibliography).

2. DB 25/14.

C0971.
Rolla, Alessandro. Italian Violinist; b. April 6, 1757, Pavia;
d. September 15, 1841, Milan.

1. Baker 7; Fetis 2/7 + Supp.; Grove 6/16 (Bibliography); Mendel; MGG
(Bibliography); Riemann 12 + Supp. (Bibliography); Schmidl.

4. Zampieri, G. L'epoca e l'arte di Alessandro Rolla. Pavia, 1941. No
copy located.

C0972.
Rollins, Sonny [Theodore Walter]. American Jazz Tenor Saxophonist.
b. September 7, 1929, New York City.

1. Baker 7; Grove-AM (Bibliography - 16 entries); Grove-Jazz; PAB-MI/2
(Bibliography); Riemann 12 + Supp. (Bibliography).

2. DB 23/24, 25/14, 29/1, 32/18, 38/17, 41/3, 44/7, 46/2, 49/5.

4. Blancq, Charles. Melodic Improvisation in American Jazz: the Style
of Theodore "Sonny" Rollins, 1951-1962. Ph.D. diss. Tulane University, 1977. vii, 263 p., plates, discography, bibliography.

Blancq, Charles. Sonny Rollins: the Journey of a Jazzman. Boston:
Twayne Publishers, 1983. 142 p., chronology, notes and references,
107-item selected bibliography, discography, index.

5. A0159, B0048.

C0973.
Romberg, Bernhard Heinrich. German Cellist; b. November 11, 1767,
Dinklage, Oldenburg; d. August 13, 1841, Hamburg.

1. Baker 7; Fetis 2/7; Grove 6/16 (Bibliography); MGG (Bibliography);
   Riemann 12 (Bibliography) + Supp. (Bibliography); Schmidl.

   Son of the talented bassoonist, Anton Romberg (b. March 6, 1742,
   Muenster; d. December 14, 1814, Muenster).

4. Schaefer, Herbert. Bernard Romberg: sein Leben und Wirken. Ein Beitrag zur Geschichte des Violoncells. Luebben: Buch- und Steindruck-
   erei, Richter & Munkelt, 1931 [Ph.D. diss. University of Bonn, 1831].
   162, xxxiii p., list of works, 56-item bibliography.

   Stephenson, Kurt. Andreas Romberg: ein Beitrag zur hamburgischen
   Musikgeschichte. Hamburg: Christians Verlag, 1938 [Ph.D. diss. University of Freiburg, 1937]. 204 p.

   Andreas and Bernhard were cousins and constant companions.

5. A0104.

   SEE: Eckhardt, J. under Justus Dotzauer (C0322.4).

   SEE: Kohlmorgen, Fritz under Jean-Louis Duport (C0342.4).

C0974.
Rosand, Aaron. American Violinist; b. March 15, 1927, Hammond, Indiana.

1. Baker 7; Grove-AM (Bibliography); PAB-MI/2 (Bibliography).

2. Strad Nov/1986.

C0975.
Rosé, Arnold Josef. Austrian Violinist; b. October 24, 1863, Jassy,
Romania; d. August 25, 1946, London, England.

1. Baker 7; Grove 6/16 (Bibliography); MGG (Bibliography); Riemann 12
   (Bibliography); Schmidl.

5. B0037.

C0976.
Rose, Leonard Joseph. American Cellist; b. July 27, 1918, Washington,
D.C.; November 16, 1984, White Plains, New York.

1. Baker 7; Grove 6/16; Grove-AM (Bibliography); PAB-MI/2 (Bibliography); Riemann 12/Supp.

   The trio with Isaac Stern and Eugene Istomin was legendary.

5. A0100.

C0977.
Rosen, Charles Wells. American Pianist; b. May 5, 1927, New York City.

1. Baker 7; Grove 6/16; Grove-AM; PAB-MI/2 (Bibliography); Riemann 12/ Supp.

   Rosen is also a brilliant musicologist and writer.

2. CL 23/3; GR 48/February; HiFi/MusAm 25/11; CK(KB) 2/2; MM 18/4, 25/7.

C0978.
Rosen, Max. American Violinist; b. April 11, 1900, Dorohoi, Romania; d. December 17, 1956, New Yrok City.

1. Baker 7; Grove-AM; PAB-MI/2 (Bibliography); Riemann 12.

5. B0061.

C0979.
Rosen, Nathaniel. American Cellist; b. June 9, 1948, Altadena, CA.

1. Baker 7; Grove-AM; PAB-MI/2 (Bibliography).

2. HiFi/MusAm 29/2; Strad Jan/1979.

C0980.
Rosenthal, Moriz. Polish Pianist; b. December 17, 1862, Lemberg (now L'vov, Ukraine); d. September 3, 1946, New York City.

1. Baker 7; Grove 6/16; Grove-AM (Bibliography); MGG (Bibliography); PAB-MI/2 (Bibliography); Riemann 12 + Supp. (Bibliography); Schmidl.

2. HiFi/SR 14/2; RS 7.

5. A0048, B0053.

   SEE: Heiles, W.H. under **Ignaz Friedman** (C0423.4).

C0981.
Rostropovich, Mstislav Leopoldovich. Soviet Cellist [stripped of his citizenship in March 1978 by the Soviet government as an "ideological renegade"]; b. March 27, 1927, Baku.

1. Baker 7 (Bibliography); Grove 6/16 (Bibliography); Grove-AM (Bibliography); MGG/Supp. (Bibliography); PAB-MI/2 (Bibliography); Riemann 12 + Supp. (Bibliography).

   He is a brilliant cellist, excellent pianist, and fine conductor.

2. GR 54/March; HiFi/MusAm 25/10, 28/2; Opera News 40/3; OPER 1970: ein Jahrbuch der Zeitschrift Opernwelt; Time October 24, 1977.

3. Rostropowitsch, Mstislaw and Galina. Die Musik und unser Leben. Bern: Scherz Verlag, 1985 [1st edition Paris, 1983]. 223 p., notes, discography, index of names.

4. Galdamovich, Tat'iana Alekseevna. <u>Mstislav Rostropovich</u>. Moskva: Gos. musykal'noe izd-vo, 1969. 125, [2] p. + 8 plates, 18 illus., 35-item bibliography, repertoire.

Ginsburg, Lev Solomonovich. <u>Mstislav Rostropovich</u>. Moskva: Muzika, 1963. 44, [1] p. + 3 plates, 5 illus.

Samuel, Claude. <u>Entretiens avec Mstislav Rostropovich et Galina Vichnevskaia sur la Russie, la musique, la liberté</u>. Paris: Editions Robert Laffont, 1983. 205, [2] p. + 4 plates, 18 illus., discography.

5. B0071.

SEE: Cairns, David. <u>Responses: Musical Essays and Reviews</u>. New York: Alfred A. Knopf, Inc., 1973.

SEE: Cowden, Robert H. under **Charles-Auguste de Bériot** (C0116.4). Entries about Galina Vishnevskaya.

SEE: Cowden, Robert H. under **Hans von Buelow** (C0193.5). Entries about Rostropowitsch.

SEE: Vishnevskaya, Galina. <u>Galina: a Russian Story</u>. Translated by Guy Daniels. New York: Harcourt Brace Jovanovich, Publishers, 1984.

C0982.
Rothwell, Evelyn. English Oboist; b. January 24, 1911, Wallingford.

1. Baker 7; Grove 6/16 (Bibliography); PAB-MI/2 (Bibliography); Riemann 12 (under Barbirolli - her husband since 1939).

4. Atkins, Harold and Peter Cotes. <u>The Barbirollis: a Musical Marriage</u>. Foreword by Janet Baker. London: Robson Books Ltd., 1983. 238 p., 28 illus., 44-item bibliography, index.

5. SEE: Cowden, Robert H. under **Hans von Buelow** (C0193.5). Entries about John Barbirolli.

C0983.
Rovelli, Pietro. Italian Violinist; b. February 6, 1793, Bergamo; d. September 8, 1838, Bergamo.

1. Baker 7; Fetis 2/7; Grove 6/16 (Bibliography); Mendel; MGG/Supp. (Bibliography); Schmidl + Supp.

C0984.
Rubinstein, Anton Grigor'yevich. Russian Pianist; b. November 28, 1829, Vykhvatinetz, Podolia; d. November 20, 1894, Peterhof, near St. Petersburg.

1. Baker 7 (Bibliography); EdS (Bibliography); Fetis 2/7 + Supp.; Grove 6/16 (Bibliography); Grove-AM (Bibliography); Mendel; MGG (Bibliography); PAB-MI/2 (Bibliography); Riemann 12 (Bibliography) + Supp. (Bibliography); Schmidl.

"According to contemporary reports, his playing possessed extraordinary power (his octave passages were famous) and insight, re-
vealed particularly in his performance of Beethoven's sonatas."
Baker 7.

2. CL 16/4; HiFi/SR 27/2; MQ 5/1, 25/4.

3. Rubinstein, Anton. A Conversation on Music. Translated by Mrs. John
   P. Morgan. New York: Chas. F. Tretbar, Publisher, 1892. 146 p.

   Rubinstein, Anton. Autobiography of Anton Rubinstein 1829-1889.
   Translated by Aline Delano. Boston: Little, Brown, and Company,
   1890 [original St. Petersburg, 1889]. Reprint 1969. xii, 171 p.,
   portrait.

   Rubinstein, Anton. Music and Its Masters. Chicago: Charles H. Sergel
   & Company, 1892 [original St. Petersburg, 1888]. 136 p.

   Interesting material on Clementi, Hummel, Field, Moscheles, Thalberg,
   Liszt, and Henschelt.

4. Barenboim, L. Nikolai Grilor'evich Rubinshtein. Moskva: Muzyka, 1982.
   276, [1] p. + 16 plates, 49 illus., notes, bibliography, index.

   Bowen, Catherine Drinker. "Free Artist": the Story of Anton and
   Nicholas Rubinstein. New York: Random House, 1939. xi, 412 p., 15
   illus., compositions by Anton, 350-item bibliography includes 66
   citations in Russian, index.

   Droucker, Sandra. Erinnerungen an Anton Rubinstein. Bemerkungen,
   Andeutungen und Besprechungen (mit vielen Notenbeispielen) in seiner
   Klasse im St. Petersburger Konservatorium. Leipzig: Verlag von Bart-
   holf Senff, 1904. 28 p.

   Hervey, Arthur. Rubinstein. London: Murdoch, Murdoch & Co., n.d.
   [1913]. 28 p.

5. A0028, A0033, A0035, A0047, A0051, B0008, B0020, B0021, B0035, B0083,
   B0102, B0109.

   SEE: Ehrlich, A. [pseud. for Albert Payne]. Schlaglichter und Schlag-
   schatten aus der Musikwelt. Berlin: Verlag von F. Guttentag,
   1872.

   SEE: Autobiography of Frederic Lamond (C0694.3).

   SEE: Norris, Gerald. Stanford the Cambridge Jubilee and Tchaikovsky.
   London: David & Charles, Inc., 1980.

C0985.
Rubinstein, Artur. American Pianist; b. January 28, 1887, Lodz, Poland;
d. December 20, 1982, Geneva, Switzerland.

1. Baker 7; Grove 6/16; Grove-AM (Bibliography); MGG (Bibliography);
   PAB-MI/2 (Bibliography); Riemann 12 + Supp. (Bibliography); Schmidl.

He was one of the towering pinnacles of 20th century keyboardists.

2. CL 8/6, 22/2, 22/10, 23/10, 26/1; GR 46/November; HiFi 13/7; HiFi/ MusAm 16/9, 26/2; HiFiRev 3/3; HiFi/SR 49/1; MM 16/10, 19/2.

3. Rubinstein, Arthur. My Many Years. New York: Alfred A. Knopf, Inc., 1980. [iii], 626 p. + 12 plates, 55 illus., index.

   Rubinstein, Arthur. My Younger Years. New York: Alfred A. Knopf, Inc., 1973. xi, [ii], 478, [1], xiii p. + 8 plates, 23 illus., index.

4. Forsee, Aylesa. Artur Rubinstein: King of the Keyboard. New York: Thomas Y. Crowell Company, 1969. vii, 178 p. + 4 plates, 8 illus., index.

   Gavoty, Bernard. Artur Rubinstein. Genève: René Kister, 1956. 30, [2] p., 24 illus., recordings.

   Khentova, Sofia Mikhailovna. Artur Rubinshtein. Moskva: Gos. musykal' noe izd-vo, 1971. 161 p., illus., bibliographical references.

   von Lewinski, Wolf-Eberhard. Artur Rubinstein. Berlin: Rembrandt Verlag, 1967. 30 p. + 15 plates, 27 illus.

   Lipmann, Eric. Arthur Rubinstein ou l'amour de Chopin. Paris: Editions De Messine, 1980. 222 p., illus.

5. A0060, B0012, B0030, B0039, B0041, B0042, B0044, B0058, B0086, B0098, B0108, B0109.

C0986.
Rubinstein, Beryl. American Pianist; b. October 26, 1898, Athens, Georgia; d. December 29, 1952, Cleveland, Ohio.

1. Baker 7; Grove-AM; PAB-MI/2 (Bibliography); Riemann 12/Supp.

C0987.
Rubinstein, Nicolai Grigor'yevich. Russian Pianist, brother of Anton; b. June 14, 1835, Moscow; d. March 23, 1881, Paris, France.

1. Baker 7 (Bibliography); Fetis 2/Supp.; Grove 6/16; Mendel; MGG (Bibliography); Riemann 12 (Bibliography); Schmidl.

   The two brothers, by introducing European methods into education and establishing the highest standards of artistic performance, played major roles in the musical culture of 19th century Russia.

4. SEE: Bowen, Catherine Drinker under Anton Rubinstein (C0984.4).

5. SEE: All entries under Anton Rubinstein (C0984).

C0988.
Russell, Pee Wee [Charles Ellsworth]. American Jazz Clarinetist; b. March 27, 1906, Maple Wood, Missouri; d. February 15, 1969, Alexandria, Virginia.

1. Baker 7; Grove 6/16 (Bibliography); Grove-AM (Bibliography); Grove-Jazz; JB; PAB-MI/2 (Bibliography).

2. DB 25/10, 30/14, 36/12.

5. A0004, A0034.

C0989.
Russo, Michel-Angelo. Italian Pianist; b. 1830, Naples; d. 1891, Naples.

1. Fetis 2/7; Mendel; Schmidl.

4. Kaiser, Carl Friedrich, comp. Michel-Angelo Russo's Biographie. Translated by Carl Friedrich Kaiser. Dresden: In Commission der Arnoldischen Buchhandlung, 1843. 16 p., portrait.

Biographical information compiled from newspaper articles.

C0990.
Ruthstroem. Bror Olaf Julius. Swedish Violinist; b. December 30, 1877, Sundsvall; d. April 2, 1944, Stockholm.

1. Baker 7; Grove 6/16; MGG (Bibliography).

C0991.
Ružičková, Zuzana. Czechoslovakian Harpsichordist; b. January 14, 1928, Plzen.

1. Baker 7; Grove 6/16 (Bibliography); PAB-MI/2 (Bibliography); Riemann 12/Supp. (Bibliography).

4. Berkovec, Jirí. Zuzana Ružičková. Praha: Supraphon, 1972. 73, [3] p. + 10 plates, phonodisk, discography, repertoire.

C0992.
Sabin, Wallace Arthur. English Organist; b. December 15, 1860, Culworth, Northamptonshire; d. December 8, 1937, Berkeley, California.

1. Baker 7; Grove-AM.

4. Rinder, Reuben R. Tribute to Wallace Arthur Sabin on the Occasion of the Memorial Services Held at Grace Cathedral, San Francisco.... San Francisco: Grabhorn Press, 1938. 15 p.

C0993.
Salmond, Felix Adrian Norman. English Cellist; b. November 19, 1888, London; d. February 19, 1952, New York City.

1. Baker 7; Grove 6/16; Grove-AM; PAB-MI/2 (Bibliography); Riemann 12.

5. B0061,

C0994.
Salzedo, Carlos Léon. American Harpist; b. April 6, 1885, Arcachon, France; d. August 17, 1961, Waterville, Maine.

1. Baker 7; Grove 6/16 (Bibliography); Grove-AM (Bibliography); MGG (Bibliography); PAB-MI/2 (Bibliography); Riemann 12; Schmidl + Supp.

4. Archambo, S.B. Carlos Salzedo (1885-1961): the Harp in Transition. Ph.D. diss. University of Kansas, 1984.

C0995.
Samaroff [née Hickenlooper], Olga. American Pianist; b. August 8, 1882, San Antonio, Texas; d. May 17, 1948, New York City.

1. Baker 7 (Bibliography); Grove 6/16; Grove-AM; PAB-MI/2 (Bibliography); Riemann 12; Schmidl (under Samarov).

2. CL 26/8; PQ 118.

3. Samaroff-Stokowski, Olga. An American Musician's Story. New York: W. W. Norton & Company, Inc., 1939. 326 p., 19 illus.

She was the wife of Leopold Stokowski from 1911 to 1923.

5. A0048, B0061.

SEE: Pucciani, D. Olga Samaroff (1882-1948): American Musician and Educator. Ph.D. diss. New York University, 1979.

C0996.
Samuel, Harold. English Pianist; b. May 23, 1879, London; d. January 15, 1937, London.

1. Baker 7; Grove 6/16; PAB-MI/2 (Bibliography).

2. RS 6, 76.

C0997.
Sándor, Arpád. American Pianist/Accompanist; b. June 5, 1896, Budapest, Hungary; d. February 10, 1972, Budapest.

1. Baker 7; Grove-AM; Riemann 12.

C0998.
Sándor, Gyoergy. American Pianist, cousin of Arpád; b. September 21, 1912, Budapest, Hungary.

1. Baker 7; Grove 6/16; Grove-AM; PAB-MI/2; Riemann 12/Supp.

2. PQ 88.

C0999.
Sanromá, Jesús María. Puerto Rican Pianist; b. November 7, 1902, Carolina; d. October 12, 1984, San Juan.

1. Baker 7; Grove-AM (Bibliography); Riemann 12 + Supp.

4. Belaval, Emilio S. El niño Sanromá: biografia mínima. San Juan de Puerto Rico: Biblioteca de Autores Puertorriqueños, 1952. 69, [2] p.

C1000.
Sapelnikov, Vasili. Russian Pianist; b. November 2, 1867, Odessa;
d. March 17, 1941, San Remo, Italy.

1. Baker 7; Riemann 12/Supp. (under Sapelnikow); Schmidl (under
Sapellnikow).

C1001.
Sarasate [y Navascuéz], Pablo Martín Melitón. Spanish Violinist;
b. March 10, 1844, Pamplona; d. September 20, 1908, Biarritz.

1. Baker 7 (Bibliography); Fetis 2/Supp.; Grove 6/16 (Bibliography);
Mendel; MGG (Bibliography); PAB-MI/2 (Bibliography); Riemann 12
(Bibliography) + Supp. (Bibliography); Schmidl.

There is a special Sarasate Museum in Pamplona which he founded.

2. ML 36/3; Strad July/1976.

4. Altadill y Torrontera de Sancho San Román, Julio. Memorias de
Sarasate. Pamplona: Imprenta de Aramendía y Onsalo, 1909. xx, 618,
CI, [iv] p. + 13 plates, 15 illus., 10 leaves of music.

Beramendi, E.F. Julián Gayarre y Pablo Sarasate. Buenos Aires:
Sebastian de Amorrortu e Hijos, 1944. 182, [1] p., 13 illus.

Mena Mateos, Jesús Joaquín. Pablo Sarasate, His Life. New York:
Hasteruga, Inc., 1963. 191 p. [typescript MS].

5. A0093, B0008, B0020, B0037, B0065, B0083, B0109.

C1002.
von Sauer, Emil George Konrad. German Pianist; b. October 8, 1862,
Hamburg; d. April 27, 1942, Vienna, Austria.

1. Baker 7; Grove 6/16 (Bibliography); MGG (Bibliography); PAB-MI/2
(Bibliography); Riemann 12; Schmidl.

3. von Sauer, Emil. Meine Welt: Bilder aus dem Geheimsache meiner
Kunst und meines Lebens. Stuttgart: Verlag von W. Spemann, 1901.
292 p.

5. B0053.

C1003.
Sauret, Emile. French Violinist; b. May 22, 1852, Dun-le-roi (Cher);
d. February 12, 1920, London, England.

1. Baker 7; Grove 6/16 (Bibliography); MGG (Bibliography); Riemann 12;
Schmidl.

C1004.
Scarpini, Pietro. Italian Pianist; b. April 6, 1911, Rome.

1. Baker 7; Grove 6/16; Riemann 12 + Supp.

C1005.
Scharrer, Irene. English Pianist; b. February 2, 1888, London;
d. January 11, 1971, London.

1. Baker 7; Grove 6/16 (Bibliography).

C1006.
Scharwenka, Franz Xaver. German Pianist; b. January 6, 1850, Samter,
Posen; d. December 8, 1924, Berlin.

1. Baker 7; Fetis 2/Supp.; Grove 6/16 (Bibliography); Mendel; Riemann
   12.

2. MQ 62/4.

3. Scharwenka, Xaver. Klaenge aus meinem Leben: Erinnerungen eines
   Musikers. Leipzig: Verlag von K.F. Koehler, 1922. 144 p. + 7 plates,
   21 illus., compositions, index of names.

C1007.
Schenck, Jean Johannes. German Viol da Gambist; baptized June 3, 1660,
Amsterdam, Holland; d. c.1715.

1. Baker 7 (Bibliography); Fetis 2/7; Grove 6/16 (Bibliography); Mendel;
   MGG (Bibliography); Riemann 12 + Supp. (Bibliography); Schmidl.

C1008.
Schiøler, Victor. Danish Pianist; b. April 7, 1899, Copenhagen;
d. February 17, 1967, Copenhagen.

1. Baker 7; Riemann 12.

C1009.
Schmidt, Annerose. German Pianist; b. October 5, 1936, Wittenberg.

1. Riemann 12/Supp.

4. Winkler, Franz. Annerose Schmidt fuer Sie portraetiert. Leipzig:
   VEB Deutscher Verlag fuer Musik, 1981. 59 p., 31 illus., chronology,
   repertoire, discography.

C1010.
Schmuller, Alexander. Dutch Violinist; b. December 5, 1880, Mozyr,
Russia; d. March 29, 1933, Amsterdam.

1. Baker 7; Riemann 12.

C1011.
Schnabel, Artur. American Pianist; b. April 17, 1882, Lipnik, Austria
(now Czechoslovakia); d. August 15, 1951, Morschach, Canton Schwyz,
Switzerland.

1. Baker 7; Grove 6/16; Grove-AM (Bibliography); MGG (Bibliography);
   PAB-MI/2 (Bibliography); Riemann 12 + Supp. (Bibliography); Schmidl.

A consummate performer of Beethoven, especially the later sonatas.

2. CL 11/7, 21/3, 22/1; PQ 84 (Special Issue); RS 2, 9, 42/43.

3. Schnabel, Artur. Music and the Line of Most Resistance. Princeton:
   Princeton University Press, 1942. Reprint 1969. 3-90, [1] p. + 2
   plates, illus.

   Schnabel, Artur. My Life and Music. New York: St. Martin's Press,
   1963 [original London: Longmans, Green and Co Ltd, 1961]. xv, 223 p.
   The 1970 reprint adds 8 plates, 19 illus., index.

   Schnabel, Artur. Reflections on Music. Manchester, 1933. No copy
   located.

4. Saerchinger, César. Artur Schnabel, a Biography. Tribute by Clifford
   Curzon. London: Cassel & Company Ltd, 1957. Reprint 1973. 354 p. + 7
   plates, 26 illus., compositions, programs, discography, index.

   Wolff, Konrad. The Teaching of Artur Schnabel: a Guide to Interpretation. London Faber and Faber, 1972. 189 p., illus., 5-item bibliography, index. 2nd edition as Schnabel's Interpretation of Piano
   Music. New York: W.W. Norton and Company, Inc., 1979.

5. A0048, A0051, B0030, B0037, B0039, B0055, B0080, D0012.

C1012.
Schneider, Abraham Alexander. American Violinist; b. October 21, 1908,
Vilma, Lithuania.

1. Baker 7; Grove 6/16 (Bibliography); Grove-AM (Bibliography); PAB-MI/2
   (Bibliography).

C1013.
Schneider, Georg Abraham. German French-horn Player; b. April 19, 1770,
Darmstadt; d. January 19, 1839, Berlin.

1. Baker 7; Fetis 2/7; Grove 6/16 (Bibliography); Mendel; MGG (Bibliography); Riemann 12 (Bibliography); Schmidl.

4. Meyer-Hanno, Andreas. Georg Abraham Schneider (1770-1839) und seine
   Stellung zur Musikgeschichte der preussischen Hauptstadt in der
   ersten Haelfte des 19. Jahrhunderts. Ph.D. diss. Free University of
   Berlin, 1956 [published Berlin, 1965]. 181, v. 62 p., bibliography.

   MGG mentions that his son, Louis Schneider, published Aus meinem
   Leben: Erinnerungen. 3 vols. Berlin, 1879.

C1014.
Schneider, Johann Gottlob. German Organist; b. October 28, 1789, Alt-
Gersdorf, near Zittau; d. April 13, 1864, Dresden.

1. Baker 7; Fetis 2/7; Grove 6/16 (Bibliography); Mendel; MGG (Bibliography); Riemann 12; Schmidl.

C1015.
Schneiderhan, Wolfgang Eduard. Austrian Violinist; b. May 28, 1915, Vienna.

1. Baker 7; Grove 6/16 (Bibliography); MGG (Bibliography); PAB-MI/2 (Bibliogrphy); Riemann 12 + Supp. (Bibliography).

2. Strad Feb/1985.

4. Fassbind, Franz. Wolfgang Schneiderhan - Irmgard Seefried: eine Kuenstler- und Lebensgemeinschaft. Bern: Alfred Scherz Verlag, 1960. 308 p., 27 illus., index of names, discography.

5. A0008, A0132, B0081, B0110.

C1016.
Schradieck, Henry [Carl Franz Heinrich]. American Violinist; b. April 29, 1846, Hamburg, Germany; d. March 25, 1918, Brooklyn, New York.

1. Baker 7; Grove 6/16 (Bibliography); Grove-AM (Bibliography); Mendel; PAB-MI/2 (Bibliography); Schmidl.

C1017.
Schub, André-Michel. American Pianist; b. December 26, 1952, Paris, France.

1. Baker 7; Grove-AM (Bibliography).

2. CL 24/6; HiFi/MusAm 31/11; KB 10/7.

5. A0075.

C1018.
Schuecker, Edmund. Austrian Harpist; b. November 16, 1860, Vienna; d. November 9, 1911, Bad Kreuznach.

1. Baker 7; Grove 6/16 (Bibliography); Grove-AM; Riemann 12; Schmidl.

The family was the basis for the standard of harp playing in America.

C1019.
Schuecker, Heinrich. American Harpist, brother of Edmund; b. November 25, 1867, Vienna; d. April 17, 1913, Boston, Massachusetts.

1. Baker 7; Grove 6/16; Grove-AM; Riemann 12.

C1020.
Schuecker, Joseph E. American Harpist, son of Edmund; b, May 19, 1886, Leipzig, Germany; d. December 9, 1938, Los Angeles, California.

1. Baker 7; Grove 6/16; Grove-AM; Riemann 12.

C1021.
Schumann [née Wieck], Clara. German Pianist; b. September 13, 1819, Leipzig; d. May 20, 1896, Frankfurt/M.

1. Baker 7 (Bibliography); Fetis 2/7; Grove 6/16 (Bibliography); Mendel; MGG (Bibliography); PAB-MI/2 (Bibliography); Riemann 12 (Bibliography) + Supp. (Bibliography); Schmidl.

   "Clara Schumann war die bedeutenste Pianistin ihrer Zeit." MGG.

2. ML 26/3; MQ 2/5.

3. Alley, Marguerite and Jean, eds. A Passionate Friendship: Clara Schumann and Brahms. Translated by Mervyn Savill. London: Staples Press Limited, 1956. 214 p.

   Litzmann, Berthold, ed. Clara Schumann, Johannes Brahms: Briefe aus den Jahren 1853-1896. 2 vols. (vol. 1, 1853-1871; vol. 2, 1872-1896) Leipzig: Druck und Verlag von Breitkopf & Haertel, 1927. Reprint 1970. 648 p., illus.; 639 p., illus., index of names.

   The English translation (New York: Longmans, Green and Company, 1927. Reprint 1971/1979) is an abridged selection of the original.

   Weissweiler, Eva with Susanna Ludwig, eds. Clara and Robert Schumann Briefwechsel: Kritische Gesamtausgabe. Band I. 1832-1838. Frankfurt am Main: Stroemfeld/Roter Stern, 1984. xxxviii, 337 p.

4. Burk, John Naglee. Clara Schumann: a Romantic Biography. New York: Random House, 1940. ix, 438 p., 12 illus., sources, index.

   Chissell, Joan. Clara Schumann: a Dedicated Spirit. New York: Taplinger Publishing Co., Inc., 1983. xvi, 232 p., 15 illus., 5 appendices including compositions and tours, index.

   Fang, Siu-Wan Chair. Clara Schumann as Teacher. D.M.A. diss. University of Illinois, 1978. 96 p., tables, list of works, appendices, discography, bibliography.

   Harding, Bertita. Concerto: the Glowing Story of Clara Schumann. Indianapolis: The Bobbs-Merrill Company, Inc., 1961. 288 p., illus., 79-item bibliography, index.

   Henning, Laura. Die Freundschaft Clara Schumanns mit Johannes Brahms: aus Briefen und Tagebuchblaettern. Zuerich: Werner Classen Verlag, 1946. 147 p., 3 illus., 13-item bibliography.

   Hoecker, Karla. Clara Schumann. Regensburg: Gustav Bosse Verlag, 1938. Revised edition 1959. 93 p. + 2 foldouts.

   Hoecker, Karla. Das Leben von Clara Schumann, geb. Wieck. Foreword by Dietrich Fischer-Dieskau. Berlin: Erika Klopp Verlag, 1975. 171 p. + 10 plates, illus., bibliography.

   Holmen, Grethe. Clara Schumann. København: Gyldendal, 1970. 219, [2] p. + 8 plates, illus., index of names, 9-item bibliography.

   Kleefeld, Wilhelm. Clara Schumann. Bielefeld: Verlag von Velhagen & Klasing, 1910. 135 p. + 3 plates, illus.

La Mara [pseud. for Ida Maria Lipsius]. Clara Schumann. Translated by
Mrs. Oscar Beringer from vol. 5 of Musikalische Studienkoepfe
(Leipzig, 1882). London: The Link (February 1884): 83-91.

Litzmann, Berthold. Clara Schumann: ein Kuenstlerleben. 3 vols.
Leipzig: Breitfkopf & Haertel, 1920. Reprint 1971. vol. 1, Maedchen-
jahre 1819-1840. x, 431 p., portrait; vol. 2, Ehejahre 1840-1856. v,
416 p., portrait; vol. 3, Clara Schumann und ihre Freunde 1856-1896.
vii, 642 p., portrait, repertoire, index of names.

Litzmann, Berthold. Clara Schumann: an Artist's Life, Based on
Materials Found in Diaries and Letters. Translated by Grace E. Hadow.
London: Macmillan & Co., Limited, 1913. Reprint 1972. xxxvi, 496 p.,
portrait, index; xii, 458 p., portrait, repertoire, index.

May, Florence. The Girlhood of Clara Schumann. London: Edward Arnold,
1912. xii, 340 p., portrait, index of names.

Pitrou, Robert. Clara Schumann. Paris: Editions Albin Michel, 1961.
252, [1] p.

Reich, Nancy B. Clara Schumann the Artist and the Woman. Ithaca (NY):
Cornell University Press, 1985. 346 p., 23 illus., catalogue of compositions, notes, 168-item bibliography, index.

Riepe, Elizabeth Young. Clara Wieck Schumann: Her Artistic Development and Influence. D.M.A. diss. University of Rochester.

Schiedermair, Ludwig. Clara Schumann: Frauenliebe und Leben aus Tagebuechern und Briefen (nach den Biographie von Berthold Litzmann).
Muenchen: Langen-Mueller Verlag GmbH, 1978. 229 p. + 4 plates, 8
illus.

Schumann, Ferdinand. Reminiscences of Clara Schumann as Found in the
Diary of Her Grandson Ferdinand Schumann of Dresden. Translated and
edited by June M. Dickinson. Rochester (NY): Schumann Memorial Foundation, 1949. 41. p., 4 illus.

Based on the author's "Erinnerungen an Clara Schumann" first published in Neue Zeitschrift fuer Musik, 84 (March 1917).

Stephenson, Kurt. Clara Schumann, 1819-1896. Bonn: Inter Nationes,
1969. 83 p. + foldout, endnotes, 18-item bibliography.

Susskind, Pamela Gertrude. Clara Wieck Schumann as Pianist and Composer: a Study of Her Life and Works. Ph.D. diss. 2 vols. University
of California/Berkeley, 1977. ii, 306 p.; i, 277 p., tables, list of
works, appendices, discography, bibliography.

5. A0023, A0047, A0051, B0083.

   SEE: Bowers, Jane and Judith Tick, eds. Women Making Music: the
   Western Art Tradition, 1150-1950. Urbana (IL): University of
   Illinois Press, 1986.

SEE: Elson, Arthur. Women's Work in Music. Boston: L.C. Page & Company, 1903.

SEE: Mueller-Reuter, Theodor. Bilder und Klaenge des Friedens: Musikalische Erinnerungen und Aufsaetze. Leipzig: Verlag Wilhelm Hartung, 1919.

SEE: Neuls-Bates, Carol under Amy Fay (C0378.5).

C1022.
Schuyler, Philippa Duke. American Pianist; b. August 22, 1932, New York City; d. May 9, 1967, Danang Bay, Vietnam.

1. Baker 7; Grove-AM (Bibliography); PAB-MI/2 (Bibliography).

Her papers and scores are in the Schomberg Center for Research and Black Culture in New York City.

2. Time June 22, 1936.

3. Schuyler, Philippa Duke. Adventures in Black and White. Foreword by Deems Taylor. New York: Robert Speller & Sons, Publishers, Inc., 1960. xv, 302 p. + 16 plates, 58 illus., index.

4. Schuyler, J. Philippa the Beautiful American: the Travelled History of a Troubadour. New York, 1969. No copy located.

5. SEE: Williams, O. American Black Women in the Arts and Social Sciences. Metuchen (NJ): The Scarecrow Press, Inc., 1978.

C1023.
Schweitzer, Albert. Alsatian Organist; b. January 14, 1875, Kaysersberg; d. September 4, 1965, Lambaréne, Gabon, Africa.

1. Baker 7 (Bibliography); Grove 6/17 (Bibliography); MGG (Bibliography) + Supp. (Bibliography); PAB-MI/2 (Bibliography); Riemann 12 (Bibliography) + Supp. (Bibliography); Schmidl + Supp.

Grove 6/17 mentions a comprehensive bibliography 1898-1967 in preparation by L. Person.

4. Jacobi, Erwin R. Albert Schweitzer und die Musik. Wiesbaden: Breitkopf und Haertel, 1975. 60 p. + 2 plates, 5 illus.

Joy, Charles R., ed. Music in the Life of Albert Schweitzer, with Selections from His Writings. New York: Harper & Brothers, 1951. rev. 1953. Reprint 1959/1971. xvii, 300 p., 10 illus., appendices, index.

Quoika, Rudolf. Albert Schweitzers Begegnung mit der Orgel. Berlin: Verlag Carl Meresburger, 1954. 96 p. + 2 plates, 5 illus., 45-item bibliography, index.

C1024.
Scobey, Jan. American Jazz Trumpeter; b. December 9, 1916, Tucumcari, New Mexico; d. June 12, 1963, Montreal, Canada.

1. Grove-Jazz; JB; LJ; PAB-MI/2 (Bibliography).

2. DB 30/31.

3. Scobey, Jan. Jan Scobey Presents He Rambled! 'til Cancer Cut Him down: Bob Scobey, Dixieland Jazz Musician and Bandleader, 1916-1963. Northridge (CA): Pal Publishing, 1976. 344 p., illus., index.

C1025.
Scott, Hazel. American Jazz Pianist; b. June 11, 1920, Port of Spain, Trinidad; d. October 2, 1981, New York City.

1. Baker 7; Grove-AM (Bibliography); Grove-Jazz; PAB-MI/2 (Bibliography).

3. Testimony of Hazel Scott Powell: Hearing before the Committee on Un-American Activities, Eighty-first Congress, second session. September 22, 1950. Washington (DC): U.S. Government Printing Office, 1951. ii, 3611-3626 p.

C1026.
Segovia, Andrés. Spanish Guitarist; b. February 21, 1893, Linares, near Jaen; d. June 3, 1987, Madrid.

1. Baker 7 (Bibliography); Grove 6/17 (Bibliography); MGG; PAB-MI/2 (Bibliography); Riemann 12 + Supp. (Bibliography); Schmidl.

   "...The renaissance of the classical guitar is largely attributable to Segovia...due...to his virtuosity...and fascinating style [and]...to his encouragement of young guitarists." Grove 6/17.

2. GR 27; HiFi 11/7; HiFi/MusAm 30/7; HiFiRev 2/2; Newsweek January 25, 1954 and January 19, 1959.

3. Segovia, Andrés. Andrés Segovia: an Autobiography of the Years 1893-1920. Translated by W.F. O'Brien. New York: Macmillan Publishing Co., Inc., 1976. 207 p., illus., index.

4. Borbi, Vladimir. The Segovia Technique. New York: The Macmillan Company, 1972. 94 p., illus.

   Clinton, George, comp. and ed., Andrés Segovia: an Appreciation. London: Musical New Services, Ltd., 1978. 99, [1] p., illus.

   Gavoty, Bernard. Andrés Segovia. Genève: René Kister, 1955. 29, [3] p., 27 illus., Decca recordings.

   Purcell, Ronald C., comp. Andrés Segovia: Contributions to the World of Guitar. Melville (NY): Belwin Mills, 1973. 43 p., 3 portraits, bibliography, discography.

   Usillos, Carlos. Andrés Segovia. Madrid: Dirección General de Bellas Artes, 1973. 139, [2] p., 18 illus., chronology, 49-item bibliography.

Wade, Graham. Segovia: a Celebration of the Man and His Music.
London: Allison & Busby Limited, 1983. 153 p., 30 illus., honors,
discography, 31-item bibliography.

5. A0129, B0012, B0041, B0042, B0044, B0058.

C1027.
Seidel, Toscha. American Violinist; b. November 17, 1899, Odessa,
Russia; d. November 15, 1962, Rosemead, California.

1. Baker 7; Grove-AM (Bibliography); PAB-MI/2 (Bibliography); Riemann
   12 + Supp.; Schmidl.

C1028.
Seligmann, Hippolyte-Prosper. French Cellist; b. July 28, 1817, Paris;
d. February 5, 1882, Monte Carlo, Monaco.

1. Baker 7; Fetis 2/8 + Supp.; Mendel; Schmidl.

C1029.
Selva, Blanche. French Pianist; b. January 29, 1884, Brive; d. December
3, 1942, St. Armand, Tallende, Puy-de-Dome.

1. Baker 7; Grove 6/17 (Bibliography); MGG (Bibliography); Riemann 12;
   Schmidl + Supp.

C1030.
Serato, Arrigo. Italian Violinist; b. February 7, 1877, Bologna;
d. December 27, 1948, Rome.

1. Baker 7; Grove 6/17; Riemann 12/Supp.; Schmidl + Supp.

4. della Corte, Andrea. Arrigo Serato violinista (1877-1948). Siena:
   Casa Editrice Ticci, 1950. unpaginated [31 + 46 p.]. 300 copies.

C1031.
Serebryakov, Pavel Alexeyevich. Russian Pianist; b. February 28, 1909,
Tsaritsin, now Volgograd.

1. Grove 6/17.

4. Rastopchina, Natal'ia Markovna. Pavel Alekseevich Serebrakov. Leningrad: Muzyka, 1970. 56 p., illus., bibliographical references.

C1032.
Serkin, Peter. American Pianist; b. July 24, 1947, New York City.

1. Baker 7; Grove 6/17; Grove-AM; PAB-MI/2 (Bibliography); Riemann 12/
   Supp.

2. HiFi/MusAm 35/1; KB 10/2.

C1033.
Serkin, Rudolf. American Pianist; b. March 28, 1903, Bohemia.

1. Baker 7; Grove 6/17 (Bibliography); Grove-AM (Bibliography); MGG/ Supp. (Bibliography); PAB-MI/2 (Bibliography); Riemann 12 + Supp.

2. CL 9/8, 26/9; GR 46/May; HiFi 11/7; HiFi/MusAm 29/5; HiFi/SR 17/2; PQ 100, 107.

5. A0060, B0030, B0058, B0110.

   SEE: Jacobson, Robert. Reverberations: Interviews with the World's Leading Musicians. New York: William Morrow & Company, Inc., 1974.

C1034.
Servais, Adrien François. Belgian Cellist; b. June 6, 1807, Hal, near Brussels; d. November 26, 1866, Hal.

1. Baker 7; Fetis 2/8 + Supp.; Grove 6/17; Mendel; MGG (Bibliography); PAB-MI/2 (Bibliography); Riemann 12 (Bibliography); Schmidl.

5. A0104.

C1035.
Sevčik, Otakar. Czechoslovakian Violinist; b. March 22, 1852, Horaž-dowitz; d. January 18, 1934, Pisek.

1. Baker 7 (Bibliography); Grove 6/17 (Bibliography); MGG (Bibliography); Riemann 12 (Bibliography) + Supp. (Bibliography); Schmidl.

2. Strad Aug/1977.

4. Dostál, Jirí, ed. Otakar Sevčik: sborník statí a vzpominek. Praha: Státni nakladatelstvi krasné literatury, hudby a umění, 1953. 186 p., 33 illus., 2 folding plates, index of names.

C1036.
Severinsen, Doc [Carl Hilding]. American Jazz Trumpeter; b. July 7, 1927, Arlington, Oregon.

1. Baker 7; Grove-AM (Bibliography); Grove-Jazz; PAB-MI/2 (Bibliography).

2. DB 36/1, 41/20, 52/11; HiFi/MusAm 20/4.

C1037.
Sgambati, Giovani. Italian Pianist; b. May 28, 1841, Rome; d. December 14, 1914, Rome.

1. Baker 7 (Bibliography); Grove 6/17 (Bibliography); Mendel (under Sgambetti); MGG (Bibliography); PAB-MI/2 (Bibliography); Riemann 12 (Bibliography) + Supp. (Bibliography); Schmidl (Bibliography).

5. B0128.

   SEE: Villanis, L.A. L'Arte del pianoforte in Italia da Clementi a Sgambati. Turin, 1907. No copy located.

C1038.
Shafran, Daniel. Soviet Cellist; b. January 23, Petrograd (Leningrad).

1. Baker 7; Grove 6/17 (Bibliography).

2. Strad Aug/1987.

4. Yampol'sky, Izrail Markovich. Daniil Shafran. Moskva: Gos. musykal' noe izd-vo, 1974. 58 p. + 5 plates, illus., discography, bibliographical references.

C1039.
Shankar, Ravi. Indian Sitarist; b. April 7, 1920, Banaras, Uttar Pradesh.

1. Baker 7; Grove 6/17; Grove-AM; PAB-MI/2 (Bibliography); Riemann 12 (Bibliography).

2. DB 32/10, 35/5; MM 15/12.

3. Shankar, Ravi. My Life, My Music. New York, 1978. No copy located.

C1040.
Shattuck, Arthur. American Pianist; b. April 19, 1881, Neenah, Wisconsin; d. October 16, 1951, New York City.

1. Baker 7; PAB-MI/2 (Bibliography).

3. Shattuck, Arthur. Memoirs. Edited by S.F. Shattuck with an account of his career by Willard Luedtke. Neenah (WI): Privately Printed, 1961. 247 p. + 24 plates, illus.

C1041.
Shaw, Artie [Arthur Arshawsky]. American Jazz Clarinetist; b. May 23, 1910, New York City.

1. Baker 7 (Bibliography); Grove 6/17 (Bibliography); Grove-AM (Bibliography); Grove-Jazz; JB; LJ; PAB-MI/2 (Bibliography); Riemann 12 + Supp. (Bibliography).

2. DB 18/13, 37/2, 53/2; JJS 1/1.

3. Shaw, Artie. The Trouble with Cinderella [an Outline of Identity]. New York: Farrar, Straus and Young, 1952. [i], 394 p.

4. Blandford, Edmund I. Artie Shaw: the Man and His Music. Hastings, Sussex: Privately Printed Mimeo, 1974. 84 p. + 20 plates, 101 illus., list of recordings.

C1042.
Shearing, George Albert. American Jazz Pianist; b. August 13, 1919, London, England.

1. Baker 7; Grove-AM (Bibliography); Grove-Jazz; PAB-MI/2 (Bibliography); Riemann 12 + Supp.

2. CL 19/6; DB 25/13, 29/27, 34/21; CK(KB) 2/4, 3/8, 7/3.

C1043.
Shumsky, Oscar. American Violinist; b. March 23, 1917, Philadelphia, PA.

1. Baker 7; Grove 6/17; Grove-AM (Bibliography); PAB-MI/2 (Bibliography).

2. GR 61/September; Strad Sept/1981, March/1987.

C1044.
Shure, Leonard. American Pianist; b. April 10, 1910, Los Angeles, CA.

1. Baker 7; Grove-AM.

C1045.
Siki, Béla. Swiss Pianist; b. February 21, 1923, Budapest, Hungary.

1. Baker 7 (Bibliography); Grove 6/17; PAB-MI/2 (Bibliography).

C1046.
Siloti, Alexander Il'yich. Russian Pianist; b. October 9, 1863, Kharkov; d. December 8, 1945, New York City.

1. Baker 7 (Bibliography); Grove 6/20 (under Ziloti); MGG (Bibliography); PAB-MI/2 (Bibliography); Riemann 12; Schmidl.

   "Er galt als einer der glaenzendsten Repraesentanten der Liszt-Schule." MGG.

3. Siloti, Alexander Il'yich. Moy vospominaniya o Franz Liste. St. Petersburg, 1911 [Edinburgh, 1913. Reprint 1986]. No copy located.

5. A0048, B0053.

   SEE: Newman, Ernest under Franz Liszt (C0740.5).

C1047.
Silver, Horace [Ward Martin Tavares]. American Jazz Pianist; b. September 2, 1928, Norwalk, Connecticut.

1. Baker 7; Grove 6/17 (Bibliography); Grove-AM (Bibliography); Grove-Jazz; JB; JRRM; LJ; Riemann 12 (Bibliography).

2. CK(KB) 2/1, 5/9; DB 25/14, 27/14, 47/11.

C1048.
Silverstein, Joseph. American Violinist; b. March 21, 1932, Detroit, MI.

1. Baker 7; Grove 6/17 (Bibliography); Grove-AM (Bibliography).

2. Strad Nov/1985.

C1049.
Simon, Abbey. American Pianist; b. January 8, 1922, New York City.

1. Baker 7; Grove-AM; PAB-MI/2 (Bibliography); Riemann 12/Supp.

2. CK(KB) 5/10.

5. A0075.

C1050.
Simon, Prosper-Charles. French Organist; b. December 27, 1788, Bordeaux; d. May 31, 1866, Paris.

1. Fetis 2/Supp.; Grove 6/17 (Bibliography); MGG (Bibliography); Schmidl.

4. Dumoulin, J.-B. Biographie de Prosper-Charles Simon. Paris: Chez L'Auteur, 1866. 29 p., portrait.

C1051.
Simonetti, Achille. British Violinist; b. June 12, 1857, Turin, Italy; d. November 19, 1928, London.

1. Baker 7; Grove 6/17 (Bibliography); Schmidl.

C1052.
Sims, Zoot [John Haley]. American Jazz Tenor Saxophonist; b. October 29, 1925, Inglewood, California; d. March 23, 1985, New York City.

1. Baker 7; Grove-AM (Bibliography); Grove-Jazz; PAB-MI/2 (Bibliography); Riemann 12/Supp.

2. DB 28/8, 43/20.

C1053.
Singleton, Zutty [Arthur James]. American Jazz Drummer; b. May 14, 1898, Bunker, Louisiana; d. July 14, 1975, New York City.

1. Baker 7; Grove 6/17 (Bibliography); Grove-AM (Bibliography); Grove-Jazz; PAB-MI/2 (Bibliography).

He fused the 1920s Chicago style with that of New Orleans' drummers and thus led the way to the swing style of Sid Catlett and others.

2. DB 7/19, 30/30.

5. A0092.

C1054.
Sivori, Ernesto Camillo. Italian Violinist; b. October 25, 1815, Genoa; d. February 19, 1894, Genoa.

1. Baker 7 (Bibliography); Fetis 2/8; Grove 6/17 (Bibliography); Mendel; MGG (Bibliography); PAB-MI/2 (Bibliography); Riemann 12/Supp. (Bibliography); Schmidl (Bibliography).

4. Pierrottet, Adele. Camillo Sivori. Milano: G. Ricordi & C., 1896. 95 p., illus.

C1055.
Slavík, Josef. Bohemian Violinist; b. March 26, 1806, Jince; d. May 30, 1833, Budapest, Hungary.

1. Baker 7; Fetis 2/8 (under Slawjk); Grove 6/17 (Bibliography - 21 entries); Mendel; MGG (Bibliography); Riemann 12/Supp. (Bibliography); Schmidl + Supp.

4. Klima, Stanislav Vaclav. Josef Slavík, 1806-1833: zivot a dílo velkého ceského houslisty. Praha: Státní nakladatelstvi krásné literatury hudby a umení, 1956. 159, [1] p. + 4 plates, 8 illus., + folding plate.

Ginzburg, Lev Solomonovich. Jozef Slavik. Moskva: Gos. musykal'noe izd-vo, 1957. 44 p., illus.

C1056.
Slenczynska, Ruth. American Pianist; b. January 15, 1925, Sacramento, California.

1. Baker 7; Grove-AM; PAB-MI/2 (Bibliography); Riemann 12/Supp.

2. CL 10/1, 11/5, 15/2; CK(KB) 7/1; KB 10/5, 11/2; PQ 122.

3. Slenczynska, Ruth and Louis Biancolli. Forbidden Childhood. Garden City (NY): Doubleday & Company, Inc., 1957. 263 p.

5. B0070.

C1057.
Smendzianka, Regina. Polish Pianist; b. October 9, 1924, Torún.

1. Grove 6/17; PAB-MI/2 (Bibliography); Riemann 12.

4. Kydrynski, Lucjan. Regina Smendzianka. Kraków: Polskie Wydawnictwo Muzyczne, 1961. 34 p., 12 illus.

C1058.
Smith, Cyril James. English Pianist; b. August 11, 1909, Middlesbrough; d. August 2, 1974, London.

1. Grove 6/17.

3. Smith, Cyril with Joyce Egginton. Duet for Three Hands. London: Angus and Robertson, 1958. Reprint 1966. 224 p., 27 illus.

C1059.
Smith, Joe [Joseph C.]. American Jazz Trumpeter; b. June 28, 1902, Ripley, Ohio; d. December 2, 1937, New York City.

1. Baker 7; Grove-AM (Bibliography); Grove-Jazz; LJ; PAB-MI/2 (Bibliog.)

C1060.
Smith, Pine Top [Clarence]. American Jazz Pianist; b. June 11, 1904, Troy, Alabama; d. March 14, 1929, Chicago, Illinois.

1. Baker 7; Grove 6/17; Grove-AM (Bibliography); Grove-Jazz; LJ; PAB-MI/2 (Bibliography).

C1061.
Smith, Willie "the Lion" [William Henry Joseph Bonaparte Bertholoff]. American Jazz Pianist; b. November 24, 1897, Goschen, New York; d. April 18, 1973, New York City.

1. Baker 7; Grove-AM (Bibliography); Grove-Jazz; JB; JRRM; LJ; PAB-MI/2 (Bibliography).

Duke Ellington's "Portrait of the Lion" (1939) says it all.

2. CK(KB) 3/10; DB 30/4.

3. Smith, Willie with George Hoefer. Music on My Mind: the Memoirs of an American Pianist. Foreword by Duke Ellington. Garden City (NY): Doubleday & Company, Inc., 1964. Reprint 1975. xvi, 318 p., notes and references, index.

C1062.
Snoer, Johannes. Dutch Harpist; b. June 28, 1868, Amsterdam; d. March 1, 1936, Vienna, Austria.

1. Baker 7; Schmidl.

C1063.
Sofronitzky, Vladimir Vladimirovich. Soviet Pianist; b. May 8, 1901, St. Petersburg; d. August 29, 1961, Moscow.

1. Baker 7 (Bibliography); Grove 6/17 (Bibliography); Riemann 12/Supp. (Bibliography).

4. Mil'shteyn, J.I. Vospominaniya o Sofronitskom. Moskva: Gos. musykal' noe izd-vo, 1970. 694 p., illus., bibliographical references.

C1064.
Soldat, Marie. Austrian Violinist; b. March 25, 1863, Graz; d. September 30, 1955, Graz.

1. Baker 7; Riemann 12; Schmidl (under Soldat-Roeger).

C1065.
Solomon [Cutner, Solomon]. English Pianist; b. August 9, 1902, London.

1. Baker 7; Grove 6/17; Riemann 12 + Supp. (Bibliography).

5. A0047, D0012.

SEE: Initial autobiography of Gerald Moore (C0822.3).

C1066.
Solway, Maurice. Canadian Violinist; b. March 10, 1908, Toronto.

1. Encyclopedia of Music in Canada.

3. Solway, Maurice. Recollections of a Violinist. Foreword by Andrés Segovia. Oakville (Ontario): Mosaic Press, 1984. 123 p. + 27 plates, 49 illus.

C1067.
Somer, Hilde. American Pianist; b. February 11, 1930, Vienna, Austria; d. December 24, 1979, Freeport, Bahamas.

1. Baker 7; Grove-AM.

2. PQ 83.

C1068.
Somis, Giovanni Battista. Italian Violinist; b. December 25, 1686, Turin; d. August 14, 1763, Turin.

1. Baker 7 (Bibliography); Fetis 2/Supp.; Grove 6/17 (Bibliography); MGG (Bibliography); Riemann 12 + Supp. (Bibliography); Schmidl (Bibliography).

5. B0020.

C1069.
Sor [Sors], Joseph Fernando Macari. Spanish Guitarist; b. February 13, 1778, Barcelona; d. July 10, 1839, Paris, France.

1. Baker 7 (Bibliography); Fetis 2/8; Grove 6/17 (Bibliography); Mendel; MGG (Bibliography); PAB-MI/2 (Bibliography); Riemann 12 (Bibliography) + Supp. (Bibliography); Schmidl.

4. Jeffrey, Brian. Fernando Sor, Composer and Guitarist. London: Tecla Editions, 1977. 197 p., illus., catalogue of works, index.

Sasser, William Gray. The Guitar Works of Fernando Sor. Ph.D. diss. University of North Carolina, 1960. xi, 177 p., bibliography.

5. A0129.

C1070.
Soriano, Gonzalo. Spanish Pianist; b. March 14, 1913, Alicante; d. April 14, 1972, Madrid.

1. Baker 7; Grove 6/17 (Bibliography); PAB-MI/2 (Bibliography).

C1071.
Sowinski, Wojciech. Polish Pianist; b. 1803? Lukaszówka, Podolia; d. March 5, 1880, Paris, France.

1. Baker 7; Fetis 2/8; Grove 6/17 (Bibliography); Mendel (under Sowinsky); MGG (Bibliography); Riemann 12 (Bibliography) + Supp. (Bibliography); Schmidl + Supp.

3. Sowinski, Wojciech. Les musiciens polonais et slaves, anciens et modernes; dictionnaire biographique.... Paris: A. Le Clerc, 1857. Reprint 1971. (Polish edition, 1874). 599 p.

Best known for his dictionary of Polish musicians which "contains about 1,000 biographies of composers, performers, theorists and others connected with Polish music from the earliest times to Sowinski's contemporaries" Grove 6/17.

C1072.
Spalding, Albert. American Violinist; b. August 15, 1888, Chicago, Illinois; d. May 26, 1953, New York City.

1. Baker 7; Grove-AM (Bibliography); PAB-MI/2 (Bibliography); Riemann 12; Schmidl.

3. Spalding, Albert. Rise to Follow, an Autobiography. New York: Henry Holt and Company, 1943. Reprint 1972/1977. 328 p., portrait, index.

He also wrote a biographical novel about Tartini, A Fiddle, A Sword, and a Lady (New York, 1953).

5. A0100, B0089.

C1073.
Spanier, Muggsy [Francis Joseph]. American Jazz Cornetist; b. November 9, 1906, Chicago, Illinois; d. February 12, 1967, Sausalito, California.

1. Baker 7; Grove 6/17 (Bibliography); Grove-AM (Bibliography); Grove-Jazz; LJ; JRRM; PAB-MI/2 (Bibliography).

2. DB 25/13.

C1074.
Spivakovsky, Tossy. American Violinist; b. February 4, 1907, Odessa, Russia.

1. Baker 7; Grove-AM (Bibliography); PAB-MI/2 (Bibliography); Riemann 12 + Supp. (Bibliography); Schmidl/Supp.

5. A0100.

C1075.
Stadler, Anton Paul. Austrian Clarinetist; b. June 28, 1753, Bruck an der Leitha; d. June 15, 1812, Vienna.

1. Baker 7; Grove 6/18; MGG (Bibliography) + Supp.; PAB-MI/2 (Bibliography); Riemann 12/Supp. (Bibliography); Schmidl/Supp.

C1076.
Stamitz, Johann Wenzel Anton. Bohemian Violinist; b. June 19, 1717, Deutsch-Brod; d. March 27, 1757, Mannheim, Germany.

1. Baker 7 (Bibliography); Grove 6/18 (Bibliography); Mendel; MGG (Bibliography); PAB-MI/2 (Bibliography); Riemann 12 (Bibliography) + Supp. (Bibliography); Schmidl.

A fine soloist, he made the Mannheim Orchestra the best in Europe, and "he virtually created the Classical sonata form." Baker 7.

C1077.
Stark, Robert. German Clarinetist; b. September 19, 1847, Klingenthal;
d. October 29, 1922, Wuerzburg.

1. Baker 7; Riemann 12; Schmidl.

C1078.
Starker, Janos. American Cellist; b. July 5, 1924, Budapest, Hungary.

1. Baker 7 (Bibliography); Grove 6/18; Grove-AM (Bibliography); PAB-MI/2
   (Bibliography); Riemann 12/Supp.

2. CL 21/9; HiFi 9/6; HiFi/MusAm 19/11, 23/2; HiFi/SR 6/6.

5. B0058, B0130.

   SEE: Grodner, Murray. Concepts in String Playing. Bloomington (IN):
      Indiana University Press, 1979.

C1079.
Staryk, Steven [pseud. **Stefan Primas**]. American Violinist; b. April 28,
1932, Toronto, Canada.

1. Baker 7; Grove 6/18; PAB-MI/2 (Bibliography); Riemann 12/Supp.

2. Strad March/1983.

C1080.
Stern, Isaac. American Violinist; b. July 21, 1920, Kremenetz, USSR.

1. Baker 7; Grove 6/18 (Bibliography); Grove-AM (Bibliography); MGG;
   PAB-MI/2 (Bibliography); Riemann 12 + Supp. (Bibliography).

2. GR 46/March; HiFi 6/5; HiFi/SR 50/2; New Yorker June 5, 1965; New
   York Times Magazine October 14, 1979; Strad Aug/1977, Nov/1985; Time
   July 7, 1980.

5. A0100, A0115, A0132, B0076.

C1081.
Stern, Leo[pold **Lawrence**]. English Cellist; b. April 5, 1862, Brighton;
d. September 10, 1904, London.

1. Baker 7; Grove 6/18 (Bibliography).

C1082.
Steuermann, Edward [**Eduard**]. American Pianist; b. June 18, 1892, Sambor,
near Lwow, Poland; d. November 11, 1964, New York City.

1. Baker 7; Grove 6/18 (Bibliography); Grove-AM (Bibliography); MGG/
   Supp. (Bibliography); PAB-MI/2 (Bibliography); Riemann 12 + Supp.
   (Bibliography).

2. HiFi/MusAm 21/6.

5. B0080.

C1083.
Stich, Václav [or Giovanni Punto]. Czechoslovakian French-horn Player;
b. September 28, 1746, Zehušice, near Cáslav; d. February 16, 1803,
Prague.

1. Baker 7 (Bibliography); Fetis 2/8; Grove 6/15 (under Punto - Bibliography); Mendel; MGG (Bibliography); Riemann 12 (Bibliography) +
   Supp. (Bibliography); Schmidl.

C1084.
Stitt, Sonny [Edward]. American Jazz Saxophonist; b. February 2, 1924,
Boston, Massachusetts; d. July 22, 1982, Washington, D.C.

1. Baker 7; Grove-AM (Bibliography); Grove-Jazz; JB; PAB-MI/2 (Bibliography).

2. DB 26/10, 33/20.

C1085.
Stojowski, Sigismund. American Pianist; b. May 14, 1869, Strzelce,
Poland; d. November 5, 1946, New York City.

1. Baker 7; Grove 6/18 (Bibliography); Grove-AM; MGG (Bibliography);
   PAB-MI/2 (Bibliography); Riemann 12 + Supp. (Bibliography); Schmidl.

C1086.
Stoltzman, Richard Leslie. American Clarinetist; b. July 12, 1942,
Omaha, Nebraska.

1. Baker 7; Grove-AM (Bibliography); PAB-MI/2 (Bibliography).

   His interest in contemporary music has led to a significant expansion of the repertoire for the clarinet.

2. DB 53/10; HiFi/MusAm 28/6.

C1087.
Stotijn, Jaap. Dutch Oboist; b. September 22, 1891, The Hague; d. April
5, 1970, The Hague.

1. Grove 6/18 (Bibliography).

3. Stotijn, Jaap. Even uitblazen. Den Haag: Albersen & Co., 1976. 64 p.,
   24 illus.

C1088.
Stradal, August. Bohemian Pianist; b. May 17, 1860, Teplitz; d. March
13, 1930, Schoenlinde, Germany.

1. Baker 7; MGG; Riemann 12; Schmidl.

4. Stradal, Hildegard. August Stradals Lebensbild. Bern: Paul Haupt,
   1934. 143 p., portrait, compositions.

C1089.
Stratton, George Robert. English Violinist; b. July 18, 1897, London;
d. September 4, 1954, London.

1. Baker 7; Grove 6/18.

C1090.
Straube, Karl Montgomery. German Organist; b. January 6, 1873, Berlin;
d. April 27, 1950, Leipzig.

1. Baker 7; Grove 6/18 (Bibliography); MGG (Bibliography); PAB-MI/2
   (Bibliography); Riemann 12 (Bibliography) + Supp. (Bibliography);
   Schmidl.

3. Straube Karl. Briefe eines Thomaskantors. Compiled by Wilibald
   Gurlitt and Hans-Olaf Hudemann. Stuttgart: K.F. Koehler Verlag, 1952.
   268, [2] p. + 8 plates, 8 illus., index of names.

   Straube, Karl. Wirken und Wirkung. Edited by Christoph and Ingrid
   Held. Berlin: Evangelische Verlagsanstalt GmbH, 1976. 283, [1] p.,
   15 illus., chronology, list of contributors, index of names.

4. Wolgast, Johannes. Karl Straube: eine Wuerdigung seiner Musikerper-
   soenlichkeit anlaesslich seiner 25jaehrigen Taetigkeit in Leipzig.
   Leipzig: Druck und Verlag von Breitkopf & Haertel, 1928. 54 p.

C1091.
Strayhorn, Billy [William]. American Jazz Pianist; b. November 29, 1915,
Dayton, Ohio; d. May 31, 1967, New York City.

1. Baker 7; Grove 6/18; Grove-AM (Bibliography); Grove-Jazz; JB; JRRM;
   PAB-MI/2 (Bibliography).

5. SEE: Entries under **Duke Ellington** (C0357.4).

C1092.
Suggia, Guilhermina. Portuguese Cellist; b. June 27, 1888, Oporto;
d. July 31, 1950, Oporto.

1. Baker 7; Grove 6/18; Riemann 12; Schmidl.

2. ML 2/2.

C1093.
Suk, Josef. Czechoslovakian Violinist; b. August 8, 1929, Prague.

1. Baker 7; Grove 6/18 (Bibliography); MGG; PAB-MI/2 (Bibliography);
   Riemann 12/Supp.

2. Strad July/1982.

C1094.
Sutton, Ralph Earl. American Jazz Pianist; b. November 4, 1922, Hamburg,
near St. Louis, Missouri.

1. Grove-AM (Bibliography); Grove-Jazz; JB; LJ; PAB-MI/2 (Bibliography).

2. CK(KB) 7/12.

4. Shacter, James D. Piano Man: the Story of Ralph Sutton. Chicago: Jaynar Press, 1975. 244 p., discography, index.

C1095.
Sykes, James Andrews. American Pianist; b. July 10, 1908, Atlantic City, New Jersey.

1. Baker 7; Grove-AM (Bibliography); PAB-MI/2 (Bibliography).

5. A0061.

C1096.
Szendy, Arpád. Hungarian Pianist; b. August 11, 1863, Szarvas; d. September 10, 1922, Budapest.

1. Baker 7; Grove 6/18 (Bibliography); MGG/Supp. (Bibliography); Riemann 12; Schmidl.

C1097.
Szeryng, Henryk. Mexican Violinist; b. September 22, 1918, Zelazowa, Poland; d. 1988 [according to MLA Notes].

1. Baker 7; Grove 6/18 (Bibliography); PAB-MI/2 (Bibliography); Riemann 12 + Supp.

2. GR 47/October; HiFi 13/4; HiFi/MusAm 33/3; Strad May/1978.

5. B0110.

C1098.
Szigeti, Joseph. American Violinist; b. September 5, 1892, Budapest, Hungary; d. February 19, 1973, Lucerne, Switzerland.

1. Baker 7; Grove 6/18 (Bibliography); Grove-AM (Bibliography); MGG (Bibliography) + Supp. (Bibliography); PAB-MI/2 (Bibliography); Riemann 12 + Supp. (Bibliography); Schmidl + Supp.

2. HiFi/MusAm 23/1, 33/2; Strad July/1977.

3. Szigeti, Joseph. Szigeti on the Violin. New York: Frederick A. Praeger, Publishers, 1970. x, 234 p., portrait, index.

   "I have tried...to set down my thoughts about violinists and violin-playing in the contemporary musical scene."

   Szigeti, Joseph. With Strings Attached: Reminiscences and Reflec-tions. New York: Alfred A. Knopf, Inc., 1947. Reprint 1979. xiii, 341, xvii p. + 8 plates, 15 illus., discography, index.

4. Soroker, Yakov L'vovich. Iozhef Sigeti. Moskva: Muzyka, 1968. 126 p. + 2 plates, illus., bibliography.

5. A0008, A0100, A0132, A0142, B0030, B0037, B0044, B0055, D0012.

SEE: Carpenter, McDonnell under **Mischa Elman** (C0359.4).

SEE: Autobiography of **Carl Flesch** (C0393.3).

C1099.
Szymanowska [née Wolowska], Maria Agata. Polish Pianist; b. December 14, 1789, Warsaw; d. July 24, 1831, St. Petersburg, Russia.

1. Baker 7 (Bibliography); Fetis 2/8; Grove 6/18; Mendel; MGG (Bibliography); Riemann 12 + Supp. (Bibliography); Schmidl.

C1100.
Tabuteau, Marcel. French Oboist; b. July 2, 1887, Compiègne; d. January 4, 1966, Nice.

1. Baker 7; Grove 6/18; PAB-MI/2 (Bibliography).

C1101.
Tacchino, Gabriel. French Pianist; b. August 4, 1934, Cannes.

1. Baker 7; Grove 6/18.

C1102.
Taffanel, Claude Paul. French Flutist; b. September 16, 1844, Bordeaux; d. November 22, 1908, Paris.

1. Baker 7; Grove 6/18; MGG (Bibliography); PAB-MI/2 (Bibliography); Riemann 12; Schmidl.

5. SEE: Imbert, Hugues under **Hubert Leonard** (C0715.5).

C1103.
Tagliaferro, Magda[lena]. Brazilian Pianist; b. January 19, 1893, Petropolis; d. September 9, 1986, Rio de Janeiro.

1. Baker 7; Riemann 12/Supp.

2. CL 21/3.

3. Tagliaferro, Magdalena. Quase tudo... (Memórias). Rio de Janeiro: p.p., 1979. 181 p. + 8 plates, 17 illus.

4. Anon. O aperfeicoamento da cultura musical, atividades de Madalena Tagliaferro no Brasil. Rio de Janeiro: Ministério da educacão e saúde, 1946. 13 p.

C1104.
Tagliavini, Luigi Ferdinando. Italian Organist/Harpsichordist; b. October 7, 1929, Bologna.

1. Baker 7; Grove 6/18 (Bibliography); PAB-MI/2 (Bibliography); Riemann 12.

C1105.
Tarr, Edward H[ankins]. American Trumpeter; b. June 15, 1936, Norwich, Connecticut.

1. Baker 7; Grove 6/18 (Bibliography); Grove-AM; PAB-MI/2 (Bibliography); Riemann 12/Supp.

C1106.
Tartini, Giuseppe. Italian Violinist; b. April 8, 1692, Pirano, Istria; d. February 26, 1770, Padua.

1. Baker 7 (Bibliography); Fetis 2/8; Grove 6/18 (Bibliography); Mendel; MGG (Bibliography); PAB-MI/2 (Bibliography); Riemann 12 (Bibliography) + Supp. (Bibliography); Schmidl + Supp.

2. Strad Sept/1980.

4. Anon. Nel giorno della inaugurazione del monumento a Giuseppe Tartini in Pirano. Trieste: Stabilimento Artistico Tipografico G. Caprin, 1896. 138 p. + 7 plates, illus.

   Elmer, M. Tartini's Improvised Ornamentation. Ph.D. diss. University of California/Berkeley, 1962.

   Goldin, M. The Violinistic Innovations of Giuseppe Tartini. Ph.D. diss., New York University, 1955.

   Guinsburg, Lev. Tartini: His Life and Times. Translated by I. Levin. Neptune City (NJ): Paganiniana Publications, Inc., 1981. 378, [3] p., 85-item bibliography, discography, index.

5. A0093, B0020, B0050.

C1107.
Tassinari, Arrigo. Italian Flutist; b. December 1889, Cento, Ferrara.

1. Riemann 12/Supp.

3. Tassinari, Arrigo. Ricordi della mia carriera artistica. Roma: A cura dell'Autore, 1969. 188 p., portrait.

C1108.
Tatum, Art[hur, Jr.]. American Jazz Pianist; b. October 13, 1910, Toledo, Ohio; d. November 5, 1956, Los Angeles, California.

1. Baker 7; Grove 6/18 (Bibliography); Grove-AM (Bibliography - 19 entries); Grove-Jazz; JB; JRRM; PAB-MI/2 (Bibliography); Riemann 12 + Supp. (Bibliography).

2. DB 22/17, 23/25, 33/21; CK(KB) 6/7, 7/10 (Special Issue); New Yorker September 7, 1968.

4. Howard, Joseph Adolph. The Improvisational Techniques of Art Tatum. 3 vols. Ph.D. diss. Case Western Reserve University, 1978. 510 p.; 835 p.; 110 p., illus., list of works, appendices, bibliography.

Howlett, Felicity A. An Introduction to Art Tatum's Performance
Approaches: Composition, Improvisation and Melodic Variation. Ph.D.
diss. Cornell University, 1983.

Laubich, Arnold and Ray Spencer. Art Tatum: a Guide to His Recorded
Music. Metuchen (NJ): The Scarecrow Press and the Institute of Jazz
Studies, Rutgers University, 1982. xxviii, 330 p., illus., chrono-
logical discography, films, 4 appendices.

5. A0006.

C1109.
Tausch, Franz Wilhelm. German Clarinetist; b. December 26, 1762, Heidelberg; d. February 9, 1817, Berlin.

1. Baker 7; Fetis 2/8; Grove 6/18 (Bibliography); Mendel; MGG (Bibliography); Riemann 12 (Bibliography) + Supp. (Bibliography); Schmidl.

C1110.
Tausig, Carl. Polish Pianist; b. November 4, 1841, Warsaw; d. July 17,
1871, Leipzig, Germany.

1. Baker 7 (Bibliography); Fetis 2/Supp.; Grove 6/18 (Bibliography);
Mendel; MGG (Bibliography); PAB-MI/2 (Bibliography); Riemann 12
(Bibliography) + Supp. (Bibliography); Schmidl.

4. Ehrlich, Heinrich. Wie uebt Man am Klavier? Betrachtungen und Rath-
schlaege nebst genauer Anweisung fuer den richtigen Gebrauch der
Tausig-Ehrlich'schen taeglich Studien. Berlin: M. Bahn-Verlag, 1879.

5. A0014, A0063, B0020, B0128.

SEE: Ehrlich, A. under Anton Rubinstein (C0984.5).

C1111.
Taylor, Billy [William]. American Jazz Pianist; b. July 24, 1921, Green-
ville, North Carolina.

1. Baker 7; Grove-AM (Bibliography – 11 entries); Grove-Jazz; JB; PAB-
MI/2 (Bibliography).

2. DB 17/16, 22/15, 22/22, 23/5, 24/9, 24/15, 25/1, 41/7, 44/20, 47/5,
52/3; CK(KB) 2/6.

5. A0025.

C1112.
Taylor, Cecil (Percival). American Jazz Pianist; b. March 15, 1933, New
York City.

1. Baker 7; Grove 6/18 (Bibliography); Grove-Jazz; JB (13 entries);
JRRM; LJ: PAB-MI/2 (Bibliography); Riemann 12/Supp. (Bibliography).

2. DB 28/22, 32/5, 42/7, 47/4; CK(KB) 5/1, 7/5; KB 11/1.

5. A0032, B0048.

    SEE: Spellman, A.B. under **Ornette** Coleman (CO255.4).

C1113.
Taylor, **Franklin.** English Pianist; b. February 5, 1843, Birmingham;
d. March 19, 1919, London.

1. Baker 7; Grove 6/18 (Bibliography); Schmidl.

C1114.
Tchicai, John **Martin.** Danish Jazz Saxophonist; b. April 28, 1936, Copenhagen.

1. Grove 6/18 (Bibliography); Grove-Jazz; JB; PAB-MI/2 (Bibliography).

2. DB 33/3.

C1115.
Teagarden, Jack [Weldon Leo]. American Jazz Trombonist; b. August 29,
1905, Vernon, Texas; d. January 15, 1964, New Orleans, Louisiana.

1. Baker 7; Grove 6/18 (Bibliography); Grove-AM (Bibliography - 14
   entries); Grove-Jazz; JB; JRRM; LJ; PAB-MI/2 (Bibliography); Riemann
   12 + Supp. (Bibliography).

He was among the finest of all jazz trombonists.

2. DB 24/5, 24/20, 26/24, 30/15; New Yorker April 2, 1984.

4. Smith, Jay D. and Len Guttridge. Jack Teagarden: the Story of a Jazz
   Maverick. London: Cassell & Company Ltd, 1960. Reprint 1976. viii,
   208 p. + 8 plates, 20 illus., selected discography, index.

   Waters, Howard J. Jack Teagarden's Music, His Career and Recordings.
   Foreword by Paul Whiteman. Stanhope (NJ): Walter C. Allen, 1960.
   ix, 222 p. + 23 plates, 62 illus., discographies, 3 appendices, 47-
   item bibliography, index of catalog numbers.

5. A0034, B0054.

C1116.
Tedesco, Ignaz **Amadeus.** Bohemian Pianist; b. 1817, Prague; d. November
13, 1882, Odessa, Russia.

1. Baker 7; Fetis 2/8; Mendel; Schmidl.

C1117.
Teichmueller, Robert. German Pianist; b. May 4, 1863, Braunschweig;
d. May 6, 1939, Leipzig.

1. Baker 7; Riemann 12 (Bibliography); Schmidl.

4. Baresel, Alfred. Robert Teichmueller und die Leipziger Klavier-
   tradition. Leipzig: C.F. Peters, 1934. 40 p., 3 illus.

C1118.
Telmányi, Emil. Hungarian Violinist; b. June 22, 1892, Arad.

1. Baker 7; PAB-MI/2 (Bibliography); Riemann 12 + Supp.; Schmidl.

3. Telmányi, Emil. Af en musikers billedbog. København: Nyt Nordisk
   Forlag Arnold Busck A/S, 1978. 319, [1] p., illus., concerts of Carl
   Nielsen's music, discography, index of names.

C1119.
Temianka, Henri. American Violinist; b. November 19, 1906, Greenock,
Scotland.

1. Baker 7; Grove 6/18 (Bibliography); Grove-AM (Bibliography); PAB-MI/2
   (Bibliography).

2. Strad Aug/1985.

3. Temianka, Henri. Facing the Music: an Irreverent Close-up of the Real
   Concert World. Preface by Yehudi Menuhin. New York: David McKay
   Company, Inc., 1973. x, 272 p. + 8 plates, 16 illus., index.

C1120.
Templeton, Alec Andrew. American Pianist; b. July 4, 1909, Cardiff,
Wales; d. March 28, 1963, Greenwich, Connecticut.

1. Baker 7; Grove-AM (Bibliography); PAB-MI/2 (Bibliography).

3. Templeton, Alec. Alec Templeton's Music Boxes. New York: Wilfred
   Funk, Inc., 1958. 164 p. + 8 plates, 26 illus.

C1121.
Tertis, Lionel. English Violist; b. December 29, 1876, West Hartlepool;
d. February 22, 1975, London.

1. Baker 7 (Bibliography); Grove 6/18 (Bibliography); PAB-MI/2 (Bibliography); Riemann 12 + Supp. (Bibliography); Schmidl.

   "He eventually became one of the most renowned viola players in
   Europe." Baker 7.

2. RS 62; Strad Aug/1984.

3. Tertis, Lionel. Cinderella No More. London: Peter Nevill Ltd., 1953.
   118 p. + 6 plates, 9 illus., index.

   Tertis, Lionel. My Viola and I: a Complete Autobiography, with...
   Other Essays. London: Paul Elek, 1974. xv, 184 p. + 5 plates, 21
   illus., works for viola, discography, index.

C1122.
Thalben-Ball, George Thomas. English Organist; b. June 18, 1896, Sydney,
Australia; d. January 18, 1987, London.

1. Grove 6/18 (Bibliography); PAB-MI/2 (Bibliography).

4. Rennert, Jonathan. George Thalben-Ball. London: David & Charles (Publishers) Limited, 1979. 175 p., 4 appendices including discography and chronology, index.

C1123.
Thalberg, Sigismond. German Pianist; b. January 8, 1812, Geneva, Switzerland; d. April 27, 1871, Posilipo, near Naples.

1. Baker 7 (Bibliography); Fetis 2/8 + Supp.; Grove 6/18 (Bibliography); Mendel; MGG (Bibliography); PAB-MI/2 (Bibliography); Riemann 12 (Bibliography) + Supp. (Bibliography); Schmidl.

2. PQ 77.

5. A0014, A0023, B0020, B0021, B0083, C0984.3.

   SEE: Spark, William. Musical Memories. London: Swan Sonnenschein & Co., 1888.

C1124.
Thibaud, Jacques. French Violinist; b. September 27, 1880, Bordeaux; d. September 1, 1953, near Mt. Cemet, French Alps.

1. Baker 7; Grove 6/18 (Bibliography); MGG/Supp. (Bibliography); PAB-MI/2 (Bibliography); Riemann 12 + Supp. (Bibliography); Schmidl.

3. Thibaud, Jacques. Un violon parle: souvenirs. Edited by Jean-Pierre Dorian. Paris: Au Blé qui Lève, 1946. Reprint 1953. 208 p.

   Thibaud, Jacques. Extraits de journaux. Edited by J.-A. Coulangheon. Paris: Imprimerie A. Gautherin, 1901. 32 p.

4. Anon. Jacques Thibaud: sa tournée en Amérique. Paris: A. Dandelot, 1904. 36 p.

5. A0008, A0142, B0010, B0028, B0037, B0053, B0089, D0012.

   SEE: Lopes Graca, Fernando under Jose Vianna Da Motta (C0279.5).

C1125.
Thomán, István. Hungarian Pianist, Father of Maria; b. November 4, 1862, Homonna; d. September 22, 1940, Budapest.

1. Baker 7; Grove 6/18 (Bibliography); MGG/Supp. (Bibliography); Riemann 12 + Supp. (Bibliography).

C1126.
Thomán, Maria. Hungarian Violinist; b. July 12, 1889, Budapest; d. February 25, 1948, Budapest.

1. Baker 7; Grove 6/18; MGG/Supp.; Riemann 12 + Supp.

C1127.
Thomas, John [Pencerdd Gwalia]. Welsh Harpist; b. March 1, 1826, Bridgend, Glamorganshire; d. March 19, 1913, London.

1. Baker 7; Grove 6/18 (Bibliography); MGG (Bibliography); PAB–MI/2 (Bibliography); Schmidl.

C1128.
Thomson, César. Belgian Violinist; b. March 17, 1857, Liège; d. August 21, 1931, Lugano, Italy.

1. Baker 7; Grove 6/18 (Bibliography); PAB–MI/2 (Bibliography); Riemann 12 + Supp.

5. B0053.

C1129.
de Thurner, Frédéric Eugène. French Oboist; b. December 9, 1785, Montbéliard; d. March 21, 1827, Amsterdam, Holland.

1. Baker 7; Fetis 2/8; Mendel; Schmidl.

C1130.
Tilney, Colin. English Harpsichordist; b. October 31, 1933, London.

1. Baker 7; Grove 6/18; PAB–MI/2 (Bibliography).

C1131.
Tortelier, Paul. French Cellist; b. March 21, 1914, Paris.

1. Baker 7; Grove 6/19 (Bibliography); MGG; PAB–MI/2 (Bibliography); Riemann 12 + Supp.

3. Tortelier, Paul with David Blum. Paul Tortelier: A Self-Portrait in Conversation with David Blum. London: William Heinemann Ltd., 1984. xvii, 270 p. + 7 plates, 26 illus., compositions, discography, index.

C1132.
Totenberg, Roman. American Violinist; b. January 1, 1911, Lodz, Poland.

1. Baker 7; Grove 6/19; Grove–AM; PAB–MI/2 (Bibliography); Riemann 12 + Supp.

C1133.
Tough, Dave. American Jazz Drummer; b. April 26, 1908, Oak Park, Illinois; d. December 6, 1948, Newark, New Jersey.

1. Baker 7; Grove–AM (Bibliography); Grove–Jazz; PAB–MI/2 (Bibliography).

2. CK(KB) 5/5.

C1134.
Tournemire, Charles Arnould. French Organist; b. January 22, 1870, Bordeaux; d. November 3, 1939, Arcachon.

1. Baker 7 (Bibliography); Grove 6/19 (Bibliography); MGG (Bibliography); PAB–MI/2 (Bibliography); Riemann 12 (Bibliography) + Supp. (Bibliography); Schmidl + Supp.

C1135.
Trampler, Walter. American Violist; b. August 25, 1915, Munich, Germany.

1. Baker 7; Grove 6/19; Grove-AM; PAB-MI/2 (Bibliography); Riemann 12/ Supp.

C1136.
Tretyakov, Viktor. Soviet Violinist; b. October 17, 1946, Krasnoyarsk.

1. Baker 7; Grove 6/19 (Bibliography).

C1137.
Tristano, Lennie [Leonard Joseph]. American Jazz Pianist; b. March 19, 1919, Chicago, Illinois; d. November 18, 1978, New York City.

1. Baker 7; Grove 6/19 (Bibliography - 13 entries); Grove-AM (Bibliography); Grove-Jazz; JB: JRRM; LJ; PAB-MI/2 (Bibliography); Riemann 12 + Supp. (Bibliography).

He excelled as a teacher and founded (1951) a unique school of jazz.

2. CK(KB) 6/1; DB 23/10, 25/22, 29/24; 29/30, 36/21.

4. McKinney, J.F. The Pedagogy of Lennie Tristano. Ph.D. diss. Fairleigh Dickinson University, 1978.

5. A0001.

SEE: Fayenz, Franco under **Charlie Parker** (C0881.5).

C1138.
Tua, Teresina Maria Felicità. Italian Violinist; b. May 22, 1867, Turin; d. October 29, 1955, Rome.

1. Baker 7; MGG (Bibliography); Riemann 12/Supp.; Schmidl.

C1139.
Tuckwell, Barry Emmanuel. Australian French-horn Player; b. March 5, 1931, Melbourne.

1. Baker 7; Grove 6/19; PAB-MI/2 (Bibliography).

2. MM 17/1; New Yorker March 14, 1977.

C1140.
Tudor, David Eugene. American Pianist; b. January 20, 1926, Philadelphia, Pennsylvania.

1. Baker 7; Grove 6/19 (Bibliography); Grove-AM (Bibliography); PAB-MI/2 (Bibilography); Riemann 12 + Supp. (Bibliography).

2. HiFi/MusAm 25/8; MM 20/12.

5. SEE: Cage, John. A Year from Monday. Middletown (CT): Wesleyan University Press, 1967.

C1141.
Tulou, Jean-Louis. French Flutist; b. September 12, 1786, Paris; d. July 23, 1865, Nantes.

1. Baker 7; Fetis 2/8 + Supp.; Grove 6/19; MGG (Bibliography); Riemann 12; Schmidl.

C1142.
Tureck, Rosalyn. American Pianist; b. December 14, 1914, Chicago, IL.

1. Baker 7; Grove 6/19; Grove-AM (Bibliography); PAB-MI/2 (Bibliography); Riemann 12 + Supp.

2. CL 19/10; CK(KB) 4/5.

5. A0069.

   SEE: LePage, Janet Weiner under Wanda Landowska (C0634.5).

C1143.
Turetzky, Bertram. American Double Bassist; b. February 14, 1933, Norwich, Connecticut.

1. Grove 6/19; Grove-AM; PAB-MI/2 (Bibliography); Riemann 12.

C1144.
Turini, Ronald Walter. Canadian Pianist; b. September 30, 1934, Montreal.

1. Baker 7; Grove 6/19; Encyclopedia of Music in Canada.

2. CL 25/4.

C1145.
Turner, Bruce. English Jazz Clarinetist; b. July 5, 1922, Saltburn, Yorkshire.

1. Grove-Jazz; PAB-MI/2 (Bibliography).

3. Turner, Bruce. Hot Air, Cool Music. London: Quartet Books Limited, 1984. 248 p. + 8 plates, 24 illus., discography, index.

C1146.
Tyner, McCoy [Saud, Sulaimon]. American Jazz Pianist; b. December 11, 1938, Philadelphia, Pennsylvania.

1. Baker 7; Grove-AM (Bibliography); Grove-Jazz; JB; JRRM; LJ; PAB-MI/2.

2. DB 40/20, 42/15, 44/17, 51/2; CK(KB) 2/5, 4/8, 7/8.

C1147.
Uninsky, Alexander. American Pianist; b. February 2, 1910, Kiev, Russia; d. December 19, 1972, Dallas, Texas.

1. Baker 7; Riemann 12/Supp.

C1148.
Urso, Camilla. American Violinist; b. June 13, 1842, Nantes, France;
d. January 20, 1902, New York City.

1. Baker 7 (Bibliography); Grove-AM (Bibliography); PAB-MI/2 (Bibliography); Schmidl.

4. Barnard, Charles. A Tribute by Charles Barnard to Camilla Urso. New York: United States Lyceum Bureau, c.1882. unpaginated [32 p.], list of repertoire.

5. A0093.

C1149.
Valenti, Fernando. American Harpsichordist; b. December 4, 1926, New York City.

1. Baker 7; Grove 6/19; Grove-AM; PAB-MI/2 (Bibliography).

2. HiFi 3/6, 4/9; CK(KB) 6/4; KB 11/10.

3. Valenti, Fernando. The Harpsichord: a Dialogue for Beginners. Hackensack (NJ): Jerona Music Corporation, 1982. 92 p.

"Many years ago I promised myself that I would never put in print anything that even vaguely resembled a 'method' for harpsichord playing and this is it."

C1150.
Varga, Tibor. Hungarian Violinist; b. July 4, 1921, Gyoer.

1. Baker 7; Grove 6/19 (Bibliography); PAB-MI/2 (Bibliography); Riemann 12 + Supp. (Bibliography).

2. Strad Feb/1987.

C1151.
von Vecsey, Franz. Hungarian Violinist; b. March 23, 1893, Budapest;
d. April 6, 1935, Rome, Italy.

1. Baker 7; Riemann 12; Schmidl + Supp.

5. B0024, B0053.

C1152.
Venuti, Joe [Giuseppe]. American Jazz Violinist; b. April 4, 1898,
Lecco, Italy; d. April 14, 1978, Seattle, Washington.

1. Baker 7; Grove-AM (Bibliography); Grove-Jazz; JB; LJ; PAB-MI/2 (Bibliography).

"Venuti is considered the most important violinist in early jazz..."
Grove-AM.

2. Strad Oct/1986.

C1153.
Verne [Wurm], Mathilde. English Pianist; b. May 25, 1865, Southampton;
d. June 4, 1936, London.

1. Baker 7; Schmidl/Supp.

3. Verne, Mathilde. Chords of Remembrance. London: Hutchinson & Co.
(Publishers) Ltd., 1936. 288 p., 47 illus., index.

C1154.
Veyron-Lacroix, Robert. French Harpsichordist/Pianist; b. December 13,
1922, Paris.

1. Baker 7 (Bibliography); Grove 6-19; PAB-MI/2 (Bibliography); Riemann
12/Supp. (Bibliography).

C1155.
Vierne, Louis. French Organist; b. October 8, 1870, Poitiers; d. June 2,
1937, Paris.

1. Baker 7; Grove 6/19 (Bibliography); MGG (Bibliography); PAB-MI/2
(Bibliography); Riemann 12 (Bibliography) + Supp. (Bibliography);
Schmidl + Supp.

3. Crawford, Jack Reed. 'Mes souvenirs' of Louis Vierne (1870-1937): an
Annotated Translation. Ph.D. diss. University of Miami, 1973. 314 p.

4. Doyen, Henri. Mes leçons d'orgue avec Louis Vierne, souvenirs et
témoignages. Paris: Editions "Musique Sacrée", 1966. 124 p., 5 illus.

Gavoty, Bernard. Louis Vierne, la vie et l'oeuvre. Paris: Editions
Albin Michel, 1943. 319 p. + 6 plates, 12 illus., index of names.

Kasouf, Edward Joseph. Louis Vierne and His Six Organ Symphonies.
Ph.D. diss. Catholic University, 1970. iii, 208 p., tables, bibliography.

C1156.
Vieuxtemps, Henri. Belgian Violinist; b. February 17, 1820, Verviers;
d. June 6, 1881, Mustapha, Algiers.

1. Baker 7 (Bibliography); Fetis 2/8; Grove 6/19 (Bibliography); Mendel;
MGG (Bibliography); PAB-MI/2 (Bibliography); Riemann 12 (Bibliography) + Supp. (Bibliography); Schmidl.

2. Strad April/1974, March 1981.

4. Bergmans, Paul. Henry Vieuxtemps. Turnhout: Etablissements Brepols,
S.A., Imprimeurs-Editeurs, 1920. 30, [1] p., portrait, 10-item Bibliography.

Kufferath, Maurice. Henri Vieuxtemps, sa vie et son oeuvre.
Bruxelles: V.J. Rozez, Librairie-Editeur, 1882. 142 p. + 2 plates,
22-item bibliography, compositions.

Radoux, J[ean].-Théodore. Vieuxtemps: sa vie, ses oeuvres. Liège:
Aug. Bénard, Imprimeur-Editeur, 1891. 166, [11] p., 14 illus., list
of compositions.

5. A0014, A0016, A0093, B0083, B0112.

C1157.
Villoing, Alexander. Russian Pianist; b. March 12, 1804, Moscow;
d. September, 2, 1878.

1. Baker 7; Fetis 2/Supp.; Schmidl.

C1158.
Viñes, Ricardo. Spanish Pianist; b. February 5, 1875, Lérida; d. April
29, 1943, Barcelona.

1. Baker 7 (Bibliography); Grove 6/19 (Bibliography); PAB-MI/2
   (Bibliography); Riemann 12 + Supp. (Bibliography).

C1159.
Viotti, Giovanni Battista. Italian Violinist; b. May 12, 1755, Fonta-
netto; d. March 3, 1824, London, England.

1. Baker 7 (Bibliography); Fetis 2/8 (Bibliography); Grove 6/19 (Bibliography); Mendel; MGG (Bibliography); PAB-MI/2 (Bibliography);
   Riemann 12 (Bibliography) + Supp. (Bibliography); Schmidl (Bibliography).

4. Boyce, Mary Frances. The French School of Violin Playing in the
   Sphere of Viotti: Technique and Style. Ph.D. diss. University of
   North Carolina, 1973. xiii, 423 p., illus., tables, appendices,
   bibliography.

   d'Eymar, Ange-Marie. Anecdotes sur Viotti, précédés de quelques
   réflexions sur l'expression en musique. Genève: Luc Sestié, 1800
   [original Milano: A.S. Zeno, 1792]. 47 p.

   Giazotto, Remo. Giovanni Battista Viotti. Milano: Edizioni Curci,
   1956. 390 p., illus., index of names, general index.

   White, C. Giovanni Battista Viotti and His Violin Concertos. Ph.D.
   diss. Princeton University, 1957.

5. A0023, A0093, B0020, B0050, B0051.

C1160.
Vivier, Eugène Léon. French French-horn Player; b. December 4, 1817,
Brionde, Haute-Loire; d. February 24, 1900, Nice.

1. Baker 7; Fetis 2/8; Grove 6/20 (Bibliography); Mendel; PAB-MI/2 (Bibliography); Riemann 12 (Bibliography); Schmidl + Supp.

3. Baker 7 mentions "...an autobiography (largely fictitious), La Vie
   et les aventures d'un corniste (Paris, 1900)".

5. A0016.

C1161.
Voigt [née Kunze], Henriette. German Pianist; b. November 24, 1808,
Leipzig; d. October 15, 1839, Leipzig.

1. Baker 7 (Bibliography); Riemann 12 (Bibliography) + Supp. (Bibliography).

C1162.
Voisin, Roger Louis. American Trumpet Player; b. June 26, 1918, Angers,
France.

1. Baker 7; Grove 6/20; Grove-AM.

C1163.
Votapek, Ralph. American Pianist; b. March 20, 1939, Milwaukee, WI.

1. Baker 7; Grove-AM; PAB-MI/2 (Bibliography).

5. A0075.

C1164.
Walcha, Helmut. German Organist; b. October 27, 1907, Leipzig.

1. Baker 7; Grove 6/20; MGG; PAB-MI/2 (Bibliography); Riemann 12 + Supp.

2. HiFi 9/7

5. B0076, B0081, B0110.

C1165.
Waller, Fats [Thomas Wright]. American Jazz Pianist; b. May 21, 1904,
New York City; d. December 15, 1943, Kansas City, Missouri.

1. Baker 7; Grove 6/20 (Bibliography); Grove-AM (Bibliography - 20
   entries); Grove-Jazz; JB; JRRM; LJ; PAB-MI/2 (Bibliography); Riemann
   12 + Supp. (Bibliography).

   One of the leading stride pianists, Waller made immaginative and
   important contributions to the evolution of jazz piano playing.

2. CK(KB) 3/2; DB 32/5; Journal of Jazz Studies 1/1, 4/1; New Yorker
   April 10, 1978.

4. Davies, John R.T. The Music of Thomas "Fats" Waller, with Complete
   Discography. London, Jazz Journal Publications, 1950/rev. 1953 by
   R.M. Cooke. 26 p.

   Fox, Charles. Fats Waller. London: Cassell & Company Limited, 1960.
   89, [1] p. + 2 plates, 4 illus., discography.

   Kirkeby, W.T. with Duncan P. Schiedt and Sinclair Traill. Ain't Mis-
   behavin': the Story of Fats Waller. New York: Dodd, Mead & Company,
   1966. Reprint 1975. 248 p. + 8 plates, 39 illus., select discography.

Machlin, Paul S. Stride: the Music of Fats Waller. Boston: Twayne Publishers, 1985. xv, 167 p., portrait, chronology, 68-item select bibliography, discography, index.

Vance, Joel. Fats Waller: His Life and Times. Chicago: Contemporary Books, Inc., 1977. viii, 179 p. + 4 plates, 10 illus., 21-item bibliography, index.

Waller, Maurice and Anthony Calabrese. Fats Waller. New York: Schirmer Books. xix, 235 p., 16 illus., recording dates and personnel, list of compositions and arrangements, index.

5. A0029, B0054.

C1166.
Warren, Samuel Prowse. American Organist; b. February 18, 1841, Montreal, Canada; d. October 7, 1915, New York City.

1. Baker 7; Grove-AM (Bibliography); PAB-MI/2 (Bibliography).

C1167.
Watts, André. American Pianist; b. June 20, 1946, Nuremberg, Germany.

1. Baker 7; Grove-AM (Bibliography); PAB-MI/2 (Bibliography); Riemann 12/Supp.

2. CL 3/1, 18/9; HiFi/MusAm 24/6, 28/12; CK(KB) 3/12, 7/5; New York Times Magazine September 19, 1971; PQ 57, 81.

5. A0060, A0069, A0075.

C1168.
Webb, Chick [William Henry]. American Jazz Drummer; b. February 10, 1909, Baltimore, Maryland; d. June 16, 1939, Baltimore.

1. Baker 7; Grove 6/20 (Bibliography); Grove-AM (Bibliography); Grove-Jazz; JB: PAB-MI/2 (Bibliography); Riemann 12 + Supp.

2. DB 29/13.

C1169.
Weber, Margarit. Swiss Pianist; b. February 24, 1924, Ebnat-Kappel.

1. Baker 7 (Bibliography); Grove 6/20; PAB-MI/2 (Bibliography); Riemann 12/Supp.

C1170.
Webster, Beveridge. American Pianist; b. May 30, 1908, Pittsburgh, PA.

1. Baker 7; Grove-AM.

C1171.
Wehle, Karl. Bohemian Pianist; b. March 17, 1825, Prague; d. June 3, 1883, Paris, France.

1. Baker 7; Fetis 2/Supp; Mendel.

C1172.
Weinrich, Carl. American Organist; b. July 2, 1904, Patterson, New Jersey.

1. Baker 7; Grove 6/20; Grove-AM; PAB-MI/2 (Bibliography); Riemann 12 + Supp.

C1173.
Weir, Gillian Constance. New Zealand Organist/Harpsichordist; b. January 17, 1941, Martinborough.

1. Baker 7; Grove 6/20; PAB-MI/2 (Bibliography).

C1174.
Weissenberg, Alexis Sigismund. French Pianist; b. July 26, 1929, Sofia, Bulgaria.

1. Baker 7; Grove 6/20; Grove-AM (Bibliography); PAB-MI/2 (Bibliography); Riemann 12/Supp.

A controversial pianist from the studio of Olga Samaroff.

2. CL 21/8; CK(KB) 7/3.

4. Breuer, Gustl. _Alexis Weissenberg: ein kaleidoskopisches Portraet._ Berlin: Rembrandt Verlag, 1977. 62 p., 25 illus., chronology, discography.

C1175.
Wells, Dicky [William]. American Jazz Trombonist; b. June 10, 1907, Centerville, Tennessee; d. November 12, 1985, New York City.

1. Grove-AM (Bibliography); Grove-Jazz; JB; LJ; PAB-MI/2 (Bibliography).

3. Wells, Dicky with Stanley Dance. _The Night People: Reminiscences of a Jazzman._ Foreword by Count Basie. Boston: Crescendo Publishing Company, 1971. vi, 118 p. + 4 plates, 18 illus., glossary, index.

C1176.
Wendling, Johann Baptist. Alsatian Flutist; b. June 17, 1723, Rappoltsweiler; d. November 27, 1797, Munich, Germany.

1. Baker 7; Fetis 2/8; Grove 6/20; Mendel; MGG (Bibliography); Riemann 12 (Bibliography) + Supp.; Schmidl/Supp.

C1177.
Whitehouse, William Edward. English Cellist; b. May 20, 1859, London; d. January 12, 1935, London.

1. Baker 7; Grove 6/20; Riemann 12; Schmidl/Supp.

3. Whitehouse, William Edward. _Recollections of a Violoncellist._ London: The Strad Office, 1930. iii, 107 p. + 5 plates, 5 illus.

C1178.
Widor, Charles-Marie-Jean-Albert. French Organist; b. February 21, 1844, Lyons; d. March 12, 1937, Paris.

1. Baker 7 (Bibliography); Grove 6/20 (Bibliography); MGG (Bibliography); PAB-MI/2 (Bibliography); Riemann 12 (Bibliography) + Supp. (Bibliography); Schmidl + Supp.

2. MQ 30/2.

5. SEE: Knauff, Theodore under William T. Best (C0128.5).

C1179.
Wieniawski, Henryk [Henri]. Polish Violinist; b. July 10, 1835, Lublin; d. March 31, 1880, Moscow, Russia.

1. Baker 7 (Bibliography); Fetis 2/8; Grove 6/20 (Bibliography); Mendel; MGG; PAB-MI/2 (Bibliography); Riemann 12 (Bibliography); Schmidl.

   "At the age of 11 he graduated with first prize in violin, an unprecedented event in the annals of the Paris Cons...Wieniawski was undoubtedly one of the greatest violinists of the 19th century..." Baker 7.

2. Strad April/1971, April/1980.

4. Desfossez, Achille. Henri Wieniawski. La Haye: Imprimerie de Belinfante frères, 1856. 29, [1] p., portrait.

   Duleba, Wladyslaw. Henryk Wieniawski: kronika zycia. Kraków: Polskie Wydawnictwo Muzyczne, 1967. 299 p., illus., notes, compositions, repertoire, discography.

5. A0028, A0093, B0024, B0102.

C1180.
Wieniawski, Joseph. Polish Pianist, brother of **Henryk**; b. May 23, 1837, Lublin; d. November 11, 1912, Brussels, Belgium.

1. Baker 7; Fetis 2/8; Grove 6/20; Mendel; MGG (Bibliography); PAB-MI/2 (Bibliography); Riemann 12 (Bibliography); Schmidl.

4. Delcroix, Léon. Joseph Wieniawski: notes biographiques et anecdotiques. Bruxelles: J.B. Katto, éditeur de musique, 1908. 15 p., portrait.

C1181.
Wild, Earl. American Pianist; b. November 26, 1915, Pittsburgh, PA.

1. Baker 7; Grove 6/20; Grove-AM; PAB-MI/2 (Bibliography).

2. CL 20/3, 25/2; HiFi/MusAm 36/2; KB 12/12; PQ 131.

5. A0055.

C1182.
Wilhelmj, August Emil Daniel. German Violinist; b. September 21, 1845,
Usingen; d. January 22, 1908, London, England.

1. Baker 7 (Bibliography); Fetis 2/Supp. (under Wilhelmy); Grove 6/20
   (Bibliography); Mendel; MGG (Bibliography); PAB-MI/2 (Bibliography);
   Riemann 12 (Bibliography); Schmidl.

5. B0035.

C1183.
Wilkomirska, Wanda. Polish Violinist; b. January 11, 1929, Warsaw.

1. Baker 7; Grove 6/20 (Bibliography); PAB-MI/2 (Bibliography); Riemann
   12/Supp.

4. Kydryński, Lucjan. <u>Wanda Wilkomirska</u>. Kraków: Polskie Wydawnictwo
   Muzyczne, 1960. 38, [1] p., 19 illus.

C1184.
Willent-Bordogni, Jean-Baptiste. French Bassoonist; b. December 8, 1809,
Douai; d. May 11, 1852, Paris.

1. Baker 7; Fetis 2/8 + Supp.; Mendel; Schmidl.

C1185.
Williams, Cootie [Charles Melvin]. American Jazz Trumpeter; b. July 24,
1910, Mobile, Alabama.

1. Baker 7; Grove 6/20; Grove-AM (Bibliography); Grove-Jazz; JB; JRRM;
   PAB-MI/2 (Bibliography); Riemann 12.

2. DB 34/9.

C1186.
Williams, John Christopher. Australian Guitarist; b. April 24, 1942,
Melbourne.

1. Baker 7; Grove 6/20.

C1187.
Williams [née Scruggs], Mary Lou [Elfrieda]. American Jazz Pianist;
b. May 8, 1910, Atlanta, Georgia; d. May 28, 1981, Durham, NC.

1. Baker 7; Grove 6/20; Grove-AM (Bibliography); Grove-Jazz; JB; JRRM;
   LJ; PAB-MI/2 (Bibliography); Riemann 12.

2. DB 24/21, 31/24, 38/11; CK(KB) 3/10.

5. A0004.

C1188.
Willmers, Rudolf. Danish Pianist; b. October 31, 1821, Copenhagen;
d. August 24, 1878, Vienna, Austria.

1. Baker 7 (Bibliography); Fetis 2/8 + Supp.; Mendel; Schmidl.

C1189.
Wilson, Teddy [Theodore Shaw]. American Jazz Pianist. b. November 24, 1912, Austin, Texas; d. July 31, 1986.

1. Baker 7; Grove 6/20 (Bibliography); Grove-AM (Bibliography); Grove-Jazz; JB; PAB-MI/2 (Bibliography); Riemann 12 + Supp. (Bibliography).

   His appointment (1950) at Julliard was an early recognition of jazz.

2. DB 26/2, 36/21, 44/4; CK(KB) 2/2.

5. A0006.

C1190.
Winding, Kai [Chresten]. American Jazz Trombonist; b. May 18, 1922, Aarhus, Denmark; d. May 6, 1983, Yonkers, New York.

1. Baker 7; Grove-AM (Bibliography); Grove-Jazz; JB; PAB-MI/2 (Bibliography); Riemann 12 + Supp.

2. DB 45/15.

C1191.
Wittgenstein, Paul. American Pianist; b. November 5, 1887, Vienna, Austria; d. March 3, 1961, Manhasset, Long Island, New York.

1. Baker 7; Grove 6/20 (Bibliography); Grove-AM (Bibliography); MGG (Bibliography); PAB-MI/2 (Bibliography); Riemann 12 + Supp. (Bibliography); Schmidl.

C1192.
Woelfl, Joseph. Austrian Pianist; b. December 24, 1773, Salzburg; d. May 21, 1812, London, England.

1. Baker 7 (Bibliography); Fetis 2/8 + Supp.; Grove 6/20 (Bibliography); Mendel; MGG (Bibliography); PAB-MI/2 (Bibliography); Riemann 12 (Bibliography) + Supp. (Bibliography); Schmidl (under Woelffl).

4. Baum, Richard. Joseph Woelfl (1773-1812): Leben, Klavierwerke, Klavierkammermusik und Kalvierkonzerte. Kassel: Baerenreiter-Verlag, 1928 [original Ph.D. diss. University of Munich, 1926]. 90 p.

C1193.
Woodward, Roger. Australian Pianist; b. December 20, 1942, Sydney.

1. Baker 7; Grove 6/20; PAB-MI/2 (Bibliography).

C1194.
Wuehrer, Friedrich. Austrian Pianist; b. June 29, 1900, Vienna; d. December 27, 1975, Mannheim, Germany.

1. Baker 7; Grove 6/20; MGG (Bibliography) + Supp. (Bibliography); PAB-MI/2 (under Wuhrer - Bibliog.); Riemann 12 + Supp. (Bibliography)

4. Wuehrer-Jungbluth, Margaretha. Befluegelte Reisen: mein Leben mit Friedrich Wuehrer. Salzburg: Verlag Anton Pustet, 1981. 280 p., 9 illus.

C1195.
Wurm, Marie. English Pianist; b. May 18, 1860, Southmapton; d. January 21, 1938, Munich, Germany.

1. Baker 7; PAB-MI/2 (Bibliography); Riemann 12; Schmidl.

C1196.
Yamash'ta [Yamashita], Stomu [Tsutomu]. Japanese Percussionist; b. March 15, 1947, Kyoto.

1. Baker 7; Grove 6/20; PAB-MI/2 (Bibliography).

C1197.
Yancey, Jimmy [James Edward]. American Jazz Pianist; b. c.1894, Chicago, Illinois; d. September 17, 1951, Chicago.

1. Baker 7; Grove 6/20 (Bibliography); Grove-AM (Bibliography); Grove-Jazz; JB; LJ; PAB-MI/2 (Bibliography).

C1198.
Yellin [née Bentwich], Thelma. Israeli Cellist; b. March 15, 1895, London, England; d, March 21, 1959, Jerusalem.

1. Grove 6/20.

4. Bentwich, Margery. Thelma Yellin: Pioneer Musician. Jerusalem: Rubin Mass Publisher, 1964. 131 p. + 7 plates, 11 illus., index.

C1199.
Yepes, Narciso. Spanish Guitarist; b. November 14, 1927, Lorca.

1. Baker 7; Grove 6/20 (Bibliography); PAB-MI/2 (Bibliography); Riemann 12/Supp.

C1200.
Yost, Michel. French Clarinetist; b. 1754, Paris; d. July 5, 1786, Paris.

1. Baker 7; Fetis 2/8; Mendel; Riemann 12; Schmidl.

C1201.
Young, Prez [Lester Willis]. American Jazz Tenor Saxophonist; b. August 27, 1909, Woodville, Mississippi; d. March 15, 1959, New York City.

1. Baker 7; EdS (Bibliography); Grove 6/20 (Bibliography - 12 entries); Grove-AM (Bibliography - 24 entires); Grove-Jazz; JB; JRRM; LJ; PAB-MI/2 (Bibliography); Riemann 12 (Bibliography) + Supp. (Bibliography).

2. DB 16/8, 18/22, 23/5, 26/9, 30/1, 36/7, 48/1; HiFi/SR 34/6.

4. Burkhardt, Werner and Joachim Gerth. Lester Young: ein Portraet. Wetzlar: Pegasus Verlag, 1959. 48 p. + 8 plates, 16 illus., discography.

Cash, B. An Analysis of the Improvisation Technique of Lester Willis Young, 1936-1942. Ph.D. diss. University of Hull (England), 1982.

Franchini, Vittorio. Lester Young. Milano: G. Ricordi & C., 1961. 91, [4] p. + 2 plates, 4 illus., discography, 14-item bibliography.

Gelly, Dave. Lester Young. New York: Hippocrene Books Inc, 1984. 94 p., 8 illus., selected discography by Tony Middleton.

Jepson, Jorgen Grunnet. A Discography of Lester Young. København: Knudsen, 1968. 45 p.

Lucky, Robert A. A Study of Lester Young and His Influence upon His Contemporaries. Ph.D. diss. University of Pittsburgh, 1981.

Paulussen, Diethelm. Untersuchungen zu den Improvisationen Lester Youngs. Ph.D. diss. University of Frankfurt/M., 1971.

Porter, Lewis. Lester Young. Boston: Twayne Publishers, 1985. xxi, 190 p., illus., chronology, notes, 111-item bibliography, discography, index.

5. A0001, A0159.

SEE: Fayenz, Franco under Charlie Parker (C0881.5).

C1202.
Ysaÿe, Eugène. Belgian Violinist; b. July 16, 1858, Liège; d. May 12, 1931, Brussels.

1. Baker 7; Grove 6/20 (Bibliography); MGG (Bibliography); PAB-MI/2 (Bibliography); Riemann 12 (Bibliography) + Supp. (Bibliography); Schmidl.

2. Strad March/1970, March/1976, Feb/1978, July/1978, April/1983.

4. Christen, Ernest. Ysaÿe. Genève: Editions Labor et Fides, 1946. 228, [5] p. + 9 plates, illus.

Ginzburg, Lev Solomonovich. Ezhen Izai. Moskva: Gos. muzykal'noe izd-vo, 1959. 198 p. + 2 plates, illus., bibliography. Translated as Ysaÿe by X.M. Danko. Neptune City (NJ): Paganiniana Publications, n.d. [1980]. 672 p., illus., discography, index.

Quitin, José. Eugene Ysaÿe, étude biographique et critique. Bruxelles: Bosworth & Co., 1938. 54 p. + 3 plates, illus., music.

Ysaÿe, Antoine and Bertram Ratcliffe. Ysaÿe: sa vie, son oeuvre, son influence d'après les documents recueillis par son fils. Préface by Yehudi Menuhin. Bruxelles: Editions L'Ecran du monde, 1948. 550 p., 78 illus., list of works, 61-item bibliography, iconography.

This was originally published in an abridged edition in 1947
[London: W. Heinemann. xi, 250 p. + 9 plates, 19 illus., works,
recordings, honors]. Reprint 1978. New translation 1980.

5. A0142, B0001, B0020, B0024, B0037, B0053, B0083, B0089, B0105, B0109.

SEE: Dressel, Dettmar. Up and Down the Scale: Reminiscences. London:
Selwyn & Blount, Paternoster House, 1937.

C1203.
Yudina, Maria Veniaminovna. Soviet Pianist; b. September 9, 1899, Nevel,
near Vitebsk; d. November 19, 1970, Moscow.

1. Baker 7 (Bibliography); Grove 6/20 (Bibliography).

C1204.
Zabaleta, Nicanor. Spanish Harpist; b. January 7, 1907, San Sebastian.

1. Baker 7; Grove 6/20; MGG (Bibliography); PAB-MI/2 (Bibliography);
   Riemann 12 + Supp. (Bibliography).

C1205.
Zak, Yakov Izrailevich. Soviet Pianist; b. November 20, 1913, Odessa;
d. June 28, 1976, Moscow.

1. Baker 7; Grove 6/20 (Bibliography).

C1206.
Zamara, Antonio. Italian Harpist; b. June 13, 1829, Milan; d. November
11, 1901, Hietzing, near Vienna, Austria.

1. Baker 7; Grove 6/20 (Bibliography); Schmidl.

C1207.
Zeisler [née Blumenfeld], Fannie Bloomfield. American Pianist; b. July
16, 1863, Bielitz, Austrian Silesia; d. August 20, 1927, Chicago, IL.

1. Baker 7 (Bibliography); Grove 6/20; Grove-AM (Bibliography); PAB-MI/2
   (Bibliography); Schmidl.

She was one of the finest women pianists of her generation.

4. Anon. Fannie Bloomfield Zeisler: an Appreciation. Chicago: Fannie
   Bloomfield Zeisler Club of Chicago, 1927. 4 p., illus.

C1208.
Zeitlin, Zvi. American Violinist; b. February 21, 1923, Dubrovnik, Yugo-
slavia.

1. Baker 7; Grove 6/20; Grove-AM (Bibliography); PAB-MI/2 (Bibliography); Riemann 12.

C1209.
Zichy, Géza [Count Vasony-Keö]. Hungarian Pianist; b. July 22, 1849,
Sztára Castle; d. January 14, 1924, Budapest.

1. Baker 7; Grove 6/20 (Bibliography); MGG (Bibliography); Riemann 12; Schmidl.

3. Zichy, Géza. Aus meinem Leben: Erinnerungen und Fragmente. 3 vols. Stuttgart: Deutsche Verlags-Anstalt, 1911-13. 171 p., 21 illus.; 149, [1] p.; vol. 3 (1920) not seen.

C1210.
Zimbalist, Efrem Alexandrovich. American Violinist; b. April 21, 1889, Rostov-na-Donu, Russia; d. February 22, 1985, Reno, Nevada.

1. Baker 7; Grove 6/20 (Bibliography); Grove-AM; MGG (Bibliography); PAB-MI/2 (Bibliography); Riemann 12 + Supp. (Bibliography); Schmidl.

2. New Yorker December 5, 1931; RS 46.

5. A0100, B0001, B0061, B0089.

C1211.
Zoeller, Karlheinz. German Flutist; b. August 24, 1928, Hoehr-Grenzhausen.

1. Baker 7; Grove 6/20; Riemann 12/Supp.

C1212.
Zukerman [née Rich], Eugenia. American Flutist; b. September 25, 1944, Cambridge, Massachusetts.

1. Baker 7; Grove-AM (Bibliography).

C1213.
Zukerman, Pinchas. Israeli Violinist, husband of Eugenia (1968-1985); b. July 16, 1948, Tel Aviv.

1. Baker 7; Grove 6/20 (Bibliography); Grove-AM (Bibliography); PAB-MI/2 (Bibliography); Riemann 12.

2. HiFi/MusAm 28/8, 34/12; Newsweek October 20, 1980; Strad June/1987.

5. B0052.

C1214.
Zukofsky, Paul. American Violinist; b. October 22, 1943, Brooklyn, NY.

1. Baker 7; Grove 6/20 (Bibliography); Grove-AM (Bibliography); PAB-MI/2 (Bibliography).

2. Strad Nov/1986.

C1215.
Zykan, Otto M. Austrian Pianist; b. April 29, 1935, Vienna.

1. Baker 7; PAB-MI/2 (Bibliography); Riemann 12/Supp.

APPENDIX I:

Reference Material

Much to my surprise, the expected authoritative entries under "virtuoso" in the standard encyclopedias (EdS, GROVE 6, HARVARD 3, MENDEL, and MGG) proved to be nonexistent. There exist, however, a limited number of other sources which are often helpful in tracking down titles by and about instrumental virtuosi and which provide biographical material not to be found elsewhere. Most of these titles would be familiar to the serious researcher but not, perhaps, to the collector or afficionado.

D0001. Adams, John L. Musicians' Autobiographies: an Annotated Bibliography of Writings Available in English 1800 to 1980. Jefferson (NC): McFarland & Company, Inc., 1982. x, 11-126 p., chronological index, title index, subject index.

   800+ titles not including reprints. The chronological index is most helpful for pinpointing related material.

D0002. Adkins, Cecil and Alis Dickinson, eds. Doctoral Dissertations in Musicology. 7th ed./2nd International ed. Philadelphia: The American Musicological Society, 1984. [x], 545 p., subject index, author index.

   A basic reference.

D0003. Angelis, Alberto de. L'Italia musicale d'oggi: Dizionario dei musicisti: compositori, direttori d'orchestra, concertisti, insegnanti, liutae, cantanti, scrittori musicali, librettisti, editori musicali ecc. 3rd ed., corredate di una appendice. Roma: Ausonia, 1928. 523, 211 p.

D0004. Aoki, K., ed. Historical Records of Great Artists. Toyko: Gramophile-Sha, 1940. 323 p., 73 illus.

   Limited edition of 1,000 copies with text in Japanese and English. Compilation of three conductors, thirty-three instrumentalists, and sixty-five singers with biographical sketches of the artists in Japanese and discographies in English. This is a very rare and important work. Not in Duckles 4 (D0010).

D0005. Bernsdorf, Eduard. Neues Universal-Lexikon der Tonkunst: fuer Kuenstler, Kunst-Freunde und alle Gebildeten. 3 vols. Dresden: (vols. 1/2) Verlag von Robert Schaefer, 1856/57; Offenbach: (vol. 3) Verlag von Johann Andre, 1861. 878 p.; 1084 p.; 912, [2] p., supp. 1865.

   Helpful for obscure artists. Not in Duckles 4 (D0010).

D0006. Brown, James D. and Stephen S. Stratton. British Musical Biog-
raphy: a Dictionary of Musical Artists, Authors and Composers, born in
Britain and its Colonies. Birmingham: Chadfield and Son, Ltd., 1897.
Reprint 1971. 11, 462, [1] p.

Full of obscure instrumentalists.

D0007. Cowden, Robert H. Concert and Opera Conductors: a Bibliography of
Biographical Materials. Westport (CT): Greenwood Press, 1987. xvi, 285
p., 2 appendices including an index to conductors in Baker 7, index of
authors and editors.

A substantial number of entries are valuable due to relationships
between conductors and instrumentalists, e.g. Olga Samaroff and
Leopold Stokowski; Evelyn Rothwell and John Barbirolli; Elly Ney
and Willem van Hoogstraten. Not in Duckles 4 (D0010).

D0008. Cowden, Robert H. Concert and Opera Singers: a Bibliography of
Biographical Materials. Westport (CT): Greenwood Press, 1985. xviii,
278 p., 2 appendices including an index to singers in Grove 6, index of
authors and editors.

A wealth of references which relate directly to many virtuosi. For
example, included in the entry for Maria Malibran (C0378) are titles
which contain important material about Auguste de Beriot.

D0009. Current Biography. New York: H.W. Wilson, 1940–

This monthly journal which has an annual accumulation gathers
biographies of 100+ individuals including musicians each year.
The occupation index makes it easy to use.

D0010. Duckles, Vincent H. and Michael A. Keller. Music Reference and
Research Materials: An Annotated Bibliography. 4th edition. New York:
New York: Schirmer Books, 1988. xv, 714 p.

The standard reference for music research materials in all languages,
Duckles 4 is most valuable for the international and national biography sections which have 190 titles, many with material related to
instrumentalists. Care must be taken in utilizing Duckles 4 as many
of the titles appear more than once, and the annotations, while helpful, do not always include important information, e.g., the cross-
indexing of periodicals in D0008. Books "printed after 1986 were not
included", e.g., D0007.

D0011. Eitner, Robert. Biographisch-bibliographisches Quellen-Lexikon
der Musiker und Musikgelehrten der christlichen Zeitrechnung bis zur
Mitte des 19. Jahrhunderts.... 10 vols. Leipzig: Breitkopf & Haertel,
1898-1904. Miscellanea Musicae Bio-bibliographica; Musikgeschichtliche
Quellennachweise als Nachtraege und Verbesserungen zu Eitners Quellen-
lexikon. Leipzig: Breitkopf & Haertel, 1912-1914.

D0012. Hamilton, David. The Listener's Guide to Great Instrumentalists.
New York: Facts On File, 1982. 136 p., 26 illus.

This is a review and annotation of "notable" recordings by artists famous for their style, technique, and tone quality. A short bio-graphical sketch introduces each artist. Keyboard: Horowitz, Cortot, Rachmaninof, Lipatti, Schnabel, Landowska, Fischer, Solomon, and Prokofiev; Brass/Woodwind: Moyse, Goosens, and Brain; Strings: Kreisler, Szigeti, Heifetz, Menuhin, Primrose, and Casals; Chamber Music: Szigeti & Bartok; Feuerman & Hess; Cortot, Thibaud & Casals; Budapest Quartet; Busch Quartet. Not in Duckles 4 (DO010).

DO013. Highfill, Jr., Philip H., Kalman A. Burnim and Edward A. Lang-hans. A Biographical Dictionary of Actors, Actresses, Musicians, Dancers, Managers and other Stage Personnel in London, 1660-1800. 12 vols. to date. Carbondale (IL): Southern Illinois University Press, 1973-

The Preface to the initial volume indicates both the scope and the nature of this absolutely monumental undertaking. The exhaustive research, particularly on obscure figures, is exemplary. Artists other than English who appeared in London are included, and any writer who is tracking an instrumentalist who did perform during this period simply must consult this work.

DO014. Hixon, Don L. and Don Hennessee. Women in Music: a Bibliography. Metuchen (NJ): The Scarecrow Press, Inc., 1975. xiii, 347 p., alphabet-ical lists by specialty.

Indexes forty-eight biographical reference works from Rodolfo Arizaga to Alexander Vodarsky-Shiraeff.

DO015. Kinkle, Roger D. The Complete Encyclopedia of Popular Music and Jazz 1900-1950. 4 vols. New Rochelle (NY): Arlington House Publishers, 1974.

Volumes two and three are devoted to biographies.

DO016. Mixter, Keith E. General Bibliography for Music Research. second edition. Detroit: Information Coordinators, Inc. 1975. 135 p.

The section on national and international biographical dictionaries is particularly helpful.

DO017. Skowronski, JoAnn. Black Music: a Bibliography. Metuchen (NJ): The Scarecrow Press, 1981. ix, 723 p., author index.

Part I, "Selected Musicians and Singers" is a veritable treasure trove of information, e.g. Louis Armstrong has entries 217-1,116; Miles Davis has 3,977-4,425; Duke Ellington has 4,440-5,682; and Andre Watts has 11,814-11,903!

DO018. Southern, Eileen. Biographical Dictionary of Afro-American and African Musicians. Westport (CT): Greenwood Press, 1982. xviii, 478 p., appendices (period of birth; place of birth; musical occupations), 183-item selected bibliography, index.

An important bibliography.

D0019. [Schmidt, Leopold]. Spemanns goldenes Buch der Musik: eine Haus-
stunde fuer Jedermann. Berlin: Vergal von W. Spemann, 1900.

    Columns 702-1312, "Tonkuenstler der Gegenwart", contain short biog-
raphies each with a portrait. Not in Duckles 4 (D0010).

ADDENDUM

Please note that these authors as well as Michael A. Keller (D0010) are
not included in the index.

D0020. Block, Adrienne Fried and Carol Neuls-Bates. Women in American
Music: A Bibliography of Music and Literature. Westport (CT): Greenwood
Press, 1979. 302 p.

    This classified bibliography of 5,024 entries is annotated and
includes an index to recordings.

D0021. Mapp, Edward. Directory of Blacks in the Performing Arts.
Metuchen (NJ): The Scarecrow Press, Inc., 1978. xv, 428 p., directory of
organizations, 64-item bibliography, classified index.

    Biographical and career information on almost 800 performers
including fourteen concert singers, twenty-five conductors, nine folk
singers, seven gospel singers, eighty-one jazz musicians, forty-two
musicians, fifteen opera singers, twenty-nine pianists, and one
hundred seventy singers.

D0022. Skowronski, JoAnn. Women in American Music: a Bibliography.
Metuchen (NJ): The Scarecrow Press, Inc., 1978. 183 p., index of names.

    Arranged chronologically.

APPENDIX II:

Index to Instrumentalists in Baker 7

This index lists the sixteen hundred twenty-two instrumentalists who are accorded an individual entry in the monumental Baker's Biographical Dictionary of Musicians (seventh edition, New York, 1984) edited by the justly legendary Nicolas Slonimsky. The major work of its kind in the United States, Baker 7 is a standard reference work consulted by persons seeking authoritative information on instrumentalists both past and present. This cross-referenced index should prove to be a timesaver for those who need information on performers not included in the 1,215 artists who have an entry in the main body of this bibliography. Any commonality with Baker 7 is indicated by the appropriate code number preceding the name, e.g. C0002 (the entry number in the Individual Virtuosi, A-Z, p. 42) before Cannonball Adderley who, fittingly for "American musical traditions", is the first virtuoso instrumentalist listed in Baker 7.

dall'Abaco, Joseph Marie
Abbado, Marcello
Abel, Carl Friedrich
Abel, Ludwig
Abell, John
Abreu, Eduardo
Abreu, Sergio
Accardo, Salvatore
Achron, Isidor
Achucarro, Joachín
Adam, Claus
Adamowski, Joseph
Adamowski, Timothee
Adams, Thomas
C0001. Adaskin, Harry
Adaskin, Murray
C0002. Adderley, Cannonball
Adeney, Richard
Adler, Clarence
C0003. Adler, Larry
Adni, Daniel
Aerts, Egide
C0004. Aeschbacher, Adrian
C0005. Agosti, Guido

C0006. Aguado y Garcia, Dionisio
C0007. Ahlgrimm, Isolde
C0008. Ahrens, Joseph Johannes
Aitken, Robert
Aitken, Webster
C0009. Alain, Marie-Claire
C0010. Alard, Jean-Delphin
C0011. Alberghi, Paolo Tommaso
Albersheim, Gerhard
C0012. Alborea, Francesco
Albrecht, Evgeny
Albrecht, Konstantin
C0013. Not in Baker 7
Alcock, John, Sr.
C0014. Alcock, Walter Galpin
Alexandrov, Anatoli
C0015. Not in Baker 7
C0016. Allen, Henry "Red"
Almeida, Laurindo
C0017. Almenraeder, Karl
Alpert, Herb
von Alpenheim, Ilse
Altenburger, Christian
Altes, Joseph-Henri

Amar, Licco
C0018. Amfiteatrov, Massimo
C0019. Ammons, Albert
Amoyal, Pierre
C0020. Anda, Geza
C0021. Andersen, Carl Joachim
C0022. Andersen, Vigo
C0023. Anderson, Lucy
C0024. André, Maurice
C0025. Andrée, Elfrida
C0026. Andreoli, Carlo
C0027. Anet, Jean-Baptiste
C0028. d'Anglebert, Jean-Henri
C0029. Anievas, Augustin
C0030. Ansorge, Conrad Eduard
Anthony, Ray
Appia, Edmond
Ara, Ugo
C0031. Aranyi, Francis
d'Aranyi, Adila
C0032. d'Aranyi, Jelly
C0033. Arban, Jean-Baptiste
C0034. Arbós, Enrique
C0035. Arbuckle, Matthew
d'Archambeau, Iwan
C0036. Argerich, Martha
C0037. Armingaud, Jules
C0038. Armstrong, Louis
Armstrong, William D.
Arnold, Richard
Aronowitz, Cecil
C0039. Arrau, Claudio
C0040. Artôt, Alexandre-Joseph
C0041. Asciolla, Dino
C0042. Ashkenazy, Vladimir
C0043. Askenase, Stefan
C0044. Atkins, Chet
C0045. Not in Baker 7
C0046. Aubert, Jacques
C0047. Auer, Leopold
C0048. Aulin, Tor Bernhard
Aus der Ohe, Adele
Austin, Florence
C0049. Ax, Emanuel
C0050. Ayler, Albert
Ayo, Felix

-B-

C0051. Babbi, Pietro Giovanni
Babin, Victor
Babitz, Sol
C0052. Bachauer, Gina
C0053. Not in Baker 7
C0054. Bachmann, Alberto

C0055. Bachrich, Sigismund
C0056. Backhaus, Wilhelm
C0057. Badura-Skoda, Paul
C0058. Baehr, Franz Joseph
C0059. Baermann, Heinrich
Baermann, Karl
C0060. Not in Baker 7
C0061. Baillot, Pierre-Marie
Bailly, Louis
Baird, Martha
C0062. Not in Baker 7
C0063. Baker, Israel
C0064. Baker, Julius
C0065. Baker, Robert Stevens
Bakfark, Valentin
Baldwin, Samuel A.
C0066. Ballista, Antonio
C0067. Balokovič, Zlatko
C0068. Balsam, Artur
C0069. Banister, Henry Joshua
Banister, John, Jr.
Barbosa-Lima, Carlos
C0070. Barcewicz, Stanislaw
C0071. Barenboim, Daniel
C0072. Bar-Illan, David
Barere, Simon
C0073. Barkel, Charles
C0074. Not in Baker 7
C0075. Barmas, Issaye
Baron, Ernst Gottlieb
C0076. Baron, Samuel
C0077. Barrère, Georges
C0078. Barret, Apollon
Barrett, Sweet Emma
Barrett, Syd
C0079. Barrière, Jean
C0080. Barrows, John
C0081. Barth, Christian Samuel
C0082. Barth, Karl Heinrich
C0083. Barth, Richard
C0084. Barthélémon, François
Bartlett, Ethel
C0085. Barwahser, Hubert
C0086. Bashkirov, Dmitri
C0087. Basie, Count
C0088. Batta, Alexandre
C0089. Baudiot, Charles-Nicolas
C0090. Bauer, Harold
C0091. Baumann, Hermann
C0092. Baumgartner, Paul
Bay, Emmanuel
C0093. Bazzini, Antonio
C0094. Bean, Hugh
C0095. Beauvarlet-Charpentier, J.
C0096. Bechet, Sidney

C0192. Brymer, Jack
      Buchbinder, Rudolf
      Buckner, Milt
C0193. von Buelow, Hans
C0194. Buhlig, Richard
C0195. Bull, John
C0196. Bull, Ole
C0197. Not in Baker 7
C0198. Buonamici, Giuseppe
C0199. Not in Baker 7
C0200. Burgin, Richard
C0201. Burmester, Willy
C0202. Busch, Adolf
C0203. Busch, Hermann
C0204. Busoni, Ferruccio
C0205. Bustabo, Guila
C0206. Buswell, James Oliver
      Byrd, Henry Roeland

-C-

C0207. Callaway, Paul
C0208. Not in Baker 7
      Calligaris, Sergio
C0209. Camden, Archie
C0210. Camidge, Matthew
C0211. Campagnoli, Bartolommeo
C0212. Campanella, Michele
C0213. Campoli, Alfredo
C0214. Capet, Lucien
C0215. Not in Baker 7
C0216. Not in Baker 7
      Carl, William Crane
C0217. Carmirelli, Pina
C0218. Carney, Harry
C0219. Carreño, Teresa
C0220. Carrodus, John Tiplady
C0221. Carter, Benny
C0222. Cartier, Jean-Baptiste
C0223. Carulli, Ferdinando
      Casadesus, Henri
C0224. Casadesus, Jean
C0225. Casadesus, Marius
C0226. Casadesus, Robert
C0227. Casals, Pablo
C0228. Cassadó, Gaspar
C0229. Castleman, Charles
      Caston, Saul
C0230. Catlett, Sid
      Cavallo, Enrica
C0231. Cesi, Beniamino
C0232. Not in Baker 7
C0233. Chasins, Abram
C0234. Cherkassy, Shura
C0235. Cherry, Don

C0236. Chopin, Frédéric
      Chorzempa, Daniel
C0237. Christian, Charlie
C0238. Not in Baker 7
C0239. Chung, Kyung-Wha
C0240. Chung, Myung-Wha
C0241. Chung, Myung-Whun
C0242. Ciccolini, Aldo
C0243. Civil, Alan
C0244. Clapton, Eric
C0245. Not in Baker 7
C0246. Clarke, Kenny
C0247. Clayton, Buck
C0248. Clement, Franz Joseph
C0249. Clementi, Muzio
C0250. Cliburn, Van
C0251. Cochereau, Pierre
C0252. Coenen, Franz
C0253. Cohen, Harriet
      Cohen, Isidore
      Cohn, Al
C0254. Cole, Cozy
C0255. Coleman, Ornette
      Collard, Jean-Philippe
      Collette, Buddy
      Collum, Herbert
C0256. Coltrane, John
      Commette, Edouard
C0257. Condon, Eddie
C0258. Not in Baker 7
      Conti-Guglia, John
      Conti-Guglia, Richard
C0259. Cooper, Kenneth
C0260. Corea, Chick
C0261. Corelli, Arcangelo
C0262. Corigliano, John
C0263. Cortot, Alfred
C0264. Cossmann, Bernhard
      Cottlow, Augusta
C0265. Couperin, Armand-Louis
C0266. Couperin, Francois
C0267. Courboin, Charles M.
C0268. Cramer. Johann Baptist
C0269. Cramer, Wilhelm
C0270. Not in Baker 7
C0271. Crossley, Paul
C0272. Crozier, Catharine
C0273. Crusell, Benhard
      Culbertson, Alexander
      Curtis, Alan
C0274. Curzon, Clifford
      Cutler, Henry S.
C0275. Czerny, Carl
C0276. Not in Baker 7
C0277. Cziffra, Gyoergy

C0357. Ellington, Duke
C0358. Ellis, Don
C0359. Elman, Mischa
C0360. Elvey, George Job
C0361. Engel, Karl
C0362. Entremont, Philippe
C0363. Epstein, Julius
Epstein, Richard
C0364. Not in Baker 7
C0365. Erdmann, Eduard Paul
C0366. Ernst, Heinrich Wilhelm
C0367. Eschenbach, Christoph
C0368. Essipoff, Anna
Esteban, Julio
C0369. Eto, Toshiya
C0370. Not in Baker 7
C0371. Evans, Bill

-F-

C0372. Fachiri, Adila
Faelten, Carl
C0373. Falcinelli, Rolande
C0374. Not in Baker 7
C0375. Farnadi, Edith
C0376. Farnam, W. Lynnwood
C0377. Farrenc, Jeanne-Louise
C0378. Fay, Amy
C0379. Feinberg, Samuel
C0380. Ferguson, Maynard
C0381. Fernández Bordas, Antonio
C0382. Ferrari, Domenico
C0383. Ferras, Christian
Ferrata, Giuseppe
C0384. Festing, Michael
C0385. Feuermann, Emanuel
C0386. Field, John
Fields, James
C0387. Not in Baker 7
C0388. Firkušný, Rudolf
C0389. Fischer, Annie
C0390. Fischer, Edwin
C0391. Fisk, Eliot
Fizdale, Robert
C0392. Fleisher, Leon
C0393. Flesch, Carl
C0394. Fleury, Louis François
C0395. Fodor, Eugene
C0396. Foldes, Andor
C0397. Not in Baker 7
C0398. Foster, Sidney
Fou, Ts'ong
C0399. Fountain, Pete
C0400. Fournier, Pierre Léon
C0401. Not in Baker 7

C0402. Fox, Virgil
C0403. Fradkin, Frederic
C0404. Fraenzl, Ferdinand
C0405. Fraenzl, Ignaz
C0406. Frager, Malcolm
C0407. Francescatti, Zino
Francesch, Homero
C0408. Franchomme, Auguste-Joseph
C0409. Not in Baker 7
C0410. Franck, Eduard
Franck, Richard
C0411. François, Samson
C0412. Frank, Claude
Frankl, Peter
C0413. Franko, Sam
Frantz, Justus
C0414. Fraser, Norman
C0415. Not in Baker 7
C0416. Freire, Nelson
C0417. Frey, Emil
C0418. Frey, Walter
C0419. Fried, Miriam
C0420. Friedberg, Carl
C0421. Friedheim, Arthur
C0422. Friedman, Erick
C0423. Friedman, Ignaz
Fries, Wulf
C0424. Friskin, James
C0425. Frugoni, Orazio
Fryer, George Herbert
C0426. Not in Baker 7
C0427. Fuchs, Joseph
C0428. Fuchs, Lillian
Fukikawa, Mayumi
C0429. Fuller, Albert

-G-

C0430. Gabrilowitsch, Ossip
C0431. Galamian, Ivan
Galla-Rini, Anthony
C0432. Gallico, Paolo
C0433. Galston, Gottfried
C0434. Galway, James
C0435. Ganz, Rudolph
Ganz, Wilhelm
C0436. Garbousova, Raya
Gardner, Samuel
C0437. Garner, Erroll
Gaultier, Denis
C0438. Gaviniès, Pierre
C0439. Gazzelloni, Severino
C0440. Gebhard, Heinrich
C0441. Gehot, Jean (Joseph)
C0442. Gelber, Bruno-Leonardo

Hasselmans, Louis
C0533. Haupt, Karl August
C0534. Hauschka, Vincenz
C0535. Hauser, Miska
C0536. Hausmann, Robert
Hautzig, Walter
C0537. Havemann, Gustav
C0538. Not in Baker 7
C0539. Hawkins, Coleman
C0540. Haynes, Roy Owen
Hays, Doris
Heermann, Hugo
Hegedues, Ferencz
Hegner, Otto
Hegyesi, Louis
C0541. Heifetz, Jascha
C0542. Heinemeyer, Ernst Wilhelm
C0543. Not in Baker 7
C0544. Hekking, Anton
C0545. Hekking, Gérard Prosper
C0546. Heller, Stephen
C0547. Hellmesberger, Georg, Jr.
C0548. Hellmesberger, Joseph, Sr.
C0549. Hemke, Frederick LeRoy
C0550. Hendrix, Jimi
C0551. Not in Baker 7
Henriot, Nicole
Henry, Harold
C0552. von Henselt, Adolph
C0553. Herman, Woody
C0554. Hermstedt, Johann Simon
C0555. Herseth, Adolph
C0556. Herz, Henri
C0557. Hess, Myra
C0558. Hess, Willy
Hesse, Adolph
C0559. Hesse-Bukowska, Barbara
Hewitt, Maurice
Heyman, Katherine Ruth
C0560. Higginbotham, J.C.
C0561. Hilsberg, Alexander
C0562. Hinderas, Natalie
C0563. Hines, Earl
C0564. Hirt, Al
C0565. Hirt, Franz Josef
C0566. Hirt, Fritz
C0567. Hodges, Edward
C0568. Hodges, Johnny
C0569. Hoelscher, Ludwig
Hoelscher, Ulf
C0570. Hoffman, Richard
Hofmann, Casimir
C0571. Hofmann, Josef
C0572. Hollaender, Gustav
C0573. Hollander, Lorin

C0574. Holliger, Heinz
C0575. Hollins, Alfred
Hollmann, Joseph
C0576. Holmes, Alfred
C0577. Holmes, Henry
C0578. Holst, Henry
C0579. Holy, Alfred
C0580. Honneger, Henri
C0581. Hopekirk, Helen
Hopkins, Claude
C0582. Horák, Josef
C0583. Horowitz, Vladimir
C0584. Horszowski, Mieczyslaw
C0585. Hrimalý, Johann
Hsu, John
C0586. Hubay, Jenoe
C0587. Hubbard, Freddie
C0588. Huberman, Bronislaw
C0589. Huenten, Franz
C0590. Hughes, Edwin
C0591. Hummel, Johann Nepomuk
Hungerford, Bruce/Leonard
C0592. Hurford, Peter
C0593. Hurwitz, Emanuel
C0594. Hutcheson, Ernest

-I-

C0595. Igumnov, Konstantin
Imai, Nobuko
Isepp, Martin
C0596. Istomin, Eugene
C0597. Iturbi, José
Iwamoto, Marito

-J-

C0598. Jackson, Milt
C0599. Jacob, Benjamin
Jacobs, Paul
Jacquet, Illinois
C0600. Jaëll, Alfred
C0601. Jaëll-Trautmann, Marie
C0602. James, Harry
C0603. Janigro, Antonio
C0604. Janis, Byron
C0605. Jarrett, Keith
C0606. Jedliczka, Ernst
Jehin, François
C0607. Jehin-Prume, Françoise
Jencks, Gardner
C0608. Jenson, Dylana
C0609. Joachim, Joseph
C0610. Johannesen, Grant
C0611. Johnasen, Gunnar

Labunski, Wiktor
C0691. Lachmund, Carl V.
Ladnier, Tommy
Lafont, Charles-Philippe
La Forge, Frank
C0692. Laidlaw, Anna Robena
Laine, Papa Jack
C0693. Lalewicz, Georg
La Marre, Jacques
Lambert, Alexander
C0694. Lamond, Frederic Archibald
de Lancie, John
C0695. Landowska, Wanda
C0696. Lang, Eddie
Langenus, Gustave
Langley, Allen Lincoln
C0697. Lanzetti, Salvatore
Lanzky-Otto, Ib
C0698. Laredo, Jaime
Laredo, Ruth
C0699. Not in Baker 7
C0700. La Rocca, Nick
C0701. de Larrocha, Alicia
C0702. Laskine, Lily
C0703. Lateiner, Jacob
C0704. Laub, Ferdinand
C0705. Lautenbacher, Susanne
C0706. Lavigne, Antoine-Joseph
Lawrence, Vera Brodsky
Laws, Hubert
C0707. Lebègue, Nicolas-Antoine
C0708. Lebrun, Jean
C0709. Lebrun, Ludwig August
C0710. Leclair, Jean Marie
C0711. Lee, Sebastian
Lefebure, Yvonne
C0712. Lefèvre, Jean Xavier
C0713. Leginska, Ethel
Lehmann, George
Lehmann, Robert
C0714. Lemare, Edwin Henry
Lener, Jenoe
C0715. Léonard, Hubert
C0716. Leonhardt, Gustav Maria
C0717. Le Roy, René
C0718. Leschetizky, Theodor
Lettvin, Theodore
Letz, Hans
Lev, Ray
C0719. Levant, Oscar
C0720. Levitzki, Mischa
Lévy, Ernst
C0721. Lévy, Lazare
C0722. Lewenthal, Raymond
C0723. Not in Baker 7

C0724. Lewis, John Aaron
C0725. Lewis, Meade "Lux"
Lewis, Ramsey
C0726. Leygraf, Hans
C0727. Lhévinne, Josef
C0728. Lhévinne, Rosina
C0729. Liberace
C0730. Libert, Henri
Licad, Cecile
Lichtenberg, Leopold
C0731. Lie, Erika
C0732. Liebling, Emil
C0733. Liebling, Georg
C0734. Lill, John Richard
Lin, Cho-Lian
C0735. Linde, Hans-Martin
C0736. Lipatti, Dinu
C0737. Lipinsky, Karol Józef
C0738. List, Eugene
C0739. Listemann, Bernhard
C0740. Liszt, Franz
C0741. Llobet, Miguel
C0742. Lloyd-Weber, David
C0743. Locatelli, Pietro
C0744. Loeillet, Jean-Baptiste
C0745. Loesser, Arthur
C0746. Loevensohn, Marix
C0747. Lolli, Antonio
C0748. Long, Marguerite
C0749. Longy, Gustave-Georges
Lopes-Graça, Fernando
C0750. de Lorenzo, Leonardo
C0751. Loriod, Yvonne
C0752. Lowenthal, Jerome
C0753. Not in Baker 7
C0754. Luboshutz, Léa
Luboshutz, Pierre
C0755. Luca, Sergiu
C0756. Luebeck, Ernst
C0757. Lupu, Radu
C0758. Luvisi, Lee
C0759. Lympany, Moura
C0760. Not in Baker 7

-M-

C0761. Ma, Yo-Yo
Macmillen, Francis
Madge, Geoffrey Douglas
C0762. Magaloff, Nikita
Maier, Guy
C0763. Majeske, Daniel
C0764. Malcuzynski, Witold
C0765. Malgoire, Jean-Claude
Malkin, Jacques

C0847. Newman, Anthony
        Newmark, John
        Newton, Ivor
C0848. Ney, Elly
C0849. Not in Baker 7
C0850. Nicols, Red
C0851. Nicolet, Aurèle
C0852. Nikolayev, Leonid
C0853. Nikolayeva, Tatiana
C0854. Noone, Jimmy
C0855. Norvo, Red
C0856. Novães, Guiomar
C0857. Nyiregyházi, Erwin

-O-

C0858. Oborin, Lev
C0859. Odnoposoff, Adolfo
C0860. Odnoposoff, Ricardo
C0861. Ogdon, John
C0862. Ohlsson, Garrick
C0863. Oistrakh, David
C0864. Iostrakh, Igor
        Olevsky, Julian
C0865. Oliveira, Elmar
C0866. Oliver, King
C0867. Not in Baker 7
C0868. Ondřiček, Franz
C0869. Oppens, Ursula
C0870. Orlov, Nicòlai
C0871. Ornstein, Leo
C0872. Orozco, Rafael
C0873. Orsi, Romeo
C0874. Ortiz, Cristina
C0875. Ory, Kid
        Oury, Anna Caroline

-P-

        Pachler-Koschak, Marie
C0876. de Pachmann, Vladimir
C0877. Paderewski, Ignacy Jan
C0878. Paganini, Niccolò
C0879. Page, Hot Lips
        Page, Jimmy
        Paratore, Anthony
        Paratore, Joseph
        Parent, Armand
C0880. Parish-Alvars, Elias
        Parkening, Christopher
C0881. Parker, Charlie
C0882. Parlow, Kathleen
C0883. Parnas, Leslie
C0884. Parratt, Walter
        Parsons, Geoffrey

C0885. Patorni-Casadesus, Regina
C0886. Pattison, John Nelson
C0887. Pauer, Ernst
C0888. Pauer, Max
C0889. Pauk, Gyoergy
C0890. Peinemann, Edith
C0891. Pelissier, Victor
        Pelton-Jones, Frances
C0892. Pembaur, Joseph, Jr.
C0893. Pennario, Leonard
C0894. Pepper, Art
C0895. Perabo, Ernst
C0896. Perahia, Murray
C0897. Perlemuter, Vlado
C0898. Perlman, Itzhak
        Perry, Edward Baxter
C0899. Persinger, Louis
        Petchnikov, Alexander
C0900. Peterson, Oscar
C0901. Petri, Egon
C0902. Not in Baker 7
C0903. Pettiford, Oscar
C0904. Pfannstiehl, Bernhard
        Pfatteicher, Carl F.
C0905. Pfundt, Ernst Gotthold
C0906. Philipp, Isidore
C0907. Phillips, Harvey
        Piastro, Josef
C0908. Piastro, Michel
C0909. Piatigorsky, Gregor
C0910. Piatti, Alfredo Carlo
        Pinnock, Trevor
C0911. Pixis, Johann Peter
C0912. Planté, Francis
        Pleshakov, Vladimir
        Pleyel, Ignaz Joseph
        Pochon, Alfred
        Pogorelich, Ivo
C0913. Pollack, Ben
        Pollikoff, Max
C0914. Pollini, Maurizio
C0915. Pommier, Jean-Bernard
C0916. Ponti, Michael
C0917. Ponty, Jean-Luc
C0918. Popper, David
C0919. Porro, Pierre-Jean
C0920. Posselt, Ruth
C0921. Postnikova, Viktoria
C0922. Potter, Philip Cipriani
C0923. Poulet, Gerard
C0924. Powell, Bud
        Powell, John
C0925. Powell, Maud
        Pressler, Menahem
C0926. Preston, Simon John

Schiff, Andras
Schiff, Heinrich
Schifrin, Lalo
C1008. Schiøler, Victor
Schloesser, Adolf
C1009. Not in Baker 7
Schmitz, Elie Robert
C1010. Schmuller, Alexander
C1011. Schnabel, Artur
C1012. Schneider, Alexander
C1013. Schneider, Georg Abraham
C1014. Schneider, Johann
C1015. Schneiderhan, Wolfgang
C1016. Schradieck, Henry
Schroeder, Alwin
Schroeder, Jaap
C1017. Schub, André-Michel
C1018. Schruecker, Edmund
C1019. Schruecker, Heinrich
C1020. Schruecker, Joseph E.
C1021. Schumann, Clara
Schuppanzigh, Ignaz
Schuster, Joseph
C1022. Schuyler, Philippa Duke
Schwarz, Boris
Schwarz, Gerard
C1023. Schweitzer, Albert
C1024. Not in Baker 7
C1025. Scott, Hazel
Seboek, Gyoergy
C1026. Segovia, Andrés
C1027. Seidel, Toscha
C1028. Seligmann, Hippolyte
C1029. Selva, Blanche
C1030. Serato, Arrigo
C1031. Not in Baker 7
C1032. Serkin, Peter
C1033. Serkin, Rudolf
C1034. Servais, Francois
C1035. Sevčik, Otakar
C1036. Severinsen, Doc
C1037. Sgambati, Giovani
C1038. Shafran, Daniel
C1039. Shankar, Ravi
C1040. Shattuck, Arthur
C1041. Shaw, Artie
C1042. Shearing, George
Sheridan, Frank
Sherwood, William H.
Shostakovich, Dmitri
C1043. Shumsky, Oscar
C1044. Shure, Leonard
Siegel, Jeffrey
C1045. Siki, Béla
C1046. Siloti, Alexander

Silva, Luigi
C1047. Silver, Horace
C1048. Silverstein, Joseph
C1049. Simon, Abbey
C1050. Not in Baker 7
C1051. Simonetti, Achille
C1052. Sims, Zoot
C1053. Singleton, Zutty
C1054. Sivori, Camillo
Slatkin, Felix
C1055. Slavík, Josef
C1056. Slenczynska, Ruth
Slobodskaya, Oda
Sloper, Lindsay
C1057. Not in Baker 7
Smeterlin, Jan
Smit, Leo
C1058. Not in Baker 7
C1059. Smith, Joe
C1060. Smith, Pine Top
Smith, Ronald
C1061. Smith, Willie "the Lion"
C1062. Snoer, Johannes
C1063. Sofronitzky, Vladimir
C1064. Soldat, Marie
C1065. Solomon
C1066. Not in Baker 7
C1067. Somer, Hilda
C1068. Somis, Giovanni Battista
C1069. Sor, Fernando
C1070. Soriano, Gonzalo
C1071. Sowinski, Wojciech
C1072. Spalding, Albert
C1073. Spanier, Muggsy
Sparnaay, Harry
Spiering, Theodore
C1074. Spivakovsky, Tossy
Spross, Charles G.
Stacy, Thomas
C1075. Stadler, Anton
C1076. Stamitz, Johann Wenzel
Standage, Simon
C1077. Stark, Robert
C1078. Starker, Janos
Starr, Ringo
C1079. Staryk, Steven
Stavenhagen, Bernhard
C1080. Stern, Isaac
C1081. Stern, Leo
Sternberg, Constantin
C1082. Steuermann, Edward
Stewart, Humphrey John
Stewart, Reginald
C1083. Stich, Jan Václav
Stillman, Mitya

Vered, Ilana
Verne, Adela
C1153. Verne, Mathilde
C1154. Veyron-Lacroix, Robert
C1155. Vierne, Louis
C1156. Vieuxtemps, Henri
C1157. Villoing, Alexander
C1158. Viñes, Ricardo
C1159. Viotti, Giovanni Battista
C1160. Vivier, Eugène-Léon
Voicu, Ion
C1161. Voigt, Henriette
C1162. Voisin, Roger
Voss, Charles
C1163. Votapek, Ralph
Vronsky, Vitya

-W-

Wadsworth, Charles
C1164. Walcha, Helmut
Wallenstein, Martin
C1165. Waller, Fats
Warren, George W.
C1166. Warren, Samuel Prowse
C1167. Watts, André
Weatherford, Teddy
C1168. Webb, Chick
C1169. Weber, Margrit
C1170. Webster, Beveridge
C1171. Wehle, Karl
C1172. Weinrich, Carl
C1173. Weir, Gillian
Weisberg, Arthur
Weiss, Franz
C1174. Weissenberg, Alexis
C1175. Not in Baker 7
C1176. Wendling, Johann Baptist
Werba, Erik
C1177. Whitehouse, William E.
Whiting, Arthur Battelle
C1178. Widor, Charles-Marie
Wiehmayer, Theodor
C1179. Wieniawski, Henryk
C1180. Wieniawski, Joseph
Wieprecht, Friedrich
Wihan, Hans
C1181. Wild, Earl
C1182. Wilhelmj, August
C1183. Wilkomirska, Wanda
Willeke, Willem

C1184. Willent-Bordogni, J.-B.
C1185. Williams, Cootie
C1186. Williams, John C.
C1187. Williams, Mary Lou
C1188. Willmers, Rudolf
Wilson, Ransom
C1189. Wilson, Teddy
C1190. Winding, Kai
Winograd, Arthur
Wirth, Emanuel
de Wit, Paul
Witek, Anton
C1191. Wittgenstein, Paul
C1192. Woelfl, Joseph
C1193. Woodward, Roger
C1194. Wuehrer, Friedrich
C1195. Wurm, Marie
Wustman, John
Wyton, Alec

-XYZ-

C1196. Yamash'ta, Stomu
C1197. Yancey, Jimmy
C1198. Not in Baker 7
C1199. Yepes, Narciso
C1200. Yost, Michel
C1201. Young Lester
C1202. Ysaÿe, Eugène
C1203. Yudina, Maria
C1204. Zabaleta, Nicanor
Zacharewitsch, Michael
C1205. Zak, Yakov
C1206. Zamara, Antonio
Zecchi, Carlo
C1207. Zeisler, Fanny Bloomfield
C1208. Zeitlin, Zvi
Zeltser, Mark
Zerrahn, Carl
C1209. Zichy, Géza
C1210. Zimbalist, Efrem
Zimerman, Krystian
Zimmermann, Agnes
C1211. Zoeller, Karlheinz
Zoellner, Joseph, Sr.
C1212. Zukerman, Eugenia
C1213. Zukerman, Pinchas
C1214. Zukofsky, Paul
Zumbro, Nicholas
Zverev, Nicolai
C1215. Zykan, Otto M.

APPENDIX III:

Index to Instrumentalists in Grove-AM

This index lists the four hundred twenty instrumentalists who have an entry in The New Grove Dictionary of American Music (London, 1986). This is the first "reference work on the music of the United States that is comprehensive in approach, academically sound, and written by a team of specialists." Numerous artists are included in this work who are either not to be found in other major reference works or who are not covered in depth elsewhere. It is a major contribution to the under-standing of "the specific character of American musical traditions." This index should prove to be most helpful to those wishing to track down their favorite performers. Some 1,215 virtuosi are accorded entries in the main body of this bibliography, and any commonality with Grove-AM is indicated by the appropriate code number preceding the name, e.g. C0002 (the entry number in the Individual Virtuosi, A-Z, p. 42) before Cannonball Adderley who, fittingly for "American musical tradi-tions", is the first virtuoso instrumentalist listed in Grove-AM.

Abercrombie, John
Achron, Isidor
Adamowski, Timothee
Adams, Pepper
C0002. Adderley, Cannonball
C0003. Adler, Larry
Aitken, Webster
Ali, Rashied
C0016. Allen, Henry "Red"
Alpert, Herb
C0019. Ammons, Albert
Ammons, Gene
Anderson, Cat
C0029. Anievas, Agustin
Appel, Toby
C0035. Arbuckle, Matthew
C0038. Armstrong, Louis
Armstrong, William D.
C0039. Arrau, Claudio
Artzt, Alice
C0044. Atkins, Chet
C0047. Auer, Leopold
C0049. Ax, Emanuel
C0050. Ayler, Albert

—B—

Babin, Victor
Bacon, Fred
Baermann, Carl
C0060. Bailey, Buster
C0062. Baker, Chet
C0063. Baker, Israel
C0064. Baker, Julius
Baker, Kenny
C0065. Baker, Robert S.
Baldwin, Dalton
Baldwin, Samuel A.
C0068. Balsam, Artur
C0072. Bar-Illan, David
Barnet, Charlie
C0076. Baron, Samuel
C0077. Barrère, Georges
C0080. Barrows, John
C0087. Basie, Count
Basquin, Peter
C0090. Bauer, Harold
C0096. Bechet, Sidney
C0102. Beiderbecke, Bix

CO104. Bellison, Simeon
Bellson, Louis
Benson, George
Benson, Joan
Berger, Karl
CO114. Berigan, Bunny
Berry, Chu
CO121. Berry, Chuck
CO129. Bethune, Blind Tom
CO134. Bigard, Barney
CO135. Biggs, E. Power
CO139. Bilson, Malcolm
CO143. Bishop-Kovacevich, Stephen
Black, Robert
Blackwell, Ed
Blaisdell, Frances
CO148. Blake, Eubie
CO149. Blakey, Art
CO150. Blanton, Jimmy
CO155. Bodky, Erwin
CO158. Bolden, Buddy
CO159. Bolet, Jorge
Borge, Victor
Bostic, Earl
Bowie, Lester
Brackeen, JoAnne
Bradford, Perry
CO173. Brailowsky, Alexander
Brauchli, Bernard
Braxton, Anthony
Brookmeyer, Bob
CO186. Brown, Clifford
Brown, Pete
Brown, Ray
CO188. Browning, John
CO189. Brubeck, Dave
Brusilow, Anshel
CO194. Buhlig, Richard
CO195. Bull, Ole
CO199. Burge, David
CO200. Burgin, Richard
Burke, Joseph
Burton, Gary
CO202. Busch, Adolf
CO206. Buswell, James Oliver
Byas, Don
Byrd, Donald

–C–

CO207. Callaway, Paul
Carl, William Crane
CO216. Carle, Frankie
CO218. Carney, Harry
CO219. Carreno, Teresa

CO221. Carter, Benny
Carter, Ron
CO227. Casals, Pablo
CO229. Castleman, Charles
CO230. Catlett, Sid
Celestin, Papa
Chaloff, Serge
Chambers, Paul
Charles, Teddy
CO233. Chasins, Abram
Cheatham, Doc
CO234. Cherkassy, Shura
CO235. Cherry, Don
CO237. Christian, Charlie
Christian, Palmer
Christie, William
CO239. Chung, Kyung-Wha
CO240. Chung, Myung-Wha
CO241. Chung, Myung-Whun
CO245. Clarke, Herbert
CO246. Clarke, Kenny
CO247. Clayton, Buck
Clements, Vassar
CO250. Cliburn, Van
Cobham, Billy
Coci, Claire
CO254. Cole, Cozy
CO255. Coleman, Ornette
Colon, Willie
Coltrane, Alice
CO256. Coltrane, John
CO257. Condon, Eddie
Cooder, Ry
CO259. Cooper, Kenneth
CO260. Corea, Chick
CO262. Corigliano, John
Cormier, Joe
Costello, Marilyn
CO267. Courboin, Charles M.
Craighead, David
CO270. Crawford, Jesse
CO272. Crozier, Catharine
Curtis, Alan
Curtis, King
Cutler, Henry S.
Cyrille, Andrew

–D–

CO278. Dameron, Tadd
CO288. Davidovich, Bella
Davis, Anthony
CO290. Davis, Ivan
CO291. Davis, Miles
Davis, Richard

-E-

-F-

-G-

Gilmore, John
C0461. Gimpel, Bronislav
C0463. Gingold, Josef
Giuffre, Jimmy
C0467. Gleason, Harold
Glenn, Carroll
C0469. Godowsky, Leopold
C0471. Goldberg, Szymon
Golde, Walter
C0472. Goldsand, Robert
Gomberg, Harold
Gomberg, Ralph
Gomez, Eddie
Gonsalves, Paul
C0475. Goode, Richard
C0476. Goodman, Benny
C0480. Gordon, Dexter
C0481. Gordon, Jacques
Gorodnitzki, Sascha
C0483. Gottschalk, Louis Moreau
C0485. Graffman, Gary
Grandjany, Marcel
C0488. Graudan, Nikolay
Graves, Milford
C0490. Greenhouse, Bernard
Greer, Sonny
Grimes, Tiny
Gross, Robert
Gruskin, Shelly
Gusikoff, Michel

–H–

C0515. Hackett, Bobby
Haden, Charlie
C0516. Haig, Al
Hall, Edmond
Hall, Robert Browne
Hamilton, Chico
Hamilton, Jimmy
C0522. Hampton, Lionel
C0523. Hancock, Herbie
Hanna, Roland P.
C0526. Harrell, Lynn
Harris, Barry
Harris, Bill
C0528. Harrison, Hazel
Harrison, Jimmy
Hart, Clyde
C0530. Harth, Sidney
C0531. Hartmann, Arthur
C0539. Hawkins, Coleman
C0540. Haynes, Roy Owen
Heifetz, Daniel
C0541. Heifetz, Jascha

C0549. Hemke, Frederick
Henderson, Joe
C0550. Hendrix, Jimi
C0553. Herman, Woody
C0555. Herseth, Adolph
C0556. Herz, Henri
Heyman, Henry C.
C0560. Higginbotham, J.C.
Higgins, Billy
C0561. Hilsberg, Alexander
C0562. Hinderas, Natalie
C0563. Hines, Earl
Hinton, Milt
C0564. Hirt, Al
C0568. Hodges, Johnny
C0570. Hoffman, Richard
C0571. Hofmann, Josef
C0573. Hollander, Lorin
Hollister, Carroll
C0581. Hopekirk, Helen
Hopkins, Claude
C0583. Horowitz, Vladimir
C0584. Horszowski, Mieczyslaw
Houseley, Henry
Hsu, John
C0587. Hubbard, Freddie
C0590. Hughes, Edwin
Hutcherson, Bobby
C0594. Hutcheson, Ernest

–I–

Innes, Frederick Neil
Isbin, Sharon
C0596. Istomin, Eugene
C0597. Iturbi, Jose

–J–

C0598. Jackson, Milt
Jackson, Tony
Jacobs, Paul
Jaffee, Michael
Jamal, Ahmad
C0602. James, Harry
C0604. Janis, Byron
C0605. Jarrett, Keith
Jenkins, Leroy
C0608. Jenson, Dylana
C0610. Johannesen, Grant
C0611. Johnasen, Gunnar
Johns, Paul Emile
C0612. Johnson, Bunk
Johnson, Charles L.
C0613. Johnson, James P.

APPENDIX IV:

Index to Virtuosi by Instrument

This index classifies the twelve hundred fifteen virtuosi who are accorded an individual entry in "Part C" by instrument. The code number preceding each name refers the reader to that artist's entry in the main body of this bibliography. Several things should be kept in mind in order to locate an artist: (1) those who have distinguished themselves on more than one instrument have a double asterisk (**) following their name and thus appear in more than one category; (2) all percussionists, regardless of instrument, are listed under "Percussion/Timpani"; (3) no distinction was made between performers of any type of music in the listing, i.e., all virtuosi on the piano are listed under that heading.

Bassoon

C0017. Almenraeder, Karl
C0120. Berr, Friedrich **
C0209. Camden, Archie
C1184. Willent-Bordogni, Jean-B.

Cello

C0012. Alborea, Francesco
C0018. Amfiteatrov, Massimo
C0069. Banister, Henry Joshua
C0079. Barrière, Jean
C0088. Batta, Alexandre
C0089. Baudiot, Charles-Nicolas
C0097. Becker, Hugo
C0122. Berteau, Martin
C0172. Braga, Gaetano
C0176. Brandukov, Anatol
C0180. Breval, Jean-Baptiste
C0203. Busch, Hermann
C0227. Casals, Pablo
C0228. Cassadó, Gaspar
C0238. Christiani, Lise
C0240. Chung, Myung-Wha
C0264. Cossmann, Bernhard
C0280. Dancla, Arnaud
C0287. Davidov, Carl
C0322. Dotzauer, Justus Johann
C0323. Dotzauer, Karl Ludwig

C0342. Duport, Jean-Louis
C0343. DuPré, Jacqueline
C0352. Eisenberg, Maurice
C0385. Feuermann, Emanuel
C0400. Fournier, Pierre
C0408. Franchomme, Auguste-Joseph
C0426. Fuchs, Carl
C0436. Garbousova, Raya
C0444. Gendron, Maurice
C0445. Gérardy, Jean
C0488. Graudan, Nicolai
C0490. Greenhouse, Bernard
C0494. Gruemmer, Paul
C0497. Gruenfeld, Heinrich
C0498. Gruetzmacher, Friedrich
C0526. Harrell, Lynn
C0527. Harrison, Beatrice
C0534. Hauschka, Vincenz
C0536. Hausmann, Robert
C0544. Hekking, Anton
C0545. Hekking, Gérard Prosper
C0569. Hoelscher, Ludwig
C0580. Honegger, Henri
C0603. Janigro, Antonio
C0645. Kindler, Hans
C0653. Kirshbaum, Ralph Henry
C0655. Klengel, Julius
C0697. Lanzetti, Salvatore

C0711. Lee, Sebastian
C0742. Lloyd-Webber, Julian
C0746. Loevensohn, Marix
C0761. Ma, Yo-Yo
C0766. Malkin, Joseph
C0776. Maréchal, Maurice
C0801. Menter, Joseph
C0841. Navarra, André Nicolas
C0843. Nelsova, Zara
C0849. Nicastro, Oscar
C0859. Odnoposoff, Adolfo
C0883. Parnas, Leslie
C0909. Piatigorsky, Gregor
C0910. Piatti, Alfredo Carlo
C0918. Popper, David
C0973. Romberg, Bernhard
C0976. Rose, Leonard Josef
C0979. Rosen, Nathaniel
C0981. Rostropovich, Mstislav
C0993. Salmond, Felix Adrian
C1028. Seligmann, Hippolyte-P.
C1034. Servais, Adrien François
C1038. Shafran, Daniel
C1078. Starker, Janos
C1081. Stern, Leo
C1092. Suggia, Guilhermina
C1131. Tortelier, Paul
C1177. Whitehouse, William E.
C1198. Yellin, Thelma

Clarinet

C0058. Baehr, Franz Josef
C0059. Baermann, Heinrich J.
C0060. Bailey, Buster
C0096. Bechet, Sidney **
C0100. Beer, Johann Joseph
C0104. Bellison, Simeon
C0120. Berr, Friedrich **
C0134. Bigard, Barney
C0146. Blaes, Arnold Joseph
C0151. Blatt, František Tadeáš
C0192. Brymer, Jack
C0273. Crusell, Bernhard Henrik
C0294. De Franko, Buddy
C0298. De Peyer, Gervase Alan
C0311. Dodds, Johnny
C0320. Dorsey, Jimmy **
C0335. Drucker, Stanley
C0399. Fountain, Pete
C0476. Goodman, Benny
C0553. Herman, Woody
C0554. Hermstedt, Johann Simon
C0582. Horák, Josef
C0636. Kell, Reginald Clifford

C0659. Klosé, Hyacinthe-Eléonore
C0712. Lefèvre, Jean Xavier
C0723. Lewis, George
C0806. Mezzrow, Mezz
C0831. Muehlfeld, Richard B.
C0854. Noone, Jimmie
C0873. Orsi, Romeo
C0988. Russell, Pee Wee
C1041. Shaw, Artie
C1075. Stadler, Anton Paul
C1077. Stark, Robert
C1086. Stoltzman, Richard
C1109. Tausch, Franz Wilhelm
C1145. Turner, Bruce
C1200. Yost, Michel

Clavecin/Keyboard

C0028. d'Anglebert, Jean-Henri
C0195. Bull, John
C0266. Couperin, F. le Grand **
C0885. Patorni-Casadesus, Regina

Cornet

C0033. Arban, Joseph J.-B.
C0035. Arbuckle, Matthew
C0102. Beiderbecke, Bix
C0158. Bolden, Buddy
C0245. Clarke, Herbert Lincoln
C0292. Davison, Wild Bill
C0401. Fox, Roy
C0513. Hackett, Bobby **
C0640. Keppard, Freddie
C0700. La Rocca, Nick
C0850. Nichols, Red
C0866. Oliver, King
C1073. Spanier, Muggsy

Double Bass

C0150. Blanton, Jimmy
C0170. Bottesini, Giovanni
C0208. Callender, Red
C0326. Dragonetti, Domenico
C0397. Foster, Pops
C0628. Karr, Gary Michael
C0648. Kirby, John
C0812. Mingus, Charles
C0903. Pettiford, Oscar
C1143. Turetzky, Bertram

Flute

C0021. Andersen Carl Joachim

C0022. Andersen, Vigo
C0064. Baker, Julius
C0076. Baron, Samuel
C0077. Barrère, Georges
C0085. Barwahser, Hubert
C0112. Berbiguier, Benoit-T.
C0157. Boehm, Theobald
C0182. Briccialdi, Giulio
C0332. Drouet, Louis
C0337. Duelon, Friedrich
C0394. Fleury, Louis François
C0434. Galway, James
C0439. Gazzelloni, Severino
C0542. Heinemeyer, Ernst Wilhelm
C0644. Kincaid, William
C0667. Koehler, Ernesto
C0717. Le Roy, René
C0735. Linde, Hans-Martin
C0750. de Lorenzo, Leonardo
C0771. Mann, Herbie
C0830. Moyse, Marcel Joseph
C0851. Nicolet, Aurèle
C0928. Prill, Emil
C0938. Quantz, Johann Joachim
C0944. Rampal, Jean-Pierre
C0953. Rémusat, Jean
C0966. Robison, Paula Judith
C1102. Taffanel, Claude Paul
C1107. Tassinari, Arrigo
C1141. Tulou, Jean-Louis
C1176. Wendling, Johann Baptist
C1211. Zoeller, Karlheinz
C1213. Zukerman, Eugenia

French-horn

C0080. Barrows, John
C0091. Baumann, Hermann
C0174. Brain, Aubrey Harold
C0175. Brain, Dennis
C0243. Civil, Alan
C0285. Dauprat, Louis-François
C0347. Duvernoy, Frédéric
C0507. Gumpert, Friedrich Adolf
C0708. Lebrun, Jean
C0891. Pelissier, Victor
C0955. Reynolds, Verne
C1013. Schneider, Georg Abraham
C1083. Stich, Václav
C1139. Tuckwell, Barry
C1160. Vivier, Eugène Léon

Guitar

C0006. Aguado y Garcia, Dionisio

C0044. Atkins, Chet
C0074. Barker, Danny
C0101. Behrend, Siegfried
C0121. Berry, Chuck
C0144. Bitetti, Ernesto
C0178. Bream, Julian
C0223. Carulli, Ferdinando
C0237. Christian, Charlie
C0244. Clapton, Eric
C0257. Condon, Eddie
C0391. Fisk, Eliot Hamilton
C0451. Ghiglia, Oscar
C0466. Giuliani, Mauro
C0513. Hackett, Bobby **
C0550. Hendrix, Jimi
C0696. Lang, Eddie
C0741. Llobet, Miguel
C0795. McLaughlin, John
C0815. Molitor, Alois Franz
C0819. Montgomery, Wes
C0820. Montoya, Carlos Garcia
C0919. Porro, Pierre Jean
C0948. Reinhardt, Django
C1026. Segovia, Andrés
C1069. Sor, Joseph Fernando
C1186. Williams, John C.
C1199. Yepes, Narciso

Harmonica

C0003. Adler, Larry

Harp

C0113. Berghout, Phia
C0125. Bertrand, Aline
C0154. Bochsa, Robert-Nicolas
C0306. Dilling, Mildred
C0308. Dizi, François-Joseph
C0364. Erdeli, Xenia
C0486. Grandjany, Marcel
C0492. Grimm, Karl Konstantin
C0579. Holy, Alfred
C0629. Kastner, Alfred
C0690. Labarre, Théodore François
C0702. Laskine, Lily
C0794. McDonald, Susan
C0838. Nadermann, Jean Francois
C0880. Parish-Alvars, Elias
C0954. Renié, Henriette
C0994. Salzedo, Carlos Léon
C1018. Schuecker, Edmund
C1019. Schuecker, Heinrich
C1020. Schuecker, Joseph E.
C1062. Snoer, Johannes

C1127. Thomas, John
C1204. Zabaleta, Nicanor
C1206. Zamara, Antonio

Harpsichord

C0007. Ahlgrimm, Isolde
C0259. Cooper, Kenneth
C0305. Dieupart, Charles **
C0325. Draghi, Giovanni
C0350. Ehlers, Alice
C0429. Fuller, Albert
C0457. Gilbert, Kenneth **
C0470. Goldberg, Johann G.
C0525. Harich-Schneider, Eta
C0616. Jones, Geraint
C0647. Kipnis, Igor
C0652. Kirkpatrick, Ralph Leonard
C0695. Landowska, Wanda
C0716. Leonhardt, Gustav Maria **
C0744. Loeillet, Jean-Baptiste
C0774. Marchand, Louis **
C0778. Marlowe, Sylvia
C0847. Newman, Anthony **
C0937. Puyana, Rafael
C0968. Roesgen-Champion, M.
C0991. Ružičkova, Zuzana
C1104. Tagliavini, Luigi **
C1130. Tilney, Colin
C1149. Valenti, Fernando
C1154. Veyron-Lacroix, Robert **
C1173. Weir, Gillian C. **

Jews' Harp

C0370. Eulenstein, Charles

Oboe

C0078. Barret, Apollon Marie-Rose
C0081. Barth, Christian Samuel
C0126. Besozzi, Alessandro
C0479. Goossens, Leon Jean
C0574. Holliger, Heinz
C0706. Lavigne, Antoine-Joseph
C0709. Lebrun, Ludwig August
C0749. Longy, Gustave
C0765. Malgoire, Jean-Claude
C0982. Rothwell, Evelyn
C1087. Stotijn, Jaap
C1100. Tabuteau, Marcel
C1129. de Thurner, Frédéric

Organ

C0008. Ahrens, Joseph Johannes
C0009. Alain, Marie-Claire
C0014. Alcock, Walter Galpin
C0025. Andrée, Elfrida
C0045. Auberlen, Samuel Gottlob
C0065. Baker, Robert Stevens
C0095. Beauvarlet-Charpentier, J.
C0099. Beckmann, Johann Friedrich
C0128. Best, William Thomas
C0135. Biggs, E. Power
C0162. Bonnet, Joseph Elie
C0197. Bunk, Gerard
C0207. Callaway, Paul
C0210. Camidge, Matthew
C0215. Capocci, Filippo
C0232. Chapuis, Michel
C0251. Cochereau, Pierre
C0265. Couperin, Armand-Louis
C0266. Couperin, François le Grand
C0267. Courboin, Charles Marie
C0270. Crawford, Jesse
C0272. Crozier, Catharine
C0295. Demessieux, Jeanne
C0307. Diruta, Girolamo
C0324. Downes, Ralph
C0339. Dunham, Henry Morton
C0344. Dupré, Marcel.
C0348. Eddy, Clarence Hiram
C0360. Elvey, George Job
C0373. Falcinelli, Rolande
C0376. Farnam, W. Lynnwood
C0402. Fox, Virgil Keel
C0446. Germani, Fernando
C0450. van den Gheyn, Matthias
C0456. Gigout, Eugène
C0457. Gilbert, Kenneth **
C0467. Gleason, Harold
C0470. Goldberg, Johann G. **
C0500. Grunenwald, Jean-Jacques
C0503. Guillon, Jean
C0504. Guilmant, Félix
C0521. Hamm, Adolf
C0533. Haupt, Karl August
C0543. Heitmann, Fritz
C0567. Hodges, Edward
C0592. Hurford, Peter John
C0599. Jacob, Benjamin
C0634. Kee, Piet
C0662. Koch, Caspar Petrus
C0675. Kraft, Walter Wilhelm
C0707. Lebègue, Nicolas-Antoine
C0714. Lemare, Edwin Henry
C0716. Leonhardt, Gustav Maria **

C0730. Libert, Henri
C0773. Marchal, André-Louis
C0774. Marchand, Louis **
C0787. Matthaei, Karl
C0808. Middelschulte, Wilhelm
C0847. Newman, Anthony **
C0884. Parratt, Walter
C0904. Pfannstiehl, Bernhard
C0926. Preston, Simon John
C0943. Ramin, Guenther
C0949. Reinken, Johann Adam
C0961. Rinck, Johann Christian
C0992. Sabin, Wallace Arthur
C1014. Schneider, Johann G.
C1023. Schweitzer, Albert
C1050. Simon, Prosper-Charles
C1090. Straube, Karl Montgomery
C1104. Tagliavini, Luigi **
C1122. Thalben-Ball, George
C1134. Tournemire, Charles
C1155. Vierne, Louis
C1164. Walcha, Helmut
C1166. Warren, Samuel Prowse
C1172. Weinrich, Carl
C1173. Weir, Gillian C. **
C1178. Widor, Charles-Marie

Percussion/Timpani

C0145. Blades, James
C0149. Blakey, Art
C0230. Catlett, Big Sid
C0246. Clarke, Kenny
C0254. Cole, Cozy
C0310. Dodds, Baby
C0540. Haynes, Roy Owen
C0615. Jones, Elvin Ray
C0617. Jones, Jo
C0618. Jones, Philly Joe
C0676. Kraft, William
C0685. Krupa, Gene
C0905. Pfundt, Ernst Gotthold
C0913. Pollack, Ben
C0957. Rich, Buddy
C0965. Roach, Max
C1053. Singleton, Zutty
C1133. Tough, Dave
C1168. Webb, Chick
C1196. Yamash'ta, Stomu

Piano

C0004. Aeschbacher, Adrian
C0005. Agosti, Guido
C0015. Alkan, Charles Henri

C0019. Ammons, Albert
C0020. Anda, Geza
C0023. Anderson, Lucy
C0026. Andreoli, Carlo
C0029. Anievas, Augustin
C0030. Ansorge, Conrad Eduard
C0036. Argerich, Martha
C0039. Arrau, Claudio
C0042. Ashkenazy, Vladimir
C0043. Askenase, Stefan
C0049. Ax, Emanuel
C0052. Bachauer, Gina
C0053. Bache, Constance
C0056. Backhaus, Wilhelm
C0057. Badura-Skoda, Paul
C0066. Ballista, Antonio
C0068. Balsam, Artur
C0071. Barenboim, Daniel
C0072. Bar-Illan, David
C0082. Barth, Karl Heinrich
C0086. Bashkirov, Dmitri
C0087. Basie, Count
C0090. Bauer, Harold
C0092. Baumgartner, Paul
C0106. Bendel, Franz
C0108. Bendix, Otto
C0110. Benoist, André
C0115. Beringer, Oscar
C0117. de Bériot, Charles-W.
C0118. Berman, Lazar
C0119. Béroff, Michel
C0124. Bertini, Henri-Jérôme
C0129. Bethune, Blind Tom
C0137. Bigot de Morogues, Marie
C0139. Bilson, Malcolm
C0141. Binns, Malcolm
C0143. Bishop-Kovacevich, Stephen
C0148. Blake, Eubie
C0152. Blumental, Felicja
C0153. Blumenthal, Jacob
C0155. Bodky, Erwin
C0159. Bolet, Jorge
C0160. Bomtempo, João Domingos
C0161. di Bonaventura, Anthony
C0163. Bordes-Pène, Léontine
C0164. Borgatti, Renata
C0165. Borovsky, Alexander
C0166. Borwick, Leonard
C0167. Bos, Coenraad Valentyn
C0168. Boskoff, George
C0169. Bosquet, Emile
C0173. Brailowsky, Alexander
C0177. Brassin, Louis
C0179. Brendel, Alfred
C0188. Browning, John

C0189. Brubeck, Dave
C0190. de la Bruchollerie, M.
C0193. von Buelow, Hans
C0194. Buhlig, Richard
C0198. Buonamici, Giuseppe
C0199. Burge, David
C0204. Busoni, Ferruccio
C0212. Campanella, Michele
C0216. Carle, Frankie
C0219. Carreño, Teresa
C0224. Casadesus, Jean
C0226. Casadesus, Robert
C0231. Cesi, Beniamino
C0233. Chasins, Abram
C0234. Cherkassky, Shura
C0236. Chopin, Frédéric
C0241. Chung, Myung-Whun
C0242. Ciccolini, Aldo
C0249. Clementi, Muzio
C0250. Cliburn, Van
C0253. Cohen, Harriet
C0260. Corea, Chick
C0263. Cortot, Alfred Denis
C0268. Cramer, Johann Baptist
C0271. Crossley, Paul Christopher
C0274. Curzon, Clifford Michael
C0275. Czerny, Carl
C0276. Czerny-Stefanska, Halina
C0277. Cziffra, Gyoergy
C0278. Dameron, Tadd
C0279. Da Motta, José Vianna
C0284. Dannreuther, Edward
C0288. Davidovich, Bella
C0289. Davies, Fanny
C0290. Davis, Ivan
C0296. Demus, Joerg
C0302. Dichter, Misha
C0304. Diémer, Louis-Joseph
C0309. Dobrzynski, Ignacy
C0312. von Doehler, Theodor
C0313. von Dohnanyi, Ernst
C0317. Domaniewski, Boleslaus
C0318. Domino, Fats
C0319. Door, Anton
C0328. Dresel, Otto
C0329. Dreyschock, Alexander
C0331. Dreyschock, Felix
C0333. Drozdov, Anatoly
C0334. Drozdowski, Jan
C0336. Drzewiecki, Zbigniew
C0338. Dulcken, Luise
C0341. Dunn, John Petri
C0345. Durlet, Emmanuel
C0349. Egghard, Julius
C0351. Ehrlich, Karl Heinrich

C0353. Ekier, Jan
C0355. Ellegaard, France
C0357. Ellington, Duke
C0361. Engel, Karl
C0362. Entremont, Philippe
C0363. Epstein, Julius
C0365. Erdmann, Eduard Paul
C0367. Eschenbach, Christoph
C0368. Essipova, Anna
C0371. Evans, Bill
C0375. Farnadi, Edith
C0377. Farrenc, Jeanne-Louise
C0378. Fay, Amy
C0379. Feinberg, Samuel
C0386. Field, John
C0387. Filtsch, Károly
C0388. Firkušný, Rudolf
C0389. Fischer, Annie
C0390. Fischer, Edwin
C0392. Fleisher, Leon
C0396. Foldes, Andor
C0398. Foster, Sidney
C0406. Frager, Malcolm
C0410. Franck, Eduard
C0411. François, Samson
C0412. Frank, Claude
C0414. Fraser, Norman
C0416. Freire, Nelson
C0417. Frey, Emil
C0418. Frey, Walter
C0420. Friedberg, Carl
C0421. Friedheim, Arthur
C0423. Friedman, Ignaz
C0424. Friskin, James
C0425. Frugoni, Orazio
C0430. Gabrilowitsch, Ossip
C0432. Gallico, Paolo
C0433. Galston, Gottfried
C0435. Ganz, Wilhelm
C0437. Garner, Erroll
C0440. Gebhard, Heinrich
C0442. Gelber, Bruno-Leonardo
C0454. Gieseking, Walter
C0455. Giesen, Hubert
C0458. Gilels, Emil
C0460. Gil-Marchex, Henri
C0462. Gimpel, Jacob
C0468. Goddard, Arabella
C0469. Godowsky, Leopold
C0472. Goldsand, Robert
C0473. Goldschmidt, Otto
C0475. Goode, Richard
C0477. Goodman, Isador
C0478. Goodson, Katharine
C0482. Gorodnitzki, Sasha

C0483. Gottschalk, Louis Moreau
C0484. Gould, Glenn
C0485. Graffman, Gary
C0489. de Greef, Arthur
C0491. Gregoir, Jacques Mathieu
C0493. de Groot, Cor
C0496. Gruenfeld, Alfred
C0505. Gulda, Friedrich
C0509. Gutmann, Adolph
C0510. Haas, Monique
C0511. Haas, Werner
C0512. Haberbier, Ernst
C0514. Haebler, Ingrid
C0516. Haig, Al
C0518. Hall, Elsie
C0520. Hambourg, Mark
C0523. Hancock, Herbie
C0524. Harasiewicz, Adam
C0528. Harrison, Hazel Lucile
C0529. Harrison, Sidney
C0532. Haskil, Clara
C0538. Hawes, Hampton
C0546. Heller, Stephen
C0551. Hennes, Therese
C0552. von Henselt, Georg Martin
C0556. Herz, Henri
C0557. Hess, Myra
C0559. Hesse-Bukowska, Barbara
C0562. Hinderas, Natalie
C0563. Hines, Earl
C0565. Hirt, Franz Josef
C0570. Hoffman, Richard
C0571. Hofmann, Josef
C0573. Hollander, Lorin
C0575. Hollins, Alfred
C0581. Hopekirk, Helen
C0583. Horowitz, Vladimir
C0584. Horszowski, Mieczyslaw
C0589. Huenten, Franz
C0590. Hughes, Edwin
C0591. Hummel, Johann Nepomuk
C0594. Hutcheson, Ernest
C0595. Igumnov, Konstantin
C0596. Istomin, Eugene
C0597. Iturbi, José
C0600. Jaëll, Alfred
C0601. Jaëll-Trautmann, Marie
C0604. Janis, Byron
C0605. Jarrett, Keith
C0606. Jedliczka, Ernst
C0610. Johannesen, Grant
C0611. Johansen, Gunnar
C0613. Johnson, James P.
C0621. Joseffy, Rafael
C0622. Kalichstein, Joseph

C0623. Kalish, Gilbert
C0624. Kalkbrenner, Friedrich
C0627. Kapell, William
C0630. Katchen, Julius
C0631. Kates, Stephen
C0632. Katin, Peter
C0633. Katz, Mindru
C0637. Kellermann, Berthold
C0638. Kempff, Wilhelm
C0639. Kentner, Louis Philip
C0641. Kessler, Joseph Christoph
C0643. Kilenyi, Edward, Jr.
C0646. King, Oliver A.
C0651. Kirkpatrick, John
C0656. Klien, Walter
C0658. Klindworth, Karl
C0661. Knorr, Julius
C0665. Kocsis, Zoltán
C0666. Koczalski, Raoul Armand
C0671. Kontarsky, Aloys
C0678. Kraus, H.J. Detlef
C0679. Kraus, Lili
C0683. Kreutzer, Leonid
C0687. Kuhe, Wilhelm
C0689. Kyriakou, Rena
C0691. Lachmund, Carl V.
C0692. Laidlaw, Anna Robena
C0693. Lalewicz, Georg
C0694. Lamond, Frederic A.
C0699. Laretei, Kaebi Alma
C0701. de Larrocha, Alicia
C0703. Lateiner, Jacob
C0713. Leginska, Ethel
C0718. Leschetizky, Theodor
C0719. Levant, Oscar
C0720. Levitzki, Mischa
C0721. Lévy, Lazare
C0722. Lewenthal, Raymond
C0724. Lewis, John Aaron
C0725. Lewis, Lux
C0726. Leygraf, Hans
C0727. Lhévinne, Josef
C0728. Lhévinne, Rosina
C0729. Liberace
C0731. Lie, Erika
C0732. Liebling, Emil
C0733. Liebling, Georg
C0734. Lill, John Richard
C0736. Lipatti, Dinu
C0738. List, Eugene
C0740. Liszt, Franz
C0745. Loesser, Arthur
C0748. Long, Marguerite
C0751. Loriod, Yvonne
C0752. Lowenthal, Jerome

C0753. Loyonnet, Paul
C0756. Luebeck, Ernst
C0757. Lupu, Radu
C0758. Luvisi, Lee
C0759. Lympany, Moura
C0762. Magaloff, Nikita
C0764. Malcuzynski, Witold
C0767. Mana-Zucca
C0768. Mandel, Alan
C0777. Marks, Alan
C0782. Martins, João Carlos
C0783. Mason, William
C0785. Masselos, William
C0788. Matthay, Tobias Augustus
C0789. Matthews, Denis James
C0797. McPartland, Margaret
C0799. Mehegan, John
C0802. Menter, Sophie
C0804. von Meyer, Leopold
C0807. Michelangeli, Arturo
C0809. Mikhasoff, Ivar Emilan
C0810. Miller, Robert
C0814. Moiseiwitsch, Benno
C0817. Monk, Thelonious
C0818. Montgomery, Little Brother
C0822. Moore, Gerald
C0823. Moravec, Ivan
C0826. Morton, Jelly Roll
C0827. Moscheles, Ignaz
C0828. Moszkowski, Moritz
C0829. Moten, Bennie
C0834. Munn, Mary Elizabeth
C0840. Nat, Yves
C0845. Neuhaus, Heinrich
C0847. Newman, Anthony **
C0848. Ney, Elly
C0852. Nikolayev, Leonid
C0853. Nikolayeva, Tatiana
C0856. Nováes, Guiomar
C0857. Nyiregyházi, Erwin
C0858. Oborin, Lev
C0861. Ogdon, John
C0862. Ohlsson, Garrick
C0869. Oppens, Ursula
C0870. Orlov, Nicolai
C0871. Ornstein, Leo
C0872. Orozco, Rafael
C0874. Ortiz, Cristina
C0876. de Pachmann, Vladimir
C0877. Paderewski, Ignacy
C0886. Pattison, John Nelson
C0887. Pauer, Ernst
C0888. Pauer, Max
C0889. Pauk, Gyoergy
C0892. Pembaur, Joseph, Jr.

C0893. Pennario, Leonard
C0895. Perabo, Johann Ernst
C0896. Perahia, Murray
C0897. Perlemuter, Vlado
C0900. Peterson, Oscar
C0901. Petri, Egon
C0906. Philipp, Isidor
C0911. Pixis, Johann Peter
C0912. Planté, Francis
C0914. Pollini, Maurizio
C0915. Pommier, Jean-Bernard
C0916. Ponti, Michael
C0921. Postnikova, Viktoria
C0922. Potter, Philip Cipriani
C0924. Powell, Bud
C0932. Prudent, Emile
C0935. Pugno, Stéphane Raoul
C0942. Rachmaninoff, Sergei
C0945. Ránki, Dezsoe
C0946. Rappoldi-Kahrer, Laura
C0950. Reisenauer, Alfred
C0951. Reisenberg, Nadia
C0958. Richter, Sviatoslav
C0959. Richter-Haaser, Hans
C0960. Ries, Ferdinand
C0962. Risler, Joseph Edouard
C0964. Rivé-King, Julie
C0969. Rogé, Pascal
C0977. Rosen, Charles
C0980. Rosenthal, Moriz
C0984. Rubinstein, Anton
C0985. Rubinstein, Artur
C0986. Rubinstein, Beryl
C0987. Rubinstein, Nicolai
C0989. Russo, Michel-Angelo
C0995. Samaroff, Olga
C0996. Samuel, Harold
C0997. Sándor, Arpád
C0998. Sándor, Gyoergy
C0999. Sanromá, Jesús María
C1000. Sapelnikov, Vasili
C1002. von Sauer, Emil George
C1004. Scarpini, Pietro
C1005. Scharrer, Irene
C1006. Scharwenka, Franz
C1008. Schiøler, Victor
C1009. Schmidt, Annerose
C1011. Schnabel, Artur
C1017. Schub, André-Michel
C1021. Schumann, Clara
C1022. Schuyler, Philippa Duke
C1029. Selva, Blanche
C1031. Serebryakov, Pavel
C1032. Serkin, Peter
C1033. Serkin, Rudolf

C1037. Sgambati, Giovani
C1040. Shattuck, Arthur
C1042. Shearing, George
C1044. Shure, Leonard
C1045. Siki, Béla
C1046. Siloti, Alexander
C1047. Silver, Horace
C1049. Simon, Abbey
C1056. Slenczynska, Ruth
C1057. Smendzianka, Regina
C1058. Smith, Cyril James
C1060. Smith, Pine Top
C1061. Smith, Willie "the Lion"
C1063. Sofronitzky, Vladimir
C1065. Solomon
C1067. Somer, Hilde
C1070. Soriano, Gonzalo
C1071. Sowinski, Wojciech
C1082. Steuermann, Edward
C1085. Stojowski, Sigismund
C1088. Stradal, August
C1091. Strayhorn, Billy
C1094. Sutton, Ralph Earl
C1095. Sykes, James Andrews
C1096. Szendy, Arpád
C1099. Szymanowska, Maria Agata
C1101. Tacchino, Gabriel
C1103. Tagliaferro, Magda
C1108. Tatum, Art
C1110. Tausig, Carl
C1111. Taylor, Billy
C1112. Taylor, Cecil
C1113. Taylor, Franklin
C1116. Tedesco, Ignaz Amadeus
C1117. Teichmueller, Robert
C1120. Templeton, Alec
C1123. Thalberg, Sigismond
C1125. Thomán, István
C1137. Tristano, Lennie
C1140. Tudor, David
C1142. Tureck, Rosalyn
C1144. Turini, Ronald Walter
C1146. Tyner, McCoy
C1147. Uninsky, Alexander
C1153. Verne, Mathilde
C1154. Veyron-Lacroix, Robert **
C1157. Villoing, Alexander
C1158. Viñes, Ricardo
C1161. Voigt, Henriette
C1163. Votapek, Ralph
C1165. Waller, Fats
C1167. Watts, Andre
C1169. Weber, Margarit
C1170. Webster, Beveridge
C1171. Wehle, Karl

C1174. Weissenberg, Alexis
C1180. Wieniawski, Joseph
C1181. Wild, Earl
C1187. Williams, Mary Lou
C1188. Willmers, Rudolf
C1189. Wilson, Teddy
C1191. Wittgenstein, Paul
C1192. Woelfl, Joseph
C1193. Woodward, Roger
C1194. Wuehrer, Friedrich
C1195. Wurm, Marie
C1197. Yancey, Jimmy
C1203. Yudina, Maria
C1205. Zak, Yakov Izrailevich
C1207. Zeisler, Fannie B.
C1209. Zichy, Géza
C1215. Zykan, Otto M.

Recorder

C0191. Brueggen, Frans

Saxophone

C0002. Adderley, Cannonball
C0050. Ayler, Albert
C0096. Bechet, Sidney **
C0218. Carney, Harry
C0221. Carter, Benny
C0255. Coleman, Ornette
C0256. Coltrane, John William
C0283. Dankworth, Johnny
C0299. Desmond, Paul
C0316. Dolphy, Eric
C0320. Dorsey, Jimmy **
C0415. Freeman, Bud
C0448. Getz, Stan
C0480. Gordon, Dexter
C0539. Hawkins, Coleman
C0549. Hemke, Frederik LeRoy
C0568. Hodges, Johnny
C0649. Kirk, Andy
C0650. Kirk, Roland T.
C0670. Konitz, Lee
C0832. Mule, Marcel
C0833. Mulligan, Gerry
C0881. Parker, Charlie
C0894. Pepper, Art
C0947. Rascher, Sigurd Manfred
C0972. Rollins, Sonny
C1052. Sims, Zoot
C1084. Stitt, Sonny
C1114. Tchicai, John Martin
C1201. Young, Prez

Sitar

C1039. Shankar, Ravi

Trombone

C0103. Belcke, Friedrich A.
C0181. Brevig, Per
C0303. Dickenson, Vic
C0321. Dorsey, Tommy
C0560. Higginbotham. J.C.
C0614. Johnson, J.J.
C0835. Murphy, Turk
C0875. Ory, Kid
C0933. Pryor, Arthur Willard
C1115. Teagarden, Jack
C1175. Wells, Dicky
C1190. Winding, Kai

Trumpet

C0016. Allen, Red
C0024. André, Maurice
C0038. Armstrong, Louis
C0062. Baker, Chet
C0107. Bendinelli, Cesare
C0114. Berigan, Bunny
C0186. Brown, Brownie
C0235. Cherry, Don
C0247. Clayton, Buck
C0291. Davis, Miles
C0314. Dokshitcher, Timofey
C0354. Eldridge, Roy
C0358. Ellis, Don
C0374. Fantini, Girolamo
C0380. Ferguson, Maynard
C0452. Ghitalla, Armando
C0459. Gillespie, Dizzy
C0555. Herseth, Adolph
C0564. Hirt, Al
C0587. Hubbard, Freddie
C0602. James, Harry
C0612. Johnson, Bunk
C0619. Jones, Quincy Delight
C0620. Jones, Thad
C0626. Kaminsky, Max
C0673. Kosleck, Julius
C0760. Lyttelton, Humphrey
C0770. Mangione, Chuck
C0772. Manone, Wingy
C0779. Marsalis, Wynton
C0796. McPartland, Jimmy
C0842. Navarro, Fats
C0879. Page, Hot Lips
C0930. Prima, Louis

C0970. Rogers, Shorty
C1024. Scobey, Jan
C1036. Severinsen, Doc
C1059. Smith, Joe
C1105. Tarr, Edward
C1162. Voisin, Roger Louis
C1185. Williams, Cootie

Tuba

C0907. Phillips, Harvey Gene

Vibraphone

C0522. Hampton, Lionel
C0598. Jackson, Milt
C0855. Norvo, Red

Violin

C0001. Adaskin, Harry
C0010. Alard, Jean-Delphin
C0011. Alberghi, Paolo Tommaso
C0013. Albu, Sandu
C0027. Anet, Jean-Baptiste
C0031. Aranyi, Francis
C0032. d'Aranyi, Jelly
C0034. Arbós, Enrique Fernández
C0037. Armingaud, Jules
C0040. Artôt, Alexandre-Joseph
C0041. Asciolla, Dino
C0046. Aubert, Jacques
C0047. Auer, Leopold
C0048. Aulin, Tor Bernhard
C0051. Babbi, Pietro Giovanni
C0054. Bachmann, Alberto
C0055. Bachrich, Sigismund
C0061. Baillot, Pierre-Maire
C0063. Baker, Israel
C0067. Balokovič, Zlatko
C0070. Barcewicz, Stanislaw
C0073. Barkel, Charles
C0075. Barmas, Issaye
C0083. Barth, Richard
C0084. Barthélémon, François
C0093. Bazzini, Antonio
C0094. Bean, Hugh
C0098. Becker, Jean
C0105. Benda, Franz
C0109. Bennewitz, Antonín
C0111. Berber, Felix
C0116. de Bériot, Charles-A.
C0123. Bertheaume, Isidore
C0127. Bessems, Antoine
C0130. Betti, Adolfo

C0131. Bezekirsky, Vasili
C0132. von Biber, Heinrich
C0133. Biernacki, Nikodem
C0136. Bignami, Carlo
C0138. Bihari, Janos
C0140. Bini, Pasquale
C0142. Birkenstock, Johann Adam
C0147. Blagrove Henry Ganble
C0156. Boehm, Joseph
C0171. Boucher, Alexandre-Jean
C0183. Bridgetower, George A.
C0184. Brodsky, Adolf
C0185. Brosa, Antonio
C0187. Brown, Eddy
C0196. Bull, Ole
C0200. Burgin, Richard
C0201. Burmester, Willy
C0202. Busch, Adolf
C0205. Bustabo, Guila
C0206. Buswell, James Oliver IV
C0211. Campagnoli, Bartolommeo
C0213. Campoli, Alfredo
C0214. Capet, Lucien
C0217. Carmirelli, Pina
C0220. Carrodus, John Tiplady
C0222. Cartier, Jean-Baptiste
C0225. Casadesus, Marius
C0229. Castleman, Charles
C0239. Chung, Kyung-Wha
C0248. Clement, Franz Joseph
C0252. Coenen, Franz
C0258. Constantin, Louis
C0261. Corelli, Arcangelo
C0262. Corigliano, John
C0269. Cramer, Wilhelm
C0281. Dancla, Jean-Baptiste
C0282. Dancla, Léopold
C0286. David, Ferdinand
C0293. De Ahna, Heinrich Karl
C0297. Dengremont, Maurice
C0300. Dessau, Bernhard
C0301. De Vito, Gioconda
C0305. Dieupart, Charles **
C0327. Drdla, František Alois
C0330. Dreyschock, Felix Raimund
C0340. Dunn, John
C0346. Dushkin, Samuel
C0356. Eller, Louis
C0359. Elman, Mischa
C0366. Ernst, Heinrich Wilhelm
C0369. Eto, Toshiya
C0372. Fachiri, Adila
C0381. Fernández Bordas, Antonio
C0382. Ferrari, Domenico
C0383. Ferras, Christian

C0384. Festing, Michael
C0393. Flesch, Carl
C0395. Fodor, Eugene
C0403. Fradkin, Fredric
C0404. Fraenzl, Ferdinand
C0405. Fraenzl, Ignaz
C0407. Francescatti, Zino
C0409. Franci, Rinaldo
C0413. Franko, Sam
C0419. Fried, Miriam
C0422. Friedman, Erick
C0427. Fuchs, Joseph
C0431. Galamian, Ivan
C0438. Gaviniès, Pierre
C0441. Gehot, Jean
C0443. Geminiani, Francesco
C0447. Gerster, Ottmar
C0449. Geyer, Stefi
C0453. de'Giardini, Felice
C0461. Gimpel, Bronislaw
C0463. Gingold, Josef
C0464. Giornovichi, Giovanni
C0465. Gitlis, Ivry
C0471. Goldberg, Szymon
C0474. Goldstein, Mikhail
C0481. Gordon, Jacques
C0487. Grappelli, Stéphane
C0495. Gruenberg, Erich
C0499. Grumiaux, Arthur
C0501. Guénin, Marie Alexandre
C0502. Guillemain, Louis
C0506. Gulli, Franco
C0508. Gusikoff, Michel
C0515. Haendel, Ida
C0517. Haliř, Carl
C0519. Hall, Marie
C0530. Harth, Sidney
C0531. Hartmann, Arthur
C0535. Hauser, Miska
C0537. Havemann, Gustav
C0541. Heifetz, Jascha
C0547. Hellmesberger, Georg, Jr.
C0548. Hellmesberger, Joseph, Sr.
C0558. Hess, Willy
C0561. Hilsberg, Alexander
C0566. Hirt, Fritz
C0572. Hollaender, Gustav
C0576. Holmes, Alfred
C0577. Holmes, Henry
C0578. Holst, Henry
C0585. Hrimalý, Johann
C0586. Hubay, Jenoe
C0588. Huberman, Bronislaw
C0593. Hurwitz, Emanuel
C0607. Jehin-Prume, Françoise

C1079. Staryk, Steven
C1080. Stern, Isaac
C1089. Stratton, George
C1093. Suk, Josef
C1097. Szeryng, Henryk
C1098. Szigeti, Joseph
C1106. Tartini, Giuseppe
C1118. Telmányi, Emil
C1119. Temianka, Henri
C1124. Thibaud, Jacques
C1126. Thomán, Maria
C1128. Thomson, César
C1132. Totenberg, Roman
C1136. Tretyakov, Viktor
C1138. Tua, Teresina Maria
C1148. Urso, Camilla
C1150. Varga, Tibor
C1151. von Vecsey, Franz
C1152. Venuti, Joe
C1156. Vieuxtemps, Henri
C1159. Viotti, Giovanni Battista
C1179. Wieniawski, Henryk

C1182. Wilhelmj, August Emil
C1183. Wilkomirska, Wanda
C1202. Ysaÿe, Eugène
C1208. Zeitlin, Zvi
C1210. Zimbalist, Efrem
C1213. Zukerman, Pinchas
C1214. Zukofsky, Paul

Viola

C0315. Doktor, Paul
C0428. Fuchs, Lillian
C0790. Maugars, André
C0931. Primrose, William
C0963. Ritter, Hermann
C1121. Tertis, Lionel
C1135. Trampler, Walter

Viola da Gamba

C1007. Schenck, Jean Johannes

Index of Authors, Editors, and Compilers

This index includes authors, co-authors, editors, and compilers. Many individual virtuosi are not included in this listing either because they did not author published material or because that material eluded my best efforts to locate it. Translators are not included although they are in the citations. References are to individual entries by category in the following order: A0001–A0165 COLLECTIVE WORKS/Books on Virtuosi; B0001–B0134 COLLECTIVE WORKS/Related Books; C0001–C1215 INDIVIDUAL VIRTUOSI, A–Z; D0001–D0019 REFERENCE MATERIALS.

About the Compiler

ROBERT H. COWDEN is Professor of Music at San Jose State University. The author of *Concert and Opera Singers: A Bibliography of Biographical Materials* (Greenwood Press, 1985), *Concert and Opera Conductors: A Bibliography of Biographical Materials* (Greenwood Press, 1987), and *The Chautauqua Opera Association 1929-1958: An Interpretative History,* Dr. Cowden has translated several operas as well as authored numerous articles and reviews published in *Arts in Society, MLA Notes, The NATS Bulletin, Opera, The Opera Journal, Performing Arts Review,* and *Theatre Design and Technology.* He is presently working on a compendium of major opera houses of the world as well as a revised and expanded edition of his bibliography of concert and opera singers which will include artists from the popular and commercial recording and concert fields.